Reconsidering Woodrow Wilson

This book is based on a conference held in collaboration with the Woodrow Wilson House, a National Trust for Historic Preservation historic site in Washington, D.C. President Wilson's Washington home is now a presidential museum that promotes Woodrow Wilson's legacy as president, educator, and world statesman.

Reconsidering Woodrow Wilson

PROGRESSIVISM, INTERNATIONALISM, WAR, AND PEACE

Edited by **JOHN MILTON COOPER JR.**

Woodrow Wilson Center Press
Washington, D.C.

The Johns Hopkins University Press
Baltimore

EDITORIAL OFFICES
Woodrow Wilson Center Press
Woodrow Wilson International
  Center for Scholars
One Woodrow Wilson Plaza
1300 Pennsylvania Avenue, N.W.
Washington, D.C. 20004-3027
Telephone: 202-691-4029
www.wilsoncenter.org

ORDER FROM
The Johns Hopkins University Press
Hampden Station
P.O. Box 50370
Baltimore, Maryland 21211
Telephone: 1-800-537-5487
www.press.jhu.edu/books/

2 4 6 8 9 7 5 3 1

Library of Congress Cataloging-in-Publication Data
Reconsidering Woodrow Wilson: progressivism, internationalism, war, and peace
/ edited by John Milton Cooper Jr.
   p. cm.
Papers from a symposium held in Washington, DC, on Oct. 28, 2006 and
cosponsored by the Woodrow Wilson International Center for Scholars.
Includes bibliographical references and index.
ISBN 978-0-8018-9074-1 (hardcover : alk. paper)
1. Wilson, Woodrow, 1856–1924—Political and social views—Congresses.
2. Wilson, Woodrow, 1856–1924—Influence—Congresses. 3. United States—
Politics and government—1913–1921—Congresses. 4. United States—Foreign
relations—1913–1921—Congresses. 5. Progressivism (United States politics)—
History—20th century—Congresses. 6. Internationalism—History—20th
century—Congresses. 7. World War, 1914–1918—Congresses. 8. Cold War—
Congresses. 9. World politics—1900–1945—Congresses. 10. Peace-building.
American—History—20th century—Congresses. I. Cooper, John Milton.
II. Woodrow Wilson International Center for Scholars.
E767.1.R43 2008
973.91'3092—dc22
                    2008015569

**Woodrow Wilson
International
Center
for Scholars**

The Woodrow Wilson International Center for Scholars, established by Congress in 1968 and headquartered in Washington, D.C., is the living, national memorial to President Wilson.

The Center is a nonpartisan institution of advanced research, supported by public and private funds, engaged in the study of national and world affairs. The Center establishes and maintains a neutral forum for free, open, and informed dialogue.

The Center's mission is to commemorate the ideals and concerns of Woodrow Wilson by providing a link between the world of ideas and the world of policy, by bringing a broad spectrum of individuals together to discuss important public policy issues, by serving to bridge cultures and viewpoints, and by seeking to find common ground.

Conclusions or opinions expressed in Center publications and programs are those of the authors and speakers and do not necessarily reflect the views of the Center staff, fellows, trustees, advisory groups, or any individuals or organizations that provide financial support to the Center.

The Center is the publisher of *The Wilson Quarterly* and home of Woodrow Wilson Center Press, *dialogue* radio and television, and the monthly newsletter "Centerpoint." For more information about the Center's activities and publications, please visit us on the web at www.wilsoncenter.org.

Lee H. Hamilton, President and Director

Contents

Acknowledgments

This volume has grown out of the conference to mark the one-hundred-fiftieth anniversary of Woodrow Wilson, which was held in Washington on October 28, 2006. The conference was cosponsored by the Woodrow Wilson International Center for Scholars, which is the official national memorial to President Wilson, and the Woodrow Wilson House, which was his last residence and is a presidential museum. We thank the president and director of the Woodrow Wilson Center, Lee H. Hamilton, and the executive director of the Wilson House, Frank Aucella, for sponsoring the conference. We also thank those others at the Woodrow Wilson Center who helped make the event possible: Kent Hughes, director of the project on Science, Technology, America, and the Global Economy; Philippa Strum, director of the Division of United States Studies; and Samuel F. Wells, associate director of the Center and director of West European Studies. At the Wilson House, we thank Mark Benbow, the resident historian.

Reconsidering Woodrow Wilson

Introduction: Wilson Revisited

John Milton Cooper Jr.

December 2006 marked the one hundred and fiftieth anniversary—the sesquicentennial—of the birth of Woodrow Wilson. By coincidence, *The Atlantic Monthly*—only months away from its own sesquicentennial—chose that month's issue to rate what its cover touted as "The 100 Most Influential Americans of All Time." Woodrow Wilson ranked tenth on *The Atlantic's* list. The only presidents who ranked ahead of him were, in this order, Abraham Lincoln, George Washington, Thomas Jefferson—three of the four faces on Mount Rushmore—and Franklin Roosevelt. The only other political leaders who ranked ahead of him were Alexander Hamilton, Benjamin Franklin, and John Marshall. The higher ranking for those seven is understandable. Five of them—Washington, Jefferson, Hamilton, Franklin, and Marshall—were Founders of the Republic, while the other two—Lincoln and Roosevelt—led the nation through its greatest crises. Interestingly, Wilson ranked ahead of his greatest rival, Theodore Roosevelt—the fourth face on Mount Rushmore—who came in fifteenth.[1]

In justifying Wilson's tenth-place ranking on its list of influential Americans, *The Atlantic* said of him, "He made the world safe for U.S. intervention, if not for democracy." Those twelve words nicely encapsulate essential elements of Wilson's historical reputation, if not of the man himself. His greatest influence, by common agreement, lay in foreign affairs, where he remains the avatar of an idealistic approach to the nation's role in the world. As *The Atlantic's* statement implies, that reputation remains controversial. Unlike the leaders who ranked ahead of him or his great rival, Wilson has not become a figure of warm, generalized adulation. Rather, nine decades after his death, he still draws sharply conflicting estimates of his accomplishments and legacies; people still admire or revile him. Clearly, then, he is a person who deserves to be revisited and examined again for who he was, what he did, and what influences he created. He is, as Winston Churchill said about him shortly after his death, "a monument to human meditation."[2]

During the year of Wilson's sesquicentennial, four institutions associated with him or his memory held conferences that looked at him and his legacies. The first of these conferences was at Princeton University, where he served as professor and president, at the school of public and international affairs named after him. This conference examined his contributions to both academic life and public affairs, including state government. The second conference was at the Woodrow Wilson Presidential Library, which is located at his birthplace in Staunton, Virginia. This conference examined him, along with Jefferson and Lincoln, in the context of race and American democracy. The final conference was at the Woodrow Wilson International Center for Scholars in Washington, and was cosponsored by the Woodrow Wilson House, Wilson's last home and now a presidential museum, also in Washington. This conference concentrated on his contributions to public life. This book presents revised versions of the papers that were given at this final conference in Washington.

All these sesquicentennial conferences about Wilson took a broader look at him and his accomplishments and shortcomings, as well as how his words and deeds have helped shape what has come afterward. In keeping with the mission of the Woodrow Wilson Center, its conference concentrated on his public career, mainly his presidency. But this conference did not neglect other aspects of Wilson's life—so both the public and other main dimensions of his career are thus covered in this book.

Part I of the book considers the overarching theme of how Wilson's career institutionalized his progressivism. In chapter 1, "Making a Case for Wilson," I use Churchill's observations about him to discuss both what a truly pivotal role he played in world affairs and what an unusual background he had for a president. His pivotal role came during World War I, and his decision to intervene—which he partially justified with the words "the world must be made safe for democracy"—was what gave rise to the characterization in *The Atlantic*. With that decision and justification, Wilson established himself as the first major interventionist president and, thereby, supposedly the premier spokesperson for an idealistic foreign policy. His background was in private life—he did not enter politics until he ran successfully for governor of New Jersey at the age of fifty-three years—just two years before he was elected president. His private career had been in academic life, as a professor at Bryn Mawr College and Wesleyan and Princeton universities and as president of Princeton. No other president has come from such a background, and, with the exception of Herbert Hoover, no other president has had anything like such a spectacularly successful career outside politics or the military.

The question that inescapably arises about Wilson's background is, How did it serve him in public life? The so-called ivory tower of academia does not enjoy much esteem as a preparation for the worldly pursuits, particularly in business or politics. Wilson struck many contemporaries as a natural leader, and it could be argued that his sojourn in academia was largely irrelevant to his performance in the state house or the White House. Wilson himself did not see it that way at all. He believed that his earlier academic studies of politics and government and his educational leadership at Princeton had given him excellent preparation for "real" politics. Chapter 2, by Trygve Throntveit, "'Common Counsel': Woodrow Wilson's Pragmatic Progressivism," agrees with Wilson's view of his academic background. This chapter examines how closely his political thinking mirrored the larger philosophical currents of American pragmatism at the time, especially as enunciated by William James, and how that thinking shaped the approaches that he would take as president.

The overweening role of foreign affairs in Wilson's presidency was something that he neither expected nor wanted. In chapter 1, I quote his remark that such a development would be "an irony of fate." Great events made that remark memorable, but the irony should not overshadow Wilson's domestic presidency. He wanted, above all else, to be a great reform legislator, and in his first term he succeeded to an extraordinary degree with his New Freedom program. The centerpiece of that program and the greatest legislative monument to his presidency was the Federal Reserve Act of 1913, and his other accomplishments included the Clayton Antitrust Act, the creation of the Federal Trade Commission, the first federal aid to farmers, a statute outlawing child labor (later overturned by the Supreme Court), and the first federal eight-hour-day law for labor. In addition, he nominated and gained confirmation after a hard fight for his appointment of Louis Brandeis to the Supreme Court—in itself a major contribution to public life. Chapter 3, by W. Elliott Brownlee, "Wilson's Reform of Economic Structure: Progressive Liberalism and the Corporation," examines his reform program and accomplishments for the nation's economy, with a special concentration on banking reform through the Federal Reserve.

If such reforms represented the brighter side of Wilson's domestic presidency, the darker side came with his handling of social issues. Part II of the book addresses the two concerns that dominated this area of his presidency: race and gender. His handling of racial discrimination has left one of the two biggest blots on his historical reputation. His administration witnessed an attempt by several Cabinet members to introduce segregation into the federal workplace and a reduction in black employment in the government. Overall, he set a tone that was at best indifferent and at worst hostile toward African Americans. To present-day eyes, he presents a puzzle. With respect to religion and ethnicity, he presented a picture of enlightenment. He not only appointed Brandeis as the first Jew to the U.S. Supreme Court, but as governor he also named the first Jew to the New Jersey Supreme Court. Before that he had appointed the first Jew and first Catholic to the Princeton faculty. Also, as president, he vetoed discriminatory immigration restriction legislation. Why such enlightened views did not extend to race is the subject of chapter 4, by Gary Gerstle, "Race and Nation in the Thought and Politics of Woodrow Wilson." This chapter rejects the argument that Wilson was simply an unreconstructed white southerner and instead introduces the concept of "racialized nationalism" to put him in a broader but not exculpatory context.

Gender presented Wilson with comparable problems, but with a happier outcome. He was no paragon of advanced views about women's emancipation, but he was no reactionary, either. His first teaching job was at a women's college, and he sent his three daughters to college. Two of them became advocates for woman suffrage and lobbied their father to support the cause. At the beginning of his political career, he ducked that issue, taking no stand and claiming that suffrage was strictly a state matter. During his presidency, however, he endorsed suffrage, first at the state level and then through an amendment to the U.S. Constitution. How and why his views evolved is the subject of chapter 5, by Victoria Bissell Brown, "Did Woodrow Wilson's Gender Politics Matter?" This chapter maintains that he eventually came to champion suffrage through a combination of principled rethinking, adroit persuasion by suffrage leaders, and political calculation.

Turning to Wilson's unexpected involvement in foreign affairs, the three chapters that make up part III of the book examine aspects of that turn of events—which constitute the seeds of what has come to be known as "Wilsonianism." Even before World War I broke out, his administration was heavily involved in Latin America. Contrary to previous Democratic attacks on their opponents' alleged "imperialism," Wilson and his first secretary of state, William Jennings Bryan, continued and expanded the interventionist policies of their Republican predecessors in the Caribbean and Central America. Revolution and civil war in Mexico presented Wilson with a special problem almost from the day of his inauguration. How he handled that problem and others in the Western Hemisphere is the subject of chapter 6, by Mark Gilderhus, "Revolution, War, and Expansion: Woodrow Wilson in Latin America." This chapter also touches on how he and his policies appeared in the eyes of leaders of other countries in this region.

Repressions of civil liberties after the United States entered the war have cast the other great blot on Wilson's historical reputation. Why this came to pass is the subject of chapter 7, by Geoffrey Stone, "Mr. Wilson's First Amendment," which addresses the seeming paradox that these repressions occurred under a president who understood and shared some of the views of critics and opponents of World War I and who predicted that hysteria and intolerance would come with entry into that war. The stakes for which Wilson played with intervention are the subject of chapter 8, by Lloyd Ambrosius, "Democracy, Peace, and World Order." This chapter examines the ideas and policies that underlie Wilson's reputation as an international idealist.

Like any strong president who oversees and tries to guide great changes, Wilson has cast a long shadow over subsequent events. Both *The Atlantic*'s rating of him and persistent uses of the term "Wilsonian" more than eighty years after his death attest to how much he still haunts those who analyze and make foreign policy. The three chapters that make up part IV of the book examine this legacy. Chapter 9, by Emily Rosenberg, "Progressive Internationalism and Reformed Capitalism: New Freedom to New Deal," treats the first twenty years after Wilson's presidency. Among other things, this chapter shows how his ideas and approaches shaped the work of influential people who had been his opponents during and after World War I. Chapter 10, by Martin Walker, "Woodrow Wilson and the Cold War: 'Tear Down This Wall, Mr. Gorbachev,'" takes up the story during the half-century from World War II to the downfall of the Soviet Union. The theme of defending and extending democracy, inspired by Wilson's rhetoric and ideas, recurred repeatedly, even among persons who did not trace their political lineage back to him and his party—most notably the person quoted in the title, Ronald Reagan. Chapter 11, by Frank Ninkovich, "Wilsonianism after the Cold War: 'Words, Words, Mere Words,'" casts a critically appraising eye over what really remains of his legacy in the most recent years. Despite recurrent invocations of his name and words and despite arguments that the George W. Bush administration is neo-Wilsonian, this chapter finds little of real substance to any legacy.

Finally, an afterword by Anne-Marie Slaughter looks at how Wilson's insights apply today. Overall, she wagers that he now would say: "Democracy must be made safe for the world." The United States thus needs to be pursuing a long-term policy of promoting liberal democracies that aspire to be *p*opular, *a*ccountable, and *r*ights-regarding—up to PAR.

The chapters in this volume range widely in subject and viewpoint. There is no general line of appraisal or approach. Some chapters are more laudatory and some are more skeptical about both the man and his thoughts and deeds. Wilson himself would have approved of this divergence. He believed in and enjoyed the flow and clash of ideas—as a friend in college called it, "the play of the mind." The fact that his reputation and legacy continue to be controversial is itself testimony to the tremendous impact that he made on his nation and the world. To view Woodrow Wilson in different lights in his sesquicentennial year is the best tribute that he could have and the one that he would have wanted.

Notes

1. "They Made America," *Atlantic Monthly*, December 2006, 60–78. A recently coined term to denote a high reputation among presidents is the "Mount Rushmore standard." By the commonly accepted measure of polls of historians and political scientists, Franklin Roosevelt meets that standard better than his distant cousin Theodore. It helped that the creator of Mount Rushmore was a friend and political follower of Theodore Roosevelt. The other two figures who ranked ahead of Wilson were Martin Luther King Jr. and Thomas Edison.

2. Ibid., 61; Winston S. Churchill, *The World Crisis* (London: Thornton Butterworth, 1927), vol. 3, 230.

Part I
Institutionalizing Progressivism

1. Making a Case for Wilson
John Milton Cooper Jr.

In 1927, three years after Woodrow Wilson died, Winston Churchill delivered a celebrated pronouncement about this American president: "Writing with every sense of respect, it seems no exaggeration to pronounce that the action of the United States with its repercussions on the history of the world depended on the workings of this man's mind and spirit to the exclusion of almost every other factor; and that he played a part in the fate of nations incomparably more direct and personal than any other man." Churchill was referring to the part that Wilson played in World War I, particularly in regard to bringing about American intervention in April 1917. It has been ninety years since that event, and the research and analysis done in those intervening decades fully vindicate Churchill's assessment. The United States entered World War I because this president decided to take the country in. Woodrow Wilson really did hold the fate of this nation and the world in his hands.[1]

Churchill also had a bit more to say about Wilson that has not become so celebrated. When he made his pronouncement, he had been reading first two published volumes of *The Intimate Papers of Colonel House*. Reading the diary entries and letters by this confidant of Wilson's prompted Churchill to add a description of the president: "Dwelling in the bosom of his domestic circle with the simplicity and frugality of [Tsar] Nicholas II, inaccessible except to friends and servitors—and very sparingly to them—towering above Congress, the Cabinet his mere implement, untempered and undinted in the smithy of public life, and guided by that 'frequent recurrence to first principles' enjoined in the American Constitution, Woodrow Wilson, the inscrutable and undecided judge upon whose lips the lives of millions hung, stands forth a monument to human meditation." It has been eighty years since Churchill's wrote these words, and, again, the intervening decades have vindicated his assessment. A seldom-flagging flood of writing about Wilson and what he wrought has indeed made him "a monument to human meditation."[2]

Wilson's Domestic Accomplishments

Churchill's words are worth remembering because they point to the two questions that need to be asked in judging Wilson as president—really any president. First, what did he accomplish while in office? Both of Churchill's statements, and particularly the first one, speak to that question. Second, what did he bring to and give to the office? The second statement speaks to that question, and a comment is in order about where Churchill was coming from. He was basically right to remark that Wilson was a solitary sort when compared to most other politicians. Relying on Colonel Edward House, Churchill exaggerated that quality of solitariness— Wilson did consult a lot with others—but Churchill was measuring Wilson against his own experience of having spent nearly all his adult life in the thick of parliamentary politics, in the House of Commons. He had great difficulty believing that without such experience anyone could be a true statesman. In his book of sketches titled *Great Contemporaries*, Churchill repeatedly passes the judgment, "The House found him out." Not only for Churchill but also for others, many of them Americans, Wilson was an odd political duck, and they had grave doubts about how good a leader he could be. Whether such doubts were well founded brings back the question of what this man brought to and gave to the presidency.

First, however, comes the question of what he accomplished. This remains the inescapable standard by which all occupants of the White House are judged. A person may have great gifts and enjoy a stellar career before and afterward, but if he, or someday she, does not measure up by the standard of accomplishment, then the judgment is failure. How does Wilson measure up by this standard?

As with most presidents, it is useful to break down the performance between domestic and foreign affairs. Domestically, the yardstick most commonly applied is legislation: Did a substantial number of significant laws get passed during this person's presidency? By this yardstick, Wilson stands extraordinarily tall. In the first eighteen months of his presidency, he oversaw and pushed through a truly staggering program of major legislation. This program goes by the name "the New Freedom." It included the first successful lowering of tariff in four decades, which was accompanied by the first permanent income tax; establishment of the Federal Reserve system; and passage of a new antitrust act, which was accompanied by creation of the Federal Trade Commission (FTC).

No one can gainsay the importance of those measures. The income tax has become the most important and, in recent decades, most controversial source of revenue for the federal government. The Federal Reserve, strengthened and centralized by subsequent reforms, has grown into possibly the most potent single factor in the American economy. The antitrust law passed in Wilson's administration—though intermittently applied—and the FTC remain the twin instruments of antitrust policy.

Wilson played a critical role in the passage of this legislation. Following a practice that he had earlier conceived as governor of New Jersey, he became the first president to plan a legislative program in advance. Likewise, he picked his shots carefully as he pressed forward with his agenda. He also kept Congress on the job. Before the 1960s, Congress seldom met for long sessions, and members never stayed almost continuously on the job as they have done in recent decades. In April 1913, a month after his inauguration, Wilson called the Sixty-Third Congress into session; with only one brief recess, he kept the senators and representatives at it for eighteen months. This was unprecedented: Congress had never met for so long at a time, not even during the Civil War.

In getting his program through, Wilson enjoyed plenty of luck, and he had a powerful political tailwind behind him. That tailwind was called "progressivism," and it gathered together a set of ideas whose time had come. The 1912 election, which swept Wilson into the White House, had been a contest between him and Theodore Roosevelt and their rival visions of progressivism, the New Freedom and the New Nationalism. Thanks to Roosevelt having split the normal Republican majority of that time, Wilson had won a huge majority in the electoral college, despite carrying only 42 percent of the popular vote. Likewise, the Republican split allowed Wilson's Democratic Party to garner a fat majority in the House of Representatives. Moreover, the Democrats were hungry after sixteen years in the political wilderness, and their hunger put them in a cooperative mood. Finally, the party's three-time presidential nominee and ideological guru, William Jennings Bryan, was at Wilson's side as secretary of state, and he provided invaluable liaison and lobbying with his followers on Capitol Hill. Clearly, those circumstances helped Wilson during those eighteen months, and this was also a time when he had comparatively few distractions from foreign affairs.

Those legislative accomplishments are well known and acknowledged even by Wilson's severest critics. That program at the outset of his administration did not, however, comprise the sum of his record as a legislative leader. In 1916, the last year of his first term, he pushed through another program. One part of that program was not strictly legislation, but it did have great policy implications and it required resourceful lobbying in the Senate. This was the nomination and confirmation of Louis Brandeis to the Supreme Court. The purely legislative parts included a federal child labor law, the first federal financial aid to farmers, regulation of maritime shipping, levying of the first graduated income tax and the first federal inheritance taxes, and an eight-hour-day law for railroad workers. This 1916 program differed from the earlier New Freedom in that it did not consist of a trio of monumental pieces of legislation but of a number of smaller but plainly significant measures. Likewise, the choice of Brandeis for the Supreme Court was, arguably, the finest single appointment any president has made.

Taken together, those two programs of the New Freedom made Woodrow Wilson one of the three great legislative presidents of the twentieth century, perhaps of all of American history. His peers are Franklin Delano Roosevelt with the New Deal and Lyndon Baines Johnson with the Great Society. It is really extraordinary to rank Wilson alongside those two presidents. Despite his good luck, he did not enjoy the advantages and assets that FDR and LBJ did. His progressive tailwind in 1913 and 1914 did not give him anything approaching the blank check from Congress that the national emergency of the Depression gave to FDR. Nor did Wilson have behind him long years of learning the ways of Congress and dominating one of its chambers as LBJ did. Here was a man who was only two years removed from private life, who had held only one elective office for two years before becoming president.

Other things make Wilson's ranking among the legislative all-stars still more extraordinary. The political circumstances at the outset of his administration were not so favorable as they might appear at first blush. The Democrats did not have a big majority in the Senate, and the very size of their House majority made it unwieldy. Wilson also had to wend his way among different programs and constituencies, particularly with the Federal Reserve. That act and the antitrust and FTC acts likewise presented great technical and policy problems in being forged into workable legislation. Efforts to lower tariffs seemed jinxed. Two of Wilson's predecessors, Grover Cleveland and William Howard Taft, had tried and failed to lower rates, and Wilson had to beat back the same protectionist guerilla tactics in the Senate that had stymied those earlier presidents.

The political circumstances in 1916 were much less favorable. Losses in the 1914 elections had greatly reduced the Democratic majority in the House, and Bryan had resigned in protest in 1915 over foreign policy. In fact, Bryan was actively opposing Wilson on military and foreign policy and openly fighting him for leadership of the Democrats. Now, too, foreign affairs provided a major distraction. In fact, even during the opening months of his administration, Wilson had to deal with the vexing situation in Mexico. After August 1914, he had to deal with World War I. With the sinking of the *Lusitania*—which was that era's equivalent to the September 11, 2001, terrorist attacks—the United States faced the threat of being sucked into the world war. Disagreement over how to face that threat prompted

Bryan to resign and to resist Wilson from what would later be called the "dovish" side. At the same time, there was "hawkish" opposition from such figures as Theodore Roosevelt and Henry Cabot Lodge.

For Wilson to get a program of major domestic legislation through Congress in those circumstances was truly phenomenal. It was as if FDR had enacted his "Second New Deal" of 1935–36 at the same time that he was dealing with the foreign policy conflict between the outbreak of World War II and Pearl Harbor, with Cordell Hull or John Nance Garner on the outside openly fighting him. Or as if LBJ had pushed through the Great Society with the Vietnam debate in full swing and Robert Kennedy actively opposing him. In short, there is simply no way to gainsay Wilson's stature as a leader in domestic legislation. He may well have surpassed FDR and LBJ in this arena.

Wilson's Accomplishments in Foreign Policy

If Wilson had been a peacetime president or one whose administration had witnessed few crises or troubles abroad, this record of domestic legislative accomplishment would make his place among successful presidents secure. Legislation was what he cared about most when he entered the White House and what he expected to devote most of his energies to pursuing. Soon after he was elected president, Wilson made an offhand remark to a former colleague on the Princeton University faculty: "It would be an irony of fate if my administration has to deal chiefly with foreign problems; for all my preparation has been in domestic matters." The first part of that remark is quoted by almost everyone who has written about Wilson because an "irony of fate" overtook him in the most significant possible way with the outbreak of World War I. The second part of the remark is equally important, because it speaks to the question of what he brought to the presidency.[3]

First, however, it is necessary to assess Wilson's accomplishments in foreign policy. Unlike in domestic affairs, he did not start out well here. Actually, his "irony of fate" began to overtake him as soon as he entered the White House. A month before his inauguration, the revolution in Mexico took a nasty turn when the liberal president Francisco Madero was overthrown and murdered in a military coup. During the next three years, Wilson thrashed around in an effort to aid the more democratic forces in Mexico. He also seems to have given in to an itch to intervene that was left over from his earlier brief fling with imperialism at the time of the Spanish-American War. An armed clash at Vera Cruz in April 1914 left 19 American sailors and marines dead and 71 wounded and 126 Mexicans dead and 195 wounded, and it sparked a nationalistic backlash in

Mexico that included the elements Wilson was trying to aid. This served as a wake-up call for him, and it steeled him to resist later demands for full-scale intervention in Mexico. The best that can be said about his early efforts in Mexico is that he learned lessons and gained valuable experience in dealing with a new phenomenon with which he and subsequent presidents would grapple: violence and revolution in less developed parts of the world.[4]

There is a sharp division between the way Wilson conducted himself in foreign policy before and after the sinking of the *Lusitania*. That event, rather than the outbreak of World War I, was the great turning point for him and one of the great turning points in American foreign policy. This was when the war became real and dangerous for the United States, and it set off the great debate between internationalism and isolationism that would last, off and on, for the next twenty-five years. For Wilson himself, one the biggest consequences of the diplomatic crisis following the sinking of that great ship was Bryan's resignation. Before then, he had treated his secretary of state as virtually an equal partner in framing and executing foreign policy. They divided the world into respective spheres of responsibility. The president looked mainly after European affairs and Mexico, while the secretary of state tended to the rest of the world, particularly Latin America. Interestingly, it was the high priest of anti-imperialism, Bryan, who played the larger role in United States intervention in the Caribbean and Central America than did the reformed imperialist, Wilson. After Bryan's resignation, Wilson managed foreign policy single-handedly and made decisions largely on his own. He treated Bryan's successor, Robert Lansing, like a glorified clerk. He did confer with Colonel House, but that man would have far less influence than he believed.

In assessing the situation right after the sinking of the *Lusitania*, Wilson confessed, "I wish with all my heart I saw a way to carry out the double wish of our people, to maintain a firm front in respect of what we demand of Germany and yet do nothing that might by any possibility involve us in the war." He was stating the classic dilemma of peace with honor. For the next two years, he would try by might and main to square that circle. In the spring of 1916, he went to the brink of war and got the Germans to back down—temporarily. At the end of that year, after he won reelection, he mounted a peace offensive that sought a compromise settlement for the war—"peace without victory"—and he pledged American participation in a postwar league of nations to enforce the peace. Germany blasted Wilson's hopes by resuming and expanding submarine warfare at the beginning of February 1917. After much agonized soul searching and desperately trying to find a way to stay out, he made the decision to intervene. As Churchill observed, this was his decision; he was not forced into the war.[5]

As a war leader, Wilson left military affairs to the professionals more than any other wartime president. He likewise delegated much of the management of the domestic war effort—not always with good results. Still, for all the fumbling and ill consequences, it was remarkable that the United States got on a military footing as fast as it did and was able to send over 2 million troops in Europe by the time the war ended. When the Germans unleashed their submarines, they calculated that they would knock the British and French out of the war long before any American forces could be brought in against them. Wilson's war leadership played a big part in foiling those calculations and winning the war for the Allies.

The president's own role during the eighteen months of American belligerency was primarily diplomatic. When the United States intervened, Wilson refused to make wholehearted common cause with the Allies. He insisted that the United States be called an "Associated Power." He also pursued a program of more limited, less punitive war aims, which he articulated on a number of occasions, particularly in the Fourteen Points in January 1918. He intended his war aims to serve two purposes. One was to restrain the Allies and, thereby, lay what he saw as a more solid foundation for future peace. The other purpose was to undermine the German will to fight, and this proved surprisingly successful. The war ended much sooner than anyone anticipated.

Wilson's record in foreign policy up to the end of World War I stands as creditable—one of the better ones among presidents. His early fumbling in Mexico and the often ill-thought interventions in the Caribbean and Central America did nothing to add to his later reputation. Like most presidents, he had little background or, as he liked to say, "preparation" in foreign affairs, and he had to learn on the job. But he did learn. By the time of the outbreak of the world war, he had begun to acquire a surer touch, and his handling of America's posture toward the war was often masterful. His peace offensive and vision of a nonpunitive settlement and league of nations were bold, exciting ventures, and they offer a teasing might-have-been for the outcome of the world war and its aftermath. During America's participation in the war, he performed creditably, and his continued pursuit of a nonpunitive settlement and new world order gave the Allied victory dimensions that it would not otherwise have had. Above all, there is no arguing with success: Wilson won his war.

Wilson's postwar performance in foreign affairs has occasioned the severest criticisms and harshest judgments of his presidency. Those criticisms and judgments have concentrated on what he did and did not do in 1919. He went to the Paris peace conference as the head of the American delegation, but he did not take any prominent Republicans or any senators with him. At Paris, he got down and bargained over the terms of the peace settlement, and he made compromises. He also played the main role in drafting the Covenant of the League of Nations. Back home, he tried and failed to sell his peace program. Ultimately, a spiteful stalemate arose between him and the Republican leadership of the Senate over the peace treaty and membership in the League. To make matters far worse, in the midst of this "League fight," he suffered a severe stroke that left him an invalid who never again fully functioned as president. That stroke caused the worst episode of presidential disability in American history. Remaining in office until March 1921, he served mainly as a roadblock and spoiler and an albatross around the neck of the Democrats, who, in 1920, suffered one of the worst electoral defeats any party has ever suffered.

The severest judgment on Wilson's presidency is that his failures in 1919 canceled out all his other accomplishments. That judgment is excessive. To give a comparison, it is like saying that the fiasco of the Embargo canceled out everything that Thomas Jefferson did previously in his two terms. It is also instructive to ask exactly what Wilson's failures in 1919 really were. Some have argued that at Paris he gave away too much to the Allies in order to get the League of Nations. With one exception—acquiescing in Japan's temporary occupation of Shantung—it is difficult to see where he traded away anything to get the League going. Another, weightier criticism is that he allowed excessive expectations to flower, but much of that was beyond his control. As for his role in the League fight at home, that is a complicated business, but one incontrovertible fact stands out. This political conflict would almost certainly have turned out differently if he had not suffered his stroke. This puts a different complexion on judging his performance. It is one thing to fault a person for failure of nerve or judgment; it is another thing to fault her or him for failures of arteries.

That is a brief examination of what Wilson accomplished as president. A final judgment of his presidency should await an examination of the other criterion for assessing presidents—what this one brought to and gave to the office.

From Academic to Political Leader

The main reason why Winston Churchill shook his head over Wilson was that, by his lights, this man had a most unusual background for a political leader—and not only by Churchill's lights. No other president has had Wilson's background and preparation. No other president has made such a quick jump from private life to the White House. In addition, Wilson came from what some commentators hold to be the worst preparation for politics: academic life. To date, Wilson is the only holder of a PhD and the only professional academic to become president.

But Wilson was not just any academic. He was a political scientist—one of a handful of truly great political scientists America has produced. He really had only one subject, which he studied with a quiet obsessiveness: How does power really work? He came to that subject as an undergraduate at Princeton, when he discovered the writings of the English journalist Walter Bagehot. Wilson added a corollary to his basic question: How can power be made to work more efficiently and more accountably in a representative system? He sought answers partly through comparisons between our separated powers and the unified powers of parliamentary systems, and he believed that the American system ought to be made more like those systems. There was nothing sentimental in that thinking. Despite his mother's birth in England and his family's Scottish background, he did not admire the Westminster Parliament because it was British. He simply thought it worked better. Later, he expanded his political vision with a newfound appreciation of Edmund Burke's anti-ideological conception of politics. In short, from his years of academic study, he gained a keen appreciation for how politics did and should work and a set of ideas about what the proper purposes of politics should be.

Wilson was that rare creature who gets to practice what he preaches. He had an interesting trial run at political leadership as president of Princeton. It was there that he first showed his penchant for bold initiatives and big plans. He ultimately lost two big battles to transform Princeton, but those defeats owed less to misjudgments or personality defects than to bad luck. How much his academic leadership foreshadowed his political leadership remains a matter for argument. He often said that after academic politics, the "real thing" was so much nicer, easier, and aboveboard. His real trial run for the presidency was the governorship of New Jersey. That was where he first drew up a legislative program in advance and where he worked primarily through his party. He would use both of those techniques again with great success in the White House.

Wilson's political leadership grew straight out of his academic studies of politics. That was really what he meant when he followed up his "irony of fate remark" by saying, "All my preparation has been in domestic matters." From an early age, he criticized the separation of powers. He once said, "Ever since I have had independent judgments of my own I have been a Federalist [!]" By that, he meant that he was a Hamiltonian, a devotee of strong centralized government. In his comparisons with parliaments, he was looking for ways to bridge that separation. He personalized the bridge-building exercise by reviving the custom that Jefferson had abandoned of addressing Congress in person. He appeared in person in front of Congress more than any other president before or since. The main reason why later presidents have not done this as much is because, first, radio and, then, television have provided other and presumably more direct means to reach a national audience. But Wilson was also more concerned with bridging the separation of powers than any succeeding president—except possibly LBJ, who went about it differently.[6]

Wilson did more than show his face and make his voice heard on Capitol Hill. In passing domestic legislation, he worked mainly through his party. The academic theorist of party government now became the practitioner of party government. He worked with his party's committee chairmen and leaders in the two houses, and he often went to the Capitol to confer with them and others. This practice paid off handsomely in the passage of his New Freedom programs during his first term.

This practice of party government also carried a price, and it partially explains why partisan conflict was so bitter in 1919. Wilson had never reached out much to Republicans, and he did not do it when choosing the delegation to the Paris peace conference. Belatedly, he did try to reach out when he came back from Paris and sought to bring senators around. He can be faulted for not trying harder and not embracing bipartisanship. As a longtime student of parliamentary systems and coalition governments, he should have appreciated how to make such things work. In his defense, it should also be noted that bipartisanship had little if any precedent during World War I. What happened twenty years later, during and after World War II, sprang in part from various people having learned "lessons" from the debacle of 1919. Bipartisanship may also be an overworked and overpraised practice. It usually involves a large degree of surrender by one of the parties involved—which is what happened in the 1940s.

By and large, Wilson's background as an academic student of politics served him extremely well as president. No other career in American history—perhaps in any country's history—has better commended the study of politics for the practice of politics.

Wilson also brought some other things to the presidency, although it is often hard to separate temperament from professional conditioning. For one thing, he was a genuinely collegial leader. Refreshingly, he knew what he did not know, and he was not ashamed to rely on people who did. He gave an early example of this when he was president of Princeton. He did not know much about science, and he gladly delegated responsibility there to his friend and right-hand man, Dean Henry B. Fine. In the White House, he delegated a great deal of responsibility to his Cabinet, and he gave the secretaries great latitude in running their departments—

with one exception. That was in foreign affairs, but even there, during his first two years, he treated Bryan as an equal partner. Wilson did what seems like an amazing thing: He treated his Cabinet members like responsible adults, he listened to them, and he let them run their own shops.

This delegation could have bad consequences. Two of the worst blots on Wilson's performance and reputation come from the attempt to impose segregation in the federal workplace and the repression of civil liberties during and immediately after the war. In both cases, he deferred to Cabinet members and let them follow their inclinations. With segregation, he did bring the effort to a halt in the face of protests. With civil liberties, the worst repressions occurred after he suffered his stroke, and it is doubtful that he knew much about what A. Mitchell Palmer was doing. Those circumstances do not excuse his shortcomings, but they do mitigate them slightly.

Nor should those shortcomings detract from Wilson's achievement. He really offers an alternative model to the commonly accepted conception of the strong president. That conception is based on FDR and LBJ, with perhaps a touch of Theodore Roosevelt thrown in as well. To be honest, the commonly accepted conception of the strong president contains large elements of bullying, manipulation, meddling, and a generally overbearing quality. Wilson showed that someone does not have to act that way to be a strong, effective president.

Another bit of background that Wilson brought to the presidency was the characteristic that bothered Churchill. Whether because of his "professorial" habits or his temperament, he was one of the most solitary presidents. He did like people, and he could mix well with them. This was true not just of the speaking platform and campaign trail—where he shone—but also of small groups and one-to-one encounters. He first demonstrated his individual charm and persuasiveness as Princeton's president. One of his recruits to the faculty later described their first meeting this way: "Had Woodrow Wilson asked me to go with him and work under him while he inaugurated a new university in Kamchatka or Senegambia, I would have said 'yes' without further question."[7]

Still, Wilson was something of a loner. He did not surround himself with people. He worked by himself a lot in his office. He also liked to turn off what he considered the business side of his mind when he was off duty. William Gibbs McAdoo, who was both his secretary of the Treasury and his son-in-law, used to irritate Wilson by trying to talk business at the family dinner table. Wilson's brother-in-law, Stockton Axson—who probably knew him better than anyone else, except his sister, Wilson's first wife, Ellen—said that this was a clash of temperaments. McAdoo was the man of affairs who was constantly attending to business, whereas Wilson was the artist who poured himself into his work with intensity and concentration, and then needed to get away from it all.[8]

Wilson showed this solitary tendency most clearly when he made major decisions. He would seek advice and listen to opinions, up to a point. But then he would closet himself, read over papers, and write memoranda and notes to himself. He also wrote his own speeches—he was the last president to do that—and he would rarely show drafts to other people. At times of crisis, such as the sinking of the *Lusitania* or the Germans' resumption of submarine warfare, his instinctive reaction was to seclude himself.

These solitary practices drew private complaints from the people around Wilson, including his secretary Joe Tumulty, Cabinet members such as McAdoo, and Colonel House. They were all more naturally gregarious types, what a later generation would call "people persons." His frequent seclusion and disinclination to seek their advice or let them in on big decisions frustrated them, and they all saw these things as shortcomings and weaknesses. It is worth asking, however, whether those complaints were right. It is difficult to point to a single wrong decision he made through failure to consult and take other people's views into account. Two of his most generally acknowledged mistakes—the failure to take Republicans or senators to Paris and the call for the election of a Democratic Congress in the 1918 elections—were matters on which he got plenty of advice. The call for a Democratic congress came in part from his bowing to pressure from party leaders. In the really big decisions, particularly the response to the *Lusitania* and the decision to intervene in the war, he seems to have had near perfect pitch in his attunement to public opinion. He believed that leaders should listen to the people, and his solitariness does not seem to have impaired his attunement to them.

There is another way to ask whether those complaints were right. The literature about how to practice politics written by practitioners is not extensive, but a common refrain in the few examples is the lament that politicians lack detachment and time to reflect. Politicians have so much coming at them so fast; they are surrounded by people who want things from them and tell them what to do. For whatever reasons—whether it was his temperament or his professorial working habits—Wilson built in as much time as he could get for reflection and keeping his bearings.[9]

One final aspect of what Wilson brought to the presidency is his religion. He was the son, grandson, and nephew of Presbyterian ministers, and he spent part of his youth on the campus of a Presbyterian theological seminary. His first wife was the daughter of a Presbyterian minister. No other president, with the possible exception of Jimmy Carter, has been so closely identified with religion. Yet this is a part of Wilson's background that is easy to misconstrue. His upbringing placed him among the most learned and liberal Protestants in America in his time. His religion was deep and profound, but it was also something that he largely took for granted. He did not believe that God spoke to him and told him what to do, and he believed strongly that politics and religion should be kept separate, even religion that promoted social reform. This separation particularly informed his approach to foreign policy. After the sinking of the *Lusitania*, when a correspondent implored him to declare war "in the name of God," Wilson told his stenographer, "War is not declared in the name of God; it is an human affair entirely."[10]

Wilson rarely invoked God in his speeches. The most notable example of such an invocation came in the last sentence of the speech that he gave to Congress asking for a declaration of war. Speaking of the values and ideals that America would fight for, he declared, "God helping her, she can do no other." As many people recognized, that was an exact paraphrase of Martin Luther's celebrated declaration, "God helping me, I can do no other." Wilson may well have been casting his nation in the role that Luther cast the individual Christian—a limited, fallible creature, who could only try to do God's will through following faith and scripture and who could not avoid sin. Wilson was really following Luther in asking his country to "sin boldly."[11]

Both Wilson's religious background and an invocation such as that revealed a sensibility that is far removed from either the self-righteous crusader or the naive idealist that he is often taken to be. He was indeed an idealist, as was nearly every political leader of that time, apart from the most hard-bitten standpatters and machine types. He kept his feet on the ground and was practical and circumspect in his programs at home and abroad. The best example of this comes with the question of trying to spread democracy in the world. In the war address, he uttered the sentence "The world must be made safe for democracy." This man was the most punctilious stylist ever to sit in the White House, and he would never have used the passive voice unless he meant to. That passive voice contains a world of difference from notions of actively imposing democracy on other peoples, especially by force. He had already tried a bit of that in Mexico and had gotten burned. Here he meant that democracy must be defended where it existed, and if America could aid others in advancing democracy, so much the better. Self-righteousness and naive idealism constitute the thrust of the term "Wilsonian" as it is usually employed. The term is a misnomer. Like Marx, who said, "I am not a Marxist, just Karl Marx," this president's ghost could say, "I am not a Wilsonian, just Woodrow Wilson."[12]

Conclusions

What, then, should be the final judgment on Wilson? By the standard of accomplishment, he towers. He was one of the greatest legislative leaders ever to sit in the White House. He conducted a largely successful foreign policy, at least up to a point. Even his great failure had a tragic grandeur and left a haunting legacy. He was not a president for all seasons. It is difficult to imagine him as a president in an "ordinary" time, if there is any such thing. If it had not been for the political upheaval caused by the progressive movements, such an outsider with such an unusual background would not have become president. If it had not been for that upheaval, he would not have enjoyed the chance to employ his penchant for boldness and preparation as a legislative leader. If it had not been for the international upheaval of World War I, he would not have employed the same penchant on the world stage. He needed demanding times, and when he got them he attempted and accomplished great things.

By the standard of contributions to the presidency, Wilson brought eloquence and depth of thought—more eloquence and depth perhaps than any other president except Abraham Lincoln. He brought an approach to leadership that has a becoming maturity and self-restraint. These were all functions of what he called "preparation." He prized self-control, and he liked dispassionate discussion. His model of public persuasion was not the evangelical one followed by Bryan and Theodore Roosevelt. Instead, and not surprisingly, his model was education. He believed in educating the public and being educated by the public.

This concept of preparation was the most important asset Woodrow Wilson brought to and tried to give to the presidency. He does not seem to have succeeded in transferring that asset. His models of leadership and persuasion have not found much of a following among his successors. The presidency has been the poorer for not having become more Wilsonian in this proper sense of that term. This professor-turned-president believed in teaching and learning, and the men and, someday, the women who sit in the White House would do well to learn from him. This man with the long jaw and pince-nez showed a way to be both good and great as president.

Notes

1. Winston S. Churchill, *The World Crisis* (London: Thornton Butterworth, 1927), vol. 3, 229.

2. Ibid.

3. Ray Stannard Baker interview with Edward Grant Conklin, June 3, 1925, Ray Stannard Baker Papers, Library of Congress, box 104.

4. In August 1914, Wilson told his secretary of war, "There are in my judgment no conceivable circumstances which would make it right for us to direct by force or by threat of force the internal processes of what is a profound revolution, a revolution as profound as that which occurred in France. All the world has been shocked ever since the time of that revolution in France that Europe should have undertaken to nullify what was done there, no matter what the excesses then committed." Wilson to Lindley M. Garrison, Aug. 8, 1914, in *The Papers of Woodrow Wilson*, 69 vols., ed. Arthur S. Link et al. (Princeton, N.J.: Princeton University Press, 1966–94), vol. 33, 367.

5. Wilson to Bryan, June 7, 1915, in ibid., 349.

6. Wilson to Albert Bushnell Hart, June 3, 1889, in ibid., vol. 6, 243.

7. Robert K. Root, "Wilson and the Preceptors," in *Woodrow Wilson: Some Princeton Memories*, ed. William Starr Myers (Princeton, N.J. : Princeton University Press, 1946), 15.

8. For this observation, see Arthur S. Link, ed., *"Brother Woodrow": A Memoir of Woodrow Wilson by Stockton Axson* (Princeton, N.J.: Princeton University Press, 1993), 218.

9. For one such observation, see Stimson Bullitt, *What It Means To Be a Politician* (Garden City, N.Y.: Doubleday Anchor, 1961), 138.

10. Entry, May 10, 1915, Diary of Charles L. Swem, in *Papers of Woodrow Wilson*, ed. Link, vol. 33, 138.

11. Wilson speech, April 2, 1917, in ibid., vol. 41, 527.

12. Ibid., 525.

2. "Common Counsel": Woodrow Wilson's Pragmatic Progressivism, 1885–1913

Trygve Throntveit

In his inaugural address of March 4, 1913, Woodrow Wilson heralded the triumph of progressivism in American politics, confirming his commitment to restore "equality" and "justice" by shielding citizens "from the consequences of great industrial and social processes which they cannot alter, control, or singly cope with." He further pledged to derive the policies of this progressive agenda not from elegant theories but from close observation of "the facts as they are." In short, he forecast the ascendancy of a humane empiricism in national politics. "We shall deal with our economic system as it is and as it may be modified, not as if it might be if we had a clean sheet of paper to write upon," he announced, "and step by step we shall make it what it should be in the spirit of those who question their own wisdom and seek counsel and knowledge." More than a "cool process of mere science," the task at hand was "to understand our time and the need of our people," determining through constant reflection "whether we be indeed their spokesmen and interpreters, whether we have the pure heart to comprehend and the rectified will to choose our high course of action."[1]

Empirical yet empathetic; reformist yet restrained—what exactly was the nature of the progressive politics Wilson brought to the White House? His injunction against drawing-board reforms sounds like the creed of a conservative, while his

The author thanks James T. Kloppenberg of Harvard University, John M. Cooper Jr. of the University of Wisconsin-Madison, and Philippa Strum of the Woodrow Wilson International Center for Scholars for feedback on early drafts of this chapter. He also thanks James Kloppenberg and John Cooper, and the organizers of the Wilson at One Hundred Fifty Conference, for presenting the opportunity to write it; and Clark Evans and the staff of the Library of Congress Rare Books Reading Room for help with much of the research behind it.

rejection of ideological rigidity created a safe distance from the "radicals" of his day. Yet his legislative accomplishments in office mark him as one of the most radical reformers to occupy the presidency. In fact, the sweeping changes he effected in office can only be understood as the product of a skeptical and deliberative yet creative and adaptive mind—as the work of a radical empiricist in politics.

That "the facts as they are" might be the basis rather than the nemesis of change was a belief characteristic of Wilson, but not endemic to him. For many leading lights of American social thought, the Darwinian revolution in natural science had recast all aspects of the human condition as historically conditioned and inherently protean phenomena susceptible to conscious manipulation. Perhaps most famously, the self-styled "radical empiricist" William James developed a method—which he dubbed "pragmatism"—for deciding philosophical, epistemological, and moral questions in a "world of pure experience," and in the process he influenced a host of liberal reformers fascinated by his work. John Dewey, Jane Addams, W. E. B. Du Bois, Herbert Croly, and Walter Lippmann were only the foremost among those who saw pragmatism as a fundamentally radical approach to human experience with transformative political implications.[2] James's theory of "corrigible" truth and vision of a deliberative "intellectual republic" taught these reformers to challenge outmoded political ideas, while his writings on ethics taught them how to replace those ideas in an interdependent society with democratic aspirations.[3] In James's view, only an "ethical republic," deliberating over as wide a range of demands as possible, could discover the relationships among individual moral ideals and determine truly social values; and even these would never be final, "until the last man has had his experience and said his say."[4] James's students in the progressive movement applied this method to political values and the institutions enshrining them, hoping not only to achieve specific reforms but also to perpetuate the experiment in interventionist government that was the essence of progressivism.[5]

James was dead by the fall of 1910, when Wilson came to national prominence as a progressive; and as governor of New Jersey, Wilson spoke more often of restoring than relativizing democratic institutions. In many ways Wilson was conservative, skeptical of reforms for which large sectors of the public were unprepared. But James, too, recognized that changes in thinking were typically incremental, constrained by a social environment shaped in turn by the past, so that "truth" developed "much as a tree grows by the activity of a new layer of cambium."[6] In his first book on government, Wilson took a similarly organic view of the institutions embodying America's political ideas. "The noble charter of fundamental law given us by the convention of 1787 is still our Constitution," he wrote, but it was "only the sap-centre of a system of government vastly larger than the stock from which it has branched."[7] Though it was Wilson's own, this conception of the state as an organic expression of political values in constant creation was eminently Jamesian. And though Wilson was no devotee of James, pragmatism provides a vocabulary uniquely suited to explaining the political philosophy and practice of a remarkably elastic thinker. Indeed, Wilson's consistent promotion of a powerful yet flexible and more truly representative national government embodied the pragmatic progressive ideal: continuous political and social reconstruction through broadly inclusive, deliberative discourse—or as Wilson called it, "common counsel."

"A Root, Not a Perfect Vine"

Political and social reconstruction were the foci of Wilson's earliest writings on government. In his dissertation at Johns Hopkins, published as *Congressional Government* in 1885, he argued that the American political system—in which "all motive and regulatory power" resided in a feckless, splintered oligarchy of standing congressional committees—required reshaping. The Constitution was "a root, not a perfect vine," whose natural development toward greater centralization had grown twisted during a century of neglect justified by strict adherence to the separation of powers. The damage must be undone so that coordinated legislative programs, formulated cooperatively by the executive and his party in Congress, and tempered by exhaustive debate, might replace the piecemeal policymaking of committees in camera. Wilson argued that only through some such analog of British cabinet government could the American system become truly "representative," empowered not only "to speak the will of the nation" but also "to lead it to its conclusions, to utter the voice of its opinions, and to serve as its eyes in superintending all matters of government."[8]

Congressional Government was inspired by Walter Bagehot's *The English Constitution* (1867), and Bagehot's historicist approach to politics left a lasting impression on Wilson. Throughout the 1880s, Wilson argued that democracy's vibrancy depended upon the deliberate adaptation of political institutions to changing social and economic conditions, rather than adherence to what Bagehot termed "the literary theory" of constitutions.[9] Wilson's second major book, *The State: Elements of Historical and Practical Politics* (1889), revealed him still as a disciple of Bagehot, committed to demonstrating the underlying premise of *Congressional Government*: that government was "merely the executive organ of society" and that this organic relationship justified changing government's form and functions as society changed. But Wilson was also influenced by another political economist of historicist leanings, his instructor at Hopkins, Richard T. Ely, and he shared Ely's simultaneously religious and scientific perspective on the state's role in promoting social change. In 1885 Wilson wrote that propagating "the supreme and peaceful rule of *counsel*," so to draw humanity toward "kinship with God" by affirming "reason over passion," was the ministry of "the modern democratic state." This divine commission, however, demanded more than proselytizing zeal. Sharing "the benefits of political cooperation" required that their mechanisms be "found by experiment, as everything else has been found out in politics."[10]

Along with Ely's disdain for what he thought to be the inhumane and unscientific rigidity of classical political economy, Wilson absorbed his teacher's interest in nonrevolutionary socialism as a source of experimental tactics for reinvigorating the "rule of counsel" in industrial America. After reading Ely's *The Labor Movement in America* (1886), Wilson gave his own vigorous nod to the salutary potential of an interventionist state in "Socialism and Democracy" (1887), arguing that self-government implied society's use of the state as a tool upon itself. There was no theoretical basis for assuming socialist methods incapable of producing democratic results, he explained, for "in fundamental theory socialism and democracy are almost if not quite one and the same," resting together "upon the absolute right of the community to determine its own destiny and that of its members."[11]

Wilson was suspicious of many socialist reform schemes, asking "not whether the community has power to act as it may please" but "how it can act with practical advantage—a question of *policy*."[12] Nonetheless, he also suspected that question must be answered, in its broadest terms, just as social democrats like Ely predicted: by translating the language of interdependence characterizing the new social science into government action. In *The State*, he endorsed a host of reforms, from regulation of monopolies to child labor laws and factory sanitation standards, all justified in terms of government's duty to maintain the health of the whole social organism. "It should be the end of government *to assist in accomplishing the objects of organized society*," he wrote. "Every means, therefore, by which society may be perfected through the instrumentality of government, every means by which individual rights can be fitly adjusted and harmonized with public duties, by which individual self-development may be made at once to serve and to supplement social development, ought certainly to be diligently sought. . . . Such is the socialism to which every true lover of his kind ought to adhere with the full grip of every noble affection that is in him."[13]

Such passages suggest that Wilson fully embraced the radical but nonrevolutionary ethos of interdependence that would mark Ely's "Wisconsin School" progressivism. Indeed, Wilson never wavered from the conviction that reconciling "individual self-development" with "social development" was government's prime directive. But his ideas about government's role in fostering what is now called "positive freedom" had by no means crystallized in 1889. As industrial violence flared in the 1890s, he found another alternative to revolution in Edmund Burke's prudent gradualism. Though rarely invoked by reformers then or now, Burke's rejection of "speculative politics" for "practical politics" seemed to Wilson the best model for achieving justice and stability in a volatile, variegated society. "Speculative politics treats men and situations as they are supposed to be," Wilson explained while ruminating on Burke in 1893, whereas "practical politics treats them . . . as they are found at the moment of contact."[14] Throughout the 1890s, Wilson promoted such "practical politics," exhorting "leaders of men" to marshal "the major thought of the nation" behind change while respecting the centripetal force of tradition. True leaders, Wilson advised in 1898, must appreciate with Burke the value of a politics that "invent[ed] nothing" yet "had the power of life in it,—and, if the power of life, the power of growth."[15]

Still, Wilson translated Burke's paeans to prudence loosely. "Burke is the apostle of the great English gospel of Expediency," he told his students in 1893. As Wilson interpreted it, this was the same "expediency" he had endorsed in *The State* to justify the catalog of regulatory responsibilities that should comprise modern government's "ministrant functions."[16] Wilson greatly admired Burke, whom he once referred to as "the Master."[17] But to make too much of this comment is to risk labeling pragmatism conservatism and obscuring Wilson's belief in the practical merits of majoritarian democracy. In fact, he considered Burke as visionary in his own way as the Jacobins he famously scorned. Though Burke's insight into the evolutionary nature of the state explained "the high purposes he had ever in view," his mistrust of the mass of Englishmen made it "impossible he should be followed so far." At the same time, Burke was "too timid. . . . He erred when he supposed that progress can in all its stages be made without changes which seem to go even to the substance."[18] In this sense, Burke failed to practice the expediency he preached. In any case, using Wilson's admiration for Burke's anti-ideological politics as evidence of a fundamentally conservative mindset is tendentious.[19] Nearly two decades after rediscovering Burke and after countless genuflections before his genius, Wilson still could say to that bastion of conservatism, the American Bar Association, "I do not fear Revolution. I do not fear it even if it comes. I have unshaken faith in the power of America to keep its self-possession."[20]

Pondering Politics

A revolution of sorts was occurring in Woodrow Wilson's own life that summer of 1910, when he delivered his speech to the American Bar Association. He had seized his chance to be a "leader of men" in 1902 by accepting the presidency of Princeton University, and he had put his leadership ideal into practice with a host of curricular and administrative reforms that made him one of America's foremost educators. By 1910, however, a series of bitter controversies culminated in his defeat in a highly publicized contest over the location of Princeton's new graduate school. By the battle's end, confidence in his leadership had so ebbed that any agenda he might have conceived for the school was foredoomed to stagnation.[21] Yet his shade-like existence in administrative limbo would not last long. Straight through the Princeton graveyard came the political express train, run by powerful interests determined to make him governor of New Jersey.

Though in a sense messengers of a new dispensation, Wilson's suitors were neither angels nor strangers. George Harvey, editor of the J. P. Morgan mouthpiece *Harper's Weekly*, and former U.S. Senator James Smith, boss of the New Jersey Democratic machine, were kingmakers who had tried to run Wilson as a candidate for senator in 1906. Harvey had been impressed with Wilson's personal magnetism since hearing his Princeton inaugural in 1902. Subsequently, he detected in Wilson's frequent strictures against hasty reform the signs of a conservative who respected the power—and perquisites—of the nation's economic elite, and who if groomed as a *presidential* candidate might break William Jennings Bryan's grip on the Democratic Party. Believing that no Democrat could repudiate the party's progressive wing and win the presidential nomination, Wilson declined to be Harvey's candidate. Still, Harvey took such a shine to Wilson that from 1906 he emblazoned each issue of *Harper's Weekly* with the words: "For President—Woodrow Wilson."[22]

Harvey and company, however, never had the bead on Wilson they thought they did; and by the time Wilson took their hand and plunged into politics he had, ironically, regained full confidence in the legitimacy and prudence of government intervention to restore the voice of "the people" to its deliberations. His flirtation with conservatism was a phase in a much longer development of his political thought culminating in his 1907 Blumenthal Lectures at Columbia University. These lectures, published as *Constitutional Government* in 1908, confirmed once and for all his commitment to an adaptive, experimental, and radically democratic politics mirroring Jamesian pragmatic ethics.[23]

The advanced positions staked out in the Blumenthal lectures—to be discussed shortly—are the more remarkable in light of the three-year period preceding them: From roughly 1904 to 1907, Wilson sympathized with a brand of political conservatism seemingly antithetical to James's "ethical republic." Though often characterized as Wilson's "states'-rights" phase, "antipopulist" would be a more accurate description. Wilson blamed demagogues in the Democratic Party for stripping the national leadership of the power to organize an effective assault on Republican hegemony. The two-party system itself, he thought, was consequently threatened. To avoid the Scylla of anarchy and the Charybdis of one-party rule, the country needed "a party of conservative reform, acting in the spirit of law and of ancient institutions," to restore efficiency and deliberation to the center of politics.[24]

Wilson's vision of "conservative reform" coincided with Harvey's goal: breaking the power of Bryan. Bryan, in Wilson's judgment, lacked a "mental rudder," whipping followers into frenzies over serious economic problems he did not understand.[25] Theodore Roosevelt's 1904 presidential win convinced Wilson once and for all that the Democrats' exile from the White House would never end while Bryan's "populists and radical theorists, contemptuous alike of principle and of experience," dominated the party. From 1905, Wilson became something of a stumper for Democratic conservatism as an alternative to both Bryan's populism and Roosevelt's "paternalism."[26] He seemed over the next two years to repudiate almost entirely the views he had expressed in *The State*.[27]

The election of 1904, therefore, caused a change in Wilson's politics. But it was a shift, not a break, in his thinking; and a leaning, not a turn, to the right. He decried "hasty" trust-busting, claiming, "We can't abolish the trusts. We must moralize them."[28] He proposed, however, not to coax moral conduct but compel it. The government should investigate the social impact of corporate practices and pass laws to "individualize" corporate morals rather than "lump and merge" executives in the larger anonymity of a "socialist" state. Democracy depended upon "individual responsibility," and, if not fostered among citizens, that ethos would never characterize a government that absorbed them. On similar grounds, Wilson criticized unions for elevating artificial equality over responsible self-government. Referring to the practice, in some trades, of limiting production to the level of the least skilled, he explained: "The objection I have to labor unions is that they drag the highest man to the level of the lowest."[29]

Though his naive understanding of unions made him question their activities, Wilson never questioned their right to exist, just as he never questioned the right of businesses to form large corporations. Economic life was an aspect of political life, and in political life organization was crucial: "Until the reformers can organize as Tammany has organized, they can never successfully keep the field against her."[30] The question was, How to cultivate the right *spirit* and *habit* of organization among the nation's citizens? Wilson's answer in the early 1900s was to begin locally, and this accounts for his reputation as a states'-rights Jeffersonian. But his argument was pragmatic, not dogmatic. Instead of invoking states'-rights theory to defend local government, he evoked the analyses of Tocqueville, which had impressed him in the 1880s. "It is easier to apply morals in limited communities than in vast states, easier for neighbors to understand one another than for fellow citizens of a continent," Wilson wrote for a Jefferson Day address in 1906. Long training in this communal application of morals had developed the habits of self-government Tocqueville identified as the lifeblood of American democracy, and Wilson believed the continued health of that democracy required a recommitment to such training. But still it was *training* in which Wilson was interested; the conditioning necessary to sustain a much larger, nobler movement toward unified national life. Even when attacking "paternalism," Wilson echoed its ostensible sponsor, Theodore Roosevelt, in urging his listeners "to think of this country as every citizen should, as a single whole, a thing to be served not merely in its parts and in its separate interests, as the States are intended to serve it, but also in its entirety as the Federal Government is intended to serve it, keeping all interests harmonious, all powers co-operative."[31]

Thus, while lauding the "spirit" of his party's patron saint, Wilson argued that Jefferson's extreme individualism and fear of government must yield to modern exigencies. It was not the "tenets" of Jefferson but "the end we are interested in, the realization of the rights of individuals and an impartial development of the people's life," and this required instilling in all citizens the "principle . . . that their object is [the] service, not of *private interests*, but of the *general development.*" This principle in turn demanded abandoning laissez-faire attitudes toward "the great undertakings which feed the industrial life of the nation." Finally, Wilson never, even at the height of his antipopulism, sought to take government out of the hands of the majority. Rather, he "would *turn again*, and turn with confidence, to the *common people* of the country," who "speak in their judgments the true and simple spirit of all just law." Even when extolling individualism, he reminded listeners that "particular interests have been suffered both to check and determine the economic growth of the United States," whereas the "Jeffersonian principle means this: all interests upon an equal footing and everyman singled out for his personal responsibility." This simultaneous critique and codification of American individualism captures the ambiguities in Wilson's thinking at the time. The following, from the same transcript, indicates the direction he was heading: "I cannot make Democratic theory out of each of you, but I could make a Democratic theory out of all of you."[32]

Wilson's political thought had evolved, then, since he wrote *The State*, notably in its emphasis on personal responsibility. But Wilson's democratic vision had always compassed this "covenantal" aspect.[33] Furthermore, neither his Burkean preference for pragmatic reform over populist revolution, nor his countervailing belief in the supreme duty of government to implement the will of the people, had changed. Alarm and ambition combined to make stability his watchword from 1904 to 1907; he feared the populist threat to party government and coveted the recognition his role as conservative spokesman garnered. By the last quarter of the decade, however, he was uncomfortable in that role and began reaffirming his support for a strong central government committed to solving the nation's social and economic ills.[34] The lectures that became *Constitutional Government* revealed much about the direction his self-correction would take him and contain the most important of the political principles he brought to his governorship and the presidency.

Wilson's intellectual affinity with pragmatic political ethics appears in his very definition of "constitutional government," in which the necessity of conflict between society and the individual is implicitly rejected: "A constitutional government is one whose powers have been adapted to the interests of the people and the maintenance of individual liberty," he wrote.[35] Though liberty was the "ultimate object of a constitutional system," Wilson insisted that "there can be no constitutional government unless there be a community to sustain and develop it—unless the nation, whose instrument it is, is conscious of common interests and can form common purposes." Such common purposes were not self-evident but "formed only by the slow processes of common counsel."[36] Thus, securing for individuals the "means of enforcing the understandings of the law" against society's encroachments depended upon two more fundamental tasks: First, "To bring the active and planning will of the government into accord with the prevailing popular thought and need"; and second, "To give to the law thus formulated under the influence of opinion . . . both stability and an incorruptible efficacy."[37]

Wilson resolved the paradox of an individual liberty at once supreme and contingent upon "prevailing" common counsel by affirming the basic principle of pragmatic ethics: the contingent nature of all values. "The ideals of liberty cannot be fixed from generation to generation," he wrote. "Liberty fixed in unalterable law would be no liberty at all. Government is a part of life, and, with life, it must change, alike in its objects and its practices." Certainly "the best practicable adjustment between the power of the government and the privilege of the individual" should be sought, but "the freedom to alter the adjustment" was, in Wilson's mind, "as important as the adjustment itself."[38] Hence the need for representative bodies and courts—the first to amend the law, the second to provide a "nonpolitical forum" in which its scope could be negotiated between the government and citizens who felt their personal ideals had been trammeled.[39]

Wilson's return to form in *Constitutional Government* also included a revived interest in organic metaphors of state development, leading him, for the first time, explicitly to claim Darwinian science as the model for his political analysis. Wilson's political Darwinism, however, was prescriptive as well as descriptive. Though all governments were organic, a truly "constitutional" government was one in which this organic principle was recognized and put to use: "Living Constitutions," he explained, "must be Darwinian in structure *and* in practice."[40] A Darwinian theory of politics thus justified constitutional experimentation on the grounds that human actions shape human constructs—and conscious action might shape them to our liking. Whether Wilson's political science bore any more resemblance to true Darwinian science than did William Graham Sumner's is debatable.[41] More important are the results of its application. The organic metaphor facilitated an account of the powers and responsibilities of government that suggested the two major themes of Wilson's governorship and presidency: the legitimacy of an interventionist state and the necessity of an activist executive.

The logic of interventionism proceeded from a constitutional government's basic function: to be the "active and planning will" of an evolving body politic. Wilson preferred that the states would take it upon themselves to make their legislatures more responsive to public opinion, thus resuming their role as crucial organs of social interpretation and action.[42] Still, one has to read states'-rights theory into *Constitutional Government* to find it. Wilson worried about "a mere act of will on the part of the government" usurping powers not implied by the Constitution in its current form; he said nothing against the states granting power to the federal government if circumstances required. Categorically prohibiting such grants of power was to hew to an "old theory of sovereignty" that had "lost its vitality."[43] The nation was an indivisible whole, and to focus its diffuse interests into political will and action required a center of power responsible to the entire mass.

In 1885 Wilson had found this power, if not responsibility, in Congress. By 1907 the "natural evolution" of government had selected the president as the coordinating organ, effecting the "close synthesis of active parts" efficient representative government required. "His is the only national voice in affairs,"

Wilson wrote of the president. "If he rightly interpret the national thought and boldly insist upon it, he is irresistible." This power entailed the responsibility to bend the other branches to the national will—not by fiat but by faithfully representing public opinion in "daily consultations" with his party and Congress.[44] By performing an epistemological function analogous to that in James's scheme of human psychology, the president could truly be the head of government—registering, interpreting, and acting upon public opinion to facilitate informed and efficient collective action. Just as the art of knowing, for the pragmatists, required the creative reconciliation of conflicting ideas and the will to test the result, Wilson believed that "synthesis, not antagonism" was "the whole art of government"; he could not "imagine power as a thing negative and not positive."[45]

Positively "Unconstitutional"

From 1908 to 1910, Wilson consistently affirmed his belief in government's "positive" power to experiment with ever more efficient means of implementing the popular will.[46] His recent personal experience of power, however, had been anything but positive. Wilson's defeats at Princeton made him receptive to outside opportunities. Furthermore, despite the reputations of his political backers, a newly reoriented Wilson was eager to take advantage of the rising tide of progressivism in the Democratic Party.[47] To his surprise and relief, Harvey and Smith seemed content to promote their candidate without extracting the expected promises. Aware of the cross-party appeal of progressivism to voters nationwide, they decided it was better to have a moderately reformist Democrat in the governor's seat—and if all went well, the White House—than a Republican.[48]

The nomination was hard-won. In 1909 Wilson had again scolded labor leaders for tolerating production limits, and most of the state's progressive newspapers portrayed him as the pawn of bosses and thrall to the J. P. Morgan financial empire.[49] Having renounced campaigning as a token of his disinterestedness, Wilson abandoned silence only once, in August, when the Federation of Labor officially denounced him as antagonistic to their cause. Asked by the editor of the *Labor Standard* to respond, he replied that he thought it "not only perfectly legitimate, but absolutely necessary that Labor should organize if it is to secure justice from organized Capital." But his profession of "hearty support" for accident insurance, just wages, and "reasonable" working hours won few converts in the labor movement.[50] Furthermore, though he and Harvey had drawn up a platform tailor-made for his party's progressives, he could not reveal it until nominated without reneging on his pledge of silence. The task of securing the nomination fell to Boss Smith, who would not rest—and on the eve of the convention did not sleep—until he had convinced the major cogs in his loosely run machine to deliver their delegates' votes, and with them the nomination, to Wilson on September 15, 1910.[51]

Wilson promptly declared independence from his sponsor. "I shall enter upon the duties of the office of Governor, if elected, with absolutely no pledge of any kind to prevent me from serving the people of the State," he told a roomful of doubtful delegates. Though "this day of re-adjustment" posed difficult questions, the means of finding answers was clear. "Government is a matter of common counsel, and everyone must come into the consultation with the purpose to yield to the general view." Though "not a warfare of interests," good government required an "implacable determination to see the right done" that recognized some interests might be sacrificed for others higher. Just as James argued that "there is always a *pinch* between the ideal and the actual" requiring that "some part of the ideal must be butchered," Wilson explained that "strong purpose, which does not flinch because some must suffer, is perfectly compatible with fairness and justice and a clear view of the actual facts."[52] He then presented what seemed to many delegates the most astounding fact of all: his platform, incorporating almost every plank in the progressive shed. It called for equalizing the tax burdens of individuals and corporations, reforming educational funding, conserving natural resources, a public utilities commission, an extended employer's liability act, an eight-hour day for government employees, increased state control over corporations, a corrupt practices act, an expanded civil service, and electoral reform. When, after ending his remarks, he was called back to the stage by an enchanted crowd, he expressed in two sentences the conviction of a generation of reformers: "We must reconstruct, by thoughtful processes, economic society in this country, and by doing so will reconstruct political organization. This reconstruction will be bigger than anything in American history."[53]

Putting economic relationships at the heart of modern politics, Wilson accepted the fundamental premise of a progressive spectrum ranging from Ely's Wisconsin School to Croly's New Nationalism. The erstwhile anti-Wilsonian Joseph P. Tumulty recalled the cry that rippled through the convention's reformist ranks: "Thank God, at last, a leader has come!"[54] Of course, the leader was not yet in office and had not led anyone anywhere. The first of these obstacles Wilson overcame with the unwitting help of a formidable critic, the *Jersey Journal* columnist George L. Record. In an exchange published in the *Trenton True American* on October 26, Wilson unequivocally endorsed Record's proposals for strengthening the public utilities commission, instituting a "drastic corrupt practices act," mandating worker's accident insurance for all industries, and instituting the direct election of senators. Then, pledging to abolish bossism through "pitiless publicity," he began the process immediately, "denouncing" efforts by Smith and others to maintain machine control. He promised never to "submit to the dictation of any person or persons" but to welcome "suggestions from any citizen" and consider them "on their merits." An open administration was the wellspring of "the regeneration of the Democratic Party which I have forecast above."[55]

Wilson's widely read reply to Record probably won him the governorship.[56] More important, the Record exchange revealed the sharpening of Wilson's progressive vision. Confronted with specific issues during the campaign, he treated them discretely rather than as political stereotypes, working out policies with a practical rather than rigidly philosophical coherence and formulating the type of coordinated yet anti-ideological agenda he had extolled since *Congressional Government*.[57] Even more significant was the effect of this pragmatic approach on his political thought in general. His campaign speeches demonstrated an increasingly sophisticated rationale for reform, consistent with his rapid reorientation over the past four years. He still believed self-government required "poise, patience, and the ability to make progress by these virtues."[58] But "progress" was his emphasis: "If any part of the body politic were to lose its impulse for progress it would die." Progress depended upon "respect for the law," but only such law as preserved "the free determination to change it." Though Republican candidate Vivian Lewis pledged to be "a constitutional Governor" who would never "coerce the Legislature into doing anything simply because it was in the interests of the people," Wilson promised to be "an unconstitutional Governor" who would do just that. Maintaining order through change, by actively expounding the conclusions of the broadest "common counsel"; this was the lens through which Wilson projected his governorship to the voters of New Jersey, who liked what they saw.[59]

Once in office, Wilson gave substance to the image in which he had cast himself. He pushed an electoral reform bill through the New Jersey Legislature, ignoring all precedent on March 13 by personally addressing a legislative caucus and convincing the shocked assemblymen to support the bill as a party measure. Soon bills on corrupt practices, utility regulation, and workers' compensation were enacted. When the legislature adjourned on April 22, Wilson could look back on a ninety-day period in which he had personally propelled the type of coordinated party government he first theorized a quarter century earlier. He had been the "leader of men" upon whom responsible government depended.[60] Moreover, compared with other major-party reformers with presidential prospects, Wilson was "much the more radical" when it came to his "social program," as the editor of *The Nation* argued. "If we interpret Gov. Wilson's attitude correctly," the editor continued, cleaning up government was "only a first step. He is deeply aroused by the failure of representative institutions to represent, and he is prepared to go far, it may seem to many too far, in his desire to make these institutions over."[61]

"A New Method and Spirit of Counsel"

Wilson's stellar first term as New Jersey's governor made him the Democrats' choice for president in 1912. He was no shoe-in: Democratic progressives saw Harvey as a monkey on his back, the machines backed Speaker of the House Champ Clark, and the nomination came only after Ellen Wilson facilitated a personal rapprochement with Bryan, who one last time was the dominant figure at the national convention.[62] But Wilson's national fame as a reformer provided the momentum that carried him to Baltimore. Once it became a four-way race, in which he alone had a major party's full support, 1912 was Wilson's year. It was also the year progressivism went national.

All four candidates in 1912 paid homage to the need for change and were in surprising agreement over the ends toward which to direct it. Even William Howard Taft, the candidate of the Republican "stand-patters," proclaimed that "the best government, the government most certain to provide for and protect the rights and governmental needs of every class, is that one in which every class has a voice."[63] Theodore Roosevelt could have spoken these words to the Progressives at Armageddon, and even "Red" Eugene Debs, the Socialists' candidate, could not have painted a rosier political picture. The question in 1912 was not whether or whither to change, but how—a question of method. "We need no revolution," Wilson declared in accepting the Democratic presidential nomination. "We need only a new point of view and a new method and spirit of counsel."[64] What exactly that method should be was a question for voters and for Wilson. How could New Jersey's democratic restoration be replicated on the national level? How could he articulate his answer so that voters found it a proposition worth testing? Wilson quite consciously asked himself these questions, but it was only after meeting Louis Brandeis that he realized how central the question of method would be to his message of reform.

This meeting occurred relatively late in the game. It was not until August 28, 1912—two months before the election—that Wilson called Brandeis to Sea Girt, New Jersey, in hopes the "people's attorney" could help him reach the people.[65]

Wilson was lucky; Brandeis had been preparing to help him for weeks, and developing the means to do so for years—means that were distinctly pragmatic. Brandeis had long been receptive to James's work and ideas, and he had developed a dialectical understanding of the relationship between the individual and society that mirrored the pragmatists'. In fact, Brandeis knew James, through their mutual friend Elizabeth Evans and as a member of the Philippine Information Society (PIS) in Boston.[66] James referred to engagements and discussions with the Brandeises on multiple occasions in correspondence from 1897 to his death, and in August 1906 he vacationed in the Adirondacks with Brandeis, at one point discussing his psychical research over tea with the lawyer.[67] Though that particular discussion may or may not have touched upon moral questions, Brandeis was familiar with James's social, ethical, and political ideas through talks at Evans' house and meetings of the PIS.

The pragmatic cast of Brandeis's thought is readily apparent. Brandeis was a radical empiricist; he believed the only useful ideas were those suggested by and successfully tested against experience. "Knowledge of the decided cases and of the rules of logic cannot alone make a great lawyer," Brandeis told a young associate in 1893. "He must know, must feel 'in his bones' the facts to which they apply."[68] In the explosive light of Homestead and Pullman, Brandeis realized that blind adherence to abstract principles was not just a professional hazard; rather, "to be controlled by logic and to underestimate the logic of facts" was a hazard to society itself. "My early associations were such as to give me greater reverence than I now have for the things that are because they are," he recalled in 1913 of his first years practicing law. "I trusted only expert opinion. Experience of life has made me democratic. I began to see that many things sanctioned by expert opinion and denounced by popular opinion are wrong."[69] This thoroughly pragmatic belief in the complementariness of empirical and democratic practice impelled every work of public service Brandeis undertook; as John Dewey wrote years later, "reference to factual context" was the hallmark of Brandeis's method. After examining the facts in 1912, Brandeis, a longtime member of the Progressive Republican League, announced that "progressives, irrespective of party affiliations, should in my opinion support Woodrow Wilson for the Presidency. He is thoroughly democratic in spirit."[70]

Though Brandeis ranked Wilson's nomination as "among the most encouraging events in American history," Wilson's dry acceptance speech was not the triumph its gubernatorial counterpart was.[71] It did, however, somewhat clarify Wilson's conception of the political tasks ahead. While endorsing his party's platform generally, he outlined no specific economic policies, asserting instead that each party's platform was but a stab at answering "great questions of right and of justice" pertaining to "the development of character and of standards of action no less than of a better business system." The salient question was, "*How* do we expect to handle the great matters that must be taken up by the next Congress and the next administration?" It was a question of means more than ends; or rather, one of means as ends. For years, "great matters" had been "handled in private conference" by "men who undertook to speak for the whole nation." Some had done so "very honestly it may be, but very ignorantly sometimes, and very shortsightedly, too." The point was that no matter how honest the men or large-spirited the objects, government by the few would always be "a poor substitute for genuine common counsel."[72]

Thus it was an *idea*, the idea that "common counsel" was the best method of government, that—if Wilson had anything to do with it—would be voted on in November; an idea, he hoped, that would distinguish the Democrats from the rivals they so resembled: the Progressive Party of Theodore Roosevelt. "No group of directors, economic or political, can speak for a people," Wilson declared, alluding to the "paternalistic" methods he attributed to the Progressives. "They have neither the point of view nor the knowledge." Wilson proposed, in effect, to apply the pragmatic method to politics by broadening the national deliberative discourse. But declaiming "common counsel" as "the meaning of representative government" was a far cry from describing how it worked. Wilson needed a policy hook, an example of how common counsel might look in action, to catch the public's attention; but tariff reform, the oldest weapon in the Democratic armory, turned to rust in his hands.[73] For the first three weeks of the campaign, there was no blade in Wilson's rhetorical scabbard—a mortal disadvantage against the oratorical onslaughts of a Roosevelt.

Brandeis armed Wilson with "principles" to parry "personalities."[74] Theirs was a meeting of like minds. "I am for Wilson because I found him in complete sympathy with my fundamental convictions," Brandeis told reporters. Wilson, meanwhile, found his hook: "Both of us," he told the press with novel clarity, "have as an object the prevention of monopoly." Brandeis briefly outlined that object. "We must undertake to regulate competition instead of monopoly," he said, alluding to Roosevelt's proposal to place trusts under government control, "for our industrial freedom and our civic freedom go hand in hand and there is no such thing as civic freedom in a state of industrial absolutism."[75] Along with a motto—"To Regulate Competition Instead of Monopoly"—both men found renewed purpose at Sea Girt. Brandeis left determined to garner Wilson the vote of every reform-minded journalist, editor, social worker, businessman, and politician he knew—a considerable number.[76] Wilson immediately hurled the fruits of his encounter with

Brandeis at Roosevelt, lauding his rival's social goals but dissenting from his "central method"—the paternal. The Progressives, he alleged, had determined upon "acting as a Providence" for the people, as if understanding their needs implicitly. "I have never known any body of men, any small body of men, that understood the United States," Wilson countered. "And the only way the United States is ever going to be taken care of is by having the voices of all the men in it constantly clamorous for recognition of what is justice as they see the light."[77]

Wilson's biggest breakthrough came in a letter from Brandeis dated September 30, 1912, indicating both the specific antitrust measures Wilson's party should promote and the principles of social analysis and political experimentation inspiring them. Simply put, the Democrats must propose to learn from experience—including failure. The social harm sustained by the Sherman Antitrust Act's failure, while revealing the statute's "defects," also "established the soundness of the economic policy which it embodies." Effectively implementing that policy required examining the economic experience of the whole nation, legislating accordingly, and institutionalizing the process, making future legislation an empirical exercise. "Experience," Brandeis wrote, had revealed many forms of economic combination that suppressed competition to an "unreasonable" degree. It was time "to utilize that experience and to embody its dictates in rules of positive law" preventing such combinations. However, experience also showed that *any* means of dominating markets "otherwise than through efficiency" were unreasonable, making it necessary to protect against anticompetitive methods yet unknown. Thus "an administrative Board" was needed, with "broad powers" of investigation and legislative initiative to be "increased from time to time as we learn from experience."[78]

Wilson's initial intention to publish the letter is obvious from his many emendations, and it demonstrates the degree to which he internalized Brandeis's arguments.[79] However, the emendations also reveal subtle but important differences in their thinking. Where Brandeis wrote of measures "by which existing trusts might be effectively disintegrated," Wilson crossed out the last word and substituted the phrase "deprived of their domination and illicit power." He also deleted a paragraph proposing retroactive punishment of combinations that, though declared illegal by the courts, had not had to pay reparations.[80] Clearly, Wilson never believed as deeply in the intrinsic superiority of a small-producer economy as did Brandeis, or in the need to wreak vengeance upon the trusts. But he was sufficiently convinced of the inherent dangers of concentrated economic power to fear both trust- and government-dominated industry as graveyards of material and social growth. Wilson's dog-eared and underscored copy of Brandeis's *Scientific Management and Railroads*, which he read around this time, also evinces the degree to which he embraced Brandeis's basic logic: Competition bred experimentation; experimentation, efficiency; efficiency, prosperity; and prosperity, the opportunities for personal development that self-governing citizens required. If competition flagged, government must restore it, find a substitute, or risk its own stagnation.[81]

Brandeis did more for Wilson than point his lance at the soft underbelly of Progressive trust policy. Brandeis articulated a pragmatic method for preserving self-government in perpetuity and not merely for restoring it in 1912. That Wilson came during his presidency to find Brandeis's proscriptions of bigness increasingly simplistic shows how thoroughly he appropriated Brandeis's method, and hints perhaps at the wider range of facts to which he applied it.[82] In any case, anchoring the issues in Brandeis's social and economic empiricism gave Wilson's campaign messages the intellectual coherence and political substance they had lacked. "We talk, and we talk in very plausible phrases, indeed, about returning the government of this country to the people of this country," he told an Indianapolis audience three days after reading Brandeis's letter. But *how*? Not simply by voting for a "Progressive." Roosevelt had tolerated "the very conditions we are trying to alter" while president, and still sought to "assuage" rather than change them by placing monopolies under government stewardship. Wilson claimed that both Roosevelt and Taft sought simultaneously to preserve monopoly power and to restore lost freedoms, an impossible denial of "what the whole country knows to be true"—that economic freedom and monopoly power had proved incommensurable, and that to restore lost freedoms required a "new freedom" from the *power* of the trusts, no matter where it resided.[83]

More than just the New Freedom's central policy promise, breaking the power of the trusts was a symbolic first step in reconstituting representative government along the lines Wilson had imagined since the 1880s: responsive to the people's will and efficient in carrying it out. Restoring government to the people meant restoring prosperity to the mass of them, giving them time and energy to participate in public life; and restoring prosperity meant opening the economic laboratory to as many enterprising souls as possible.[84] Herein lay the real difference between Wilsonian and Rooseveltian progressivism. As Wilson realized, the immediate objects of each candidate, similar or dissimilar, were less important than the "engineering principles of liberty" each applied to politics.[85] Whereas Roosevelt's emphasis on national unity as the repository of national strength led him to define citizenship as self-sacrifice, and leadership as the ability to elicit such sacrifices, Wilson defined citizenship as self-government, in which self-sacrifice and enlightened self-interest played equally important roles. The task of a leader was to encourage the examination of interests that revealed convergent goals, facilitate the discussions that determined the sacrifices required to attain them, and translate the conclusions into policies embodying them—to promote, in short, "a common understanding and a free action all together."[86] Ultimately Wilson's was a vision of democracy a plurality of Americans shared on election day in 1912.

"Liberal in Purpose, and Effective in Action"

Once president, Wilson continued to believe in an empiricist, pragmatic approach to politics, and in the paramountcy of widely participatory deliberative discourse in an interdependent society. In 1913 and 1914, Wilson pushed the entire New Freedom program through the Sixty-Third Congress, rationalizing the tariff, establishing the Federal Reserve, and restricting the powers of trusts, attempting at each step to mitigate the possible stultifying effects of his statutory measures by creating flexible investigatory commissions with constructive powers. Seeking a balance between private initiative and public supervision of the economy, Wilson attempted to loosen the stranglehold of vested interests on American trade, credit, consumer prices, and the labor market, to allow Americans at least a little more latitude in the use of their dollars and hours, and thus more control over their role in national life.[87] This Herculean effort to clean and rebuild the Augean stables of the American economy was succeeded by a cascade of social justice measures beginning in 1915. Rural credits, child labor restrictions, a government worker's compensation act, and a redistributive income tax were all passed or in passage before the Democrats unveiled their 1916 platform—a platform pledging to fulfill every remaining social justice promise of the Progressive Party in 1912.[88] Just as effective in convincing social justice progressives of Wilson's zeal for the "ethical republic" was his nomination of Brandeis to the Supreme Court in January 1916, followed by a giant and successful presidential push for confirmation.[89] To the pragmatist Walter Lippmann of *The New Republic*, these efforts evinced the commitment to an "Integrated America" that progressives once looked for in Roosevelt. It also demonstrated surprising adaptability. "Wilson," wrote Lippmann in October, "is evolving under experience and remaking his philosophy in the light of it," thus "temporarily at least creating, out of the reactionary, parochial fragments of the Democracy, the only party which at this moment is national in scope, liberal in purpose, and effective in action."[90]

It has not been the purpose of this chapter to demonstrate the "influence" of pragmatism on Wilson's thinking. Wilson never cited James or Dewey in any letter or speech, though he had met both and was aware of their ideas through James's essays and Dewey's prominence in reform circles.[91] Moreover, self-consciously pragmatist progressives like Herbert Croly for years thought Wilson of a wholly different species, if not outside the progressive genus altogether. When Wilson, after his epic legislative victories in the Sixty-Third Congress, began talking as if his program of economic reorganization might alone usher in the post–Progressive Era in America, Croly wrote in *The New Republic* that such "extravagant claims" only showed how grossly the president "misconceived the meaning and the task of American progressivism."[92] Yet within two years, Croly was supporting Wilson's reelection in 1916. Prompted by his coeditor Lippmann, Croly came to realize that Wilson's agenda as president bespoke an intellectual orientation strikingly congruent with their own pragmatic progressivism, which emphasized that society was a growing thing, that the state must grow and change with it, and that the political, economic, and social spheres were as interdependent as the individuals inhabiting them.

In 1916 yet another pragmatist progressive, John Dewey, contended in *The New Republic* that Wilson had abandoned the atomistic dogma of Democratic tradition for what could justly be termed a pragmatic approach: "He has appreciated the moving forces of present industrial life and has not permitted the traditional philosophy to stand in the way of doing things that need to be done."[93] As Wilson himself explained in a folksier way in 1916, he believed the central challenge of politics could be expressed "in the formula, 'get together.' Try to understand what the common task is and all take part in it in the same spirit." Ultimately, "politics" was "nothing but a systematic attempt to keep the law adjusted to the real facts" of society—and "you cannot understand society unless you understand the component parts."[94] Here, as throughout his career, Wilson underscored the clear philosophy of social interdependence, communal inquiry, and political experimentation encapsulated in his concept of "common counsel." In other words, he articulated a pragmatic progressivism, one that by 1917 had transformed politics in America and was soon to do the same beyond its borders.

Notes

1. "An Inaugural Address," March 4, 1913, in *The Papers of Woodrow Wilson*, 69 vols., ed. Arthur S. Link et al. (Princeton, N.J.: Princeton University Press, 1966–94) (hereafter, *PWW*), vol. 27, 151.

2. The standard account of this epistemological revolution and its influence in transatlantic social-scientific and political discourse is James T. Kloppenberg, *Uncertain Victory: Social Democracy and Progressivism in European and American Thought, 1870–1920* (New York: Oxford University Press, 1986). The remarkable degree to which these discourses affected public policy and encouraged state interventionism in America, Europe, and the British Dominions is explored by Daniel T. Rodgers, *Atlantic Crossings: Social Politics in a Progressive Age* (Cambridge, Mass.: Harvard University Press, 1998).

3. The description of truth as "corrigible" and the call for an "intellectual republic" are given by William James, "The Will to Believe" (orig. pub. 1896), in *Pragmatism and Other Writings*, ed. Giles Gunn (New York: Penguin Books, 2000), 207, 218. Along with "The Will to Believe," the following essays, taken together, best elucidate James's ethics and should be read as a group: "On a Certain Blindness in Human Beings" (1889), "What Makes a Life Significant" (1889), "The Moral Philosopher and the Moral Life" (1891), and "Is Life Worth Living?" (1895), all in ibid.

4. James, "Moral Philosopher," 251, 242; see also 243–45, 248–51, 253–60; cf. James, "Is Life Worth Living," 236, 238–40. The above distillation of James's ethics suggests an ambitious argument that cannot be pursued here. The subject is elaborated by Trygve Throntveit, "Related States: Pragmatism, Progressivism, and Internationalism in American Thought and Politics, 1880–1920," doctoral dissertation, Harvard University, May 2008.

5. Definitions of "progressivism" proliferate. Almost all who adopted the label, however, rejected the laissez-faire approach to politics and economics they thought dominated yet enervated public life in America and agreed on the basic responsibility of the state to create conditions of economic and social justice. What such conditions were and how to realize them were questions that different participants in the progressive movement answered in various and sometimes contradictory ways; what distinguished "pragmatist progressives" such as John Dewey, Herbert Croly, and Walter Lippmann was their conscious willingness to exploit the fecundity of the progressive critique by interrogating its myriad hypotheses, experimenting with many, and avoiding dogmatic adherence to any.

6. William James, "What Pragmatism Means" (1907), in *Pragmatism and Other Writings*, ed. Gunn, 31, 33.

7. Woodrow Wilson, *Congressional Government* (Cleveland: Meridian Books, 1965; orig. pub. 1885), 28, 29.

8. Ibid., 30, 31, 195.

9. "His book has inspired my whole study of our government," Wilson wrote to his fiancée Ellen Axson on January 1, 1884, in *PWW*, vol. 2, 641. Wilson quotes Bagehot in *Congressional Government*, 30.

10. Woodrow Wilson, *The State: Elements of Historical and Practical Politics* (Boston: D. C. Heath, 1909; orig. pub. 1889), 576; Woodrow Wilson, "The Modern Democratic State" (1885), in *PWW*, vol. 5, 90, 92. "The Modern Democratic State" was never published; its brevity suggests it was a kind of memorandum on democratic theory to which Wilson expected to refer in later years, and in fact it did anticipate

themes to which he returned throughout his academic and political career. See the editorial note in ibid., 54–58.

11. Woodrow Wilson, "Socialism and Democracy" (unpublished, 1887), in *PWW*, vol. 5, 561–62. There is no satisfactory explanation as to why this essay was never published. For the timing of its composition, see the editorial note following its transcription in ibid., 563. Wilson's copy of *The Labor Movement in America* (New York: T. Y. Crowell, 1886) is preserved in his personal library at the Library of Congress (hereafter, WL LC), along with a copy of Ely's *French and German Socialism in Modern Times* (New York: Harper & Brothers, 1883). This last Wilson read multiple times, at least once while writing *The State*. The book is signed and dated "Woodrow Wilson, 1883" and inscribed on p. 262: "Oct. 24th, 1883 / November 9th, 1883 / May 29th, 1888."

12. Wilson, "Socialism and Democracy," 562. For an example of Wilson's skepticism concerning particular socialist programs, see his marginal note regarding cooperatives on p. 208 of Ely's *Labor Movement in America*, reproduced in *PWW*, vol. 5, 558.

13. Wilson, *The State*, 634–36; the quotations are on 633, 631–32. Here, and unless noted, the emphasis was in the original.

14. "Edmund Burke: The Man and His Times," c. August 31, 1893, in *PWW*, vol. 8, 341, 342. Wilson reread Burke's *Reflections on the Revolution in France* in the early 1890s and came to appreciate the wisdom it offered Americans in the midst of their own social and political turmoil; see the long editorial note in *PWW*, vol. 8, 313–18. Burke's belief in a slowly but steadily evolving body of law as the most rational agent of legal change also absorbed Wilson's interest, as is clear from his detailed lecture notes for July 2–10, 1894, in ibid., 597–99; and his notes for lectures on public law from ca. September 22, 1894–January 20, 1895, in *PWW*, vol. 9, 5–106.

15. T. H. Vail Motter, ed., *Leaders of Men, by Woodrow Wilson* (Princeton, N.J.: Princeton University Press, 1952), 41; Woodrow Wilson, "Edmund Burke: A Lecture," February 23, 1898, in *PWW*, vol. 10, 421.

16. "Burke: The Man and His Times," in *PWW*, vol. 8, 342; Wilson, *The State*, 614–15. John Milton Cooper Jr. makes this case in succinct, penetrating fashion: John Milton Cooper Jr., *The Warrior and the Priest: Woodrow Wilson and Theodore Roosevelt* (Cambridge, Mass.: Harvard University Press, 1983), chap. 4, esp. 53, 55–56. Evidence from Wilson's personal copy of Burke's *Works* (inscribed "1883") shows that Wilson had always read Burke in this light: Almost every passage marked indicates Wilson's interest in what James would have called the "pragmatic" ideas therein. "The spirit of practicability, of moderation, and mutual convenience will never call in geometrical exactness as the arbitrator of an amicable settlement," read one such passage, marked in Burke's "Speech on American Taxation" of 1774. It continued, "Consult and follow your experience." Edmund Burke, *The Works of the Right Honorable Edmund Burke*, 7th ed., 12 vols. (Boston: Little, Brown, 1881), vol. 2, 71, WL LC; and passim, esp. vols. 1–3.

17. Motter, *Leaders of Men*, 45. In this passage, Wilson approvingly quoted Burke's adage that "to follow, not to force, the public inclination—to give a direction, a technical dress, and a specific sanction, to the general sense of the community, is the true end of legislation." This is indeed the crux of Wilson's message in "Leaders of Men," and

his criticism of Burke is largely confined to the latter's failure to put his philosophy into practice. The quotation from Burke is marked in Wilson's personal copy of Burke's *Works*, vol. 2, 225, in Burke's "Letter to the Sheriffs of Bristol." The original quotation reads ". . . the true end of legisla*ture*."

18. Motter, *Leaders of Men*, 27, 28–29; "Burke: The Man and His Times," in *PWW*, vol. 8, 340. Wilson is known to have delivered "Leaders of Men" on January 20, 1898, at a benefit held in the University Place Church at Princeton, and again on May 24, 1898, at the University School in Bridgeport, Connecticut. He may well have recycled the address on other occasions throughout the decade. See Motter, "Introduction," in *Leaders of Men*, 4, 9.

19. The descriptor "anti-ideological," referring to Burke's politics as understood by Wilson, is borrowed from Cooper, *Warrior and the Priest*, 53. A particularly vehement argument for the fundamental conservatism of Wilson's political science is Vincent Ostrom, *The Intellectual Crisis in American Public Administration* (Tuscaloosa: University of Alabama Press, 1974), claiming specifically that Wilson's "theory of administration was no less than a counter-revolutionary doctrine" (133). For most of the past fifty years, more nuanced arguments for Wilson's conservatism have prevailed, though the literature is contradictory. In *The American Political Tradition and the Men Who Made It* (New York: Alfred A. Knopf, 1948), Richard Hofstadter made Wilson the archetypal "conservative as liberal," admitting that Wilson's philosophy left "room . . . for reform" but claiming it was fundamentally "Manchesterian" in its acceptance of "conventional laissez-faire" (239–41). In contrast, the most recent comprehensive analysis of Wilson's thought stressing his political conservatism—Niels Aage Thorsen, *The Political Thought of Woodrow Wilson* (Princeton, N.J.: Princeton University Press, 1988)—emphasizes Wilson's admiration for Burke and Hamilton in concluding that Wilson's political science replaced "the majoritarian idea of 'the people' as the principle of legitimacy with an idea of the nation," and that his most important legacy was "the creation of reasoning, metaphors, and concepts that support[ed] . . . the systematic accumulation of power" by the state (218, 233). Yet, Wilson preferred reform over revolution in politics and economics, admired Hamilton's efforts to consolidate federal power in the early republic, and thought the populist Jefferson "a great man, but not a great American," as he wrote in 1893. Yet Wilson concluded in the same essay that Hamilton's scorn for democracy was un-American, and during the campaign of 1912 compared what he considered Hamilton's plutocratic tendencies to contemporary obstacles preventing the mass of "the people" from participating in government. See Woodrow Wilson, "A Calendar of Great Americans," c. September 15, 1893, in *PWW*, vol. 8, 374, 369; and Woodrow Wilson, "A News Report of a Campaign Address in Baltimore," April 30, 1912, in *PWW*, vol. 24, 374.

20. Woodrow Wilson, "The Lawyer and the Community," August 31, 1910, in *PWW*, vol. 21, 81. The address was delivered in Chattanooga.

21. Henry W. Bragdon, *Woodrow Wilson: The Academic Years* (Cambridge, Mass.: Harvard University Press, 1967), is the standard account of Wilson's life and thought

from 1875 to 1910; on his Princeton presidency, see 269–384. Cooper's more favorable evaluation of Wilson's reforms and the efficacy of his leadership is, however, a compelling riposte to Bragdon's charges of antimodernism and intransigence, respectively; see Cooper, *Warrior and the Priest,* chap. 7, esp. 89–90, 97–101.

22. *Harper's Weekly* cover slogan quoted in Cooper, *Warrior and the Priest,* 121. A detailed account of the events described in this paragraph is Arthur S. Link, *Wilson: The Road to the White House* (Princeton, N.J.: Princeton University Press, 1947), 97–106.

23. Woodrow Wilson, *Constitutional Government in the United States* (New York: Columbia University Press, 1908).

24. Woodrow Wilson, "An Address on the South and the Democratic Party," November 30, 1904, in *PWW,* vol. 15, 548. This address was delivered at the Waldorf-Astoria Hotel in New York City to the Society of the Virginians.

25. Wilson is quoted in Link, *Road to the White House,* 96.

26. Wilson, "Address on the South," 547. For Wilson's denunciation of the then-current administration's trend toward "paternalism," see Woodrow Wilson, "A News Report of an Address to the Southern Society of New York," in *PWW,* vol. 15, 336–37; and the "Credo" Wilson drafted for the New York *Sun* in August 1907, printed in *PWW,* vol. 17, 336–37.

27. See Wilson's speeches at New Rochelle, N.Y., February 27, 1905; Detroit, March 31, 1905; and New York, April 16, 1906—all in *PWW,* vol. 16, as cited below.

28. Woodrow Wilson, "A News Release of a Speech on Thomas Jefferson," c. April 13, 1906, in *PWW,* vol. 16, 359–62.

29. Woodrow Wilson, "An Address at New Rochelle, New York," February 27, 1905, in *PWW,* vol. 16, 15.

30. Woodrow Wilson, "An Address at Detroit," March 31, 1905, in *PWW,* vol. 16, 43.

31. Wilson, "News Release of a Speech on Thomas Jefferson," 362; Woodrow Wilson, "A News Report of an Address to the Southern Society of New York," December 15, 1906, in *PWW,* vol. 16, 529–30. In Wilson's copy of *Democracy in America,* the following passage is marked: "When the members of a community are forced to attend to public affairs, they are necessarily drawn from the circle of their own interests, and snatched at times from self-observation. As soon as a man begins to treat of public affairs in public, he begins to perceive that he is not so independent of his fellow-men as he had at first imagined, and that, in order to obtain their support, he must often lend them his co-operation." Alexis de Tocqueville, *Democracy in America,* trans. Henry Reeve, 2 vols. (London: Longmans, Green, 1875), vol. 2, 94, WL LC. For more on Tocqueville's belief that the commitment to individual liberty and the historical necessity of local self-government encouraged an ethic of egalitarian reciprocity among Americans, see James T. Kloppenberg, "The Canvas and the Color: Tocqueville's 'Philosophical History' and Why It Matters Now," *Modern Intellectual History* 3, no. 3 (2006): 495–521; and James T. Kloppenberg, "Tocqueville, Mill, and the American Gentry," *The Tocqueville Review / La Revue Tocqueville* 27, no. 2 (2006): 351–80.

32. Woodrow Wilson, "News Release," in *PWW*, vol. 16, 360–61, 362 (emphasis added); Woodrow Wilson, "Address on Thomas Jefferson," April 16, 1906, in ibid., 366–67. August Heckscher briefly treats the "peace" Wilson made with Jefferson along complementary lines, giving slightly more weight to Wilson's admiration for Jefferson as a "practical man of action," despite his philosophizing. See August Heckscher, *Woodrow Wilson* (New York: Charles Scribner's Sons, 1991), 150–51.

33. Wilson suffered a series of strokes from 1896 on, including a moderately severe one in 1906. Wilson's emphasis on "the transformed, renewed, morally purified" individual after his 1906 stroke is analyzed by John M. Mulder, *Woodrow Wilson: The Years of Preparation* (Princeton, N.J.: Princeton University Press, 1978), 240–44; the quotation is on 240. Though noting Wilson's rejection of laissez-faire government, Mulder overemphasizes Wilson's individualist views, especially in his brief analysis of *Constitutional Government*. Though the extent of Wilson's commitment to individual responsibility and fear of overregulation is fully demonstrated in Mulder's survey of Wilson's speeches and writings from this period, his belief in social interdependence and the ultimate supremacy of the federal government over the states persists, and *Constitutional Government* is a clear harbinger of their return to prominence in his thought. The effects of all Wilson's strokes on his character and thinking, including the crippling one he suffered in 1919 at the height of his fight with the Senate over the Treaty of Versailles, are analyzed extensively by Edwin A. Weinstein, *Woodrow Wilson: A Medical and Psychological Biography* (Princeton, N.J.: Princeton University Press, 1981).

34. See, e.g., Woodrow Wilson, "Politics," July 31, 1907, in *PWW*, vol. 17, 309–25, a reprisal of an earlier critique of "State Rights," reprinted December 20, 1899, in *PWW*, vol. 11, 303–48. Wilson, to be sure, was still playing seesaw; see his conservative "Credo" of 1907, cited in note 26 above.

35. Wilson, *Constitutional Government*, 2, 18, 25, 30.

36. Ibid., 18, 25, 30.

37. Ibid., 23–24; see also 14.

38. Ibid., 4–5.

39. Ibid., 18, 142–43, 170–72.

40. Ibid., 20, 57; emphasis added.

41. According to Richard Hofstadter, Sumner's thinking was Darwinian in conceiving "rights" as "evolving folkways crystallized in laws" and in recognizing that in "other times and places other mores have prevailed, and still others will emerge in the future." Yet Hofstadter also notes that the "geological tempo" at which Sumner believed this emergence occurred resulted in a "scorn for all forms of meliorism and voluntarism" that prevented him from being a "consistent evolutionist," prepared to accept the "decline of laissez-faire . . . as a new trend in the development of the mores." Wilson's Darwinian politics, in contrast, evinced the "pragmatic bias" Hofstadter and others attribute to Lester Frank Ward's sociology, which distinguished "between physical, or animal, purposeless evolution and mental, human evolution decisively modified by purposive action," and thus "replaced an older passive determinism with a positive body of social theory adaptable to the uses of reform." Hofstadter's view of Sumner has

been challenged by Robert C. Bannister, who claims that Hofstadter bought in to the bogeyman caricature of Sumner conjured by Ward and other "reform Darwinists"; and by Bruce Curtis, who argues that Sumner's focus on group rather than individual conflict led him at the end of his life to see cooperation as natural and to endorse government restraint of monopolies. In any case, it is safe to say that Sumner's, Ward's, and Wilson's various "Darwinisms" all exceeded the fundamentally descriptive (rather than prescriptive or proscriptive) aims of the theory of natural selection developed by Charles Darwin in *On the Origin of Species* (1859). See Richard Hofstadter, *Social Darwinism in American Thought* (Boston: Beacon Press, 1992; orig. pub. 1944), 59–61, 65, 68; Robert C. Bannister, *Social Darwinism: Science and Myth in Anglo-American Social Thought* (Philadelphia: Temple University Press, 1979); Bruce Curtis, *William Graham Sumner* (Boston: Twayne, 1981); Clifford H. Scott, *Lester Frank Ward* (Boston: Twayne, 1976); and Edward C. Rafferty, *Apostle of Human Progress: Lester Frank Ward and American Political Thought, 1841–1913* (Lanham, Md.: Rowman & Littlefield, 2003).

42. Wilson, *Constitutional Government,* 170–72, 188–92, 195–97.

43. Ibid., 170–71, 178.

44. Ibid., 54–81; the quotations here are on 54, 59, 68, 81.

45. Ibid., 106. Arthur Link, stressing what he claims was Wilson's "plea for dynamic state [as opposed to federal] action," specifically contrasts the ideas in *Constitutional Government* with "the Herbert Croly type of progressive thought," ignoring the book's emphasis on active adaptation of institutional forms to sociopolitical circumstances. Link, *Road to the White House,* 109–10.

46. See Wilson's speech in New York, December 9, 1908, in *PWW*, vol. 18; his speeches in Chicago, February 12, 1909, and Baltimore, February 19, 1909, in ibid., vol. 19; and again in New York, January 18, 1910, in ibid., vol. 20.

47. For a thoughtful analysis of the relative weight of intellectual temperament and personal advantage in Wilson's embrace of progressivism (giving greatest weight to the former), see Cooper, *Warrior and the Priest,* 122–27. For more on the change in progressives' fortunes and its effect on Wilson, see Link, *Road to the White House,* 122–23.

48. See the selection from William O. Inglis, "Helping to Make a President," in *Woodrow Wilson: Reform Governor*, ed. David W. Hirst (Princeton, N.J.: Van Nostrand, 1965), 7–9. Inglis was a writer hired by Harvey to help publicize Wilson's candidacy; his account appeared during Wilson's second presidential campaign in three issues of *Collier's Weekly* in October 1916. For Wilson's impressions, which corroborate Inglis's account, see his letters to David B. Jones and Edward W. Sheldon on June 27 and July 11, 1910, in *PWW*, vol. 20, 543–45, 572–73. Wilson responded to the only "conditions" of Boss Smith's support with devious ambiguity: "I would be perfectly willing to assure Mr. Smith that I would not, if elected governor, set about 'fighting and breaking down the existing Democratic organization and replacing it with one of my own.' The last thing I should think of would be *building up a machine of my own*"; Wilson to John Harlan, June 23, 1910, in ibid., 540 (emphasis added).

49. "Baccalaureate Address," June 13, 1909, in *PWW*, vol. 19, 245; Hirst, *Woodrow Wilson*, 35–36.

50. Wilson to Edgar Williamson, August 23, 1910, in *PWW*, vol. 21, 59–61.

51. On the convention, see Cooper, *Warrior and the Priest*, 164–65; and Link, *Road to the White House*, 155–66.

52. Woodrow Wilson, "A Speech Accepting the Democratic Gubernatorial Nomination," September 15, 1910, in *PWW*, vol. 21, 91–92, 92–93; James, "Moral Philosopher," 254–55.

53. Woodrow Wilson, quoted in "A News Report of Impromptu Remarks to the Democratic State Convention," in *PWW*, vol. 21, 119. The party platform is reprinted in ibid., 94–96.

54. Joseph P. Tumulty, *Woodrow Wilson as I Know Him* (Garden City, N.Y.: Doubleday, Page, 1921), 21–22. Tumulty was a dissident Democrat who had opposed Wilson's nomination but changed his mind immediately upon hearing Wilson speak. Tumulty later became Wilson's personal secretary in the White House and a close friend.

55. George Lawrence Record to Wilson, October 17, 1910, and Wilson to Record, October 24, 1910, in *PWW*, vol. 21, 338–39, 406–11; Hirst, *Woodrow Wilson*, 97–100.

56. Record thought the letter clinched the campaign, as did many old-guard Republicans. It clearly swayed New Jersey's independents and New Idea Republicans: On November 8, Wilson won a plurality of almost 50,000 and carried fifteen of twenty-one counties, many of which went Democratic for the first time. Hirst, *Woodrow Wilson*, 106, 113.

57. This analysis closely follows that of Cooper, *Warrior and the Priest*, 172.

58. Woodrow Wilson, quoted in "A News Report of a Speech at Jersey City, New Jersey," September 20, 1910, in *PWW*, vol. 21, 147.

59. Woodrow Wilson, "A Speech in St. Peter's Hall in Jersey City," September 28, 1910, in *PWW*, vol. 21, 191, 190; Woodrow Wilson, "A Campaign Address in Trenton, New Jersey," in ibid., 229–30; Woodrow Wilson, "The Final Address of the Campaign Delivered in Newark, New Jersey," in ibid., 565.

60. As Arthur Link put it, Wilson "was truly a prime minister in the state." Link, *Road to the White House*, 249.

61. *The Nation*, August 17, 1911, 137.

62. Ellen Wilson's efforts in the spring of 1911 to reconcile Bryan and Wilson are described in Link, *Road to the White House*, 317–18. For Wilson's growing appeal to Bryan's supporters, the increasing closeness between the two politicians, and Bryan's role in securing Wilson's nomination, see ibid., 318–26, 352–57, 433–62.

63. William Howard Taft, "The Judiciary and Progress: Address of Hon. William H. Taft at Toledo, Ohio, Friday Evening, March 8, 1912," Washington, G.O.P., 1912, 3. Despite his genuine belief in popular government, the thrust of Taft's message was to condemn Roosevelt's proposal for a process of judicial recall, on grounds that the courts were responsible to the law rather than to public opinion.

64. Woodrow Wilson, "A Speech Accepting the Democratic Nomination in Sea Girt, New Jersey," August 7, 1912, in *PWW*, vol. 25, 6.

65. On Wilson's prenomination campaign and presidential campaign before August 28, see Link, *Road to the White House*, 309–488; Cooper, *Warrior and the Priest*,

177–86, 191–93; and James Chace, *1912: Roosevelt, Wilson, Taft, and Debs—The Election That Changed the Country* (New York: Simon & Schuster, 2004), 128–42, 209–15, 227–29.

66. Brandeis's wife, Alice Goldmark Brandeis, was the sister of James's longtime friend Pauline Goldmark, and both Louis and Alice were extremely close friends with Elizabeth Evans, the widow of Glendower Evans, both of whom had long ago formed close ties with the Jameses. In 1897, Evans invited both the philosopher and the people's attorney to her home on Otis Place in Boston, and after the Spanish-American War, Evans recruited Brandeis to join the PIS. See William James to Elizabeth G. Evans, July 29, 1897, and James to Pauline Goldmark, April 18, 1899, in *The Correspondence of William James*, ed. Ignas K. Skrupskelis and Elizabeth M. Berkeley, 12 vols. (Charlottesville, Va.: University Press of Virginia, 1992–2004), vol. 8, 288, 515. On the Brandeises and Evanses, and the latter couple's ties to the Jameses, see Allon Gal, *Brandeis of Boston* (Cambridge, Mass.: Harvard University Press, 1980), 10, 150. Brandeis may also have come into contact with James through the Filene's department store's Filene Cooperative Association, a pioneering workers' insurance and comanagement organization for which both Brandeis and James were enlisted as occasional speakers; Gal, ibid., 60–61.

67. See William James to Pauline Goldmark, November 17, 1903, in *Correspondence of William James*, ed. Skrupskelis and Berkeley, vol. 10, 330; James to Goldmark, June 30, 1904, in ibid., 426; and James to Alice Howe Gibbens James, August 30, 1906, and to Margaret Mary James, September 1, 1906, in ibid., vol. 11, 263–64.

68. Louis D. Brandeis to William H. Dunbar, February 2, 1893, copy in the Felix Frankfurter Papers, Library of Congress microfilm edition, reel 15.

69. Ibid.; Louis D. Brandeis, interview in the *New York Times Annalist*, 1913, in *Brandeis on Democracy*, ed. Philippa Strum (Lawrence: University Press of Kansas, 1995), 35. On Brandeis's reaction to the violence that erupted at the Carnegie steelworks in Homestead, Pa., in 1892, and to subsequent clashes between labor and management, see Philippa Strum, *Brandeis: Beyond Progressivism* (Lawrence: University Press of Kansas, 1993), 24–27.

70. John Dewey, "Mr. Justice Brandeis," *Columbia Law Review* 33 (1933): 175; Dewey was reviewing Felix Frankfurter, ed., *Mr. Justice Brandeis* (New Haven, Conn.: Yale University Press, 1932). Brandeis quoted in the *New York Times,* July 11, 1912. Brandeis's full statement, which was sent to newspapers nationwide, was reprinted in *The Democratic Textbook, 1912* (New York: Democratic National Committee, 1912), 182.

71. *New York Times,* July 11, 1912. The "solemn note" and "few cheers" that greeted Wilson's speech were noted by the *Times* on the front page of the August 8, 1912 edition.

72. Wilson, "Speech Accepting the Democratic Nomination in Sea Girt," 11, 4–6; emphasis added.

73. Ibid., 7. On the tariff issue's failure to enthuse the electorate, see Chace, *1912*, 192.

74. Wilson characterized the contest between him and Roosevelt in these terms, in a conversation with his daughter Eleanor during the campaign; see Eleanor Wilson McAdoo, *The Woodrow Wilsons* (New York: Macmillan, 1937), 172.

75. Reported in the *New York Times*, August 28, 1912, reprinted in *PWW*, vol. 25, 56–58. For the Progressive platform on business, see ibid., editorial note 1.

76. See, e.g., Brandeis to Theodore Wehle, Dickinson S. Miller, and Arthur K. Stone, all September 4, 1912; Sen. Moses E. Clapp (Chairman of the Interstate Commerce Committee) to Brandeis, September 7, 1912, and Brandeis to Clapp, September 11, 1912; Edward T. Hartman (Secretary of the Massachusetts Civic League) to Brandeis, September 12, 1912; Brandeis to Brand Whitlock (Mayor of Toledo, Ohio), September 28, 1912—all in the Louis Dembitz Brandeis papers, University of Louisville microfilm edition (hereafter, LDB UL), reel 29. Brandeis's important articles were "Trusts, Efficiency and the New Party" and "Trusts, the Export Trade, and the New Party," *Collier's Weekly*, September 14, 1912, 14–15, and September 21, 1912, 10–11; and two essays titled "Concentration" and "Trusts and the Interstate Commerce Commission," printed as editorials in Norman Hapgood's column, *Collier's Weekly*, October 5, 1912, 8–9. On Brandeis's authorship of the *Collier's* editorials, see Hapgood to Brandeis, August 29, 1912, LDB UL, reel 29.

77. Woodrow Wilson, "A Labor Day Address in Buffalo," September 2, 1912, in *PWW*, vol. 25, 75.

78. "Suggestions for Letter of Governor Wilson on Trusts," encl. in Brandeis to Wilson, September 30, 1912, in *PWW*, vol. 25, 289, 290, 291–94.

79. See ibid., and editorial note 1. In the event, Wilson did not publish the letter, perhaps deciding against issuing another's words under his own name. Kendrick A. Clements, in his fine short biography of Wilson, downplays the influence of Brandeis's letter on Wilson's thinking, noting that his Princeton colleague David B. Jones had offered similar suggestions in earlier correspondence. The quotation from Wilson by which Clements substantiates Jones's influence, however, is from the Buffalo address quoted above, delivered September 2—just days after Wilson met Brandeis at Sea Girt. Furthermore, while Brandeis's influence on Wilson was indeed most apparent in the latter's "approach to reform," Clements's claim that Wilson paid little attention to the actual measures proposed in Brandeis's letter ignores Wilson's numerous emendations and the later policy initiatives that reflected this cross-fertilization. E.g., after Wilson proposed a Federal Trade Commission in 1914, Brandeis wrote to his brother that Wilson had "paved the way for about all I have asked & some of the provisions specifically are what I got into his mind at my first interview." See Kendrick A. Clements, *Woodrow Wilson: World Statesman* (Chicago: Ivan R. Dee, 1999), 81–82, 82 n. 20, 85; and Brandeis, quoted in Strum, *Beyond Progressivism*, 87.

80. Woodrow Wilson, "Suggestions," in *PWW*, vol. 25, 290, 292.

81. See Wilson's copy of Brandeis, *Scientific Management and Railroads* (New York: Engineering Magazine, 1912), WL LC. *Scientific Management* comprised selections from what was originally a brief presented by Brandeis on January 3, 1911, to the Intestate Commerce Commission (ICC), and it consisted of Brandeis's commentary along with transcriptions of hearings in front of the ICC from roughly June 1910 to January 1911. The hearings were ordered by the ICC after a group of railroads east of the Mississippi River and north of the Ohio River jointly raised freight rates. Brandeis

represented the Traffic Committee of the Trade Organizations of the Atlantic Seaboard in the public investigation ordered by the ICC. About half the brief, the half making up the book, was devoted to the argument that scientific management of railroads would produce efficiencies obviating the need for rate hikes. Because, unlike the passenger service and manufacturing sectors, freight service was relatively uncompetitive, Brandeis argued that scientific management would have to serve as an equivalent force producing the efficiency that competition naturally induces. Brandeis built his case upon empirical observation of other industries that had adopted such management techniques, which indicated that scientific management made higher profits and lower rates, as well as higher wages and safer working conditions, possible at the same time.

82. In this rare instance, I disagree with Cooper, who gives due credit to Brandeis's importance in the campaign but explains it solely in terms of "furnishing a tactical opening and live ammunition" by suggesting the trusts be Wilson's focus. Though I concur with Cooper's statements that Wilson "did not share Brandeis' belief that bigness was itself an economic evil" nor his "preference for decentralized government," I find his claim one page later of much greater significance: "In short, [Wilson proclaimed that] democratic government must remain self-government, no matter how complex the economic and social problems became. That was the point Brandeis had helped Wilson to grasp and with which he flayed Roosevelt for much of the 1912 campaign." Cooper, *Warrior and the Priest*, 194–95.

83. Woodrow Wilson, "A Campaign Address in Indianapolis Proclaiming the New Freedom," October 3, 1912, in *PWW*, vol. 25, 321, 323–24, 329.

84. See, e.g., Woodrow Wilson, "A Portion of an Address in Kokomo, Indiana," October 4, 1912; Woodrow Wilson, "Remarks to the Women's Democratic Club in Omaha, Nebraska," October, 5, 1912; Woodrow Wilson, "A Call in Denver for a 'Second Emancipation,'" October 7, 1912; Woodrow Wilson, "A Campaign Address in Topeka, Kansas," October 8, 1912—all in *PWW*, vol. 25.

85. Woodrow Wilson, "A Campaign Address in Cleveland," in *PWW*, vol. 25, 411.

86. Woodrow Wilson, "A Public Letter," October 19, 1912, in *PWW*, vol. 25, 434.

87. Detailed accounts of Wilson's three major New Freedom initiatives are given by Arthur S. Link, *Wilson: The New Freedom* (Princeton, N.J.: Princeton University Press, 1956), chaps. 6, 7, 13. The fact that the United States began moving toward a war economy not long after the passage of the New Freedom reforms makes it difficult to assess their efficacy. Certainly, the vaunted antitrust measures—the Clayton Act of 1913 and the Federal Trade Commission Act of 1914—failed to restructure the American economy as Wilson had predicted, though they did curb abuses that had proliferated under the Sherman Act, restrict injunctions against striking unions, and provide regulatory and investigative tools put to even greater use by later administrations. Meanwhile, Wilson was criticized for appointing prominent businessmen to the Federal Reserve Board and thus "Legalizing the 'Money Power,'" as Senator Robert M. La Follette wrote in *La Follette's Weekly*, December 27, 1913, 1. Yet the Federal Reserve Act of 1913 was one of twentieth-century America's most important pieces of constructive legislation, abolishing the private monopoly over credit in America, extending

benefits to farmers and other Americans far from Northeastern financial centers, and providing, especially after overhauls in the 1930s, an elastic yet stable currency for a growing and changing economy. Finally, to recoup revenue, the Underwood-Simmons Tariff Act of 1913 instituted the first graduated income tax in American history and paved the way for the more sharply progressive income tax provision of the Revenue Act of 1916.

88. See Woodrow Wilson, "Draft of the National Democratic Platform of 1916," c. June 16, 1916, in *PWW*, vol. 37, 190–201. Wilson's text regarding the social justice measures propounded was in most cases adopted word for word at the national convention in Saint Louis; compare to "The Democratic Platform of 1916," in *National Party Platforms*, ed. Kirk H. Porter (New York: Macmillan, 1924), 373–88. Unfortunately, racial justice never commanded Wilson's attention, though contrary to popular belief, he did not believe in the innate inferiority of blacks and never compared D. W. Griffith's film *The Birth of a Nation* to "writing history with lightning." (Indeed, he insisted that he had "at no time expressed his approbation" of the film and in 1918 described it privately as a "very unfortunate production." See Wilson to J. P. Tumulty, April 28, 1915, in *PWW*, vol. 33, 86; Wilson to Tumulty, c. April 22, 1918, quoted in *PWW*, vol. 47, 388 n. 2.) Still, despite the support of the NAACP and the pro-Wilson efforts of racial democrats W. E. B. Du Bois, William Monroe Trotter, and Oswald Garrison Villard in 1912, Wilson reneged on a private promise to appoint a National Race Commission for fear of antagonizing Southern representatives. Meanwhile he approved, though did not initiate, a systematic attempt to segregate federal offices spearheaded by his postmaster general, Sidney Albert Burleson, ostensibly in the interest of both white and black employees. Ultimately Wilson halted Burleson's segregation scheme, but he never at any point thought the plight of blacks in the United States was an urgent matter requiring the attention of the national government. On the race commission, see Wilson to Villard, August 21, 1913, in *PWW*, vol. 28, 202; and Oswald Garrison Villard, *Fighting Years: Memoirs of a Liberal Editor* (New York: Harcourt, Brace, 1939), 236–38. On segregation in the government, see ibid., 237–42; W. M. Trotter, "Federal Segregation under Pres. Wilson," *Boston Guardian*, October 25, 1913; and Link, *New Freedom*, 246–54. The story of Wilson's rapture over *The Birth of a Nation* is convincingly discredited in *PWW*, vol. 33, 142 n. 1, and esp. 267 n. 1, in which Dixon's intention to deceive Wilson and Wilson's lack of interest in the film are substantiated.

89. The most thorough treatment is Alpheus T. Mason, *Brandeis: A Free Man's Life* (New York: Viking Press, 1946), 465–508.

90. Walter Lippmann, "The Case for Wilson," *New Republic*, October 14, 1916, 263. For Lippmann's views on the task of national progressivism and Roosevelt's failures at it, see Lippmann, "Integrated America," ibid., February 19, 1916, 62–63.

91. Wilson met James when the latter was awarded an honorary degree at the Princeton Sesquicentennial in 1896. "The Will to Believe" had been published in June of that year (in the *New World*, vol. 5, 327–47), giving Wilson ample time to read James's cultural bombshell before meeting him at the Princeton festivities beginning October 20. The case that Wilson did in fact read James in 1896 and again in 1915 is beyond the

scope of the present argument but is demonstrated in Throntveit, "Related States." For Princeton's Sesquicentennial Celebration, see the newspaper reports reprinted in *PWW*, vol. 10, 9–11, and the extensive collection of archival materials relating to the event in the Seeley G. Mudd Manuscript Library at Princeton University. As for Dewey, he and Wilson attended Johns Hopkins together, and Dewey is among a group of mutual "J.H.U. friends" mentioned in Albert Shaw to Wilson, May 23, 1887, in *PWW*, vol. 5, 507.

92. Herbert Croly, "Presidential Complacency," *New Republic*, November 21, 1914, 7.

93. John Dewey, "The Hughes Campaign," ibid., October 28, 1916, 320.

94. Woodrow Wilson, "An Address in Chicago to Nonpartisan Women," October 19, 1916, in *PWW*, vol. 38, 484–85.

3. Wilson's Reform of Economic Structure: Progressive Liberalism and the Corporation

W. Elliot Brownlee

We are in a temper to reconstruct economic society.
—Woodrow Wilson, 1910[1]

In his first eighteen months in office, President Woodrow Wilson led in enacting a sweeping set of reforms: the Underwood Tariff Act (1913), the Federal Reserve Act (1913), the Federal Trade Commission Act (1914), and the Clayton Act (1914). Virtually all the many scholars who have evaluated these reforms, and those that followed in their wake during the era of World War I, have concluded that the reforms represented important efforts to manage the clash between the democratic ideals of the republic and the realities of a new corporate capitalism. But these scholars have differed, sometimes widely, as they have sought to balance an image of Wilson as a champion of democratic reform against another image—one of him as affirming and helping to consolidate a new corporate-industrial order.[2]

Most scholars have discussed Wilson's balancing act in the context of either monographs focused on specific economic policies or sweeping studies of Wilson and his times. The former have often lost touch with Wilson and the latter have often given the economic issues cursory treatment. In this chapter, which undertakes a reevaluation of Wilson's program to advance both capitalism and democracy at home, I attempt both to sharpen our understanding of Wilson's intentions and to explore how they shaped the most important structural reforms of the two terms of his administration. The chapter surveys his intentions and accomplishments in the four areas of tariffs, taxes, central banking, and antitrust during the New Freedom; the transformation of his programs during World War I; and the nature of his long-term legacy for domestic reform.[3]

My exploration begins by noting that from the late 1890s Wilson centered his thinking about economic issues on the role of the corporation in American society. More specifically, he focused on a problem that was economic in its source but robustly political in its nature: the submersion of the individual within corporate society. He asked a key question: How was it possible to restore individual opportunity within that society without losing the economic benefits of the modern corporation? The problem and question, which he posed at the very outset of his national career, were, in part, classically liberal, based on his deep attachment to the economic program of British liberals, including their embrace of economic growth and the celebration of individual enterprise. But the problem and question were republican in formulation as well, based on a deep American hostility toward concentrations of power and a passion for restoration of civic virtue to the republic. As Wilson struggled to find concrete solutions and answers, he worked to square classical liberalism with republicanism. How he did that largely defined his progressivism, lent it a distinctive democratic cast, and helped account for his reform accomplishments.

The war, however, forced Wilson to abandon much of his progressive program—particularly tariff and antitrust reform. In fact, during the war he had to strengthen the position of large-scale, vertically integrated corporations and had no time or power to resume democratic reform after the war. It was this wartime retreat (and not inherent weaknesses in the New Freedom) that channeled much of Wilson's earlier reform into the corporate liberalism that has continued as one of the powerful themes in the development of American political culture. However, the war also provided the occasion to advance democratic reforms in the realm of public finance. These reforms became the most powerful and long-lived elements in Wilson's democratic legacy, in some ways gathering even greater strength during the New Deal and World War II and proving to be surprisingly durable during the antigovernment counterattacks of the last thirty years.

Finding "Prudent and Practicable Lines of Action"

The business historian Alfred D. Chandler Jr. has written that "after 1897 began the largest and certainly the most significant merger movement in American history." The movement, he added, "reached its climax between 1899 and 1902."[4] Woodrow Wilson watched this movement closely and, in the latter year, reflected on its social and political implications in writing the concluding chapter of his five-volume *A History of the American People*. He cited the example of the "great consolidation of iron-mining properties, foundries, steel mills, railroads, and steamship lines" by Carnegie Steel in 1897 and declared: "It was this new aspect of industry that disclosed the problems Republican and Democratic statesmen were to face for the coming generation." He noted that "the concentration of capital was no new thing." For twenty years, the growth of corporate consolidations had been "familiar" and stimulated farmers and workers to organize in order to protect themselves. "Great strikes . . . were but the reflex of what was taking place in Wall Street." But, Wilson noted, in 1897, "the new scale" upon which business grew "now began to be effected made it seem a thing novel and unexpected." He went on: "Thoughtful men" saw that "these vast aggregations of capital, these combinations of all the processes of a great industry in the hands of a single 'Trust'. . . might abuse to the undoing of millions of men" and result in "the permanent demoralization of society itself and of the government which was the instrument of society in the conduct of its united interests." In response, he said, leaders of the two major parties were searching for some middle way between the "very conservative beginning" of reform represented by the Interstate Commerce Act and proposals for government ownership of industry and railroads. But, as yet, neither party saw "prudent and practicable lines of actions" that would preserve "the processes which were adding so enormously to the economy and efficiency of the nation's productive work" while protecting "the liberty of the individual or the freedom and self-respect of the workingman."[5]

Wilson thus posed two different requirements for finding a "middle way" between contemporary corporate capitalism, which had buried the individual, and socialism, which could not restore individual opportunity and would stifle the productive elements of corporate capitalism. In 1902, he did not pose any "prudent and practicable lines of action." During the next ten years, however, as he assumed the presidency of Princeton University, discovered opportunities to participate in national politics, and became a candidate for major office, he worked to define a concrete policy agenda.[6] The search for the middle way that he called for in 1902 required a pragmatic approach, a flexible adjustment to shifting political and economic conditions. The emergence of progressive reform movements created opportunities for him to lead what amounted to a national search for the same kind of middle way. Part of his strategic success in identifying and seizing these opportunities was his ability to articulate the goals of these movements, often redefining them during his quest for the presidency.

Wilson's quest led to a multifaceted program of reform of tariff, tax, banking, and antitrust law. At the core of each of the four reforms were antimonopoly elements designed to contain the power of corporate capitalism and thereby stimulate economic opportunity and justice. But the reforms had other components, ones also designed to expand economic opportunity. Tariff reform, would, Wilson hoped, promote a general economic expansion by stimulating gains in productive efficiency and enhancing markets for American exports. Banking reform would have the same effect by increasing the supply of capital to ambitious investors and, at the same time, it would promote financial stability that could moderate episodes of unemployment and inflation. With this program he led the Democratic Party to an electoral victory in 1912. That victory, coupled with his well-worked-out economic program and shrewd political leadership, led to the remarkable reforms of his first term.

Attacking Protective Tariffs, Which Had "Monopoly for Father"

The starting point for Wilson's path toward a middle way was his desire to reform the tariff. Among all the programs of economic reconstruction that he championed, tariff reform was the one in which he had the longest-standing interest, and the one he had developed most fully in his own mind. His enthusiasm for tariff reform extended back to his youthful adulation of the architects of British liberalism and their commitment to the principle of free trade.[7] At the age of sixteen or seventeen, he hung a picture of his favorite liberal leader, William Gladstone, above his desk, as he did again at Princeton. Four decades later, in the White House, he apparently reread John Morley's three-volume *Life of Gladstone*.[8]

One of Wilson's first public political statements came in 1882 with testimony before the Tariff Commission. He called for "a tariff for revenue merely" and emphasized tax equity, observing that "farmers and others" were "paying these duties for the benefit of a few manufacturing classes."[9] In private, he put the matter even more strongly. Tariffs were, he said, "taxes of the most burdensome sort withal, for their weight falls most directly and most heavily on the poor and is least felt by the rich." Wilson explained how this had happened: The tariffs had "Monopoly for father."[10] Thus, while British liberals had attacked the power of monopolies in land, Wilson would attack corporate monopolies. He added an efficiency argument to the one for equity: "I maintain that manufacturers are made better manufacturers whenever they are thrown upon their own resources and left to the natural competition of trade than when they are told, 'You shall be held in the lap of the government, and you need not stand upon your feet.' Such theories discourage skill, because it puts all industries upon an artificial basis."[11]

In the 1880s, Wilson and others who held such views confronted a powerful, national commitment to a protectionist trade policy. This commitment blocked efforts to emulate British liberals, who had launched the shift of their nation toward free trade more than a half century earlier, during the 1820s. Keeping protectionism in place was a powerful coalition of groups: manufacturers who worried about competition from British manufacturers; the beneficiaries of federal programs, such as Civil War pensions, that the tariff revenues funded; workers who attributed high wages (relative to European wages) not so much to American productivity or labor shortages as to the ability of the tariff to shield them from the competition of cheap foreign labor; and investment bankers who valued the way in which high tariffs helped conserve American reserves of foreign exchange and facilitate the servicing of America's foreign debts.

During the late 1890s, however, the wall of protectionism began to crack. For one thing, British loyalty to free trade began to wane, to a large extent because of the increasing competitive power of German and American producers. Previously, American exporters enjoyed the benefits of free trade without having to sacrifice domestic protection.[12] Increasing problems in exporting, particularly to Britain or British-controlled markets, such as Canada and much of Latin America, led many American exporters to become attracted to what one historian has called tariff "revisionism."[13] They favored negotiating reciprocal trade agreements and empowering a federal tariff commission to expedite the process. The leaders in "revisionism" were organizations that represented relatively small manufacturers, merchants, and shippers. America's most advanced industrial corporations and investment bankers did not lead this movement for tariff reform, and few saw reason to even participate in it. Tariff "revisionism" promoted some dabbling in reciprocal trade agreements between 1897 and 1909, but, because of the continuing power of protectionists, accomplished relatively little in the way of tariff reduction.[14]

As "revisionism" acquired a following, inflation and corporate consolidations fueled more popular calls for drastic reductions of tariffs. Attacks on the tariff became sufficiently powerful to cause a major rift within the Midwestern Republican Party, which became attracted to the "Iowa idea" that denounced the tariff for fostering corporate monopolies. The division within the Republican Party enabled protectionists to pass the Payne-Aldrich Act in 1909. It restored a conventional protectionist program and, in turn, created an opportunity for Democrats—just at the time when Wilson entered electoral politics.[15]

Since 1882, Wilson had rarely discussed high tariffs. In 1902, in the last volume of his *A History of the American People*, he had reiterated, without adding any new ideas, the essence of his testimony two decades earlier. "Protective tariffs," he wrote, "deliberately extended the favors of the government to particular undertakings; only those who had the capital to take advantage of those favors got rich by them; the rest of the country was obliged to pay the costs in high prices and restricted competition."[16] But when Wilson became a contender for higher office, he took up the tariff issue again. He did not, however, encourage the "revisionist" program of negotiated trade agreements and treaties. Instead, he seized on the issue that he hoped would resonate with traditional, republican hostility to concentrations of power. He stressed the connections between the tariff and monopoly power in industry, suggesting that protective tariffs and monopoly worked hand in hand to encourage each other's hold on the nation. The threat to republican institutions, he warned in 1909, was particularly severe. Through the process of developing "entrenchments of Special Privilege," business organizations that were "national in their scope and control . . . have as powerful a machinery ready to their hand as the Government itself."[17] As his presidential ambitions took hold, he fleshed out his case against protection and placed tariff reform at the top of his agenda. "The tariff question, he declared in 1911, "is at the heart of every other economic question we have to deal with, and until we have dealt with that properly we can deal with nothing in a way that will be satisfactory and lasting."[18]

He continued to emphasize the potential for tariff reform to create a more equitable tax burden and to curtail monopoly power, but he also developed a new point: Reducing tariffs would promote the growth of exports, even without engaging in reciprocal trade agreements. Tariff reform would do so in two ways. First, it would enhance economic efficiency. "We conquered the world once by our visions," he told a group of bankers in 1910. Now, he said, "we shall have to make the conquest of men . . . by a new ideal of endeavor, by new willingness to submit our brains and our ingenuity to the universal pressure of the eager action of a world drawn together by the all the instrumentalities of trade."[19] He made a similar pitch for efficiency in 1912 to real estate investors: "By protecting ourselves from foreign competition—from the skill and energy and resourcefulness of other nations—we have felt ourselves at liberty to be wasteful in our own processes."[20] Second, tariff reform, in the process of encouraging Americans to buy abroad, would enable foreigners to purchase more American goods. "All trade is two-sided," he told the Commercial Club of Omaha. "If America is to insist upon selling everything and buying nothing, she will find that the rest of the world stands very cold and indifferent to her enterprise."[21]

During the 1912 campaign, Wilson's tariff positions seemed to distinguish him from his competitors. William Howard Taft became identified with the conventional protectionist approach while Theodore Roosevelt failed to generate significant traction with a "revisionist" message. Regardless of the real political effects, Wilson won the White House with a clear mandate for an across-the-board, significant rollback in tariff rates, and passage of the Underwood Act was the swift consequence.[22]

The Underwood Tariff slashed tariff rates on dutiable goods, on the average, by about one-third and expanded the list of free products to include food products, sugar, leather, and wool, and sugar (the last phased in over four years). Wilson's proposed expansion of the free list had threatened to cause defections of congressional Democrats, but Wilson insisted on a party discipline behind the expansion of the free list over a broad range of products. He had understood that if he allowed any defections, more were certain to follow. He turned back efforts by Democrats in Congress to provide protection on leather, wool, cotton textiles, tobacco, and lumber. He was generally true to a principle that he had espoused in 1909: Customs duties ought to be levied on "the things which are not of primary necessity to the people in their lives or their industry, things, for the most part, which they can do without suffering or actual privation."[23] The only compromise he made was on the phased-out tariff on sugar. He agreed to it to protect revenues while the income tax, included in the Underwood legislation partly to replace tariff revenues, proved itself. As a consequence of the Underwood Tariff, rates became lower than they had been at any time since the Civil War.

In slashing tariffs, Wilson preferred to proceed, as the economist Frank Taussig wrote, "in more or less rough and ready fashion of compromise, not of any close calculation or accurate information."[24] Wilson had made clear his intention to do so, and his trust in representative democracy, in 1911: "In the somewhat rough and ready and experimental estimates that it will be necessary to make, the judgment of an experienced committee of Congress is as good a guide as the judgment of a professional board. The question is then one of statesmanship."[25] Thus, Wilson rejected the call for so-called scientific tariff making by a commission of experts. It was, he thought, merely an excuse to delay substantive reform and maintain the status quo until the Republicans could return to power in Congress and enable protectionists to capture the regulatory process. Wilson's intent was to create, instead, a precedent and process for incremental but sustained and across-the board cuts in tariffs.[26] The cuts, he hoped, would culminate in a tariff for revenue only. The public would, Wilson believed, see the benefits of such cuts and compel the president and Congress to vanquish protectionism.

The Graduated Income Tax:
Toward a "More Just" Fiscal Policy

The Underwood Tariff included a provision that restored a graduated income tax to the federal tax code and set rates that were somewhat more progressive than those enacted during the Civil War and in 1893. This tax was an important milestone in a long movement to reform federal taxation according to the "ability to pay."[27] However, of all the movements that contributed to the accomplishments of Woodrow Wilson's first term, this one owed the least to his campaigning for the presidency. He had rarely mentioned income taxation when he defined the "New Freedom."

Wilson had, in fact, long admired the way that British liberals had made an income tax the primary means to replace tariff revenues. He appreciated, in particular, Robert Peel's restoration of income taxation (as well as tariff revisions) in 1844 and Gladstone's later sponsorship of both indirect and direct taxes.[28]

In 1894, when President Grover Cleveland coupled tariff reform with the enactment of a progressive income tax, and in 1895, when the Supreme Court struck down the tax, Wilson made no public comment. He did not participate in the subsequent debate over restoring the tax except to criticize the Supreme Court in 1902.[29] The reason for Wilson's silence is something of a mystery, but it was most likely his political pragmatism at work. He probably failed to see any effective way to engage either Roosevelt, who came out in favor of progressive income and estate taxation in 1908, or President Taft, who played to both conservatives and progressives in 1909 by supporting both an "excise tax" on corporate profits and submission of the Sixteenth Amendment to the states (where conservatives hoped to defeat it). Supporting this interpretation is the fact that, in 1911, as governor of New Jersey, Wilson did press the state legislature to ratify the Sixteenth Amendment. He told some very recalcitrant state senators that the income tax would enable the federal government to make its fiscal policy "more just" and "more nicely" adjusted "to the interests of the people at large."[30] And his silence on the income tax in the campaign of 1912 mirrored Roosevelt's. They, as well as the framers of their party platforms, were of like mind on the need to revive income taxation. The broad consensus among Democrats, Progressives, and many Republicans, and the ratification the Sixteenth Amendment in 1913, meant that the passage of the income tax provision required relatively little Wilsonian leadership.

By supporting the 1913 income tax, Wilson moved beyond the nineteenth-century British liberals, who were often troubled by graduated rates, and into the realm of progressivism.[31] But Wilson did not move as radically toward a graduated income taxation as had David Lloyd George and his Liberals in the "People's Budget" of 1909 or, for that matter, as far as William Jennings Bryan and Senator Robert M. La Follette wished.[32] It is not entirely clear exactly what Wilson expected of a graduated income tax, in terms of its long-term revenue capacity or its progression. Wilson urged caution on Furnifold M. Simmons, chair of the Senate Finance Committee. "Individual judgments will naturally differ," Wilson wrote, "with regard to the burden it is fair to lay upon incomes which run above the usual levels."[33] Wilson's caution most likely reflected his recognition that estimation of both tariff and income tax revenues was highly uncertain; that forecasts of tariff revenues were nearly as difficult to make; and that postponing a debate over tax rates made eminent good sense until it was clear what tax revenues were at stake. Wilson's most important role in creating the modern progressive income tax would come during World War I.

Central Banking and a "Democracy of Credit"

The third major movement that Wilson sought to shape in his quest for the "middle way" was one that sought the creation of a modern central bank. Like the enactment of freer trade and income taxation, the creation of central banking had been a major accomplishment of nineteenth-century British liberals. The reform represented a response to two structural problems embedded in the financial systems of the world's most powerful nation-states. The first was the instability inherent in systems of fractional-reserve banking and the second was the instability apt to result from uncertainty about the relative values of the currencies used by nations engaged in international markets.

To address the first problem, in Britain—and, in fact, all the major European economies—large banks or associations of banks developed at least some capacity to support weaker banks, and thus the entire banking system, when they encountered crises in depositor confidence. These banks became central banks when, acting at the center of their financial systems, they had the ability to act as "lenders of last resort" for other banks. In the case of England, during the nineteenth century, the Bank of England, chartered by the Crown in 1694 to assist the government in wartime finance, increasingly played this role. These central banks often also acquired the ability to create money in the form of bank notes. The Bank of England had this ability from its inception, and then, in 1844, partly to assist the bank in strengthening the financial system at its center, the government of liberal Robert Peel gave the bank a monopoly on the issuance of bank notes.[34]

To address the second problem—the stabilization of world currency markets—Britain had adopted a gold standard to set exchange rates among currencies. In the early nineteenth century, to strengthen the gold standard, the Bank of England took on the responsibility of maintaining a fixed ratio between the value of the pound sterling and the value of gold.

The United States, however, lagged far behind Britain and the continental nations in adopting central banking. The antimonopoly ideology of republicanism was a crucial factor. It was at odds with the adoption in America of the banking program of the British liberals. Since the earliest days of the republic, hostility to, and fear of, large concentrations of financial power had inhibited the development of powerful banks. Consequently, the First and Second banks of the United States had only limited capacity to protect weak banks and, thus, to act as central banks. Moreover, Andrew Jackson won his war against the Second Bank. The banks chartered under the national banking system created during the Civil War had played an even more restricted role in the realm of central banking. Compounding the difficulty in coping with episodes of financial stringency was the restriction, by the National Banking acts, of the currency-issuing capacity of national banks to their holdings of federal bonds. As a consequence, between the 1870s and World War I, the United States endured banking crises "when they were a historical curiosity in other countries," as one economic historian has put the matter.[35]

The financial crises in late-nineteenth-century America would have been even more severe had the Bank of England and other European central banks not pitched in to help protect American gold reserves. However, to do so, the central banks had to limit the extent to which they could act as lenders of last resort in protecting their own domestic banking systems. The conflict became even more difficult to manage as the U.S. economy expanded to become, by the beginning of the twentieth century, the world's largest. Gold flows to and from the United States had become huge, and potentially even more disruptive to the world financial and commodity markets. In 1907, in the face of what the Bank of England decided was excessive demand on the part of American borrowers for credit, the bank raised discount rates sharply and discouraged British investors from lending to Americans. This was the only post–Civil War crisis in which the Bank of England had not helped to ease a credit crunch in America by becoming what amounted to a lender of last resort.[36]

During the 1907 crisis, J. P. Morgan and other New York investment bankers pioneered in acting as lenders last resort, forming, in effect, a kind of loose, informal central bank. They eased the crisis somewhat but were not able to fend off a stock market crash, numerous bank failures, and the onset of an economic recession. In response, the most powerful financial leaders in America began to think hard about how to increase their power within the gold standard world and, at the same time, contribute to international economic stability. In the process, they came to focus on the need to create an American central bank.[37]

The leading bankers, anticipating popular hostility, began their campaign in a low-key, often covert fashion. They worked largely within the framework of the National Monetary Commission, created by Congress in 1908 and chaired by Senator Nelson Aldrich. After a trip to Europe, where he became firmly committed to central banking, Aldrich secretly convened the commission's most important meeting at a private retreat at Jekyll Island, off the coast of Georgia. At the meeting, Aldrich, Frank Vanderlip, the vice president of National City Bank, and Paul Warburg, a partner in the investment banking house Kuhn, Loeb, and Company, led in the design of an English-style central bank and a public relations campaign, including the creation of a National Citizens' League, to sell it to the American public and Congress. The "Aldrich plan," submitted to the Senate in January 1912 by the National Monetary Commission, provided for the creation of a "National Reserve Association." The association, or central bank, would be a private entity that would have federal authorization to issue notes that would have the status of currency or legal tender.[38] The public relations campaign mobilized massive business support for the Aldrich plan, although not among "Main Street" bankers.[39]

Wilson became a candidate for president as this movement, and a potentially great political conflict over concentrated financial power came to a head. Previously, Wilson had not articulated any detailed views on central banking. However, he understood and appreciated the role of central banking in providing economic stability. He admired Walter Bagehot, the most respected English theoretician of central banking during the late nineteenth century, and in 1898 Wilson had reviewed Bagehot's *Lombard Street*, his most important analysis of central banking and the role of the Bank of England.[40] In his five-volume history of the United States, Wilson had praised the Second Bank of the United States as having "proved itself to be an agency of adjustment and control." That bank, he wrote, "had steadied and facilitated every legitimate business transaction and rid the money markets of its worst dangers."[41] In addition, he praised the gold standard and detailed Cleveland's problems in managing the currency without a central bank.[42] And, even before the financial crisis of 1907, he began complaining about the "inelasticity" of the currency.[43] During the crisis, he lamented that the Treasury had no control over the financial situation and blamed the crisis on "the abominable money system under which we are staggering." He noted that "the European currency system is far better than our own."[44]

As Wilson began to campaign for the presidency, however, he deemphasized reform on behalf of "elasticity" and instead stressed the need for reform that would confront what he regarded as monopoly power in finance, rooted in Wall Street investment banks. In 1911 he declared: "The great monopoly, in this country is the money monopoly." He called for its destruction. "For if it is not destroyed," he said, "the whole fabric will sooner or later fall, and in that fall the innocent and guilty will suffer alike.[45] He repeated this message over and over during the 1912 campaign and in *The New Freedom* declared: "The great monopoly in this country is monopoly of big credits. So long as that exists, our old variety and freedom and individual energy of development are out of the question."[46] In the campaign, he did not publicly offer his own plan but denounced the "Aldrich plan" because it would create a central bank that would be private, a bank beyond the control of the federal government. The plan, Wilson said, "confirms the present power of small groups of American bankers to dominate the new system."[47] And he promised that "the control exercised over any system we may set up should be, so far as possible, a control emanating, not from a single special class, but from the general body and authority of the nation itself."[48]

As president, Wilson struggled to satisfy what he regarded as the pressing need for central banking while at the same time answering calls for a Democratic— and democratic—alternative to the Aldrich plan. Wilson's attacks on a monopoly of money papered over significant disagreements within his own party. At one end of a spectrum of opinion, Bryan and his supporters regarded support for central banking by Democrats as a fundamental betrayal of principles and, more concretely, the platform of the Democratic Party platform of 1912. At the other end, Colonel Edward House and Wilson's business supporters, most notably Warburg and his partners at Kuhn, Loeb, favored the Aldrich plan.[49]

In bridging the spectrum, Wilson developed two principles. The first was that the new central banking system had to be decentralized in ways that would prevent control of the system by bankers, especially the powerful New York banks, and perhaps even reduce the financial influence of Wall Street, and would enhance the availability of capital, particularly for borrowers in the South and West. Adopting the first principle would, Wilson declared, create a "Democracy of Credit." He explained that "the evil we are most bent upon correcting" was "the present concentration of reserve and control at the discretion of a single group of bankers or by a locality of banking interests."[50] Wilson's second principle was that the federal government must play a dominant role in determining the fundamental policy decisions made by the new central banking system. He insisted that "the control of the system of banking and of issue which our new laws are to set up, must be public, not private, must be vested in the Government itself, so that the banks may be the instruments, not the masters, of business and of individual enterprise and initiative."[51] In short, Wilson intended to use the opportunity provided by the adoption of central banking to democratize the financial system.

During the first half of 1913, Wilson persuaded Democratic leaders, including Carter Glass and Robert T. Owen, the respective chairs of the House and Senate banking committees, to embrace his principles. The Glass-Owen Bill that became the administration's bill in June 1913 created not one central bank but at least twelve, located throughout the nation. The Aldrich plan had called for bank branches; in the Glass-Owen Bill, each of these branches became a full-fledged, independent central bank. Also, the bill put the Federal Reserve Board, which coordinated the work of the regional banks and had the final authority over setting the discount rate, firmly under the control of the federal government by establishing the membership of the board as consisting of the secretary of the Treasury, the comptroller of the currency, and five appointees, including the board's chair, selected by the president and confirmed by the Senate. Wilson hoped that this mechanism would help offset the tendency of the regional governing board to fall under the influence of local bankers as well keep national, public financial goals primary in the operation of the new system.

Wilson's two central principles, and particularly the establishment of the system as a public institution, guaranteed the hostility of almost all Wall Street investment bankers and much of the rest of the banking community. Even the New York bankers, like Warburg, who were Democrats and had supported Wilson's election, objected to his modifications of the English model for central banking. But the support that Wilson's compromise principles won for Glass-Owen among both Democratic and Republican progressives enabled Wilson and the congressional leadership to pay little attention to the bankers' complaints. They followed the advice that Louis Brandeis offered in June: "The conflict between the policies of the administration and the desires of the financiers and of big business, is an irreconcilable one." Brandeis went on: "Concessions to the big business interests must in the end prove futile. The administration can at best have only their seeming or temporary cooperation."[52] Neither Wilson nor Congress agreed to any significant pro-banking amendments to the bill. Major compromises with financial capitalism over the nature of democracy in twentieth-century America were not on Wilson's legislative agenda.

This interpretation of Wilson's role in crafting the Federal Reserve, however, may seem inconsistent with what followed: Wilson's nomination of the first members of the Federal Reserve Board. In June 1914, Wilson proposed some candidates, including Warburg, whom the banking community, including the New York bankers, regarded favorably. When Democrats in the Senate attacked Warburg, who was vulnerable because of his identification as a New York investment banker, and Thomas D. Jones, a director of International Harvester, known as the "Harvester Trust," Wilson leaped to their defense. Only after spending a good deal of his political capital in the contests over confirmation did Wilson prevail. How is Wilson's behavior in the appointment process consistent with the way in which he shaped the legislation? Is this evidence that his interest in banking reform was largely symbolic, and that he intended, once the regulatory system was created, to allow the regulated industry to capture the regulatory board?

The inconsistencies between Wilson's nominees to the board and the principles that guided him during the legislative process were, in fact, more apparent than real. It is true that Wilson knew that business would approve of his appointees. He wanted to cut off conservative counterattacks on the financial reforms, and he thought that his business appointees would help do that. But, above all, he believed that his appointees would carry out their responsibilities in a way that would honor the democratic reforms. With the exception of Warburg and Jones, Wilson avoided any nominees who were associated with major corporations. The three other nominees had ties to either Secretary of the Treasury William A. McAdoo or Secretary of the Interior Franklin K. Lane and had all vigorously supported the Glass-Owen Bill. Like McAdoo, William P. G. Harding, president of the National Bank of Birmingham, resented the power of New York bankers and wanted the new system would expand the supply of credit available to southern enterprise. Charles S. Hamlin was an assistant secretary of the Treasury under McAdoo, and Adolph C. Miller, a finance economist at the University of California, served as an assistant to Lane, who was a close friend of McAdoo. Moreover, Wilson recognized the potential power on the board of its two ex-officio members: the secretary of the Treasury and the comptroller of the currency. The Federal Reserve Act, in fact, made the secretary of the Treasury chair of the board. Both of them, McAdoo and John Skelton Williams, raised the hackles of most Wall Street bankers. Finally, it is important to remember that Wilson trusted both Warburg and Jones. Wilson knew Warburg from New York politics, and from extensive consultations over banking reform. Wilson knew Jones from his service as a Princeton trustee. Regardless of whether or not Wilson was naive, he had great personal confidence in the moral character of both men and believed that on the board they would meet his high expectations for carrying out the public interest.[53]

On one level, the Federal Reserve Act represented an effort by Woodrow Wilson to complete, just as European nations had, the *old*, nineteenth-century liberal agenda. Like the British liberals whom he emulated, Wilson believed that a central bank, as well as ending protection, would benefit all participants in the economy and greatly energize the enterprise of small producers and traders. On another level, the act represented a *reconstructed* liberalism—a progressivism— by virtue of incorporating Wilson's democratic principles. It was the implementation of these principles that the New York investment bankers resisted, even at the risk of indefinitely postponing the enactment of central banking; the bankers wanted only the *old*, nineteenth-century package. In effect, Wilson had brought traditional republican principles to bear on the issue of central banking in a way that resolved the long-standing American tension between those principles and the liberalism inherent in the enactment of central banking. In other words, with regard to central banking, Wilson squared republicanism with classic liberalism. This formulation, at the heart of his progressivism, became a powerful force for reform, promising both a broadening of economic opportunity and a containment of the power of American corporations. Central banking had arrived in the United States and, to a large extent because of Wilson, did so with key features that reflected the nature of American democracy as much as the force of industrial capitalism.

Antitrust: "Legal Regulation" versus "Executive Regulation"

In the realm of antitrust reform, just as in tariff and banking reform, Wilson had an opportunity to impose his own distinctive stamp: the definition of progressivism as a reconstructed liberalism—a liberalism that integrated American republican ideals with classical liberalism. In the process of using the law to attack concentrations of corporate power on behalf of both competition and civic virtue, he staked out a progressive position, and he led in enacting reform that was more radically antimonopolistic than the corporate program of the British Liberals.[54]

Wilson began proposing solutions to the general problem of monopoly power in 1907, earlier than he took up the "money trust" issue in a serious way. For a decade or more, the power of the trusts had become the dominant domestic issue in American politics, and President Theodore Roosevelt had taken tentative steps to address the question—cautious prosecutions under the Sherman Antitrust Act, limited railroad regulation, and investigations under the aegis of the new Bureau of Corporations. Wilson ignored these initiatives but spoke out when it became politic for him to distinguish his position from that of Bryan. While Bryan campaigned for the presidency on a radical reform of the Sherman Act, Wilson proposed more rigorous enforcement of existing law and focusing on the behavior of individuals, not corporations. His initial emphasis was on criminal prosecutions of corporate leaders. Wilson held them personally responsible for antitrust violations. "One really responsible man in jail," Wilson asserted in 1907, "one real originator of the schemes and transactions which are contrary to public interest legally lodged in the penitentiary, would be worth more than one thousand corporations mulcted in fines, if reform is to be genuine and permanent."[55] Later that year, he wrote: "Corporations cannot be moralized. Morals belong to individuals, and a law which strikes at corporate action itself will be entirely ineffectual unless it reaches the individuals who originate that action and are truly responsible for it."[56] Wilson was no doubt trying to stand on the conservative side of Bryan, who was calling for the dissolution of trusts when they controlled more than half the market for their products. But Bryan also proposed criminal prosecutions for corporate lawbreakers. And, Wilson's position was an honest and passionate one, rooted in his religious as well as his republican values. As the historian John Mulder has suggested, Wilson's "rhetoric had the sound of a zealous reformer."[57] (And, from a twenty-first-century perspective, formed in the wake of Enron et al., the rhetoric has a certain appeal.) Moreover, Wilson soon moved toward Bryan by calling for reform of the law as well as aggressive prosecutions. In early 1908, he wrote that the rise of the "great corporations and trusts" requires "adjustments and re-formulations of the law, which the courts have not had the power or the courage to make and which must therefore be made by legislation."[58] He said the same thing two years later. In drafting a platform for the Democratic Party of Pennsylvania, he proposed "legislation which will define and forbid those acts and practices on their part, and those methods in the organization and control, which have proved destructive of free competition and detrimental to the people's interest."[59]

When Wilson became a presidential candidate, he complicated his message by acknowledging that some, perhaps even many, of these consolidations had advanced economic efficiency and, therefore, national prosperity. In 1911, in an interview with the *New York Times*, Wilson had said: "Looked at from the side of business organization, the trusts are chiefly a means of economy and efficiency." However, he still maintained that corporate consolidations had gone too far.

In fact, he probably included the reference to efficiency to soften what followed in that same interview: "But along with their efficient organization goes a tremendous power and they have used that power to throttle competition and establish virtual monopoly in every market that they have coveted." He believed that "the methods by which the greater trusts have driven competitors out of business are well-known" and that "these methods can be made criminal offenses and the monopolistic use of trusts can be stopped by the punishment of every person who tries to make uses of their power."[60]

During the presidential campaign of 1912, Wilson sharpened his views. He welcomed the Supreme Court's dissolution of Standard Oil and American Tobacco in 1911, under the Sherman Act, but he wanted more demanding standards than "the rule of reason" the Court pronounced in those cases. Perhaps under the influence of Brandeis, Wilson hinted that he would be willing to break up some large corporations in addition to attempting to modify the behavior of corporate leaders.[61] However, he did not fully share Brandeis's condemnation of bigness. Wilson drew a distinction between big business and the trusts, and he declared that he would focus on limiting the power of the latter. A trust, he said, "is not merely a business that has grown big. I am not afraid of a business that has grown big. I don't care how big it grows by the intelligence and skill and even by the audacity in business of the men who are in charge of it." But "a trust is an arrangement to get rid of competition, and a big success is business that has survived competition by conquering in the field of intelligence and economy."[62] And he warned of the need to break up interlocking directorates. They amounted to "the combination of the combinations," he said, and they represented "a community of interest more formidable than any conceivable combination in the United States."[63]

In the course of the campaign, Wilson set himself apart from Roosevelt and the Progressives. Wilson clearly believed that the nation needed greater protection from corporate monopolies than did Roosevelt and the Progressives. And Wilson rejected Roosevelt's proposal to create an independent executive instrument—a Federal Trade Commission (FTC)—to restrain monopolies. Wilson's emphasized his general preference for "legal regulation" over "executive regulation." The latter, he feared, could lead to abuses of power and capture by the regulated interests. He invoked a republican principle that he had articulated earlier. "Must we fall back on discretionary executive power?" he had asked in 1908. "The government of the United States was established to get rid of arbitrary, that is, discretionary executive power." He went on: "If we return to it, we abandon the very principles of our foundation, give up the English and

American experiment and turn back to discredited models of government."[64] Two years later, in a similar vein, he stressed the theme of capture. "Having created trusts," he wrote, "the dominant party has tried to 'regulate' them, but its regulation has threatened to transfer the actual control of business to the government itself, and may in the long run only cement the partnership and corrupt: only making it the more necessary that the interests should maintain the party and control the government."[65] During the campaign, he warned voters about the Progressives' preference for an FTC and the threat of their paternalism to the republic: "I tell you the difference in my formula and theirs: I believe in government by the people, and they believe in government for the people. . . . Government for the people is sooner or later autocracy and tyranny, no matter whether it is benevolent or not."[66]

After Wilson assumed the presidency, progressives across the two parties faced the hostility of the giant corporations and their representatives as progressives advanced their two competing programs. They faced significant problems from other groups, as well. Perhaps even more powerful than the large corporations were small manufacturers and the organizations that represented them. To be sure, small manufacturers wanted greater protection from the monopoly power of giant industry. But they also wanted protection from Sherman Act judgments as they sought to increase their own market power through trade associations and other cooperative devices. Labor unions were in a similar dilemma. They wanted to check corporate power, on the one hand, but they wanted protection for themselves from antitrust prosecutions under the Sherman Act, on the other hand.

In light of the major division among progressives and small business representatives over antitrust legislation, Wilson delayed taking it up until he had resolved the major issues surrounding tariff and banking reform. The administration began by sponsoring two bills, which the House passed in June 1914. The Clayton Bill clarified and strengthened the definition of unfair competition, and the Covington Bill provided for an Interstate Trade Commission that would be advisory. In the House deliberations, the Wilson administration satisfied both small business and labor leaders, including Samuel Gompers and the executive committee of the American Federation of Labor, that the Clayton Act would not threaten their organizing efforts.[67]

In the Senate, Wilson's antitrust program immediately encountered severe opposition from the nation's largest corporations and, more threatening to its survival, from three groups of progressives. The most serious was opposition from progressives, both Democrats and Republicans, who wanted to give a large role to the FTC. These progressives included George Rublee, a key adviser to Brandeis on antitrust and a follower of Roosevelt; Brandeis himself, despite his earlier support for Wilson's emphasis on strengthening the Sherman Antitrust Act; and the bipartisan leadership of the Senate Commerce Committee, which would take up the Clayton and Covington bills first. These progressives worried that primary reliance on a detailed specification of the methods of unfair competition would fail to capture important monopolistic devices, particularly as business applied its creative energy to avoiding the law. The second group of opponents consisted of representatives of small business who worried that the Clayton Bill would interfere with their efforts to form trade associations and to regulate their industries, defining the rules of fair trade. The third dissident interest, far less organized, was that of consumers concerned about issues like price discrimination, fair trading, and false or misleading advertising.[68]

The legislative approach that all the progressive groups favored was (1) to limit the Clayton Bill to only a very general definition of unlawful trade practices, leaving crucial matters of interpretation to the courts; and (2) to strengthen the Covington Bill by turning the FTC into an independent agency and giving it the power to issue "cease and desist" orders to prevent unfair competition. The large industrial corporations were more favorable to this approach than to Wilson's because it might open the door for them to capture the regulatory process, but they remained fundamentally hostile.

These progressives were sufficiently powerful to force Wilson to reconsider his position. Contributing to their power were three new worries in Wilson's political calculations: fear of an economic recession, concern over a backlash by large corporations following Wilson's victories in tariff and banking reform, and fear of what would happen to Democratic candidates in 1914 if Congress failed to pass an antitrust program. (These worries may also help account for Brandeis's shift of position on the best approach to antitrust.) Consequently, Wilson adopted the approach of the dissident progressives and himself led a led a coalition of Democrats and progressive Republicans to enact the amended measures. He had not shifted from assaulting monopoly power. He still would have preferred an antitrust covenant ensconced in law, but he hoped that what he regarded as the more fragile instrument of a regulatory commission would nonetheless reinforce tariff and banking reforms in countering monopoly power. In the last analysis, he had less impact on the final outcome of the movement for antitrust reform than he did on the movements for tariff and banking reform. But he pushed Congress in an antimonopolistic direction—further than Roosevelt probably would have if he had held the presidency in 1914.

World War I: Thwarted Tariff and Antitrust Reforms

By 1914, in less than two years, Woodrow Wilson had led in the creation of structural economic reform that was more ambitious than any since the sweeping program of the Republicans during the Civil War. But international contingencies intervened to prevent any comprehensive testing of the potential of his program.

World War I wrecked Wilson's assumption that the world that would be sufficiently peaceful for the United States, in league with Britain, to move in the direction of free trade. As early as 1916, under wartime pressure, Wilson and Congress departed from the approach of the Underwood Tariff. They amended the terms of the Underwood Act to keep the revenue-rich sugar tariff in order to help finance preparedness. They provided protective tariffs for American chemical companies, who anticipated price cutting and dumping from German competitors. And they created a Tariff Commission to create more flexibility in negotiating with the warring European powers.[69] Then mobilization for war, followed by postwar inflation and depression, so dislocated agriculture and industry and increased economic insecurity that Wilson's antitariff coalition broke down with the enactment of the Emergency Tariff Act of 1921 and the Fordney-McCumber Tariff of 1922.[70] Wilson's abandonment of freer trade during World War I had been only tactical, but there was no significant resumption of Wilson's policy until the Reciprocal Trade Agreement Act of 1934, and rates did not return to their 1913 levels until the late 1950s.[71]

If anything, however, the wartime experience strengthened Wilson's free trade convictions. In crafting the third of his Fourteen Points, he made his most eloquent and concise statement for free trade—one that called for "the removal, so far as possible, of all economic barriers and the establishment of an equality of trade conditions among all the nations consenting to the peace and associating themselves for its maintenance." This was more than economics. Wilson declared that "what we ourselves are seeking is a basis which will be fair to all and which will nowhere plant the seeds of such jealousy and discontent and restraint of development as would certainly breed fresh wars."[72]

Mobilization for entry into World War I also set back Wilson's antitrust policy. The FTC was slow to organize, and then World War I swept the FTC away from close investigation of domestic corporations, in part because the mobilization of industry by the War Industries Board relied heavily on corporate voluntarism and encouraged collaborations among corporations, large and small. The FTC moved into work that advanced mobilization, and then, pressed by Secretary of Commerce William Redfield, into the investigation of potential competition with foreign cartels during the postwar world. The commission focused on assisting small manufacturers who were interested in making their trade associations more powerful in international trade, and in 1918, Congress responded by passing the Webb-Pomerene Act, which exempted export trade associations from antitrust laws and assigned oversight of their activities to the FTC. During the 1920s, the FTC finally tried to live up to Wilson's expectations. But the Supreme Court, through the 1920 U.S. Steel decision, along with Republican administrations, successfully prevented the FTC from impeding the new wave of mergers that swept through industry. During the New Deal, Wilsonian ideals provided inspiration to efforts to energize the Justice Department behind antitrust actions. However, mobilization for World War II and immediate postwar worries about a return to Depression conditions stifled any chance of a more aggressive approach to antitrust. Nonetheless, it is possible, as Alfred Chandler has argued, that the Clayton Act and the FTC have enhanced competition. They have done so, according to Chandler, by effectively preventing cartel-like agreements among corporations "to set prices and output." Chandler has found that such agreements became "standard business practice in other industrializing nations." Consequently, after World War II, large, vertically integrated firms in the United States competed "functionally and strategically for market share more vigorously" than firms in Europe and Japan.[73]

Wartime Finance and the Advanced Wave of Progressivism

World War I derailed the antitariff and antitrust campaigns of the Wilson administration, but it did provide an opening for Wilson to advance the democratic components of the two other major economic reforms: the Federal Reserve Act and the graduated income tax. The need to tax and borrow on an enormous scale, and to do so rapidly, gave Wilson the leverage to use the Federal Reserve and the tax system not only to help finance the war but also to contain corporate power.

To Wilson, determining from whom the federal government would borrow was a matter of good political economy. He concluded that the Treasury needed to avoid becoming dependent on the nation's wealthiest citizens, lest control of the state pass to a small class of capitalists who might be able to redistribute even more heavily in their favor. As McAdoo put the matter, "In a democracy, no one class should be permitted to save or to own the nation."[74] Wilson and McAdoo preferred to borrow from individuals rather than corporations, especially large banks, and to borrow as much as possible from middle-class Americans. To do this, the Wilson administration utilized the central, democratic control that Wilson had imposed on the Federal Reserve. He turned it into a source of easy finance for those, especially middle-class Americans, who wanted to lend money to the federal government by purchasing Liberty Loan bonds. Whatever the merits of this program as economic policy, the administration succeeded in placing the Liberty Loans deep within the American middle class.

As important to Wilson as the composition of the nation's wartime creditors was the degree of reliance on them. Once again, he made a strategic decision, based on considerations of political economy as well as marketplace economics, to rely as heavily as possible on taxation. This approach, however, put his administration at odds with business leaders, especially Wall Street bankers, who wanted the federal government to borrow at high levels and later pay the costs of the war from taxes. They hoped that after the war administrations and Congresses would be less inclined to tax progressively. But Wilson got his way. Tax revenues paid for essentially all the costs of war preparedness in 1916 and early 1917. And, ultimately, the ·United States financed a higher percentage of its war costs through taxation, more than one-third, than did any other combatant nation.[75]

Another large issue of political economy was the question of who would pay the wartime tax bill. In the process of answering this, the Wilson administration embarked on a dramatic transformation of tax policy. Wilson decided, in essence, that the federal government ought to use the tax system not simply to finance the war effort but also to undertake a significant redistribution of income and a major assault on the power of large, monopolistic corporations.

The Wilson administration launched this tax policy with a preparedness measure, the Revenue Act of 1916.[76] Wilson and McAdoo worked with insurgent Democrats in the House, led by Representative Claude Kitchin of North Carolina, who chaired the House Ways and Means Committee and served as the House majority leader, to mobilize and direct Populist and single-tax hostilities toward concentrations of wealth and power. The result was the first significant tax on personal incomes; a doubling of the 1913 tax on corporate incomes; an excess profits tax on munitions makers; and the beginnings of the modern estate tax. As Arthur Link correctly concluded, "No nation in modern times, not even Great Britain in David Lloyd George's "Tax on Wealth" of 1909, had imposed such heavy burdens on incomes and inheritances during peacetime."[77] The Revenue Act of 1916 provided a model that the Wilson administration not only followed throughout the war but also planned to continue to follow after the war. With the act, the graduated income tax had come into its own in modern America.

At the heart of the anticorporate tax policy was a corporation tax—an excess-profits tax with an antimonopoly twist. Instead of defining the excess profits of corporations as those above prewar levels, as the excess-profits tax of the British Liberals did, the American tax took a more radical approach. It defined excess profits as those above and beyond those that a "reasonable" rate of return would produce. Anything above that "reasonable" rate would be monopoly profits.[78] This was not, therefore, a tax that could be passed forward to consumers or the federal government or passed backward to workers. And the tax involved aggressive, and ongoing, investigations into corporate and industry behavior in order to determine what constituted reasonable rates of return. The high rates (ranging, under the Revenue Act of 1918, from 30 to 65 percent on profits above a "normal" rate of return) produced about two-thirds of all federal tax revenues raised during World War I. Moreover, as one Treasury staff member put it, the excess-profits tax had "the manifest advantage . . . of becoming a permanent part of the Government's revenue system, and can be used, if need be, as a check upon monopolies or trusts earning exorbitant profits."[79] Indeed, making the tax a permanent part of the tax code, as a means of socializing monopoly profits and controlling monopoly power, was exactly what both Kitchin and the Wilson administration had in mind.

Almost overnight, the modest income tax of 1913 became a massive effort to impose shared sacrifice during wartime, permanently redistribute social power, and expand economic opportunity. This shift revealed that Wilson had not given up on his effort to use the law to shape corporate behavior. In fact, as the war went on, and as he was unable to resist the power of business within the mobilization bureaucracy, he became increasingly attracted to the antimonopoly potential of excess-profits taxation. He believed it worked and liked the fact that it did not rely primarily on administrative regulation. Thus, although defeated during World War I in his effort to attack monopoly through the "legal regulation" of the Sherman Act and the commerce clause, he succeeded, at least for a time, in doing so through the exercise of the taxing power.

His administration failed, however, to sustain this most radical of its fiscal reforms. During the elections of 1918 and 1920, the investment banking community and the leaders of the Republican Party led the way in blaming the wartime tax program for causing serious inflation and accusing the South of having foisted the income tax on the rest of the nation. This campaign turned the Democrats out of power and won popular support for the repeal, in 1921, of the excess-profits tax.

The rest of the "soak-the-rich" program of progressive income taxation survived, however. It did so partly because of the enormous revenue capacity of the tax. But it was also because Wilson, through his handling of wartime finance, had reinforced and enhanced Americans' belief in the justice of taxing according to the criterion of "ability to pay." In deference to the power of this ideal, as well as to protect the important new source of revenue, Andrew Mellon, the secretary of the Treasury from 1921 to 1932, pragmatically cast his support behind preservation of the progressive income tax.

Wilson's wartime finance program had effects on policy and politics well beyond the 1920s. In shaping New Deal tax policy after 1935, Roosevelt and his Treasury relied heavily on Wilsonian precedents for taxing corporations and wealthy individuals. In fact, the New Deal architects of the most radical anticorporate tax, the undistributed profits tax, based it explicitly on the excess-profits tax of World War I. During World War II, Roosevelt, remembering the backlash to the excess-profits tax and chastened by the backlash to the undistributed profits tax, fell back on a more conventional treatment of wartime profits. But he pushed the graduation of the personal income tax to record levels of progressivity, both as a wartime measure on behalf of shared sacrifice and a permanent reform. Roosevelt also followed Wilson's example by seeking to fund a high proportion of wartime expenses out of tax revenues. During the 1950s, Democrats and Republicans reached a kind of consensus on the fundamentals of tax policy—a consensus that even further strengthened the progressive commitment to income taxation according, in principle, to "ability to pay." And this consensus has proven to be surprisingly durable, surviving, more or less, even the powerful antigovernment counterattack of the last thirty years.

World War I advanced, as well, the Wilsonian approach to management of the Federal Reserve. In the process of implementing the Wilsonian borrowing program, the Federal Reserve acquired the expertise and the resources to play a more powerful role by way of both mobilizing resources and shaping general economic conditions. In addition, Wilson had established a pattern of executive and legislative dominance over the Federal Reserve that would have permanent effects. Subsequently, the Federal Reserve would often play its roles according to scripts written by the president and Congress, under the influence of democratic pressures, just as Wilson had intended. In subsequent wars, the Federal Reserve would place the interests of the Treasury first and foremost. In the 1920s, the Federal Reserve gained a measure of autonomy when the skillful Benjamin Strong successfully emulated the tactics that the Bank of England had pioneered. But after Strong's death in 1929, the Federal Reserve abused its free rein by embarking on disastrous policies that made the Great Depression unusually severe in the United States. President Herbert Hoover was unwilling to use the executive leverage that Wilson had provided, but President Franklin

Roosevelt, through both formal restructuring and informal political pressure, resumed Wilson's efforts to establish democratic control over the Federal Reserve. Under this kind of pressure, the Federal Reserve System generally placed the goal of high or full employment above international stability. Ultimately, in 1971 under "Nixonomics," this democratic pressure contributed by the decision to abandon the gold standard altogether. After World War II, the Federal Reserve gradually increased its political independence, but it did so by paying close attention to, and cultivating, popular support.[80]

Wilson's Attacks on Monopoly: The Meaning of Progressivism

In summary, Woodrow Wilson led in forging a broadly ambitious program of economic restructuring. Wilson intended his four major reforms—freer trade, central banking, antitrust regulation, and redistributive taxation—to fulfill a huge range of progressive purposes. These included broadening economic opportunity, stabilizing the business cycle, promoting industrial efficiency and competitiveness, expanding export markets, redistributing ill-gotten gains, and protecting republican political institutions. British liberals greatly influenced the development of Wilson's agenda, but he added significant republican dimensions to their program. These dimensions expressed community values and transformed the program into his own, his characteristic brand of progressivism. The most important theme within this distinctive Wilsonian progressivism was the containment and even reduction of the monopoly power of great corporations. The theme ran throughout all the four programs, and it was bound up with all the other progressive themes. Wilson no doubt aimed his political appeal primarily at middle-class Americans, but his definition of the middle class was broad and, in any case, he regarded the benefits of this program as ones that Americans across all class lines would enjoy. The breadth of his antimonopoly program, coupled with the rigor of its redistributional methods, put Wilson on the advanced boundary of progressivism, where it bordered social democracy.[81]

Where, if anywhere, does one find the theme of "corporate liberalism" within Wilsonian progressivism? Certainly Wilson regarded his entire program as beneficial to capitalism, and much of the program, particularly freer trade and central banking, as beneficial for some large corporations. Moreover, in framing an antitrust program, Wilson accepted the legitimacy of large corporations when they brought significant productivity gains and did not unfairly choke off opportunities for smaller enterprise. But his definition of monopoly was broad, both in the "New Freedom" message and in his tax program. More generally, whatever interest Wilson had in legitimizing the new corporate order was very much secondary. His focus was on containing and then shrinking monopoly power, which he regarded as far reaching and threatening to the republic, rather than on persuading the American public to accept monopoly power. And he was constantly worried about monopoly capture of the regulatory institutions created by progressives. Consequently, it is not surprising to find that the nation's major corporations, both industrial and financial, were largely absent in the roll call of forces supporting Wilson's most progressive measures.

Still, one might argue that Wilson's programs, regardless of their intentions, had the effect, or served the function, of legitimating corporate capitalism. But if so, it was primarily as a consequence of elements not of the New Freedom but of the procorporate policies that his administration adopted during World War I. Much of the antimonopoly agenda of his New Freedom collapsed, a casualty of World War I, and he felt compelled to replace his earlier tariff and antitrust policies with approaches that were more favorable to powerful special interests, including those of the large-scale, vertically integrated corporations. Even then, however, his administration went in the opposite direction. During World War I, it advanced the cause of progressive taxation in significant ways. If anything, the tax initiatives damaged the reputation of American corporations and helped keep alive popular anticorporate hostility at least through the 1930s. The first corporate liberal to significantly enhance the legitimacy of American corporations through taxation was not Woodrow Wilson but Secretary of the Treasury Mellon, who deliberately accepted some of the Wilsonian tax program in order to fend off radical attacks on corporate treasuries along Wilsonian lines.

In evaluating Wilson as a corporate liberal, one ought to consider as well that, in the absence of the two world wars and the Great Depression, the New Freedom program, especially its tariff reforms, might have turned out to have been effective in achieving Wilson's goals. Even its antitrust reform might have made a difference along the lines that Wilson intended. By taking hold before the capitalism of the large corporations had time to put down deep roots in the political economy, Wilsonian antitrust reform might have fostered a smaller-scale, leaner, suppler, and more efficient corporate economy.[82] Finally, one might argue that Wilson's principled distaste for paternalistic government represented his realism as well as idealism and, if implemented in a sustained way, might have helped impede the capture of regulators by the regulated. In short, absent the world wars, an even stronger strain of Wilsonian progressivism might have infused the genome of government in the twentieth century. Consequently, by the beginning of the twenty-first century, the international search for trade liberalization and equity, governmental efficiency, financial stability, and the effective regulation of multinational corporations might have been advanced by a full generation. This kind of thinking is highly speculative, of course, but, if it is based on a more accurate perception of Woodrow Wilson's democratic intentions, it might help inspire and inform efforts to undertake yet another reconstruction of American liberalism.

Notes

1. Woodrow Wilson, "The Lawyer and the Community: An Address in Chattanooga, Tennessee to the American Bar Association," August 31, 1910, in *The Papers of Woodrow Wilson*, 69 vols., ed. Arthur S. Link et al. (Princeton, N.J.: Princeton University Press, 1966–94) (hereafter, *PWW*), vol. 21, 66.

2. In the historiography of this issue, the most influential scholars have been Arthur S. Link and Martin Sklar, both of whom developed nuanced positions, resting between the extremes of "progressive" or "corporatist." See, especially, Link's *Wilson: The New Freedom* (Princeton, N.J.: Princeton University Press, 1956), and Martin Sklar, "Woodrow Wilson and the Political Economy of Modern United States Liberalism," *Studies on the Left* 1, no. 3 (1960); and Martin Sklar, *The Corporate Reconstruction of American Capitalism, 1890–1916: The Market, Law, and Politics* (Cambridge: Cambridge University Press, 1988), particularly the chapter titled "Woodrow Wilson and the Corporate-Liberal Ascendancy," 393–430.

3. In focusing on tariff, tax, banking, and antitrust reform in this chapter, I do not take up much of the progressive economic legislation that Wilson supported in 1916, including, among others, the Federal Farm Loan Act, the Child Labor Act, the Workmen's Compensation Act, and the Adamson Act. Arguably, the purposes of these measures were more modest in scope.

4. Alfred D. Chandler Jr., *Scale and Scope: The Dynamics of Industrial Capitalism* (Cambridge, Mass.: Harvard University Press, 1990), 75. For nearly three decades, the most influential history of industrial reorganization through World War I has been Chandler's *The Visible Hand: The Managerial Revolution in American History* (Cambridge, Mass.: Harvard University Press, 1977), 207 ff. For a thorough survey of scholarly assessments of Chandler's work, see Richard R. John, "Elaborations, Revisions, Dissents: Alfred D. Chandler Jr.'s *The Visible Hand* after Twenty Years," *Business History Review* 71 (Summer 1997): 151–200.

5. Woodrow Wilson, *A History of the American People* [5 vols.], *Vol. 5, Reunion and Nationalization* (New York: Harper & Brothers, 1902), 265–68.

6. On the timing for Wilson's return to the issues he had raised in 1902, see John Milton Cooper Jr., *The Warrior and the Priest: Woodrow Wilson and Theodore Roosevelt* (Cambridge, Mass.: Harvard University Press, 1983), 119–22.

7. The most thorough analysis of the intellectual influences on Wilson's economic ideas is William Diamond, *The Economic Thought of Woodrow Wilson* (Baltimore: Johns Hopkins Press, 1943).

8. Cooper, *Warrior and the Priest*, 22, 397. On Wilson's devotion to Gladstone, see also Robert E. Kelley, *The Transatlantic Persuasion: The Liberal-Democratic Mind in the Age of Gladstone* (New York: Alfred A. Knopf, 1969), 145–46.

9. Woodrow Wilson, "Testimony Before the Tariff Commission," September 22, 1882, in *PWW*, vol. 2, 140–43.

10. Woodrow Wilson, "Government by Debate," unpublished essay, ca. December 4, 1882, in *PWW*, vol. 2, 196–97.

11. Wilson, "Testimony Before the Tariff Commission," 143.

12. On this free ride, see David Lake, *Power, Protection, and Free Trade: International Sources of U.S. Commercial Strategy, 1887–1939* (Ithaca, N.Y.: Cornell University Press, 1988), 92. Lake, however, may attribute too much intentionality to American exporters and policy makers who took the free ride.

13. Paul Wolman, *Most Favored Nation: The Republican Revisionists and U.S. Tariff Policy, 1897–1912* (Chapel Hill: University of North Carolina Press, 1992).

14. Neither Wolman, in *Most Favored Nation*, nor Lake, in *Power, Protection, and Free Trade*, cites specific evidence of large industrial firms taking a leadership role in tariff reform, including the Republican revisionism, before World War I.

15. The best account of the Payne-Aldrich Tariff remains Frank W. Taussig, *The Tariff History of the United States: The Eighth Revised Edition* (New York: Capricorn Books, 1964), 361–408. (The eighth edition appeared in 1931.)

16. Wilson, *History of the American People*, vol. 5, 189.

17. Wilson, "The Tariff Make-Believe," *North American Review*, 190 (October 1909), reprinted in ibid., 128, 138.

18. Wilson, "Interview," *New York Times*, December 24, 1911, in *PWW*, vol. 23, 611.

19. Wilson, "An Address in Atlantic City to the New Jersey Bankers' Association," May 6, 1910, in *PWW*, vol. 20, 420.

20. Wilson, "An After-Dinner Address to the Real Estate Men of Boston," January 27, 1912, in *PWW*, vol. 24, 84. In promoting tariff reform as means of stimulating exports, Wilson did not, however, indicate that he was aware, as Lake has suggested, of Britain's movement away from free trade and the consequence disappearance of the "free rider" benefits to the United States. David Lake, "The State and American Trade Strategy in the Pre-Hegemonic Era," in *The State and American Foreign Policy*, ed. G. John Ikenberry et al. (Ithaca, N.Y.: Cornell University Press, 1988), 51–56; and Lake, *Power, Protection, and Free Trade*, 153–59.

21. Wilson, "A Nonpartisan Talk to the Commercial Club of Omaha," October 5, 1912, in *PWW*, vol. 25, 341.

22. On the legislative history of the Underwood Tariff, see Link, *New Freedom*, 177–97; and Taussig, *Tariff History*, 409–46.

23. Wilson, "Tariff Make-Believe," 145.

24. Taussig, *Tariff History*, 423.

25. Wilson, "Progressive Democracy Is Remedy for Evils of Tariff and Trusts, Says Woodrow Wilson," *New York Times*, December 24, 1911, in *PWW*, vol. 12, 611.

26. Wilson may well have had in mind the incremental program of the British liberals. The repeal of the Corn Laws in 1846 marked roughly the halfway point in the reduction of the average tariff rate, which began in the 1820s. See Martin Daunton, *Trusting Leviathan: The Politics of Taxation in Britain, 1799–1914* (Cambridge: Cambridge University Press, 2001), 169.

27. For a survey of the history of the "ability to pay" criterion, see W. Elliot Brownlee, "Social Philosophy and Tax Regimes in the United States, 1763 to the Present," *Social Philosophy & Policy* 23 (Summer 2006): 1–27.

28. For Wilson's comments on Gladstone's 1861 budget, see Wilson, "Testimony Before the Tariff Commission," 140; and Wilson, *Congressional Government: A Study in American Politics*, c. January 24, 1885, in *PWW*, vol. 4, 80. In the latter, Wilson described Gladstone as the "greatest of English financiers." On Gladstone's 1861 budget, see Daunton, *Trusting Leviathan*, 171–72.

29. Wilson, *History of the American People*, vol. 5, 227–30.

30. Woodrow Wilson, "To the Legislature of New Jersey," February 26, 1912, in *PWW*, vol. 24, 216; and Woodrow Wilson, "To the Legislature of New Jersey," March 20, 1911, in *PWW*, vol. 22, 511. The New Jersey Senate did not approve the amendment until February 4, 1913.

31. On Gladstone's ambivalence with regard to graduated income taxation, see Daunton, *Trusting Leviathan*, 98–99, 243, 246, 321–22.

32. See ibid., 360–74; and Link, *New Freedom*, 193–94.

33. Wilson to Furnifold M. Simmons, September 4, 1913, in *PWW*, vol. 28, 254.

34. For a fine survey of central banking, particularly the role of the Bank of England, before 1913, see Allan H. Meltzer, *A History of the Federal Reserve, Volume 1: 1913–1951* (Chicago: University of Chicago Press, 2003), 19–64.

35. Michael D. Bordo, "The Impact and International Transmission of Financial Crises: Some Historical Evidence, 1870–1933," *Rivista di Storia Economica* 2 (1985): 73.

36. For superb analyses of how the gold standard worked in practice, see Meltzer, *History of the Federal Reserve*, 19–64; Barry Eichengreen, *Globalizing Capital: A History of the International Monetary System* (Princeton, N.J.: Princeton University Press, 1996), 3–44; and Barry Eichengreen, "U.S. Foreign Financial Relations in the Twentieth Century," in *The Cambridge Economic History of the United States, Volume III: The Twentieth Century*, ed. Stanley L. Engerman and Robert E. Gallman (Cambridge: Cambridge University Press, 2000), esp. 464–75. On the role of the Bank of England during the 1907 crisis, see R. S. Sayers, *The Bank of England: 1891–1944* (Cambridge: Cambridge University Press, 1976), 43–46, 54–60.

37. On Morgan's informal role as central banker, see Vincent P. Carosso, *The Morgans: Private International Bankers, 1854–1913* (Cambridge, Mass.: Harvard University Press, 1987), 528–49. For histories of banking reform during the late nine-

teenth and early twentieth centuries, see James Livingston, *Origins of the Federal Reserve System: Money, Class, and Corporate Capitalism, 1890–1913* (Ithaca, N.Y.: Cornell University Press, 1986); Richard T. McCulley, *Banks and Politics during the Progressive Era: The Origins of the Federal Reserve System, 1897–1913* (New York: Garland, 1992); and Elmus Wicker, *The Great Debate on Banking Reform: Nelson Aldrich and the Origins of the Fed* (Columbus: Ohio State University Press, 2005), 22–41. The best analysis of the international interests of American bankers is J. Lawrence Broz, *The International Origins of the Federal Reserve System* (Ithaca, N.Y.: Cornell University Press, 1997), esp. 132–59.

38. Wicker provides one of the best summaries of the work of Nelson Aldrich and the National Monetary Commission. See Wicker, *Great Debate on Banking Reform*, 52–69.

39. Major industrial corporations joined in this support but were not, as James Livingston claims, leaders in this movement. This was partly because, as Thomas McCraw and Alfred D. Chandler suggest, corporations had been shifting to internal sources (retained earnings) for financing mergers. See Thomas K. McCraw, *Prophets of Regulation: Charles Francis Adams, Louis D. Brandeis, James M. Landis, and Alfred E. Kahn* (Cambridge, Mass.: Harvard University Press, 1984), 114; Chandler, *Visible Hand*, 373–74; and Livingston, *Origins of the Federal Reserve System*, 66–67, 183.

40. Woodrow Wilson, "Walter Bagehot: A Lecture," February 24, 1898, in *PWW*, vol. 10, 439. On Wilson's study of banking issues, see Diamond, *Economic Thought of Woodrow Wilson*, 51, 101.

41. Wilson, *History of the American People*, vol. 4, 47.

42. Ibid., vol. 5, 253–56.

43. Woodrow Wilson, "Two News Reports of Addresses in Chattanooga, Tennessee," October 27, 1906, in *PWW*, vol. 16, 475.

44. Woodrow Wilson, "An Interview in the *New York Times*," November 24, 1907, in *PWW*, vol. 17, 520.

45. Woodrow Wilson, "Money Monopoly Is the Most Menacing, Wilson's Warning," Philadelphia *North American*, June 16, 1911, speech in Harrisburg, Pa., in *PWW*, vol. 23, 157.

46. Woodrow Wilson, *New Freedom* (New York: Doubleday, Page, 1913), 185.

47. Woodrow Wilson, "A Call in Denver for a 'Second Emancipation,'" October 7, 1912, in *PWW*, vol. 25, 380.

48. Wilson, "A Speech Accepting the Democratic Nomination in Sea Girt, New Jersey," August 7, 1912, in *PWW*, vol. 25, 14.

49. The following discussion of the Federal Reserve Act relies heavily on Link, *New Freedom*, 199–240, for the details of the legislative history.

50. The "Democracy of Credit" quotation is from Joseph P. Tumulty, *Woodrow Wilson as I Know Him* (New York: Doubleday, Page & Company, 1921), 172. The longer quotation is from Wilson, "An Interview on the Banking and Currency Bill," June 23, 1913, in *PWW*, vol. 27, 569.

51. Wilson, "An Address on Banking and Currency Reform to a Joint Session of Congress," June 23, 1913, in *PWW*, vol. 27, 573.

52. Louis D. Brandeis to Wilson, June 14, 1913, in *PWW*, vol. 27, 521.

53. On the appointment of the board members, see Link, *New Freedom*, 451–57; and William Gibbs McAdoo, *Crowded Years: The Reminiscences of William G. McAdoo* (Boston: Houghton Mifflin, 1931), 278–81. Link overestimates the role Colonel House played in the appointment process and underestimates McAdoo's influence.

54. For this comparative point, see Keller, "Regulation of Large Enterprise: The United States Experience in Comparative Perspective," in *Managerial Hierarchies, Comparative Perspectives on the Rise of Modern Industrial Enterprise*, ed. Alfred D. Chandler Jr. and Herman Daems (Cambridge, Mass.: Harvard University Press, 1980), 172. See also Tony Freyer, *Regulating Big Business: Antitrust in Great Britain and America, 1880–1990* (New York: Cambridge University Press, 1992).

55. Wilson, "Address" (at Jamestown Exposition), July 4, 1907, in *PWW*, vol.17, 256.

56. Wilson, "A Statement to the *New York Times*," November 27, 1907, in *PWW*, vol. 17, 526.

57. John Mulder, *Woodrow Wilson: The Years of Preparation* (Princeton, N.J.: Princeton University Press, 1978), 244. Mulder discusses Wilson's more general search for individuals "who had been transformed, renewed, morally purified to serve others." Ibid., 240, 232–44. Also see Diamond, *Economic Thought of Woodrow Wilson*, 73–77.

58. Woodrow Wilson, "Law or Personal Power," Remarks at the National Democratic Club, New York, April 13, 1908, in *PWW*, vol. 18, 264. On Bryan's antitrust position in 1908, see Paul W. Glad, *The Trumpet Soundeth: William Jennings Bryan and His Democracy, 1896–1912* (Lincoln: University of Nebraska Press, 1960), 88–92.

59. Wilson, "A Draft of a Platform for the Democratic Party of Pennsylvania," April 4, 1910, in *PWW*, vol. 20, 316.

60. Wilson, "Interview," *New York Times*, December 24, 1911, in *PWW*, vol. 23, 613.

61. On the influence of Brandeis on Wilson during the 1912 campaign, see Link, *New Freedom*, 423–24; Philippa Strum, *Louis D. Brandeis: Justice for the People* (Cambridge, Mass.: Harvard University Press, 1984), 196–200; Philippa Strum, *Brandeis: Beyond Progressivism* (Lawrence: University Press of Kansas, 1993), 84–85; and McCraw, *Prophets of Regulation*, 110–12.

62. Wilson, "A Campaign Address in Sioux City, Iowa," September 17, 1912, in *PWW*, vol. 25, 152. In making this distinction, Wilson was wrestling with the same problem that Chandler has sought to address: determining the relative importance of efficiency-driven vertical integration and market control in corporate consolidations. See Chandler, *Visible Hand*, 331–39. Naomi Lamoreaux has argued effectively that the corporations that Wilson worried about did, in fact, organize initially to obtain market control rather than achieve greater efficiency. See Naomi Lamoreaux, *The Great Merger Movement in American Business, 1895–1904* (Cambridge: Cambridge University Press, 1985). She also concluded that "the scholarly debate on the relationship between industrial concentration and efficiency has been inconclusive." Ibid., 184. It is not surprising that Wilson was imprecise about the relationship.

63. Wilson, "An Address in Washington at a Jackson Day Dinner," January 8, 1912, in *PWW*, vol. 24, 11–12.

64. Wilson, "Law or Personal Power," 264.

65. Wilson, "To First Voters," June 26, 1910, in *PWW*, vol. 20, 504.

66. Wilson, "An Address to the Workingmen in Fall River, Massachusetts," September 26, 1912, in *PWW*, vol. 25, 266–67.

67. The best accounts of the framing of antitrust legislation are Link, *New Freedom*, 423–44; and McCraw, *Prophets of Regulation*, 80–126.

68. On consumer interests, see Morton Keller, *Regulating a New Economy: Public Policy and Economic Change in America, 1900–1933* (Cambridge, Mass.: Harvard University Press, 1990), 32–33. On their overlap with those of small business, see McCraw, *Prophets of Regulation,* esp. 101–8.

69. On the creation of a tariff commission, see William H. Becker, *The Dynamics of Business-Government Relations: Industry and Exports, 1893–1921* (Chicago: University of Chicago Press, 1982), 86–89; Joseph F. Kenkel, *Progressives and Protection: The Search for a Tariff Policy, 1866–1936* (New York: University Press of America, 1983), 91–117; Arthur S. Link, *Wilson: Confusions and Crises, 1915–1916* (Princeton, N.J.: Princeton University Press, 1964), 341–45; and Wolman, *Most Favored Nation*, 195–208.

70. For a good summary of the postwar wave of protectionism, see Peter H. Lindert, "U.S. Trade and Trade Poliy in the Twentieth Century," in *The Cambridge Economic History of the United States: Volume III, The Twentieth Century*, ed. Stanley L. Engerman and Robert E. Gallman (Cambridge: Cambridge University Press, 2000), 457–58. For analysis of this episode, see Barry Eichengreen, "The Political Economy of the Smoot-Hawley Tariff," *Research in Economic History*, 1989, 1–43.

71. For the long-term trends, see Lake, *Power, Protection, and Free Trade*, 154.

72. Wilson to Sidney Mezes, November 12, 1917, in *PWW*, vol. 45, 17.

73. The quotation is from Chandler, *Scale and Scope*, 79. On the history of the FTC from its creation through the 1920s, see Susan Wagner, *The Federal Trade Commission* (New York: Praeger, 1971), 20–27; McCraw, *Prophets of Regulation* 126–35, 142–52; and Keller, *Regulating a New Economy*, 39–40, 113–14. On the mobilization and corporations, see Robert D. Cuff, *The War Industries Board* (Baltimore: Johns Hopkins University Press, 1973). On the FTC and the Webb-Pomerene Act, see Wolman, *Most Favored Nation*, 198–204; Burton I. Kaufman, *Efficiency and Expansion: Foreign Trade Organization in the Wilson Administration, 1913–1921* (Westport, Conn.: Greenwood Press, 1974), 206–27; and Carl P. Parrini, *Heir to Empire: United States Economic Diplomacy, 1916–1923* (Pittsburgh: University of Pittsburgh Press, 1969), esp. 8–9, 28–31. (Wolman, Kaufman, and Parrini, I believe, have overestimated the role of large corporations in the passage and implementation of the Webb-Pomerene Act.)

74. William G. McAdoo, "Memorandum in Explanation of the Proposed War Loan Bill," August 1917; McAdoo to George Cooksey, October 22, 1917, in William G. McAdoo Papers, Library of Congress (LC).

75. On World War I finance, see W. Elliot Brownlee, *Federal Taxation in America: A Short History, Second Edition* (Washington and New York: Woodrow Wilson Center Press and Cambridge University Press, 2004), 58–72.

76. W. Elliot Brownlee, "Wilson and Financing the Modern State: The Revenue Act of 1916," *Proceedings of the American Philosophical Society* 129 (1985): 173–210. For a contrasting view of Wilson's role, see Arthur S. Link, *Wilson: Campaigns for Progressivism and Peace, 1916–1917* (Princeton, N.J.: Princeton University Press, 1965), 64–65. Link wrote: "Wilson, insofar as we know, had had no part in this, one of the most significant achievements of the progressive movement."

77. Ibid., 65.

78. The Wilson administration supported radical excess-profits taxation in part because some of its members found single-tax ideas attractive. The intellectual transition from one to the other was easy to make because, in principle, both taxes represented taxes on returns that resulted from monopoly power. In single-tax theory, taxation should reach to the "economic rent" that flowed from the "site value" of land. The most influential single-tax advocates within the administration were Oscar Crosby, McAdoo's closest adviser within the Treasury, and Secretary of the Interior Franklin Lane. Although the single-tax leader in Congress, Warren Worth Bailey, complained that Wilson's cabinet focused too much on income taxation and too little on taxation of property, he also noted: "These chaps [Wilson's cabinet] are all land value taxers." See Warren Worth Bailey to William M. Reedy, July 24, 1917, in Warren Worth Bailey Papers, Seeley G. Mudd Library, Princeton University. In May 1917, Wilson himself urged McAdoo to consider the proposal of George L. Record, who championed the single-tax in New Jersey, for a federal tax on "the value of land." Wilson told McAdoo that Record was "a man of somewhat erratic temper but of very clear grasp of some fundamental things." T. W. Gregory to McAdoo, March 1, 1917; George Record to Wilson, May 3, 1917, Wilson to McAdoo, May 8, 1917, in McAdoo Papers, LC.

79. I. J. Talbert, Head of Law Division, Commissioner of Internal Revenue, to George R. Cooksey, Assistant Secretary of the Treasury, August 8, 1917, in McAdoo Papers, LC.

80. Cf. Martin Sklar's assertion that the Federal Reserve Act insulated the system and the board "from national party politics and executive fiat." Sklar, *Corporate Reconstruction,* 423.

81. The social-justice initiatives launched in 1916 may locate Wilson on the same boundary. See n. 3 above.

82. For suggestions that many business historians, following in the wake of Alfred Chandler's battleship (*The Visible Hand*), may have exaggerated the efficiency gains associated with the great merger movements, see John, "Elaborations, Revisions, Dissents," 187 ff. and Gavin Wright, "Regulation in American History: The Human Touch," *Reviews in American History 14* (June 1986): 163–68.

Part II
Race, Speech, and Gender

4. Race and Nation in the Thought and Politics of Woodrow Wilson

Gary Gerstle

In both the domestic and international arenas, Woodrow Wilson stands as one of the giants of American history. While president, he became a key architect of modern liberalism. Internationally, he elaborated an ambitious and compelling vision of a world without war, where every people would have the right to independent statehood and self-governance. We have known for some time that millions of people in France and Italy turned out to greet Wilson when he arrived in Europe in 1918 to begin fashioning the international institutions that would make his vision a reality. Now we are learning that millions beyond Europe, in places such as colonial India and war-torn China, were similarly inspired. Wilson's dream of a world transformed flamed out in 1919 and 1920. Nevertheless, it remains the case that no other American president has ever sparked the breadth or intensity of international optimism and adulation that Wilson did when he sailed to Europe in 1918 to establish a new kind of world order.[1]

Yet, in matters of domestic race relations, the characteristics we associate with Wilson—boldness, passion, an insistence on social justice—are difficult to find. He was timid, cold, practically indifferent to questions of racial justice, and incapable of summoning rhetoric that might inspire and transform racial problems seemingly no deeper or more intractable than those besetting

The author thanks Philippa Strum for inviting him to the September 2006 Woodrow Wilson Center's One Hundred Fiftieth Anniversary Symposium on Woodrow Wilson. The author also thanks Mary-Elizabeth Murphy for her extraordinary research assistance. Murphy is a University of Maryland graduate student whose work will soon make its own contribution to our understanding of the Wilsonian moment in American politics and race relations. Lloyd Ambrosius, Victoria Brown, John Milton Cooper, Michael Kazin, Erez Manela, and Eric Yellin gave valuable feedback on an earlier version of the chapter. The author is grateful to them all.

the system of international states. He was deeply racist in his thought and politics, and apparently he was comfortable with being so.

Much has been written about Wilson's racial attitudes. One popular school of thought, associated with Arthur S. Link, grounds his racism in his white southern heritage. In this view, virtually no white southerners of Wilson's time were prepared to regard blacks as their equals, with the same claims as whites on the promise of American life—liberty, equality, and opportunity. If they could not overturn two results of the Civil War—the defeat of the Confederacy and the destruction of slavery—white southerners still believed that they could return blacks to a subordinate and servile position vis-à-vis whites. Indeed, the years of the South's reintegration into the nation, 1890–1925, were also the years when segregation became legal, blacks were disenfranchised in the southern states, lynchings soared to all-time highs, and numerous states outlawed interracial marriage.[2]

Wilson was not a rabid white supremacist who condoned or celebrated lynchings and other forms of violence designed to terrorize blacks and keep them in their place. His sympathies were drawn instead to the moderate white, elite southerners who viewed segregation as a progressive arrangement that upheld social peace by keeping whites and blacks at a safe distance from each other. Still, these moderates never put blacks on the same plane as whites, viewing the former as an inferior population of questionable worth as Americans, and expecting them to remain so for a very long time. Thus, when Wilson assumed the presidency in 1913 and appointed to his Cabinet more white southerners than had served in any other presidential Cabinet since before the Civil War, it hardly seems surprising that his administration moved quickly to resegregate the federal civil service. As Link remarked long ago, Wilson "was characteristically a Southerner in his attitude toward the Negro."[3]

In many respects, Wilson was a man of his region and his time. He was born in Staunton, Virginia, in 1856, and he lived his first eighteen years in Augusta, Georgia, and Columbia, South Carolina, where his father, Dr. Joseph Ruggles Wilson, was first minister of the First Presbyterian Church (Augusta) and then a professor at the Presbyterian Theological Seminary (Columbia). When war broke out in 1861, Joseph cast his lot with the Confederacy and, in his personal act of secession, helped to found the Southern Presbyterian Church that broke away from the national church that same year. Later, the church where he was the minister was used by the Confederate army as a military hospital and a stockade. When the family moved to Columbia after the war had ended, it encountered a city still devastated by General William Sherman's march to the sea in 1865.

Woodrow's boyhood, then, was thoroughly intertwined with the South at war. He developed deep attachments to the culture and pride of the South on the one hand while being extensively exposed to the destructiveness and suffering caused by war on the other. Though his family never owned slaves, it relied for household labor on black servants both before and after the Civil War. The South's culture, race relations, and devastation from war left lasting impressions on him.[4]

However, we cannot understand Woodrow entirely in terms of his residence in and experience of the South. His family also had strong northern roots. His father had lived in Ohio for twenty-nine years before coming to Virginia. Woodrow's six Wilson uncles in Ohio, Iowa, Indiana, Pennsylvania, and New York were Republicans, opposed to slavery, and Unionist. Several of them were high-ranking officers in the Union Army. Their brother Joseph's ardent Confederate sympathies did not sit well with them.[5]

We do not know much about Woodrow's attraction to the northern branch of his family. We do know, however, that once Woodrow earned his doctorate in political science from Johns Hopkins University, he chose three northern towns as the places in which to ply his professional trade: Middletown, Connecticut; Bryn Mawr, Pennsylvania; and Princeton, New Jersey. Moreover, one of his earliest essays, written when he was at the University of Virginia Law School from 1879 to 1882, suggests that both the South and the North exerted pulls on him. "Because I love the South," he wrote, "I rejoice in the failure of the Confederacy. . . . Even the damnable cruelty and folly of Reconstruction was to be preferred to helpless independence."[6] The love of the South comes first in this formulation. But not many sons of the South in the late nineteenth century would have expressed joy about the Confederacy's collapse. Wilson did so because another love competed in his mind with his love of the South, and that was a love of what northerners called the Union, and what Wilson, the southerner, called the nation: a country stretching from the Atlantic in the East to the Pacific in the West, from Canada in the North to the Gulf of Mexico in the South. Nothing could be allowed to violate the integrity of this nation; nothing could be allowed to divide the American people to the point where they would kill each other and tear the nation apart—not slavery, states' rights, or regional pride. The place of the South was in the nation, not apart from it. Wilson partook fully of Abraham Lincoln's argument that the claims of the nation on the loyalties of all Americans were supreme and inviolable.

Biographers of Wilson like to emphasize the sea changes he underwent during his career, from professor to politician, from conservative to progressive, from a student of Congress to an advocate of world parliaments.[7] But he never strayed from the love of the American nation that appeared in his earliest writings in the 1870s and 1880s. He viewed secession as a foolish and illegitimate act.[8] He believed that an economic system grounded in slavery could never have held its own against the free labor economic system of the North. Moreover, Wilson liked to imagine a future in which the South would become like the North in its commitment to free labor, industry, immigration, and economic dynamism. This stance in the 1880s and 1890s marked him as a man of the New South. But this appellation does not quite get it right, for Wilson saw himself as a man of the "New Nation," a nation that had become possible for the first time as a direct result of the South's 1865 defeat. Wilson's love of nation, and his insistence on the priority of the nation over the states, drew on Unionist and even Republican sentiments. Thus we can begin to see that descriptions of him as simply a white southern man of his time do not quite work. We cannot assume that we can understand everything about him by referring to his identity as a white southerner. Indeed, Wilson developed a dynamic notion of American nationality that celebrated America both for the varieties of its peoples and for its ability to fuse the best traits of each people into one culture. This view is not one we commonly associate with white southerners of Wilson's era.

That Wilson advanced a bold and inclusive theory of American nationality makes his failure to find a place in this theory for blacks all the more consequential. Few were as perturbed by his inflexibility on this matter as were leaders of the African American community. They were drawn to Wilson by the power, daring, and apparently liberality of the man's political imagination. And though they were repeatedly disappointed by him, they kept on coming back to him, hoping against hope that this man who seemed to promise America and the world so much would embrace the cause of African American equality. He never would.

Making the American Nation

Trained as a political scientist in the 1870s and 1880s, Woodrow Wilson turned his energies to historical writing in the 1890s, publishing *Division and Reunion* in 1893 and the multi-volume *History of the American People* in 1902.[9] Though both works aimed to be comprehensive in their coverage of politics and society in American history, they also were organized around a central theme: the making of the American nation. More particularly, Wilson wanted to tell the story of how all the people who settled or who had been born in America came to see themselves as part of one nation, one economic system, "knit and united for a common history of achievement."[10] Familiar figures played their parts in Wilson's rendition of America's rise: the intrepid English colonizers of the sixteenth and seventeenth centuries who explored the New World; the brave frontiersmen of the eighteenth century who cleared the land of Indians and began the westward push; and that special generation of Founders who engineered America's break with Britain and then devised a magnificent Constitution. But, in Wilson's telling, none of these groups and individuals did enough to give Americans the common consciousness, the unity of thought and feeling, that were so essential to successful nationhood. That unity and consciousness were a product of three seminal nineteenth-century events: First, northerners developed a new theory of nationality in response to the nullification crisis of 1830 and the emerging southern doctrine of states' rights, making national allegiance paramount and casting secession from the Union as illegitimate.[11] Second, the market revolution that had burst forth in the 1820s and 1830s was rendering America, almost overnight, a country "bound together by railway and telegraph, busy with enterprises which no State or section could imprison within local boundaries, quick and various, as in the old days, but now at last conscious of its unity and its organic integrity."[12]

The third factor promoting nationalism was the ordeal of secession, war, and Southern defeat. From Wilson's nationalist perspective, the Civil War was both inevitable and necessary. It was inevitable because the leaders of the white South, the plantation owners who also dominated the region's political class, were too proud to give up their way of life without a fight; it was necessary because "economic and social difference between the states" had grown so large that it "threatened to become permanent, standing forever in the way of homogeneous national life."[13] Thus, the Civil War, despite the horrendous suffering it caused, was a positive development, for it had allowed American nationalism to flourish to a degree it had never previously achieved. As he assessed the significance of the war for American nationality, Wilson could barely contain his enthusiasm. "National consciousness," he wrote, had been "disguised, uncertain, latent until that day of sudden rally and call to arms." Now it was "cried wide awake by the voices of battle, and acted like a passion . . . in the conduct of affairs. All things took their hue and subtle transformation from it. . . . The stage was cleared for the creation of a new nation."[14] And when the South was finally defeated and then welcomed back into the Union in 1877, America finally stood upon the threshold of greatness. A hundred years after the country's birth, Wilson declared, the "national spirit was aroused and conscious now at last of its strength."[15]

Wilson's celebration of national strength and unity was not unusual among those in the United States and elsewhere who had taken upon themselves the task of writing the history of their nations. Indeed, history as a discipline arose to tell the story of nations' rise, and most members of this early generation of historians in the United States and Europe (of which Wilson was a member) wrote about their nations in similarly romantic and teleological ways, as though the whole point of history was to reveal the paths their countries pursued to national consolidation and distinction. It was generally assumed by these late-nineteenth-century scholars, as Eric Hobsbawm shrewdly pointed out some years ago, that the great nations were those that were large in territory and population, and robust in their economic activity.[16] Equally important was an emphasis on national homogeneity in thought and feeling. Indeed, in the fixation on homogeneity, we can detect the fear everywhere driving nationalists: that the very real heterogeneity within every nation's borders put these entities at chronic risk of cultural division and political failure.[17]

Wilson partook fully of this obsession with homogeneity, a word that recurs again and again in his writing.[18] In his telling, the constitutional polity to which America aspired, one that prized individual freedom and self-government, required self-discipline, maturity, and virtue from its citizens. Drawing on conservative, even Burkean, notions of community, Wilson argued that these characteristics would be strongest among people who already possessed "a distinct consciousness of common ties and interests, a common manner and standard of life and conduct, and a practiced habit of union and concerted action in whatever affected it as a whole." Individuals in cohesive communities would be better able to discern their common purpose and sacrifice or restrain their own interests at critical moments for the sake of the general welfare and the rule of law. The conflict and friction that were endemic features of human social interactions could thus be kept within bounds. People would then be "free" to pursue their lives in relative independence, and government could be both effective and unobtrusive.[19]

There would seem to be a basic contradiction between Wilson's political theory, which posited that only settled and homogeneous societies could achieve effective self-government, and the historical reality of America, which, as a result of immigration, seemed to be perpetually composed of diverse groups of newcomers. Wilson's theory might have led him, by the 1890s, to join the many conservatives, South and North, who wanted to limit full citizenship to those who were descended from the country's original Anglo-Saxon core. But he would meet these conservatives only halfway; he fully sympathized with their desire to bar non-Europeans, most notably blacks, from the

American polity, but he rejected their desire to bar further immigration from the non-Anglo-Saxon parts of Europe or to treat those southern and eastern Europeans already in the United States as second-class citizens.

Wilson's pro-European immigrant stance may have been rooted in the immigrant character of his own family. Other than Andrew Jackson, no other president possessed an immigrant background as proximate as that of Wilson. His mother, née Janet E. Woodrow, had been born in England in 1826 to Scottish parents, the Reverend Thomas and Marion Woodrow. The entire Woodrow family, including the parents, Janet, and her six siblings, immigrated to New York in 1836 and soon after moved on to Ohio. Wilson's paternal grandfather, James Wilson, was a Scots-Irish immigrant from Northern Ireland, as was his paternal grandmother, who became Mrs. Margaretta Wilson while the two still lived on the Emerald Isle. The married couple emigrated to Philadelphia when they were young, also moving on to Ohio, where they raised eight children.[20] Wilson developed a lifelong pride in the contributions of the Scots, the Scots-Irish, and the Celts to American democracy and nationality. Wilson might have drawn a sharp line between the contributions of seventeenth- and eighteenth-century immigrants from the British Isles and Germany who had come at earlier moments in American history and those from eastern and southern Europe who began arriving in such large numbers in the 1880s and 1890s. On at least one occasion, he did just that. But his conviction about the centrality of immigrants to the making of America usually overcame whatever nativist reflexes he possessed. Indeed, his position on immigration was progressive for a man of his regional and class background.

Wilson believed, on the one hand, that European immigrants often became more ardently patriotic than the native born, and thus they revivified American ideas during periods of nationalist languor. On the other hand, he argued that America's strength emerged from the ability of different strains of European immigrants to fuse their cultures and values together and produce a new mold. The homogeneity that Wilson so valued was the product, by his own account, of periodic episodes of cultural renewal, with diversification of the population through immigration leading to new and ever stronger fusions. He never used the word "hybridity" to describe this second process, and he only embraced the notion of America as a "melting pot" in the twentieth century. But his recognition of the centrality of this process to the making of America is apparent in his earliest historical writings and in his coverage of the earliest periods of American history.

In granting immigrants a central role in the making of the American nation, Wilson endowed his previously static and conservative theory of nationhood with a dynamic and progressive quality. His contemplation of the issues of diversity in America helped him to imagine how a League of Nations might work—how, in other words, a world of culturally different nations might successfully support an international government grounded in shared constitutional principles and a common political culture. And it makes his refusal to allow non-Europeans to participate in these processes of cultural interpenetration and fusion all the more significant, consequential, and, in the eyes of his African American contemporaries, infuriating. For these contemporaries believed they had found in Wilson not an unthinking white southerner but a bold thinker who would fashion an American nation where blacks would finally be granted their full rights.

Wilson laced his argument about how America emerged from the melding or hybridization of different European peoples throughout the pages of his *History of the American People*. In describing the English seamen of the sixteenth century, he noted how many of them came from Devonshire in southwest England, "in the midst of that group of counties . . . in which Saxon mastery did least to destroy or drive out the old Celtic population." The "sense of mystery and . . . ardor of imagination" that he associated with the Celts thus "enriched the sober Saxon mind," and it was this mixture of imagination and sobriety that made the English explorers such a clever, diligent, and successful group.[21] In describing the settlement of British North America, Wilson invariably praised those colonies where the most extensive mixtures of European peoples had occurred: Pennsylvania in the seventeenth century, where the French, Dutch, Swedes, Germans, Finns, and Scots-Irish mixed with the English; Massachusetts in the eighteenth century, where the arrival of the Scots-Irish allowed it to transcend its pinched Puritan character; South Carolina, where the settlements of "Scots-Irish, Huguenots, and Swiss Palatine Germans" made the colony as diverse as Pennsylvania and New York; and Georgia, where Wilson admired the mixing of "Italians skilled in silk culture," "sober German Protestants," and "clansmen from the Scottish Highlands."[22]

Even the arrival of hundreds of thousands of impoverished Irish Catholics in the early nineteenth century, which triggered the first major nativist movement in American history, did not elicit anti-immigrant comments from Wilson. There is barely a trace of anti-Catholicism in his writings, and though he recognized the social strains that this massive immigrant wave placed on American institutions, he insisted on seeing it in positive terms. The nation-building prowess of Jacksonian America, he believed, rested in critical ways on the "great tide of immigration" that washed over the country in the antebellum years.[23]

Wilson did succumb briefly to the widespread prejudice expressed against the new immigrants of the 1890s, those from eastern and southern Europe. In one notorious passage in the last volume of his *History of the American People*, he demeaned the new immigrants as men coming out "of the lowest class from the south of Italy and men of the meaner sort of Hungary and Poland, men out of the ranks where there was neither skill nor intelligence." It was "as if the countries of the south of Europe were disburdening themselves of the more sordid and hapless elements of their population; and they came in numbers which increased from year to year."[24] He would pay dearly for having published this passage, at no time more so than in the election of 1912, when his Progressive Party opponents distributed the offending statement to Poles, Italians, and Hungarians in the major industrial cities of the Northeast and Midwest, creating an uproar in those communities.[25]

Wilson was compelled to spend much more time than he wished writing letters to irate members of these immigrant groups, trying to persuade them that this passage was an aberration.[26] Indeed, he was right to do so, and his speeches to immigrant groups once he became president reveal the depths of his appreciation for the contributions that all European immigrants had made to the United States and his belief that their arrival had invariably invigorated and renewed American democracy and freedom. In a July Fourth oration given in Philadelphia in 1914, he declared: "We opened our gate to the world and said: 'Let all men who wish to be free come to us and they will be welcome.' We said, 'This independence of ours is not a selfish thing for our own exclusive private use. It is for everybody to whom we can find the means of extending it.'"[27]

Also, in 1915, in a speech to immigrants who had just been sworn in as American citizens, Wilson expressed his appreciation to them for bringing to America a regard for patriotic ideals that often exceeded that of the native born; in the process, they had made themselves a vital source of American democratic renewal. "This is the only country in the world," he exclaimed, that experiences a "constant and repeated rebirth," and the credit went to the "great bodies of strong men and forward-looking women out of other lands" who decided to cast their lot with America."[28] That same year, he reprimanded a Daughters of the American Revolution audience clamoring for immigration restriction: "Some of the best stuff of America has come out of foreign lands, and some of the best stuff in America is in the men who are naturalized citizens of the United States."[29] These are the kinds of sentiments that twice led him to veto immigration restriction bills.[30]

Wilson expected twentieth-century immigrants, like the ones who had come before them, to Americanize. "We have brought out of the stocks of all the world all the best impulses and have appropriated them and Americanized and translated them into the glory and majesty of a great country," he declared in 1914.[31] He was not as intolerant of Old World cultures as was his Progressive rival, Theodore Roosevelt. Wilson said: "I certainly would not be one even to suggest that a man cease to love the home of his birth and the nation of his origin—these things are very sacred and ought not to put out of our hearts." Nevertheless, he expected immigrants to become "in every respect and with every purpose of your will thorough Americans."[32] He uttered those words in 1915, before the time when war pressures would impel him and his administration to insist rigidly on "100 percent Americanism." The excesses of this campaign for conformity were real, but they should not distract us from understanding the durability of Wilson's conviction that immigrants were a dynamic, essential force in the making of the American nation and American democracy.[33] At times, he even went so far as to suggest that a democratic community without sources of foreign replenishment would lose its ardor for liberty and freedom. As he asserted in 1915, "a nation that is not constantly renewed out of new sources is apt to have the narrowness and prejudice of a family; whereas, America has this consciousness, that on all sides it touches hearts with all the nations of mankind."[34] Here we see him beginning to build the bridge in his own thought from America as a pacific home to a wide array of immigrant groups to a world where countless nations could live together in peace, governed by the rule of law. His belief that diversity was a currency that, in America, had facilitated new and higher forms of hybridized national consciousness helped to nurture in him a hope that an international diversity of national identities and interests could be similarly transformed into a common global consciousness.

This is not a man easily passed off as just another white southerner, as a man whose entire body of thought was shaped by the region where he had been born and by the regional experience of slavery, secession, and war. His ability to use America's encounter with immigrants to develop a dynamic theory of hybridized homogeneity and self-government reveals the independence, boldness, and creativity of his political imagination. And those characteristics make his refusal to think creatively about America's race problem all the more frustrating and maddening. This is not just my judgment but also the judgment that his African American contemporaries made as a result of their encounters with him during his presidency. But before we consider their views, we need to explore Wilson's racial attitudes.

Race and Nation

What immediately strikes a reader of Woodrow Wilson's *History of the American People* is the dissimilarity between his treatment of European immigrants and his treatment of African immigrants and their descendants. The curiosity and empathy that are so central to his discussion of Europeans is missing from his discussion of African Americans. He does not seem to regard them as suitable citizens for America's cultural or political community. Nowhere does he allow them to play a positive role in fashioning the American nation, let alone enter the assimilatory mainstream that was creating hybridized Americans. He grounded his negative view of slavery almost entirely in his conviction that it was holding the white South back economically and sundering the white nation into two incompatible parts, not that it was morally wrong for some humans to hold others in bondage. To the contrary, he found virtue in the system of plantation slavery: "There was almost always moderation," he wrote, "a firm but not unkindly discipline, a real care shown for their [the slaves'] comfort and welfare." Masters taught their slaves handicrafts and meted out justice fairly, he claimed. They treated their domestic slaves with "affection and indulgence" and did everything they could to avoid breaking up slave families. They behaved responsibly and dutifully toward field slaves, even though the latter were "indolent" and "like a huge family of shiftless children" who often did not earn their keep. Where the masters managed their plantations, in other words, slavery proved to be, in his view, a humane system.[35]

That African Americans may have suffered, either materially or psychologically, from chattel slavery is not a thought to which Wilson gives expression. Once he moves into the history of Reconstruction (1865–1877), his analysis is driven alternately by his contempt for African Americans and their aspirations to be free and self-governing and by anger at northern whites who actually believed that the South and America could be reconstructed by putting "the white men of the South . . . under the Negroes' heels."[36] The freedmen, he wrote, "had the easy faith, the simplicity, the idle hopes, the inexperience of children. Their masterless, homeless freedom made them the more pitiable, the more dependent, because under slavery they had been shielded, the weak and incompetent with the strong and capable." Given their limits, it was hardly surprising that many swelled the ranks of "vagrants, looking for pleasure and gratuitous fortune." Nor was it surprising that the freedmen became easy targets for carpetbaggers "swarming out of the North" to fatten their wallets on southern misfortune. These northern adventurers, Wilson wrote, "became the new masters of the blacks," who could not, of course, become their own masters. They (the carpetbaggers) "gained the confidence of the Negroes, obtained for themselves the most lucrative offices, and lived upon the public treasury."[37] In small southern towns, freedmen themselves became the officeholders, even though they were "men who could not so much as write their names and who knew none of the uses of authority except its insolence." In these towns, Wilson intoned, the "policy of the [Republican] congressional leaders wrought its own perfect work of fear, demoralization, disgust, and social revolution" and brought the South to the edge of ruin.[38] For him, the demoralization caused by Reconstruction seemed to outweigh what slavery itself had produced.

To a student of American history, Wilson's account of Reconstruction's "horrors" hardly constitutes a surprise. The tale of nefarious northern opportunists allying with credulous southern freedmen to prostrate the white South had become, by the early twentieth century, the dominant view of Reconstruction not just in the South but throughout the country.[39] It was used to justify the extreme measures that whites in the South had used to regain their power, extol the virtues of white supremacy, and argue for the return of African Americans to conditions of servitude. It would take the civil rights revolution of the 1950s and 1960s to overturn the authority of this interpretation and allow historians to explore the period with fresh ideas and questions. Today, as a result, we recognize this earlier view of Reconstruction for what it was: a racist exercise meant to justify the white South's quest to regain its power and to shape the white supremacist terms under which it would be reunited with the rest of the nation. This racism informed public opinion throughout the country when Wilson was writing his history of America. As I have argued elsewhere, the tradition of racial nationalism, of viewing the United States as a nation suitable only for people of white European descent, was growing stronger in the late nineteenth and early twentieth centuries, not weaker. Thus Wilson's attempt to imagine an American nation in which blacks had no place was not extreme for the time. Few white readers of his work would have challenged him on the veracity or integrity of his interpretation.[40]

In his *History of the American People*, Wilson occasionally seems to group blacks with the animal world. A drawing of an aged African American man depicts him with monkey features. Underneath the drawing, this caption appears: "A Superannuated Darky in Richmond Virginia."[41] (See illustration on next page.) Wilson used the term "darkey" (or "darky") freely and publicly. As late as 1910, when campaigning for the New Jersey governorship, he organized his comments to a group of more than one thousand supporters around the parable of an "old darkey" and a mule who would not obey him.[42] In 1903, while president of Princeton University, he elicited a hearty laugh from a group of Princeton alumni in Baltimore by telling them a "coon" joke. Why, he asked, did the groundhog go back in its hole that February? Because he "was afraid

the President of the United States," a reference to
Theodore Roosevelt, "would put a 'coon' in it."
This joke ridiculed Roosevelt's decision to
appoint a black man, William Crum, a "coon," to
the position of collector of the Port of
Charleston.[43] Wilson seems to have stopped
telling these stories in public once he became
governor, but some evidence suggests that he still
told them in private throughout the years of his
public service as governor and then as president.[44]

More frequently, Wilson represented blacks
not as animals but as children and as lacking the
traits usually associated with adults—conscience,
knowledge, discipline, maturity, and the ability to
understand abstract concepts such as freedom and
responsibility. In his worst moments, he framed
their childishness as inborn and unalterable. In
his better moments, he believed that he and other
elite white southern men had a paternal responsi-

Drawing of an African American man
appearing in Wilson's *History
of the American People*, vol. 8, 153.

bility to oversee "Negro development" and to prepare them for the day when
they would reach adulthood and earn full membership in the American polity.

In a seminal speech that Wilson gave in 1897 at the Hampton Institute, a
Virginia vocational school for blacks similar in mission to Tuskegee, for the
first time he merged his traditional southern paternalism with a nascent
Progressive conception of society as a machine that would only work well if its
component parts were properly adjusted to each other. The nominal topic of
his speech was "liberty," but his real message was that segregation offered all
Americans, white and black, the best opportunity for racial peace and social
advancement. "What is the liberty of society?" he asked. It was not to grant
everyone within that society opportunity to do as they wished. It was not to
enjoy the basic freedoms of speech, religion, mobility, and opportunity. Nor
was it to enjoy the right to vote or the right to enter any public place. No, liberty meant "the subjection of men to the right laws of society, and their adjustment one to another in the life of communities." "The search after freedom,"
he intoned, "is the search after the best adjustment."[45]

Wilson did not specify the "right laws" to which he was referring, but it seems
likely that he had in mind the Jim Crow legislation whose constitutionality the
Supreme Court had just upheld in its famous 1896 *Plessy v. Ferguson* decision.[46]

Like many southern white moderates, he viewed segregation as the best hope for racial peace and social progress in the South.[47] By calling for the "best adjustment," he was not suggesting that the Jim Crow laws be implemented slowly because of the manifold difficulties involved in engineering a complete separation of the white and black races. Instead, he wanted to habituate blacks to segregation and to acclimatize them to the notion that their movement toward political and social equality would have to proceed at an infinitesimally slow pace. "No man ought to be impatient to see it speedily effected," he warned. "It must come from day to day. Any man who expects to bring the millennium by a sudden and violent storm of reform is fit for a lunatic asylum. . . . It takes infinite patience to learn a trade, to read a book; it takes infinite patience to solve [even] a simple problem." Using the metaphor of a machine to describe the complexity, interconnectedness, and fragility of society, he said: "The freedom of the machine comes from the perfect adjustment of all its parts." Without such perfect adjustment, the machine "would go to pieces and every part would suffer its separate destruction."[48]

In this Hampton Institute speech, Wilson laid out the principles that would guide his approach to black-white relations throughout his political career: first, that segregation served the interests of white and black Americans and should remain in force for many years to come; second, that blacks could aspire to equality and freedom as long as they understood that achieving that goal would require from them "infinite patience"; and third, that blacks could not themselves determine the pace of racial change. This was the job of a third party, perhaps a group of wise and well-intentioned white men of the South, perhaps the government, who would take it upon themselves (or itself) to balance the aspirations of blacks against the interests of other communities of Americans.

The sentiments animating Wilson's 1897 Hampton speech mirrored those undergirding the famous Atlanta Exposition address that Booker T. Washington had given two years earlier. In that 1895 speech, Washington had controversially accommodated himself and his black supporters to the emerging Jim Crow regime, declaring that they understood "that the agitation of questions of social equality is the extremest folly, and that progress in the enjoyment of all the privileges that will come to us must be the result of severe and constant struggle rather than of artificial forcing."[49] Wilson early on recognized his affinity to this group of conservative black leaders (including, in addition to Washington, men such as Robert Russa Moton, president of the Hampton Institute) who had accepted segregation as the best strategy for black progress and black-white comity.

Wilson publicly demonstrated his support for Washington by inviting him to attend his installation as Princeton University president in 1902. At the installation itself, Washington was asked to don his academic robes and march with the other 150 invited guests—a great honor, no doubt, for Washington, the only black guest who seems to have been invited. But Washington still had to endure the humiliation of segregation. Wilson and his handlers had determined that Washington should not be housed with a Princeton faculty member, as was the case with every other visiting dignitary, and that he could not be asked to join the other guests at either of the two installation dinners hosted by Wilson and his wife.[50]

Officially, of course, Washington had to accept these arrangements, for he had himself declared that "in all things purely social we [the white and black races] can be as separate as the fingers."[51] But this proud man must have been burning up inside as he trudged in the evenings to a black boardinghouse in town and made plans for his separate dinners. Wilson seems not to have been discomfited by this arrangement. Nor was he troubled by the fact that no African Americans would be accepted for undergraduate study at Princeton University during the years of his presidency. In his eyes, Princeton's status as a lily-white institution was in the nature of things. In 1909, he instructed an assistant to write a young African American who had inquired about applying to his university that "it is altogether inadvisable for a colored man to enter Princeton." None would until 1947.[52]

The Politics of Race, 1912–19

Given Woodrow Wilson's unwavering support for segregation, it seems surprising, at first glance, that in the fall of 1912, when he had become the Democratic nominee for president of the United States, a group of militant black leaders decided to cast their lot with him. This group included W. E. B. Du Bois, editor of the National Association for the Advancement of Colored People's paper, *The Crisis*; William Monroe Trotter and the Reverend J. Milton Waldron, both of the National Independent Political League; and Bishop Alexander Walters of the African Zion Church and president of the National Colored Democratic League. These men were not ignorant of Wilson's past record on race, but they were willing to give him a chance to show that his future record would be different. They no longer saw a place for blacks in a Republican Party headed by conservative William Howard Taft, and they were angry with Theodore Roosevelt for excluding southern black delegates from participation in the Progressive Party convention in 1912.[53] They had also become intrigued with Wilson and with his ambitious reform program, the New Freedom. Because Wilson seemed to have changed his politics so much since the late nineteenth century with regard to economic reform, these black leaders allowed themselves to hope that he was also in the process of changing his views on the race question.

During the campaign itself, Wilson seemed solicitous of black views. He granted Trotter and Waldron a meeting with him in July 1912 and a group of New Jersey black leaders an audience two weeks later. At an August meeting with Oswald Garrison Villard, editor of the progressive *New York Evening Post* and one of the country's leading white advocates for racial equality, Wilson assured Villard that he would "be President of all the people, that he would appoint no man to office because he was colored, any more than he would appoint him because he was a Jew or Catholic, but that he would appoint him on his merits."[54] And then, in late October, only a few weeks before the election, Wilson sent a public letter to Bishop Walters that seemed to indicate that he had embraced the cause of Negro rights. Wilson began the letter by assuring "my colored fellow-citizens of my earnest wish to see justice done to them in every matter, not mere grudging justice, but justice executed with liberality and cordial-group feeling." He then complimented "colored people" for making "extraordinary progress toward self-support and usefulness" and indicated his desire to see blacks "encouraged in every possible and proper way." He concluded by making this pledge: "Should I become President of the United States they [blacks] may count on me for absolute fair dealing and for everything which I could assist in advancing the interests of their race in the United States."[55]

This letter actually promised very little to blacks. It did not uphold the principle of racial equality, call for an end to segregation, denounce lynching, or commit Wilson to giving blacks the share of government appointments to which they had become accustomed under Republican administrations. But in Wilson's pledge "for absolute fair dealing," African American leaders thought they detected the same passion for social justice that Wilson had infused into his New Freedom campaign. Thus, many blacks voted for him in 1912, hoping that, were he to be elected, they would be among the beneficiaries. Wilson's "personality gives us hope," Du Bois wrote at the time. "He will not advance the cause of oligarchy in the South, he will not seek further means of 'Jim Crow' insult, he will not dismiss black men wholesale from office, and he will remember that the Negro in the United States has a right to be heard and considered."[56] Du Bois and other black leaders would soon be bitterly disappointed.

Rumors that Wilson and his administration intended to reintroduce segregation into the federal civil service began circulating within a few days of the election. By the spring of 1913, two of Wilson's Cabinet appointees, Albert Burleson, the postmaster general, and William A. McAdoo, the secretary of the Treasury, both white southerners, were segregating their departments. Instituting segregation meant undertaking two broad initiatives: first, separating white and black employees at work and lunch and in dressing rooms and restrooms; and second, making sure that no white employees were working under black supervisors. Imposing segregation was bound to provoke a quick and sharp reaction from blacks, because jobs in the federal service at both the entry and supervisory levels were among the best ones available to blacks anywhere in the United States. Moreover, many of these jobs were held by elite members of black society, for whom not just a paycheck but status in their home community was at stake.[57]

Black leaders began inundating Wilson with telegrams, letters, and petitions protesting the resegregation of the federal civil service.[58] They charged that Wilson had broken his campaign pledge for "absolute fair dealing" and, by supporting segregation, had violated the American principle of equality. The volume and fury of the protests took Wilson by surprise, and he felt compelled to answer his critics. In the process, he revealed himself to be the segregationist he was, and the holder of the same principles regarding black progress that he had first revealed during his Hampton Institute speech in 1897.

In a letter to Villard in July 1913, Wilson wrote that segregation was being implemented "as much . . . [for] the Negroes as for any other reason, with the approval of some of the most influential Negroes I know, and with the idea that the friction, or rather the discontent and uneasiness, which had prevailed in many of the departments would thereby be removed." The friction to which he referred was real; whites formed majorities in most federal departments in which blacks worked, and many of them did not want to work in integrated circumstances or under the authority of a black supervisor. By the spring of 1913, the leaders of a white supremacist group of federal employees, the euphemistically named National Democratic Fair Play Association, along with their southern allies in Congress (including Senator James K. Vardaman of Mississippi), had seized the opportunity given to them by Wilson's electoral victory to press their case for "protecting" the rights of whites in federal employment. By the summer of 1913, they had worked their supporters into a frenzy, convincing them that many white female federal employees risked assault by the predatory black males who worked alongside or over them.[59]

Wilson thus did have a fractious federal work force to deal with, and he felt constrained in his search for a solution by having pressure applied to him simultaneously by the black egalitarian left and the white supremacist right. His solution was the classic one preferred by Southern white moderates of his era: to stress that segregation was the best way forward, that this policy "would be in the interest of colored people, as exempting them from friction and criticism in the departments," and that he had the support of influential and clear-thinking black leaders.[60]

That Wilson responded by extolling the virtues of segregation infuriated Villard who, until this time, had been Wilson's close ally. "How I wish your Administrative heads who have brought about this thing," Villard wrote Wilson, "could for forty-eight hours be blacked up and compelled to put themselves in the Negro's place—how differently they would feel!"[61] Wilson pleaded with Villard for understanding, and when Villard refused to give it to him, he stopped corresponding with him, leaving McAdoo to present the administration's case.

In an October 27, 1913, letter to Villard, McAdoo defended the administration's segregationist position one more time. McAdoo insisted that he was "without prejudice against the Negro" and that he possessed "every desire to help him." But he would not countenance integration, "the enforced and unwelcome juxtaposition of white and Negro employees when it is unnecessary and avoidable without injustice to anybody, and when such enforcement would serve only to engender race animosities detrimental to the welfare of both races and injurious to public service." Like his boss, McAdoo's approach to the question of black opportunities in federal employment was dominated by a determination to reduce friction and promote adjustment. Like his boss, he had convinced himself that he was guided by the purest of motives, for he was without "prejudice against the Negro."[62]

It remained for the militant and mercurial William Monroe Trotter to break through Wilson's and McAdoo's facade of best intentions. At a first meeting between Trotter and Wilson in November 1913, Trotter had laid out his objections to segregation in the federal civil service. The meeting was cordial. Though Wilson made no hard promises, Trotter and his delegation came away from the meeting believing that Wilson would do something to reverse his administration's segregationist policy.[63] By the time of their second meeting in November 1914, sentiments on both sides had hardened. Trotter once again delivered an impassioned plea to end segregation in federal employment. Wilson responded to Trotter as McAdoo had done to Villard, expressing both his sincere interest in the well-being of blacks and his conviction that segregation was in their best interests. Trotter refused to back down or show Wilson the deference that the president expected was his due. To the contrary, Trotter took offense at Wilson's attempt to smother him and his delegation in paternalist good feeling. "We are not here as wards," he admonished Wilson. "We are here as full-fledged American citizens, vouchsafed equality of citizenship by the federal Constitution. Separation and distinction marking, because of a certain blood in our veins . . . is something that must be a humiliation."[64]

Trotter refused to accept the notion that segregation was due to some abstract "friction between the races." It was due instead to "race prejudice on the part of the official who puts it into operation." Trotter was referring here not to Wilson himself but to the heads of the various government departments. But then Trotter confronted Wilson directly: "Mr. President, we are sorely disappointed that you take the position that the separation itself is not wrong, is not injurious, is not rightly offensive to you."[65]

Wilson was furious at the temerity of this black man who had dared to speak to him this way in the White House. "Your tone," Wilson stiffly told Trotter, "offends me. . . . You are the only American citizen that has ever come into this office who has talked to me in a tone with a background of passion that was evident. . . . You have spoiled the whole cause for which you came."[66] A few minutes later, the meeting was over. Trotter of course was never invited back to the White House. Wilson later regretted that he had lost his temper but not that he had stood his ground.[67] Nothing would convince him that segregation was not in the interests of both the black and white races.

Nevertheless, the protests by blacks and their white allies seem to have had some effect on the Wilson administration, if only to slow down the spread of segregationist policy into departments that, by 1914, it had not yet reached. Also, some evidence suggests that the Wilson administration felt pressured by 1914 to make a greater effort to maintain the number of blacks in appointive federal offices at levels relatively similar to the number in previous presidential administrations. In 1914, the Wilson administration, for example, backed the reappointment of Robert H. Terrell as a municipal judge in Washington despite the opposition of radical white supremacists in Congress.[68] But black protests did not shake Wilson from his belief in the virtue of segregation or cause him to question his conviction that it would be a century or more before blacks would be ready for full equality with whites. Nor did the intensity of black protests over federal service segregation in 1914 cause Wilson to be wary about allowing his name to be used as an endorsement for D. W. Griffith's racist film about Reconstruction, *The Birth of a Nation*, when it was released to great fanfare in early 1915.[69] In 1916, few blacks voted to give Wilson a second term. Du Bois, who in 1912 had resigned from the Socialist Party to register as a Democrat and vote for Wilson, now advised his fellow African Americans to vote for the Socialist Party candidate.[70]

World War I seemed to force the door toward a redress of racial inequalities ajar once more. A desire to enlist all Americans in support of a war about which many remained skeptical impelled some members of the Wilson administration to reach out to African Americans. Secretary of War Newton Baker, called to

Washington after having served as the progressive mayor of Cleveland, was the administration figure who led the way. Baker would not challenge the principle of segregation in the armed forces, but he did succeed in addressing black concerns in a number of other areas. He won Wilson's assent to the appointment of Emmett J. Scott, a Tuskegee Institute officer and a close friend of Booker T. Washington, as special assistant to the secretary of war in charge of relations between the U.S. military and black community. Baker increased the number of black infantry regiments and the number of black officers serving in the army. He won clemency for ten black soldiers sentenced to death as a result of their participation in a 1917 riot in Houston.[71]

In general, Wilson kept his distance from racial issues during wartime, preferring to let his Cabinet officials address them. But the East St. Louis race riot of July 2, 1917, temporarily stripped him of his detachment. Tense relations between the city's white and black populations had exploded into violence, leading to the deaths of almost fifty people, 80 percent of them black, and the destruction of large areas of the city's black residential areas. Throughout this terrifying day, in which whites inflicted deaths on blacks through lynching and other forms of torture, the city police and National Guardsmen did almost nothing to restore order. A disturbed Wilson had written Attorney General Thomas Gregory asking him to see whether "any instrumentality of the Government . . . could be effectively employed to check these disgraceful outrages."[72] The directness and passion of Wilson's words stand in contrast to most of his previous comments on the race question. Given the progressive character of Secretary Baker's initiatives regarding black soldiers and the way in which the East St. Louis riot appeared to puncture Wilson's complacency about the race issue, it is possible to construe wartime pressures along with popular longings for democracy that Wilson's wartime idealism had unleashed as creating a climate in which those committed to racial equality might make some headway. This was certainly the stance taken by Du Bois, who believed that if blacks joined wholeheartedly in Wilson's war for democracy abroad they would advance the cause of racial democracy at home.[73]

But once again, Du Bois and other black leaders were mistaken. It took a full year after the East St. Louis riot for Wilson to denounce the evils of racial mob violence in public, and that denunciation came only after months of pressure from black leaders and Secretary Baker, and in response to an anti-American German propaganda campaign designed to expose the racial evils of American life.[74] Even then, Wilson refused to authorize a federal investigation of the riot or to use the constitutional war powers that he so readily deployed against political radicals, German sympathizers, and "slackers" to construe white violence against blacks as a threat to the war effort and to subject its perpetrators to prosecution.[75]

In truth, the war had done more to worsen than to improve race relations in the United States. The military enforced segregation in its ranks and, as a rule, excluded black servicemen from combat duties for the duration of the war. The Wilson administration's decision to nationalize the trains under McAdoo's supervision created an opportunity to extend the principle of segregated train cars to every part of the nation. Conditions of wartime mobilization had increased tensions between the white and black races, not just in East St. Louis but in most urban centers of industrial production in the North and West. The mass migration of southern blacks to these centers generated far more black-white interaction than had been customary at workplaces, in neighborhoods, and on systems of public transportation. These interactions, in turn, increased interracial tension and then interracial violence, most of it directed by whites against blacks. In 1919 alone, seventy-one blacks were lynched as race riots tore through twenty-six American cities. Wilson gave one eloquent and impassioned speech denouncing mob violence in 1918 but then fell mute on the subject. The terrifying race riots in Washington and Chicago in 1919 did not elicit any public comment from him.[76]

If they had, it would not likely have been enough to satisfy blacks. Wilson never regarded blacks as his equals. His approach to questions about race was almost always grounded in a language of adjustment. He stressed reducing friction and managing interactions between two races that, he believed, would have been better off not inhabiting the same space. He rarely talked about the rights of blacks, and he never talked about Negroes being merged into or enriching American nationality. On one occasion, he did grant that blacks had human souls and were, in that respect, "absolutely equal" to whites.[77] But he rarely granted blacks the status of "Americans." In truth, he never believed that blacks belonged in or to America. They were a problem population to be managed in the best possible and most humane fashion but never to be joined with those groups of European descent who constituted the American nation. In his eyes, blacks had made no contribution to the making of the American people. Given this stance, it is hardly surprising that by the time Wilson sailed for Europe with the eyes of the world upon him, many African Americans had turned their gaze away from him, convinced that he would never support their quest for equality, participation, and integration. Bitter and angry, these blacks were in the process of turning to a different kind of savior, Marcus Garvey, who promised them what Wilson would not: full membership in a proud nation. Garvey's nation, of course, was to be African, not American.[78]

More surprising is the number of black leaders who, in 1919, still had not given up on Wilson. Robert Moton was hoping that Wilson would issue him a personal invitation to participate in the Paris peace conference.[79] Trotter knew that such an invitation would never come his way, but that did not stop him from going to France in 1919 and asking Wilson for an audience. Wilson ignored Trotter's overtures.[80] Du Bois was in France for the peace conference, too, and he sought a meeting with Wilson as well. That he did not achieve, but he did gain an interview with Wilson's key aide, Colonel Edward House, to press his case for the importance at Versailles of addressing the future of Africa and its peoples. Du Bois won nothing from House, and he would later report that "here as elsewhere my conception of Wilson as a scholar was disappointed. At Versailles he did not seem to understand Europe nor European politics, nor the world-wide problems of race."[81] Throughout the negotiations at Versailles, Wilson showed little inclination to extend his principles of self-determination and equality among nations to nonwhite nations beyond Europe, most famously in his refusal to support a Japanese request that article 21 of the League of Nations Covenant be amended to outlaw any discrimination in national or international affairs on the basis of race or nationality.[82]

It seems noteworthy that Du Bois, as late as 1919, still had a capacity to be "disappointed" by Wilson on matters of race. Du Bois, after all, had already experienced two major disappointments with this Democratic president: first, in 1913, when Wilson failed to deliver on his 1912 election promise to promote black interests; and then in 1918, when Wilson had made it clear that he had no intention of using his "war for democracy" to push hard for racial equality in the United States. Why, then, did Du Bois even bother to petition Wilson in 1919? Why did he still seem to hope that this man, so opposed to racial equality, would now deliver?

Du Bois may have gone to Versailles simply because he recognized that, quite apart from what Wilson did or did not believe or do, the peace conference and the establishment of a League of Nations were events of world historical importance. But it may also have been the case that Du Bois and other black leaders could not give up on Wilson because they saw him as an unusually bold and imaginative politician—"a scholar" in Du Bois's parlance—whose vision of a hybridized American nationality and whose desire to use his insights about America to pursue a dream of world peace, international justice, and self-determination expressed their own deepest aspirations. Black leaders refused to concede, in other words, that Wilson was simply another white southerner unable to rise above the popular prejudices of his era, region, and race. They wanted to believe in Wilson, they wanted to be part of his vision of a dynamically diverse America. They saw him welcome European immigrants into his American nation, and they saw him extend his sympathies to nonwhite Mexicans who were struggling to make a democratic revolution in their own country.[83] They demanded again and again that he demonstrate the same solicitude and sympathy for African Americans in their struggle for equality. They never got what they wanted, but they apparently never gave up hoping that they would. Wilson infuriated and disappointed black leaders to no end. He should us, too.

Wilson's thoughts and actions on the race question earn him a spot on a roster of distinguished white Americans who were apostles for American democracy while being racists at the same time. From the very beginning of the American republic, as I have argued elsewhere, the United States propagated, alongside its civic creed, a racial nationalism that conceived of the country in racial terms, as a home for white people, which meant those of European origin and descent. From Thomas Jefferson to Theodore Roosevelt, Woodrow Wilson, and even, arguably, Franklin Roosevelt, many of those who fashioned America's universalist and democratic political creed were also the architects of its racial nationalism—a paradox that has been one of the most fascinating, enduring, and disturbing aspects of U.S. history.[84] It took a very long time, about two hundred years, for the hold of racial nationalism on the American political imagination to be broken and for the nation to commit itself to true equality.

In every period of U.S. history, we can find individuals and groups who have sought to overturn America's tradition of racial nationalism. We can certainly identify such people in Woodrow Wilson's time. But Wilson himself was not among them. As much as he celebrated diversity and hybridity, he always believed that only peoples of European descent could partake of the American experiment in democracy and freedom. His progressivism aimed to ensure that America would continue to be a white republic.

Notes

1. Erez Manela, "Imagining Woodrow Wilson in Asia: Dreams of East-West Harmony and the Revolt against Empire in 1919," *American Historical Review* 111 (December 2006): 39 pars., http://www.historycooperative.org/journals/ahr/111.5/ manela.html; Thomas J. Knock, *To End All Wars: Woodrow Wilson and the Quest for a New World Order* (New York: Oxford University Press, 1992); John Milton Cooper, Jr., *Breaking the Heart of the World: Woodrow Wilson and the Fight for the League of Nations* (New York: Cambridge University

Press, 2001); Lloyd E. Ambrosius, *Woodrow Wilson and the American Diplomatic Tradition: The Treaty Fight in Perspective* (New York: Cambridge University Press, 1987).

2. Arthur S. Link, *Wilson: The Road to the White House* (Princeton, N.J.: Princeton University Press, 1947). On the South's reintegration into the nation on white supremacist terms, see John W. Cell, *The Highest Stage of White Supremacy: The Origins of Segregation in South Africa and the American South* (New York: Cambridge University Press, 1982); Joel Williamson, *A Rage for Order: Black-White Relations in the American South Since Emancipation* (New York: Oxford University Press, 1986); David W. Blight, *Race and Reunion: The Civil War in American Memory* (Cambridge, Mass.: Harvard University Press, 2001); Glenda Elizabeth Gilmore, *Women and the Politics of White Supremacy in North Carolina, 1896–1920* (Chapel Hill: University of North Carolina Press, 1996); and Rachel F. Moran, *Interracial Intimacy: The Regulation of Race and Romance* (Chicago: University of Chicago Press, 2001).

3. Link, *Wilson: Road to the White House*, 3. Link would later modify this view. See Arthur S. Link, "Woodrow Wilson: The American as Southerner," *Journal of Southern History* 36 (February 1970): 3–17. On segregation as a progressive arrangement, see Cell, *The Highest Stage of White Supremacy*, chaps. 4–7; and William A. Link, *The Paradox of Southern Progressivism, 1880–1930* (Chapel Hill: University of North Carolina Press, 1992).

4. Link, *Wilson: Road to the White House*, 1–2; Erick Montgomery, *Thomas Woodrow Wilson: Family Ties and Southern Perspectives* (Augusta: Historic Augusta, Inc., 2006). On the question of slavery and the Wilson family: In Staunton, the family's household servants seem to have been slaves leased to it by the Presbyterian Church. In Augusta, the servants were free blacks, probably from the town's sizable free black community. Conversation with John Milton Cooper, Friday, January 19, 2007; Montgomery, *Thomas Woodrow Wilson*, 39.

5. Montgomery, *Thomas Woodrow Wilson*, 61–63; Link, "Woodrow Wilson: American as Southerner," 5; Anthony Gaughan, "Woodrow Wilson and the Legacy of the Civil War," *Civil War History* 43 (September 1997): 225–42, used in Web version, http://find.galegroup.com/itx/printdoc.do?&prodld=ITOF&userGroupName=loc_ma...W XHK.

6. Gaughan, "Woodrow Wilson and the Legacy of the Civil War," 1; Link, *Wilson: Road to the White House*, 3.

7. See, e.g., Link, *Wilson: Road to the White House*; Arthur S. Link, *Wilson: The New Freedom* (Princeton, N.J.: Princeton University Press, 1956); and Arthur S. Link, *Woodrow Wilson and the Progressive Era, 1910–1917* (New York: Harper & Brothers, 1954).

8. This is apparent even in Wilson's small book on Robert E. Lee, in which he casts the South's greatest hero as a reluctant secessionist. Woodrow Wilson, *Robert E. Lee: An Interpretation* (Chapel Hill: University of North Carolina Press, 1924).

9. Woodrow Wilson, *Division and Reunion* (New York: Longmans, Green, 1921; orig. pub. 1893); Woodrow Wilson, *History of the American People, Documentary Edition* (New York: Harper & Brothers, 1917; orig. pub. 1902), 10 vols. The inclusion of

numerous illustrations, maps, and primary documents expanded this 1917 edition from its original five volumes (in the 1902 edition) to ten.

10. Wilson, *History of the American People*, vol. 7, 30.

11. Ibid., vol. 7, 23–28; vol. 8, 58.

12. Ibid., vol. 8, 58.

13. Gaughan, "Woodrow Wilson and the Legacy of the Civil War," 5–6 of Web version.

14. Wilson, *History of the American People*, vol. 8, 121. Wilson further asserted: "The motives of politics, the whole theory of political action; the character of government, the sentiment of duty, the very ethics of private conduct were altered [by war] as no half century of slow peace could have altered them." Ibid.

15. Wilson, *Division and Reunion*, 286.

16. E. J. Hobsbawm, *Nations and Nationalism since 1780: Programme, Myth, Reality* (New York: Cambridge University Press, 1990).

17. "The real question after all," Wilson remarked to the Southern Society of New York in 1904, "is nationality, the getting to understanding alike and thinking alike." This had to be the goal of all great nations. Gaughan, "Woodrow Wilson and the Legacy of the Civil War," 6; Gary Gerstle, "Race and Nation in the United States, Cuba, and Mexico, 1880–1940," in *Nationalism in the Americas*, ed. Don Doyle and Marco Pamplona (Athens: University of Georgia Press, 2006), 272–303.

18. See, e.g., Wilson, *Division and Reunion*, 273; and Woodrow Wilson, *The State: Elements of Historical and Practical Politics* (Boston: D. C. Heath, 1889), 296.

19. Woodrow Wilson, *Constitutional Government in the United States* (New York: Columbia University Press, 1947; orig. pub. 1908), chap. 1; the quotation is on 26.

20. Montgomery, *Thomas Woodrow Wilson*, 5–11.

21. Wilson, *History of the American People*, vol. 1, 25–26.

22. Ibid., vol. 2, 136; vol. 3, 49–51; 64–65.

23. Ibid., vol. 7, 132–35.

24. Ibid., vol. 10, 98–99.

25. Link, *Wilson: Road to the White House*, 384–90; Hans Vought, "Division and Reunion: Woodrow Wilson, Immigration, and the Myth of American Unity," *Journal of American Ethnic History* 13 (Spring 1994), http://sas.epnet.com/DeliveryPrint Save.asp?tb=0&_ug=sid+C3638CC0-7606-4EC... WXHK, 3–5. See also *The Papers of Woodrow Wilson*, ed. Arthur S. Link et al., 69 vols. (Princeton, N.J.: Princeton University Press, 1966–94) (hereafter, *PWW*), vol. 24, 131–32, 241–43, 299–303, 404–7.

26. Ibid.

27. Woodrow Wilson, "Be Worthy of the Men of 1776," Address at Independence Hall, Philadelphia, July 4, 1914, in *The Public Papers of Woodrow Wilson, Authorized Edition, The New Democracy: Presidential Messages, Addresses, and Other Papers (1913–1917)*, 2 vols., ed. Ray Stannard Baker and William E. Dodd (New York: Harper & Brothers, 1926), vol. 2, 143.

28. Wilson continued: "And so by the gift of the free will of independent people it is being constantly renewed from generation to generation by the same process by which it

was originally created. It is as if humanity had determined to see to it this great Nation, founded for the benefit of humanity, should not lack for the allegiance of the people of the world." Woodrow Wilson, "Too Proud to Fight," address to several thousand foreign-born citizens, after naturalization ceremonies, Philadelphia, May 10, 1915, in *Public Papers of Woodrow Wilson, Authorized Edition, The New Democracy*, ed. Baker and Dodd, 318–22.

29. Woodrow Wilson, "Be Not Afraid of Our Foreign-Born Citizens," Address to the Daughters of the American Revolution, Washington, October 11, 1915, in ibid., 375–81.

30. On the vetoes, see Vought, "Division and Reunion," 7–8.

31. Woodrow Wilson, "Men Who Think First of Themselves Not True Americans," Address Delivered at the Unveiling of the Statue of Commodore John Barry, Washington, May 16, 1914, in *Public Papers of Woodrow Wilson, Authorized Edition, The New Democracy*, vol. 1, 110.

32. Wilson, "Too Proud to Fight," 319. On Theodore Roosevelt's intolerance of Old World cultures, see Gary Gerstle, *American Crucible: Race and Nation in the Twentieth Century* (Princeton, N.J.: Princeton University Press, 2001), chap. 2.

33. On the World War I campaign for conformity, see ibid., chap. 3.

34. Wilson, "Too Proud to Fight," 321.

35. Wilson, *History of the American People*, vol. 8, 50–53. Wilson did write in harsh terms about large antebellum plantations located in remote areas and owned by absentee masters. These enterprises, Wilson noted, were managed by "brutal [white] men, themselves mere hired drudges, who cared for nothing but to get the exacted stint of work out of" the slaves. But Wilson then used his critique of the masterless plantations to defend those plantations where the masters did reside. Ibid., 52.

36. Ibid., vol. 9, 38.

37. The "ignorance and credulity" of the blacks "made them easy dupes." Ibid., 18–20, 46–52.

38. Ibid., 49–52.

39. This view came to be associated with William Dunning, John W. Burgess, and their students, who made up the "Dunning School." See William A. Dunning, *Reconstruction, Political and Economic 1865–1877* (New York: Harper & Brothers, 1907); John W. Burgess, *Reconstruction and the Constitution, 1866–1876* (New York: Charles Scribner's Sons, 1902); and Claude G. Bowers, *The Tragic Era* (Cambridge, Mass.: Harvard University Press, 1929).

40. On the new post–civil rights revolution interpretation of Reconstruction, see Eric Foner, *Reconstruction: America's Unfinished Revolution, 1863–1877* (New York: Harper & Row, 1988), and Steven Hahn, *A Nation under Our Feet: Black Political Struggles in the Rural South from Slavery to the Great Migration* (Cambridge, Mass.: Harvard University Press, 2003). This interpretation had been laid out fifty years earlier by W. E. B. Du Bois in *Black Reconstruction in America, 1860–1880* (New York: Simon & Schuster, 1992; orig. pub. 1935). The historical profession, however, largely ignored Du Bois's work. On the growing strength of racial nationalism in the late nineteenth and early twentieth centuries, see Gerstle, *American Crucible*, chaps. 1–3.

41. Wilson, *History of the American People*, vol. 8, 153.

42. *PWW*, vol. 21, 390–91.

43. Ibid., vol. 14, 358.

44. See the excerpt from the Diary of Raymond Blaine Fosdick from December 8, 1918, when he, President Wilson, and the American delegation to the Versailles Peace Conference were sailing for France. Fosdick reports on how he and President Wilson "swapped negro stories, his easily out-rivaling mine," while taking a break from their work on the Paris Peace Conference. Reproduced in ibid., vol. 53, 340–41.

45. Ibid., vol. 10, 127–34.

46. *Plessy v. Ferguson: A Brief History with Documents*, ed. Brook Thomas (New York: Bedford Books, 1997).

47. See Cell, *Highest Stage of White Supremacy*; Michael McGerr, *A Fierce Discontent: The Rise and Fall of the Progressive Movement in America, 1870–1920* (New York: Oxford University Press, 2003).

48. *PWW*, vol. 10, 127–34.

49. Booker T. Washington, *Up from Slavery: An Autobiography* (New York: Penguin Books, 1986; orig. pub. 1901), 155–56.

50. Louis R. Harlan and Raymond W. Smock, eds., *The Booker T. Washington Papers*, 13 vols. (Urbana: University of Illinois Press, 1972–84), vol. 6, 548. The editors of the Washington papers report that Washington did attend a luncheon sponsored by the Henry Gurdon Marquand family and may have attended a Princeton class of 1879 dinner the night of Wilson's inaugural. But Washington received no invitation to the dinners that the Wilsons themselves hosted.

51. The quoted phrase is from Washington's 1895 Atlanta Exposition address, reproduced in *Up From Slavery*, 155–56.

52. *PWW*, vol. 15, 462. By the time of Wilson's Princeton presidency, several African Americans had earned advanced degrees from various departments at Princeton or from the independently run Princeton Theological Seminary; and at an earlier time, several African Americans had studied privately with Princeton President John Witherspoon. But none had been formally admitted to the jewel of Princeton, the undergraduate student program, a prohibition that Wilson reinforced.

53. Gerstle, *American Crucible*, chap. 2.

54. From the diary of Oswald Garrison Villard, August 14, 1912, in *PWW*, vol. 25, 25–26.

55. Ibid., 448–49. Wilson wrote the letter on October 21, 1912.

56. Quoted by David Levering Lewis, *W. E. B. Du Bois: Biography of a Race, 1868–1919* (New York: Henry Holt, 1993), 423.

57. On the history of blacks in the federal civil service, see Eric Yellin, "In the Nation's Service: Racism and Federal Employees in Woodrow Wilson's Washington," PhD dissertation, Princeton University, 2007. See, also, Mary-Elizabeth Murphy, "'How Our Girls Are Humiliated': African Americans Protest Civil Service Segregation in the Jazz Age, 1921–1929," seminar paper, University of Maryland, 2005, in the author's possession.

58. A total of 20,000 people in thirty-six states signed one antisegregation petition delivered to Wilson in November 1913 by William Monroe Trotter and other black leaders; in *PWW*, vol. 28, 491–500.

59. Ibid., 185–88. Yellin, "In the Nation's Service," provides the best treatment of the fight over federal civil service segregation during the Wilson administration.

60. Letter from Wilson to Villard, August 29, 2006, in *PWW*, vol. 28, 245–46.

61. Letter from Villard to Wilson, September 18, 2006, in ibid., 289–90.

62. Letter from McAdoo to Villard, October 27, 1913, in ibid., 453–55.

63. Christine A. Lunardini, "Standing Firm: William Monroe Trotter's Meetings with Woodrow Wilson, 1913–1914," *Journal of Negro History* 64 (Summer 1979): 244–64. Lunardini both reproduces transcripts of Trotter's meetings with Wilson in their entirety and provides insightful commentary on those meetings through a series of detailed notes.

64. Trotter spelled out for the president the humiliation that, he argued, was at segregation's core. Segregation, Trotter declared, "creates in the minds of others that there is something the matter with us—we are not their equals, that we are not their brothers, that we are so different that we cannot work at a desk beside them, that we cannot eat at a table beside them, that we cannot go in the dressing room where they go, that we cannot use a locker beside them, that we cannot even go into a public toilet with them." Ibid., 259.

65. Ibid., 260.

66. Ibid., 260.

67. Ibid., 263 n. 5.

68. Ibid., 263–64 n. 6; letter from Villard to Wilson, March 5, 1914; letter from John Sharp Williams to Wilson, March 31, 1914; and letter from Wilson to Williams, April 2, 1914; all in *PWW*, vol. 29, 319, 377, 394.

Eric Yellin's examination of a sample of randomly selected black federal employees suggests that most of those who suffered demotions or dismissals under Wilson experienced them during the first year and a half of Wilson's presidency (March 1913–October 1914). This suggests that the rate of demotion and dismissal slowed after Trotter's second meeting with Wilson. See Eric S. Yellin, "'President of All the People': Woodrow Wilson and White Man's Democracy," paper delivered at Annual Meeting of the American Historical Association, Atlanta, January 2007, 6.

For more on segregation of the federal service under Wilson, see Yellin, "In the Nation's Service"; Kathleen Long Wolgemuth, "Woodrow Wilson's Appointment Policy and the Negro," *Journal of Southern History* 24 (November 1958): 457–71; Kathleen L. Wolgemuth, "Woodrow Wilson and Federal Segregation," *Journal of Negro History* 44 (April 1959): 158–73; Henry Blumenthal, "Woodrow Wilson and the Race Question," *Journal of Negro History* 48 (January 1963): 1–21; Morton Sosna, "The South in the Saddle: Racial Politics during the Wilson Years, *Wisconsin Magazine of History* 54 (Autumn 1970): 30–49; Cleveland M. Green, "Prejudices and Empty Promises: Woodrow Wilson's Betrayal of the Negro, 1910–1919," *The Crisis* 87 (November 1980): 380–88; Kenneth O'Reilly, "The Jim Crow Policies of Woodrow Wilson, *Journal of Blacks in Higher Education* 17 (Autumn 1997): 117–19; Nancy J. Weiss, "The Negro and the New Freedom: Fighting Wilsonian Segregation," *Political Science Quarterly* 84 (May 1969), 61–79.

69. Wilson was not quite the cheerleader for *The Birth of a Nation* that his good friend and indefatigable *Birth* promoter, Thomas Dixon Jr., made him out to be.

The famous quotation that Dixon attributed to Wilson after the president watched the film in the White House—that the film was like "writing history with lightning. . . . My only regret is that it is all so terribly true"—seems to have been as much Dixon's creation as a faithful reporting of Wilson's actual words. (Scholars do not even agree on what Dixon alleged the president to have said, with John Hope Franklin quoting the words cited above and Arthur Leming quoting a somewhat different variant: "My one regret is that it is all too true.") When April 1915 protests against the film in Boston began to cause Wilson political trouble, his handlers put out the word that Wilson had never endorsed the film.

Nevertheless, Wilson did like the film and had written Griffith in March 1915 to congratulate him on "a splendid production." *The Birth of a Nation*—based on Thomas Dixon Jr.'s book *The Clansman: An Historical Romance of the Ku Klux Klan* (New York: Grosset and Dunlap, 1905)—told a story of Reconstruction very similar to the one Wilson had written for *History of the American People*. Indeed, on several occasions the film quotes lines from Wilson's *History*. Wilson did not, however, glorify the Klan as both Dixon and Griffith had done. On the politics of this film, see John Hope Franklin, *"The Birth of a Nation*: Propaganda as History," in *Race and History: Selected Essays, 1938–1988*, ed. John Hope Franklin (Baton Rouge: Louisiana State University Press, 1989), 16; Arthur Leming, "Myth and Fact: The Reception of *The Birth of a Nation*," *Film History* 16 (2004): 122; Michael Rogin, "'The Sword Became a Flashing Vision': D. W. Griffith's *The Birth of a Nation*," *Representations* 9 (Winter 1985): 150–95; and Thomas R. Cripps, "The Reaction of the Negro to the Motion Picture *Birth of a Nation*," *Historian* 25 (May 1963): 344–62.

70. Lewis, *W. E. B. Du Bois*, 522–23.

71. George Creel, head of the Committee on Public Information, William B. Wilson, secretary of labor, and Herbert Hoover, director of the wartime Food Administration, also showed interest in improving circumstances of African Americans. Jane Lang Scheiber and Harry N. Scheiber, "The Wilson Administration and the Wartime Mobilization of Black Americans, 1917–1918," *Labor History* 10 (Summer 1969): 433–59. On rioting in Houston and its aftermath, see also Robert V. Haynes, *A Night of Violence: The Houston Riot of 1917* (Baton Rouge: Louisiana State University Press, 1976); and *PWW*, vol. 44, 41–42, 62, 77–78; vol. 45, 546–47; vol. 48, 323; vol. 49, 324–28, 401–2.

72. Letter from Woodrow Wilson to Attorney General Thomas Gregory, in *PWW*, vol. 43, 116. On the St. Louis riot, see, Elliott M. Rudwick, *Race Riot at East St. Louis: July 2, 1917* (Carbondale: Southern Illinois University Press, 1964).

73. Lewis, *W. E. B. Du Bois*, 525–80. Also see Mark Ellis, "'Closing Ranks' and 'Seeking Honors': W. E. B. Du Bois in World War I," *Journal of American History* 79 (June 1992): 96–124; William Jordan, "'The Damnable Dilemma': African-American Accommodation and Protest during World War I," *Journal of American History* 81 (March 1995): 1562–83; and Jonathan Rosenberg, "For Democracy, Not Hypocrisy: World War and Race Relations in the United States, 1914–1919," *International History Review* 21 (September 1999): 592-625.

74. Scheiber and Scheiber, "Wilson Administration," 456–57. For the text of Wilson's speech, see "A Statement to the American People," July 26, 1918, in *PWW*, vol. 49, 97–98. See also the July 25, 1918, letter from John R. Shillady, secretary of the NAACP, to Woodrow Wilson, urging him to denounce lynching in his address to the American people; ibid., 88–89.

75. On the powers that Congress gave Wilson to prosecute, discipline, and punish those whose actions were deemed to threaten the war effort, see chapter 7 in the present volume by Geoffrey Stone; David M. Kennedy, *Over Here: The First World War and American Society* (New York: Oxford University Press, 1980); and Gerstle, *American Crucible*, chap. 3.

76. Scheiber and Scheiber, "Wilson Administration," 457; Letter from William Harrison and Others, National Race Congress, to Woodrow Wilson, October 1, 1918, in *PWW*, vol. 51, 191–93; William M. Tuttle Jr., *Race Riot: Chicago in the Red Summer of 1919* (New York: Athenaeum, 1970); Adriane Lentz-Smith, *The Great War for Civil Rights: African American Politics, World War I, and the Origins of the Civil Rights Movement* (Cambridge, Mass.: Harvard University Press, forthcoming).

77. Wilson uttered these words in his meeting with Trotter in 1914. Quoted by Lunardini, "Standing Firm," 258.

78. On the turn to Garvey, see Judith Stein, *The World of Marcus Garvey: Race and Class in Modern Society* (Baton Rouge: Louisiana State University Press, 1986).

79. Scheiber and Scheiber, "Wilson Administration," 451.

80. Blumenthal, "Woodrow Wilson and the Race Question," 9; Rosenberg, "For Democracy, Not Hypocrisy: World War and Race Relations in the United States, 1914–1919," 592–93; Stephen R. Fox, *The Guardian of Boston: William Monroe Trotter* (New York: Athenaeum, 1970), 223–30.

81. Kenneth M. Glazier, "W. E. B. Du Bois's Impression of Woodrow Wilson," *Journal of Negro History* 58 (October 1973): 459.

82. The relevant language of the original Japanese proposal read as follows: that every state participating in the League be required to accord all "alien nationals . . . equal and just treatment in every respect, making no distinction, either in law or in fact, on account of race and nationality." When the explicit use of the words "race and nationality" proved to be too radical for those who were designing the Covenant, the Japanese altered their amendment to say, simply, that article 21 endorsed "the principle of equality of nations and just treatment of their nationals." The amendment, in both versions, was motivated in the first instance by Japan's desire to secure nondiscriminatory treatment of its people who had emigrated to the United States and Latin America, and to Australia, New Zealand, Canada, and other parts of the British Commonwealth. But beyond this self-interest, Japan was acting on the principle that the League of Nations ought to commit itself explicitly to the universal application of its "equality of nations" principle.

Wilson seems to have been receptive to this amendment until he encountered sustained opposition to it from Australians and New Zealanders and also from the leaders of anti-Asian organizations in the western United States. He then refused to accept it under any circumstances, even when the League of Nations Commission, in April 1919, formally approved the watered-down version by a vote of 11 to 6. Paul Gordon Lauren, "Human Rights in History: Diplomacy and Racial Equality at the Paris Peace Conference," *Diplomatic History* 2 (summer 1978): 264, 269; Kristofer Allerfeldt, "Wilsonian Pragmatism? Woodrow Wilson, Japanese Immigration, and the Paris Peace Conference," *Diplomacy and Statecraft* 15 (2004): 545–72; Naoko Shimazu, *Japan, Race and Equality: The Racial Equality Proposal of 1919* (London: Routledge, 1998). For more general analyses of the influence of racial considerations on the 1919 peace conference, see chapter 8 in this volume by Lloyd Ambrosius; Lloyd E. Ambrosius, *Wilsonianism: Woodrow Wilson and His Legacy in American Foreign Relations* (New York: Palgrave Macmillan, 2002); and Erez Manela, "'People of Many Races': The World Beyond Europe in the Wilsonian Imagination," paper presented to Fourth Biennial Woodrow Wilson National Symposium, Woodrow Wilson Presidential Library, Staunton, Va., September 2006.

83. David J. Hellwig, "The Afro-American Press and Woodrow Wilson's Mexican Policy, 1913–1917," *Phylon* 48 (Fourth Quarter, 1987): 261–70.

84. Gerstle, *American Crucible*. Also see Edmund Morgan, *American Slavery, American Freedom* (New York: W. W. Norton, 1975); and Rogers M. Smith, *Civic Ideals: Conflicting Visions of Citizenship in U.S. History* (New Haven, Conn.: Yale University Press, 1997).

5. Did Woodrow Wilson's Gender Politics Matter?

Victoria Bissell Brown

Woodrow Wilson presided over the culmination of American women's seventy-two-year campaign to gain suffrage, and he is the only U.S. president to ever put an ounce of political capital on the line for that cause. Wilson's evolving relationship with the woman suffrage movement would seem to offer historians an excellent opportunity to explore the president's views on party government, presidential leadership, congressional power, state versus federal authority, and democratic idealism and democratic pragmatism—not to mention patriarchal views on the much-debated marriage of female domestic duty, feminine ways of knowing, and political participation. Yet in a two-foot stack of biographies and political analyses on Wilson, numbering some 5,470 pages, there appear just 148 sentences on woman suffrage. Remove the three pages that Kendrick Clements and Eric Cheezum devoted to the topic in their 2003 study for the *Congressional Quarterly Press* and there remain just 98 sentences on Wilson and woman suffrage in a body of seventeen books.[1] Without the enormously useful article "Woodrow Wilson and Woman Suffrage: A New Look," by Christine Lunardini and Thomas J. Knock, published in the *Political Science Quarterly* back in 1981, the suffrage cupboard in the Wilson kitchen would be mighty bare.[2]

Arguably, this lack of attention to Wilson and woman suffrage is reasonable because his evolving stance on the issue never decided an election in which he had a stake. In the presidential race of 1912, when the Progressive Party platform touted its unprecedented support for "equal suffrage for men and women alike," Wilson's Democratic Party platform was silent on the subject and the candidate certainly tried to be.[3] Still, when the votes were counted, Wilson, not Theodore Roosevelt, was victorious in five of the six western states that had enfranchised women; only California went for the prosuffrage Progressive Party. Even more dramatically, in 1916, Wilson ran on a Democratic Party platform that reflected the president's by-then-familiar position that woman suffrage was a matter for each state to decide. Wilson held firm to that position despite Charles Evans Hughes's endorsement of a federal suffrage amendment; despite the National Woman's Party's attacks on Wilson and the Democratic Party for failing to support such an amendment; and, most important, despite the fact that women were enfranchised in twelve states by 1916, states that accounted for 91 of 531 electoral votes. Yet again, when the votes were counted in 1916, it was Wilson, not Hughes, who swept the female-enfranchised western states, winning ten of the twelve states in which women could vote. And, finally, in the midterm congressional election of 1918, after President Wilson had come out in favor of a federal woman suffrage amendment to the Constitution, his heavy lifting to move the Democratic Party over to this new position did nothing to stop the wartime shift in congressional power from the Democrats to the Republicans.

From a purely electoral viewpoint, then, Woodrow Wilson's stance on his era's most tangible measure of gender politics mattered very little.

Those scholars who study and write about the woman suffrage movement would not agree with this conclusion. The number of sentences and pages that they devote to documenting President Wilson's alternately discouraging and encouraging role in the story of woman suffrage are simply too numerous to count. The bulk of those pages are devoted to descriptions of woman suffragists' lobbying efforts at the Wilson White House, Wilson's complicity in the abuse of imprisoned prosuffrage picketers in 1917, and his subsequent lobbying for congressional endorsement of a federal amendment in 1918. But here, again, it is arguable that Wilson's stance on female enfranchisement—though an investment of political capital on his part—was not decisive. The Democratic House of Representatives did vote in favor of a federal amendment the day after Wilson endorsed that route to suffrage, but the Democratic U.S. Senate twice refused the president's entreaties to support the amendment. It was the electoral replacement of antisuffrage with prosuffrage senators, not Woodrow Wilson's congressional lobbying or rhetorical skills, that turned the senatorial tide on woman suffrage and sent the amendment on to the states for ratification. Suffragists' energies may have been better spent in senatorial campaigns than in lobbying Wilson.[4]

But the history of human experience is as much about process as it is about outcomes. Thus, it is from the process whereby Wilson evolved from an opponent of woman suffrage to a supporter of state-by-state enfranchisement to a supporter of the federal woman suffrage amendment that we stand to learn much about his leadership style, his negotiation of political principle and political practicality, his management of the South and race, and his identification with the social justice agenda of the era's progressives—not to mention his assumptions about the female half of the human race and his relationships with the leaders of the divided woman suffrage movement.

These substantive themes receive scant attention in the discussion of suffrage in the Wilson literature. The general thrust of that literature is well represented by the Clements and Cheezum claim that "Wilson came to support suffrage" "belatedly and reluctantly."[5] This assessment echoed Clements's earlier claim that woman suffrage, like Prohibition, was "thrust upon Wilson more than sought by him."[6] That position is consistent with woman suffrage comments scattered over a half century that conjure up the image of Wilson as a schoolboy being dragged by the scruff of his neck to dancing class. John Morton Blum wrote of a "struggle" in Wilson's "heart" between attitudes toward women "that had long shaped his thinking" and prosuffrage actions "that politics demanded." David Morgan declared Wilson's support of suffrage to be "Wilson's tribute to political necessity, if not political conviction." Arthur Link wrote in the same year, 1971, that Wilson's support of suffrage represented one of those "concessions he had been compelled to make" when faced with "political forces" that were "too dangerous for any politician to oppose."[7]

A decade later, Lunardini and Knock agreed that Wilson conducted himself as an "astute politician" during the suffrage campaign, but they added the argument that his support for the federal amendment was "obviously an act of sincerity," and they quoted Wilson's own claim that his judgment in the matter was "based on the highest consideration of both justice and expediency."[8] Lunardini elegantly advanced that analysis in her 1986 suffrage study by claiming that President Wilson found support of the federal amendment to be "both necessary and palatable."[9] Sally Hunter Graham's 1984 critique of Wilson's harsh conduct toward suffrage picketers denied any "altruistic" motives in his support of the federal amendment, and John Cooper's dozen lines on woman suffrage in *The Warrior and the Priest* emphasized the political expediency in the path Wilson took on suffrage. But when Cooper returned to the subject in *Pivotal Decades*, he reaffirmed the Lunardini and Knock position that Wilson endorsed the woman suffrage amendment "partly in an effort to gain votes from women in the states where they had won the vote, and partly out of newfound conviction."[10]

There is so much in the data to recommend the emphasis on political motives in describing Wilson's support for woman suffrage that any attempt to revise that emphasis must tread carefully. Indeed, a revision need not reduce the emphasis on political motives. But it must address the lingering implication that political motives are incompatible with sincerity, that evidence of Wilson's very political reasons for supporting, first, a state approach to woman suffrage and, later, a federal approach somehow cancels the evidence of his "newfound conviction." This lingering implication assumes that Wilson's initial opposition to a federal amendment was tantamount to total opposition because the state-by-state approach was so difficult and protracted. It also assumes that Wilson failed to stop the violence against prosuffrage White House picketers in 1917 because he still opposed their cause.

These assumptions waft through both the Wilson and suffrage literature; suspicion that a political motive precludes a sincere conviction never amounts to a well-supported argument, but it persists simply because the topic of Wilson and suffrage has received so little analysis. The suggestion that Wilson did not really think women *should* be voters but was forced to support suffrage because so many women *were* voters leaves the impression that Wilson was political bedfellows with woman suffragists but never respected them in the morning. The lack of attention to this story is odd because the suggestion that Wilson endorsed woman suffrage but did not actually believe women should be voters constitutes quite a serious charge. It means that Wilson's public prosuffrage position concealed his private agreement with antisuffragists. Such a charge deserves investigation, if only to remind ourselves just what it meant to be an antisuffragist in the first two decades of the twentieth century.

Between 1900 and 1920, as women were gaining the vote all over the United States, antisuffragists reiterated an intertwining set of arguments against female enfranchisement: They argued that the female body was too weak to endure the burden of voting; they argued that the female mind was too irrational and emotional to vote responsibly; they argued that female dependence meant woman suffrage merely doubled the votes of fathers and husbands; they argued that female enfranchisement would cause women to wear the pants in the family; they argued that women could not be political actors and take care of their homes and families; they argued that women were too moral to be effective in politics; they argued that political corruption would destroy female morality; they argued that women did not want the vote; they argued that women would sacrifice their civic effectiveness by becoming partisan; they argued female voting would make no difference in American politics; and they argued that women would vote in a militant bloc either to impose a conservative agenda of temperance and sexual restraint or to enact a leftist agenda of proworker welfare spending. In sum, antisuffragists argued that woman suffrage would destroy women, destroy the American family, and destroy American government.

The ostensibly savvy, certainly cynical notion that within Woodrow Wilson's political body there beat the heart of an antisuffragist carries with it the powerful charge that Wilson was willing to jeopardize womanhood, the American family, and the state by supporting woman suffrage and thereby gaining a few votes for the Democratic Party. Once unpacked, the charge appears ridiculous and demands a closer look at Lunardini's careful observation that Wilson found the endorsement of woman suffrage to be both "necessary and palatable."[11]

Wilson's Conversion to Woman Suffrage

Woodrow Wilson underwent the most public and important male conversion to woman suffrage in U.S. history. His endorsement did not make woman suffrage happen in 1920; woman suffragists did that. But his endorsement in the years between 1915 and 1918 gave the cause a legitimacy that fueled momentum within suffragists' ranks, and that momentum put suffrage over the top in a final burst of progressive energy. So Wilson's conversion mattered at the time, and the steps in that conversion process, which is to say the evolution of Wilson's gender politics, matter to us because they represent the change that had to occur and did occur in many men's minds, especially in the decade between 1910 and 1920.

Like millions of other American men, Wilson had to accept the antipatriarchal notion that a normal, natural, kind, loving, and respectable person could be both a female and a political actor. That was step number one, and it was a big step. It opened the door to the assertion that woman suffrage would not destroy the family, would not overturn traditional gender roles, and would not weaken democracy or the U.S. government. We know the importance of this simple set of ideas because the literature from the time makes abundantly clear that few men who supported woman suffrage were signing on for a full-scale feminist revolution. What they did sign on for was the argument that a woman could be a wife, a mother, and a voter. The contemporary literature also makes clear that some men, and it appears Wilson was among them, went beyond basic acceptance of woman suffrage to the positive, if essentialist, belief that feminine difference in thinking and values would interject a desirable improvement in debate and legislation. But it was the basic agreement that womanhood, femininity, and maternalism were consistent with political advocacy that was crucial to the embrace of woman suffrage. Once a man like Wilson crossed that conceptual line, he could stop treating woman suffrage as a slightly distasteful, private, moral matter and could start treating it as a matter-of-fact, public, political matter, to be viewed—like all such matters—with an eye toward expedience and electoral gain.

From this angle, Wilson's very political handling of woman suffrage serves as evidence that he had been persuaded by the logic of woman suffrage. There is no need to deduct his political interests in the suffrage movement from the sum of his conviction; conversion to woman suffrage required, first and foremost, a willingness to treat suffragists as political actors in a political arena. The evidence that he played politics—especially race politics—with woman suffrage, or behaved in a duplicitous manner in specific instances, or greatly favored one group of suffragists over another, or took revenge on those suffragists he disliked is all part of the story of this politician's regrettable handling of the movement, but it is not evidence that he did not support the fundamental goal of the movement.

This preliminary review of the published letters, memos, news reports, and speeches seeks to demonstrate that there is more to this story than a belatedly aggressive, politically strategic endorsement of female enfranchisement. The evidence here is intended to persuade those who spend their scholarly lives in the Wilson archives to cease avoiding woman suffrage as if it were a boyish case of sexual insincerity and, instead, pursue it as a serious example of Wilson's evolution as a party leader, chief executive, and social justice progressive.

THE EARLY YEARS

Northern women had been demanding the U.S. vote for a half-dozen years when Woodrow Wilson was born in 1856. But in his southern, white, patriarchal culture, the demand for woman suffrage was exotic at best and treacherous at worst. His diary entry, at age twenty, that "universal suffrage is at the foundation of every evil in this country" was probably as much a comment on black men voting as on white or black women voting, but the youthful spirit of the sentiment is clear nonetheless: enfranchisement could and should be limited for the sake of the common good.[12] Wilson's comments about gender in the 1880s and 1890s suggest that he was acutely aware of the expansion of women's public lives and uncomfortable with the implications of that trend. He disdained any defeminizing of women's demeanor or public style, he vigorously opposed any critique of women's familial role, and he regarded that private role as determinative of women's public role.

A "chilled, scandalized feeling" came over Wilson whenever he saw women speaking in public in the 1880s, but he could still derive "whimsical delight" from female speakers who were "attractive" and "motherly," "natural, spontaneous, [and] graceful," who controlled the floor "by affection" rather than "the exercise of presidential authority," who were "round" and "jolly" rather than "stiff" or, heaven forbid, "self-assertive."[13] Feminine style mattered to him, if only as a signifier that women happily embraced the belief that they have "mental and moral gifts of a sort and of a perfection that men lack." This, he explained to his beloved Ellen three months before their marriage, meant that a woman's proper and happy role was as a "supplement [to] a man's life." The liberal in him argued that this gender difference implied no hierarchy, no subordination—it was as much his job to complete her life as it was her job to complete his—the only difference was that, for "society to exist," women had duties as housekeepers and mothers which could not be abandoned. Any woman who could not "preserve her individuality in the family . . . simply has no individuality worth preserving," wrote the unwed male graduate student from his private study. To claim the contrary, in the false name of independence, was "to pervert the truth," a statement fervently punctuated by an exclamation point. So certain was the young Wilson that female independence was a "pernicious falsehood" that he promised to lecture on "the principles lying at the foundation of the institution of the family" when he took up his new duties as a faculty member at Bryn Mawr College. He fancied that those remarks "will be hard to forget."[14]

Once settled at Bryn Mawr, however, Wilson was disappointed to encounter "a painful absenteeism of mind" among his female students. "Passing through a vacuum," he found that his "speech generates no heat." He was open to the possibility that this student apathy was due in part to "undergraduateism, not all to femininity," but it did not occur to him that it might be due to the role prescribed for women and the struggle Bryn Mawr students faced in trying to imagine where they would fit in that role.[15]

In the two decades that passed between Wilson's stint at Bryn Mawr and his academic and political careers in New Jersey, American women defied, daily, the assumption that domestic life was incompatible with political life. Wives and mothers went to meetings, chaired committees, gave speeches, wrote legislation, circulated petitions, voted in various local elections, and voted in general elections in Wyoming, Colorado, Idaho, Utah, and, by the end of 1911, Washington and California. The argument that women simply could not manage the demands of home life and the duties of citizenship was dangerously susceptible to the empirical test, and antisuffrage men like Wilson were challenged to square the evidence with their own sentimental attachment to the idea that women could not "supplement" men's lives at home and pursue public activism.

The published record of Wilson's handful of comments on women's civic role between 1908 and 1912 call to mind an observation made by Colonel Edward House several years later that whenever Wilson was unwilling to give the "real" reasons for a position, he offered "evasive or foolish reasons."[16] Given all the evidence of female activity in the public sphere, it was certainly foolish for Wilson to claim, in a 1908 letter, that women should not be enfranchised because

> women, whether by nature or circumstance, draw their conclusions about public affairs from logical reason, whereas safe and wise conclusions in such affairs can be drawn only from experience—experience of the world—such as women have not had and cannot have unless drawn entirely into the open and safe-guarded in no way. Married women could never get the necessary experience unless the present constitution of the family and the present division of duties between husband and wife is to be absolutely altered.[17]

Just six months earlier, in an interview, Wilson had observed that women in Princeton were actively engaged in all manner of "public questions," but there he evaded the suffrage implications of that civic experience by claiming that a female preference for "goodness" over "ability" and a susceptibility to "charm of manner" were traits of mind that unfit women, in Wilson's eyes, for suffrage.[18]

As Wilson positioned himself for a presidential run in 1912, he made his first public efforts to juggle his cherished notions of gender separatism with the unavoidable fact of gender integration in civic life. He admitted in a letter in the spring of 1911 that his "personal judgment" was "strongly against" woman suffrage. "I believe," he explained to a male correspondent, "that the social changes it would involve would not justify the gains that would be accomplished by it."[19] The flaw in the argument, of course, was that the "social changes" Wilson feared were already happening—women were already operating outside the confines of their role as family "supplement." Just four months earlier, he had strained to persuade the female members of the Consumer's League of New Jersey that they did not need the vote to go about their fine, voluntary work; they were "in a sense," he claimed, "a pre-eminent legislature," one that did "not depend on theory" but, instead, went out and got "the facts" and presented them to "the lawmaking powers." For public consumption, then, Wilson had dropped his private claim that women were too reliant on logic, on theory, to be effective citizens; his own experience forced him to admit that women were gaining the civic experience voters needed. He praised the members of the Consumers' League for "taking part in a vital process" of citizenship, showing their "true patriotism" by "seeing that your fellow beings are treated properly."[20]

If women's civic activism represented gains for women as citizens and for their "fellow beings" in the wider community, and if that activism moved women outside the family, then what could be the "social changes" that Wilson feared in woman suffrage? Until the Wilson archives yield up more clues, the only sensible conclusion is that he shared with other men of his generation the competing (and largely unconscious) desires to have a liberal society in which white women could move about freely as citizens yet still preserve the illiberal boundaries of gender segregation as a formal delineator of separate spheres. Male suffrage was the most convenient, least coercive tool men had to achieve these dual goals. Though lacking the vote, women could still perform as free citizens in their own way—a feminine, supplemental, voluntaristic, unselfish way—carrying out "principles of mercy and justice." Wilson told the Consumers' League members that he was "ready to aid you in any way," though he was not ready to aid them by lifting the gender boundary of suffrage and liberate women to move from a "pre-eminent legislature" to a real legislature.[21]

WOMAN SUFFRAGE AND POLITICS

In the presidential campaign of 1912, Teddy Roosevelt had the corner on the woman suffrage market. The Progressive Party platform endorsed woman suffrage not simply to win women's votes in the West, though this outcome was certainly hoped for. More immediately, the party supported woman suffrage because Roosevelt's insurgent base was comprised of prosuffrage reformers, male and female, and those reformers, along with Roosevelt, firmly believed that women's votes were requisite to enact the other social justice planks in the Progressive platform. To say that Roosevelt embraced woman suffrage for political reasons is to say that he sought the votes—and the voters—he thought would support his progressive program. But it is worth noting, as a reminder of what counted as "progressive" in 1912, that the Progressive Party platform simply supported "equal suffrage to men and women alike"; it made no mention of the method by which that goal was to be achieved, and it made no commitment to a state approach or a federal approach.[22] In 1912, a candidate's particular approach was not a measure of conviction; simply supporting woman suffrage in a national presidential campaign was a great step forward.

But while Roosevelt had progressive crowds, literally, singing from Jane Addams songbooks, Wilson tried in vain to avoid the whole subject of woman suffrage. His base was not comprised of social justice suffragists; his cultural and political circles did not significantly overlap with that crowd. The Democratic Party platform was as silent on the matter as the Republican, and Wilson relied on that official platform silence to justify his own. Even when he was publicly teased about using his "diplomatic skill" to "evade the question" of woman suffrage, he refrained from taking a firm position.[23] Even when Oswald Garrison Villard warned him in August of the possibility that "Roosevelt would gain enormous advantage in the woman suffrage states" with his prosuffrage position, Wilson sent Villard away with the distinct impression that he would "prefer defeat to stultifying himself by coming out for a measure in which he does not believe."[24]

What is intriguing about Wilson's stance on suffrage in 1912, however, is not Villard's report of the candidate's opposition but Wilson's own direct statements of confusion. The *Pittsburgh Post* reported an exchange in which a woman suffragist named Mary Bakewell told him to "lay the jokes aside" and declare himself. Pushed into a corner, Wilson took either the honest or the clever way out, telling Bakewell that woman suffrage "is a big question and I am only half way through it." Wilson's transparent effort to charm Bakewell by claiming that "my mind works somewhat slowly," tempts dismissal of the whole exchange. Still, his insistence that "on this subject I really have not come to any conclusion" hangs in the air and takes on some credibility when read alongside a letter Wilson wrote four months later, and just three days after his conversation with Villard, to Governor Eugene Foss of Massachusetts. In that private letter to a political ally, Wilson affirmed his belief that "it would be best" not to "bring the woman suffrage question into the national campaign." But he then added two comments that presaged his suffrage stance for the coming years: First, he described woman suffrage as a state, not a national question, and declared that "as a state question, I am heartily in favor of its thorough discussion and shall never be jealous of its submission to a popular vote." Second, he added that his "own judgment in the matter is in an uncertain balance. I mean my judgment as a voting citizen."[25]

It was hard to maintain that "uncertain balance" in the midst of a political campaign, and hard to keep free white women cordoned off in their separate, if public, sphere, as Wilson learned at the Brooklyn Academy of Music, where Maud Malone rudely interrupted his heroic oratory condemning political control by "small bodies of men." Malone wanted to know the candidate's views on the political control men exercised over women. A different politician in an earlier time might have lectured Malone on woman's place in the home, but the moment for that stance was past; Wilson and other liberals had allowed white women to roam free over the civic landscape, preserving gender difference with the suffrage barrier. But here was Malone climbing right over that barrier, and here, too, were the men in the audience shouting her down, forcing Wilson to insist that "we have no right to be rude to a woman." In his pathetic attempt to bring chivalry into a din of sexist fury, Wilson called Malone "madame" and "lady" and expressed his "hope" that she would "not consider it a discourtesy" if he declined "positively" to answer her question, making the flimsy excuse that it was "not pertinent to the national campaign." He then watched, impotently, as Malone was hustled off to jail.[26] This was, it appears, his first opportunity to witness the tensions between chivalry, democracy, and protest. It would not be his last.

In the whole underwritten history of Wilson and the woman suffrage movement, one of the most frequently told stories is about an event he did not attend: the woman suffrage parade in Washington on March 3, 1913, the day before his first inauguration. As the story goes, he arrived in Washington that day but was deprived of welcoming crowds because everyone was gathered along Pennsylvania Avenue to watch and, in some cases, violently disrupt the dramatic spectacle of 5,000 women marching in organized units, wearing white dresses, and carrying yellow banners that laid claim to their right to vote. The parade marked two developments that would shape Wilson's presidential experience with the woman suffrage movement. First, it signified the movement's coming of age as an unrelenting lobby with high visibility in the nation's capital. Second, and quite related, it sparked the movement's split into two hostile camps: the National American Woman Suffrage Association (NAWSA), soon to come under Carrie Chapman Catt's leadership, and the Congressional Union, precursor to the National Woman's Party, under the leadership of Alice Paul.[27]

The division within the suffrage movement would prove enormously important in Wilson's second term in office. But in his first term, it was the movement's determined lobbying that marked, and undoubtedly influenced, his conversion to public support of female enfranchisement. The story of his relationship with woman suffrage in the years between 1913 and 1916 centers around his notably frequent—and often awkward—meetings with woman suffrage lobbyists and his somewhat surprising but nonetheless decisive shift over to the prosuffrage ranks during the New Jersey referendum on suffrage in the fall of 1915.

Before Wilson's move into the White House, U.S. presidents had met with woman suffrage lobbyists a total of three times: once during William McKinley's tenure, and twice during Teddy Roosevelt's. Woman suffragists met with President Wilson six times during his first term in office, and nine times during his second term.[28] The coincidence of Wilson's presidency with the movement's maturity as a national lobby motivated the suffragists to seek these frequent meetings because they wished to educate the president.[29] But the suffrage movement was not so strong in these years that Wilson had to agree to the meetings— or the education. Indeed, he could have cited two good reasons to refuse such meetings. First, he took the pristine view that, as leader of a political party whose platform took no stand on woman suffrage, *he* could take no stand; second, he continued to insist that woman suffrage was a state matter, not a federal matter and, therefore, not a presidential matter.

Still, we have written reports describing Wilson's meetings with prosuffrage delegations in March 1913, December 1913, February 1914, June 1914, January 1915, December 1915, and January 1916. The evidence from those meetings—the five that occurred before Wilson had declared his "yes" vote in the New Jersey referendum and the two that occurred after his vote—indicates his difficulty interacting with political women in a comfortable, egalitarian way. None of his clumsy efforts at combining masculine charm with paternalistic control worked to disarm or silence the suffrage delegations. Nevertheless, he kept on meeting with those delegations, and he kept trying to convince them that his refusal to take a position was reasonable.[30]

Alice Paul, the young Quaker who had organized the preinaugural suffrage parade, led the first, small suffrage lobby to Wilson's White House in March 1913, just days after the parade. The women in attendance at that painfully awkward meeting later reported that they sat in four chairs arranged in a row, while the president sat facing them, like a schoolteacher. Wilson then asked the women for more information on their cause, patronizingly and duplicitously claiming that woman suffrage "had never been brought to his attention."[31] Assuming that story quickly made the rounds in suffrage circles, it can only have increased advocates' determination to educate the new chief executive. In late 1913, *The Literary Digest* reported on suffragists' second meeting with Wilson, where he pleaded no authority to influence the creation of a House committee on woman suffrage. This claim sparked an exchange with the Reverend Anna Howard Shaw, head of the delegation from the NAWSA:

> I inquired if I might ask him a question. He said I might. I said: "Mr. President, since you cannot present our case to Congress, and since we have no committee in the House, who is to speak for us there?" He returned laughingly that he had found us well able to speak for ourselves. Whereupon I said, "But not authoritatively. Have we any one, Mr. President, to present our case

with authority to Congress?" He hesitated a moment, the muscles of his face twitched: I was dreadfully frightened myself, and I do believe he was as much frightened; but he didn't evade the question; he answered squarely, "No." And to my mind that "No" was the most important thing in the interview.

The effort at flattery—commending the NAWSA women for being able to speak for themselves as he had commended the Consumers League members for serving as a "pre-eminent legislature"—did not work any better in a face-to-face meeting with NAWSA than it had worked with Mary Bakewell or Maud Malone.[32] Wilson was much happier when his suffrage visitors were deferential. In February 1914, a working-class delegation of 25 Women's Trade Union League members addressed the president in the White House, while another 375 waited outdoors. Responding to Miss Rose Winslow's apology for not making a graceful speech in such august company, Wilson gallantly said he "did not see why she should be so nervous as presidents are perfectly human."[33] But "his face took on a deeper color" when another member of the delegation charged him with "gunning for votes" during the campaign, when he offered suffragists hope of his support.[34]

Six months later, when a delegation of 500 women from the now-prosuffrage General Federation of Women's Clubs marched to the White House and assembled in the East Room, the president's face again "changed" when irritated by insufficient female deference. He had delivered his brief address to the women, asserted his convictions that as a party leader and supporter of states' right to decide on suffrage, he was powerless to help them and, at the conclusion, "looked relieved." But two General Federation leaders quickly drew him into a substantive debate about the merits of a federal amendment approach to woman suffrage, during which he was forced to concede that federal amendments are subjected to state ratification, so states are not silenced in that process. According to *The Suffragist* report of the debate, "the President spoke with distinct annoyance. . . . The President was plainly disconcerted. He stepped back. . . . He replied frigidly, . . . 'I have tried to answer your question, and I do not think it quite proper that I submit myself to cross-examination.'" So the once "perfectly human" president was now far too human to withstand what the *New York Times* later bemoaned as inappropriate hectoring, heckling, and even hissing of the president of the United States. Editorial claims that male delegations do not catechize the commander in chief were met by suffragists' reminder that men did not need to approach the president so aggressively; they could address the president with a "proper" instrument: the vote.[35]

If masculine flattery and paternal authority were not working with the suffrage delegations, neither were Wilson's two principled, political arguments: first, that he had no right, as leader of the Democratic Party, to take a position on any issue, including woman suffrage, that was not defined in the party's 1912 platform; second, that all questions pertaining to suffrage should be decided in individual states, not at the federal level. The first position was consistent with his long-held desire to import British-style party discipline into the American system but was not consistent with his own conduct in office. As the New York *Evening Post* noted in December 1913, Wilson urged Congress to enact a federal law for presidential primaries, even though the Democratic platform urged such legislation be confined to the states.[36] And though Jane Addams was too diplomatic to mention it when she wrote to thank Wilson for vetoing the 1915 Immigrant Literacy Bill, the Democratic platform was as silent on that subject as on woman suffrage.[37] Try as he might to persuade the suffrage delegations that he was "not a free man" to speak on their issue because the Democratic platform did not speak on their issue, no one in the suffrage camp was buying the argument.[38] NAWSA's Anna Howard Shaw argued that "he is mistaken in considering himself the spokesman of his party. He should be the spokesman of his country now." Shaw followed that claim with some slick calculations intended to show that more than half of Wilson's Democratic vote total came from states where women had the vote or whose legislatures had supported woman suffrage.[39]

By June 1914, when Wilson debated the members of the General Federation of Women's Clubs, he was no longer relying on his representative-of-the-party argument to defend his refusal to take action on woman suffrage. In his opening remarks on that occasion, he took what he regarded as a big, candid step toward the women by admitting that the platform was silent on woman suffrage because the Democratic Party believed such matters were best handled at the state level and revealed himself even further by personally aligning with the party's position. "I can only say," he added, "that since you turned away from me as a leader of a party and asked me my position as a man, I am obliged to state very frankly . . . that the best way of settling this thing [is] by the states."[40]

No wonder the president was disconcerted at that June meeting; his self-conscious step toward honest endorsement of the state approach was met with rebuke because he would not embrace a federal approach. Just two years earlier, the Progressive Party had not been required to endorse a particular approach to suffrage, but now the ground was shifting. As woman suffrage gained momentum, those who advocated a state-by-state approach began to look obstructionist. In 1915, Mary Beard and Florence Kelley issued a report that concluded that a state-by-state approach was futile; the southern states would never enfranchise their female citizens.[41]

The Senate vote on the woman suffrage amendment in March 1914 was the first one in history, an indicator of the movement's growing presence in Washington. That vote made clear, in case it had not already been clear, that opposition to a federal suffrage amendment, silence in the Democratic Party platform, and reticence in the White House were all about the South and, when it came to woman suffrage, the South was as much about race as it was about gender. In the Senate debate that March, John Williams and James Vardaman, both of Mississippi, proposed amendments to the woman suffrage amendment that limited enfranchisement to white women only.[42] In a region where black men had already been disenfranchised, racist white men might have felt confident that woman suffrage did not mean black women voting, but so intertwined were the region's fears of gender and racial equality that no historian has ever devised a formula for untying the two.[43] In that 1914 Senate vote, only four of the South's twenty senators joined the majority of thirty-five in supporting woman suffrage. The other sixteen southern senators voted "nay," either because they feared black women voting or because they feared white women voting. (It did not matter that a majority of U.S. senators supported the measure; a federal amendment requires a two-thirds endorsement by the Senate.) Less than a year later, when the House unsuccessfully took up a federal woman suffrage amendment, the "yea" votes by region ranged from 100 percent support in the Pacific Coast delegations down to 40 percent support in the border state delegations—and from that 40 percent support there was then a precipitous drop to 2 percent support in the southern delegations.[44]

Fortunately for Wilson, white woman suffragists were no more anxious to confront the race question lying at the center of their movement than he was. So he was never publicly accused of jeopardizing white and black women's interests in order to mollify his party's solid South. The woman suffrage movement itself had been torn by this issue ever since Elizabeth Cady Stanton and Lucy Stone parted company over "the Negro's hour" back in 1869. And the feud between Carrie Chapman Catt and Alice Paul in 1914 and 1915 was due, in part, to Catt's fear that by pressing too exclusively for a federal approach, Paul would stir up all the racial hornets and jeopardize the progress made in the northern states since the Colorado victory of 1893.[45]

Young women like Alice Paul scoffed at the presumption of progress in the woman suffrage movement in 1915, but for elders like Wilson and Catt, the progress in the states was quite remarkable. Between 1910, when Washington State enfranchised women and 1914, when Nevada did so, six other states embraced woman suffrage, including states with significant electoral college delegations: California, Kansas, and Illinois. Wilson was a politician and, like all politicians, he was impressed by votes, impressed by victories. Back in 1908, he had argued dismissively that women did not really want the vote and did not use it when they had it. Experience had proved him wrong. Women were campaigning to vote by the thousands, in parades and picnics, wearing scarves and buttons, hats and hankies, belts and sashes. Fashionable, funny, feminine women were marching their mothers and their children through the streets of small towns and big cities to claim the franchise.[46] Indeed, Wilson's own daughters, Margaret, Jessie, and Eleanor, were in their late twenties by 1915 and all had become their father's in-house advocates for women's right to vote. Colonel House recorded in his diary, in December 1915, that "Margaret very much desired me to convert her father to her belief that it was desirable for Congress to legislate regarding Woman's Suffrage. I expressed myself as favorable to Woman's Suffrage but thought it inadvisable for her father to act as she desired."[47] The day before House's conversation with Margaret, representatives from the Woman Voters' Convention, completing a cross-country motor tour, had arrived at the White House to present the president with an 18,000-foot petition bearing 500,000 signatures in favor of a federal amendment guaranteeing woman suffrage.[48]

In Wilson's lived experience, all his substantive objections to woman suffrage had been overturned by 1915: Women were electioneering and voting, with enthusiasm, and the American family was still intact, women were still women, and neither state governments nor the federal government had been shattered by feminine blows. Increasingly, in fact, Wilson was inclined toward the view that any progressive president who wished to enact a social justice agenda would need the votes of women to succeed. When a delegation of Democratic Party women met the president at the White House in January 1915, they cleverly read back to him a flowery paean to women's civic activism, which he had delivered as a candidate in 1912. At that time, he had observed that

> it is artificial to divide life up into sections; it is all of one piece. . . . So when the women, who are in so many respects at the heart of life, begin to take an interest in politics, then you know that all the lines of sympathy and intelligence and comprehension are going to be interlaced . . . so that our politics will be of the same pattern with our life. This, it seems to me, is devoutly to

be wished, . . . [and] I, for myself, rejoice that [women] have come to our assistance; they will be as indispensable as they are delightful.

By the time the Democratic women had completed the quote, "a ripple of amusement ran around the circle of auditors, and the President laughed outright."[49] Not for the last time, women skewered Wilson with his own oratory, and his own logic—and, this time, they made him laugh at their skill. For it was clear that, by his own reasoning, women had to be granted the vote; the phony barrier of suffrage segregation simply could not hold.

So did Wilson really say at breakfast, on the morning before his meeting with the Democratic women, that "suffrage for women will make absolutely no change in politics—it is the home that will be disastrously affected. Somebody has to make the home and who is going to do it if the women don't?" His houseguest, Nancy Saunders Toy, recorded those words in her diary, adding with pleasure that the "suffragists came and went without a crumb of comfort," thus revealing where she stood on the issue.[50] But we wonder if, while Wilson was chewing his toast, Toy herself had not opined on the disastrous effects of woman suffrage and the president had graciously nodded and affirmed that hers was, indeed, a valuable perspective. We wonder because the Democratic women had not actually left the White House without a "crumb of comfort." True, Wilson had reaffirmed his belief that "changes of this sort ought to be brought about State by State," insisted that he would hold this view on "any other thing connected with Suffrage," granted that his listeners "unanimously disagree with me" but hoped they would respect his adherence to his own principled reading of the Constitution. He had also stated, however, that his position resulted from "no attitude of antagonism" toward the goal of woman suffrage; indeed, he said, "nobody can look at the fight you are making without great admiration," adding that he was "certainly" among those who admired "the tenacity and the skill" with which suffragists were pursuing their goal.[51] If this was masculine flattery, it was also a politician's effort to give credit to others gathered on the political field.

THE TURNING POINT

The turning point in Woodrow Wilson's suffrage story came not in January 1918 when he announced his support for the federal amendment. That was a tactical shift, not a fundamentally new position on women's right—and capacity—to vote. The turning point came ten months after his breakfast with Nancy Toy. In early October 1915, Wilson obeyed the logic of his own experience and states' rights principle by announcing that he would vote in favor of woman suffrage in the upcoming New Jersey referendum. Was the timing of this endorsement of woman suffrage designed to offset female critiques of his same-day announcement of his engagement to Edith Galt? Possibly. But why care about female critiques if you are not already viewing women as voters? To argue that Wilson would endorse suffrage as a legitimate activity for half the nation's citizenry simply to gain goodwill for his marriage to his second antisuffrage wife is to trivialize the cause of woman suffrage and rather seriously underestimate the ideological significance of his conversion to the logic of that cause.[52] By late 1915, he had come to the end of his "uncertain balance" and worked his way through the problem: Women were in public life to stay, they were effective there, and many of the suffragists he was meeting seemed, for the most part, quite willing to operate in civic life as women, as wives, as mothers, as keepers of the hearth and tenders of the moral flame. Wilson had come to see that he could hold on to his sentiments about women's distinct role in life without defending an outmoded suffrage boundary that was doomed to collapse anyway.

Wilson's endorsement did not matter in the New Jersey referendum—or in the New York, Massachusetts, and Pennsylvania referenda held that same season. All of them went down in defeat. Woman suffrage was making progress, but not that much progress. Wilson may have seemed backward to those suffragists who sought a federal solution to their problem, but he was obviously ahead of the majority of male voters in New Jersey, New York, Massachusetts, and Pennsylvania.

The story of Wilson and suffrage, between his vote in the New Jersey referendum in the fall of 1915 and his support for a federal amendment in January 1918, is not a story about whether the president *believed* in woman suffrage. Antisuffragists' persistent attempt to argue that the president's opposition to a federal amendment meant that he was still on their side could not make it so and does not count as evidence of anything but their desperation.[53] Wilson had announced his side on woman suffrage in New Jersey, and thereafter described himself as "a very sincere advocate of the extension of suffrage to women."[54] The post-1915 story is about method, timing, and tactics; it is about deference to the racial and gender politics of the South and the direction of the Democratic Party; and it is about war and protest and the rage Wilson felt at suffragists who were unwilling to keep the home fires burning and his loyalty to those suffragists who were.

Wilson authored the woman suffrage plank in the Democratic Party's platform of 1916. "We recommend," stated the plank in its entirety, "the extension of the franchise to the women of the country by the States upon the same terms as men."[55] From Wilson's perspective, the word "recommend" gave the plank authentic force, but now that he was in the suffrage camp he had to explain to prosuffrage, proamendment Democrats why he still held off on a federal approach. In these exchanges, he was a politician talking to other politicians. When Harriot Stanton Blatch and a delegation of prosuffrage Democratic women met with him in late July to urge support for the federal amendment, he replied that "the Negro question" precluded that option for the Democratic Party. Countering Blatch's argument that female enfranchisement "would increase not decrease the proportion of white to black voters," the president noted that "in two states the blacks would still preponderate." But even as he bowed to the racial concerns of his southern colleagues, he placated others with hints at the possibility of federal action. "I got the most that it was feasible to get on the suffrage question from the St. Louis Convention," he told one suffrage activist, adding that he "must for the time rest content with that or else lose the really extraordinary confidence which the working forces of the party have reposed in me."[56]

Southern Democrats continued to urge the president to hold fast on the federal amendment question in the name of white supremacy and states' rights, and Wilson's inclination to do so is evident in his handling of Senator Charles S. Thomas, Democrat of Colorado, who chaired the Senate Committee on Woman Suffrage. In the wake of the Democratic Convention, Thomas asked the president to explain why he should continue to chair the committee or support the federal amendment given that his party's platform so clearly opposed a federal approach. Wilson's reply served to keep control of this prosuffrage, proamendment party member, who represented a state where women had been voting since 1893. The president insisted that the senator could "with perfect consistency remain at the head of the committee so long as what you do in that committee is consistent with the position of the party, as I am sure it will be."[57] In none of these exchanges did Wilson question the assumption that women should, in principle, vote. His contingencies were entirely racial, regional, and procedural.

Heading into the 1916 campaign, Wilson was positioned to be persistently battered by Alice Paul's newly established National Woman's Party (NWP). The NWP was fiercely devoted to a federal amendment and subscribed so thoroughly to Wilson's philosophy of party leadership that it set about to hold the party in power—the Democratic Party—responsible for women's national disenfranchisement and to do that by campaigning against Wilson in every state where women had the vote.[58] Meanwhile, he had to contend with Charles Evans Hughes's decision to support a federal amendment and thereby depart from the Republican Party platform, which favored (but did not recommend) woman suffrage, deferring to "the right of each state to settle this question for itself."[59]

If he were going to realize any political gain from his prosuffrage position, Wilson needed an ally in the 1916 election, and he found a powerful one in the 2-million-member NAWSA and its new president, Carrie Chapman Catt.

Catt's "Winning Plan" for suffrage, like Paul's plan, aimed at using the power of states in which women were enfranchised to lobby Congress for a federal amendment. Unlike Paul, however, Catt intended to continue campaigning for suffrage in individual states and rather than try to force President Wilson to support a federal amendment, Catt intended to win him over to the federal strategy by cooperating with him.[60] In the dramatic meeting that finalized the split between Catt and Paul and their respective followers, they had argued bitterly over Paul's intention to stage a partisan campaign against the Democrats in 1916. Insisting that woman suffrage needed support from both parties, that the Republican Party platform was no better than the Democratic, and that a focus on Democrats was foolish given southern intransigence, Catt forced Paul out of NAWSA with the promise, "I will fight you to the last ditch."[61] As it turned out, that last ditch circled Wilson's White House, and the fight began in earnest in the 1916 election.

Even after four years of interacting with woman suffrage leaders, Wilson was still vague about their names and alignments. As late as July 1916, Joseph Tumulty had to assure him that Catt and the women of NAWSA were not in Alice Paul's camp, were not of the "heckling" variety.[62] But the record from the 1916 campaign makes clear that Wilson sorted out the good girls from the bad girls when it was politically necessary and made sure to affiliate himself with Catt and the good girls of NAWSA. The Reverend Anna Howard Shaw, the former president of NAWSA, who had once tutored Wilson on women's need for genuine "authority" within the government and chastised him for his party loyalty, now pushed NAWSA to pass "strong resolutions condemning the action of [Alice Paul's] Woman's Party."[63] To aid in that effort, Shaw and Catt invited Wilson to speak to the NAWSA convention meeting in Atlantic City on September 8, 1916. He accepted the invitation and, for the first time, met with woman suffragists on their turf, not his. From the stage of the New Nixon Theater, he brought 4,000 cheering women to their feet by announcing, "I have not come to fight against anybody but with somebody."[64]

The two notable features of Wilson's NAWSA speech were his very brief effort to link the logic of woman suffrage to the logic of progressive politics and his repetitive effort to convince his audience and, perhaps, himself that woman suffrage was so inevitable that a state approach was not an impossible obstacle course.

Tearing a page from Teddy Roosevelt's 1912 playbook, Wilson argued that industrialization and urbanization had altered "the whole nature of our political questions," making them social, not legal, questions—"questions with regard to the relations of human beings to one another." The unspoken link between that assertion and Wilson's reference to woman suffrage as a "gathering force" was the assumption that women's natural role was to manage "the relations of human beings to one another." But if industrial, urban America needed women's votes, it could wait to for those votes to come, one state at a time. Indeed, Wilson said, he got "a little impatient" with all the talk about methods by which the "gathering force" would "prevail."[65]

The record does not reveal if Wilson really believed that a state approach alone would win suffrage for all American women, or if he thought it was the most politically realistic route to a federal amendment, or if he was willing to live with black and white women's disenfranchisement in the South for the sake of Democratic Party harmony. His campaign speech at the NAWSA convention certainly did not hint at the third possibility, but it gave plenty of support to those who believed a state approach would produce victory, one way or another. "We feel the tide," he told the crowd, "we rejoice in the strength of it, and we shall not quarrel in the long run as to the method of it." The inevitability of woman suffrage was Wilson's theme that evening, not the slow, grinding process of his recommended state approach. "The astonishing thing about the movement which you represent," he argued, "is not that it has grown so slowly, but that it has grown so rapidly." Determinedly cheerful about women's seven-decade, uphill battle, Wilson promised that "the forces of nature are steadily working . . . the tide is rising to meet the moon," the "conquering power" of woman's cause would "beyond any peradventure, be triumphant." Therefore, he abruptly concluded, "you can afford to wait a little while."[66]

Shaw, born one year before the suffrage movement began in 1848, responded, impulsively, from the podium, "We have waited long enough to get the vote. We want it now. I want it to come during your administration." Catt, characteristically, more politic, told the president, "You touched our hearts and won our fealty when you said you had come here to fight with us." She was probably reflecting the mood in the room, but if there were any dissenters, they were quiet. Catt had warned the convention participants earlier in the day that NAWSA's officers would record the names of anyone who dared to hiss the president that evening and would send those names on to Washington.[67]

Proamendment Democrats had worried, during this 1916 presidential race, that Wilson's insistence on the state method and Paul's unrelenting campaign for a federal amendment and against the Democrats would cost him votes among already-enfranchised women. Ellen Duane Davis warned him in August that "the votes of men and women in the twelve voting states will be solidly for Mr. Hughes." Wilson, running on a peace platform and refusing to be an "angler" for proamendment votes, expressed faith in the "good sense and public spirit" of women voters; he was, he insisted, "perfectly confident that the belligerent women of the [NWP] could not command the women of the country how they should vote."[68] He was also, as Home Cummings, vice chair of the Democratic National Committee, observed, "the best kind of tactical politician," whose faith in democracy meant faith that "somehow people will judge aright."[69]

Wilson's confidence that his suffrage strategy would work, or not matter, proved accurate in 1916. Hughes won in only two suffrage states, Illinois and Oregon. Wilson's sweep of the western states reinforced his 1914 observation that "a different part of America now decides," which could mean that the party leadership no longer dictated obedience to the South.[70] At the same time, women's support for Wilson reputedly put him over the top in California and thereby secured his victory.[71] This naturally strengthened his loyalty to those women who had, themselves, been enfranchised by the state approach and had turned away from the "belligerent" Paul to vote for Wilson, his peace platform, and, presumably, his approach to woman suffrage.

Endorsing a Federal Amendment:
On Toward Suffrage

Wilson's first postelection woman suffrage meeting, on January 9, 1917, was with a delegation of 300 members of the NWP, headed by Alice Paul. It did not go well. The president entered the East Room smiling, but he was not happy. These were the "heckling" women, the ones who had dogged his heels in the west during the campaign, the ones who had unfurled a banner asking "Mr. President: What Will You Do for Woman Suffrage?" during Wilson's annual address before Congress just four weeks earlier.[72] There had been cranky negotiations about the date and duration of the meeting, whose ostensible purpose was to present the president with resolutions passed at a memorial service for the beloved, recently deceased NWP heroine, Inez Milholland. And, indeed, the speech delivered to the president that day by Sara Bard Field, an NWP officer, was deeply sentimental, weaving Milholland's death into a motif of waste: the "waste of maternal force" on the "wasteful struggle" to win suffrage state by state. Field pleaded for "a favorable word" from the president in support of a federal amendment; "we cannot believe that you are our enemy, or are indifferent to the fundamental righteousness of our demand."[73]

Wilson was furious over being manipulated into making a political statement at what he thought was a memorial service. His stiff, patronizing remarks to these women, the ones who had called the Democratic Party to account in the previous election, presumed to tutor them about the role of parties in a "self-governing country." It was, he lectured, "really through the instrumentality of the Parties that things can be accomplished," and those suffragists who did not understand his need to defer to his party's platform were a source of "surprise" and "regret" to him.[74]

The words were the same as they had been for years—party governance and reliance on state enfranchisement—but the music was all wrong. A report in *McCall's Magazine* described the president's manner as "chilled," "cold," and "icy." He was fed up; he had said and done all he was going to say or do on this matter and, having won the election and defeated Paul and her NWP by running on the Democratic Party platform, he resented demands based on "righteousness." But the NWP was fed up, as well. Infuriated by the president's stubborn stance and rigid tone, NWP members decided to set up daily pickets at the White House with banners that repeated the question first unfurled in Congress: "Mr. President: What Will You Do for Woman Suffrage?"[75]

In the months between January and June of 1917, Wilson was shifting his entire identity and that of his administration from counseling "peace without victory" to waging "a war to end all war." Woman suffrage was hardly his top priority; the war was. Paul's strategy for persuading the president to endorse a federal amendment was to be single-minded and unrelenting, not to fashion her campaign to fit the wider political climate. As a Quaker, she was against the war; as a suffragist, she simply did not care about it—everything was about suffrage.[76] On this point, Catt agreed, but her single-minded suffrage focus dictated a different strategy. Though she had been a member of the Woman's Peace Party, she earned instant ejection from that tiny circle of pacifists when she personally endorsed the president's war message and pledged that NAWSA would do everything in its power to support the war effort.[77] Now all Catt's energies were bent on standing with the president against his enemies—especially Paul. In early May, just four weeks after Wilson's war message to Congress, Catt wrote to the president to assure him that it was the NWP, not NAWSA, that was pushing for consideration of a federal suffrage amendment during the special session of Congress occasioned by the war. NAWSA thought it "only fair," knowing the "overwhelming pressure upon you in pushing through immediate war measures" to "wait yet a while longer" and "not press for suffrage" at this time.[78]

The war and Paul's White House pickets gave Catt the opportunity to be supportive, nurturing, and self-sacrificing toward the president, just the qualities he liked most in a woman. In allying NAWSA with Wilson and against Paul, Catt behaved as if she had overheard Colonel House's advice on how to handle the president: "Never begin by arguing. Discover a common hate, exploit it, get the President warmed up and then start on your business."[79] Catt used Wilson's animosity toward Paul to win his support of the thing Paul most wanted: endorsement of a federal amendment.

As early as her May 1917 letter assuring the president that NAWSA would not bother him about woman suffrage at this dire time, Catt slipped in the hope that "our willingness to serve our country even only half armed would appeal to the men with whom you and we must deal in Congress as a good and sufficient reason for our enfranchisement—possibly as a war measure—when you are less pressed than at the moment."[80] So now the idea was on the table: a federal suffrage amendment as a war measure. Instead of ignoring the war, as Paul decided to do, Catt harnessed it to her suffrage campaign.

The first sign that NAWSA was using the right approach with the president came only a week after Catt's letter when Wilson, for the first time, expressed to Congress an opinion about a suffrage measure. Helen Gardener, an equally effective presidential masseuse from NAWSA, followed up Catt's letter with a note affirming that organization's "major activities" had been "placed in abeyance at your call to arms." But, Gardener added, the "*only* request" NAWSA was making of this wartime Congress was creation of a House committee on woman suffrage so that "sane progress" could be made, presumably in legislative halls, not on the streets outside the White House. "Is it asking too much," Gardener wondered, to "urge you to make known" to Representative Edward Pou (D-N.C.), chair of the House Rules Committee, that the president approved of the appointment of such a committee? Gardener noted that NAWSA had been seeking this "machinery" for years, though she did not remind Wilson that he had implied support for it back in 1913.[81] Four days later, Wilson wrote to Pou, allowing as how "strictly speaking, it is none of my business," but referencing the "admirable spirit" of Gardener's letter and revealing his alignment with NAWSA by arguing that establishment of the committee would be "an act of fairness to the best women who are engaged in the cause of woman suffrage."[82]

Invidious comparisons to the White House suffrage picketers were helping NAWSA and the woman suffrage cause but only solidifying Wilson's hostility to the pickets. Before the war, he had been politely tolerant of the daily demonstrations, famously offering the women tea on a cold day (and just as famously being turned down).[83] But once the war began, he grew to resent the NWP's banners, which used quotations from his prodemocracy speeches to mock his antiamendment stance. Wilson's negative reaction does not constitute evidence that he was insincere in supporting woman suffrage; it is, rather, additional evidence for his biographers' bulging case file indicating that he did not like criticism in general and certainly did not like unladylike street demonstrations in wartime.[84] Everything about the wartime suffrage pickets offended Wilson— except their fundamental goal. Hence, his susceptibility to Catt's blandishments; he wanted to be told that he was still a good suffragist even though the women in the street were calling him a hypocrite.

Arrests of woman suffrage picketers began in June 1917 and continued through the summer and into the fall. In all, over two hundred women were arrested and ninety-seven sentenced to time in jail. Charged with obstructing traffic, the detained women were initially held for a few days in the District of Columbia jail; by mid-July, as the war-fevered street violence against the picketers increased, the suffragists were being sent to Occoquan Workhouse in Virginia for as much as sixty days. In reply to an antipicket letter from Dee Richardson, who had herself been arrested for physically attacking a picketer while calling her a "dirty yellow traitor," the president pointed to his "pride" in "obeying the law." He went on to express his hope that the picketers' unseemly, untimely conduct "should not lead us to irregular action ourselves."[85]

By the time Wilson wrote those words, however, irregular action was already under way. Woman suffragists, including Shaw, who thought the picketing was "foolishness" were in communication with Joseph Tumulty, George Creel, and *Washington Times* editor, Arthur Brisbane, about managing the news of the pickets. Wilson endorsed these plans by suggesting that the pickets get no front page coverage, no big headlines. "A bare, colorless chronicle of what they do should be all that is printed. That constitutes part of the news, but it need not be made interesting reading."[86] Here again, Wilson's unsavory action does not count as evidence that he had suddenly turned against white female enfranchisement; it serves as additional evidence that he was willing, in wartime, to limit freedom of the press. So, too, his passive acceptance of the arrests testifies less to his stand on suffrage in 1917 than it does to his stand on free speech—and his hostility to the NWP.[87]

There is no evidence that Wilson directly ordered the arrests of picketers, and there is testimony from Louis Brownlow, District of Columbia commissioner, that Wilson opposed the arrests because he did not want to give "these women their accolade of martyrdom."[88] In July, Wilson pardoned a few prisoners, but he was rebuked with the reply that women did not want his "presidential benevolence, but American justice."[89] Whether in reaction to that rebuke or not, he did not stop the arrests; nor did he stop the increasing mistreatment of the suffrage prisoners.

The president had ready access to news of the violence being visited upon the women on the picket line, in the hands of the police, and in prison custody. He chose not to act upon it. News was being smuggled out and printed in *The Suffragist* and other newspapers (because the story was too rich to reside on back pages). Wives of prominent men were going to jail, and those men were telling Wilson that something had to be done.[90] Dudley Field Malone, Wilson's appointee as collector of the Port of New York, gave him a full report of conditions in July and pleaded with his president and longtime ally to support a federal amendment and put an end to the pickets. Wilson held fast to his party principles, conditions at Occoquan worsened, and Malone resigned in September. Wilson claimed surprise at his old friend's "disloyalty."[91]

Representative Charles A. Lindbergh, the father of the young pilot and a Republican from Minnesota, sent the president a lengthy, detailed description in August of the women's mistreatment, "within sight and sound of your office." Lindbergh held Wilson responsible for the government's actions because "you have assumed an attitude of leadership in this country that approaches the absolute." Having taken on such complete wartime power, argued Lindbergh, Wilson was duty-bound to exercise it on behalf of the suffragists. When Wilson forwarded the Lindbergh report to Newton Baker, he admitted little confidence in this antiwar member of Congress but admitted, too, that he did "not feel quite at liberty to let [the report] pass."[92] So Wilson appointed Dr. W. Gwynn Gardiner to conduct an investigation of conditions at Occoquan and soon declared Gardiner's wholly superficial, wholly inaccurate report to be "useful and I must say very satisfactory."[93] The president expressed no skepticism over Gardiner's claim that the women on hunger strike in Occoquan swallowed the feeding tube "willingly" and experienced "no more than the ordinary discomfort attending such a course of feeding."[94] Back in 1914, Wilson had told the working-class suffragist Rose Winslow not to be afraid of speaking to him because "presidents are perfectly human." But when that same Winslow smuggled out reports from jail, in the fall of 1917, telling of the vomiting and the pain that accompanied forced feeding, her "perfectly human" president was deaf to her pleas.[95]

Meanwhile, Catt had the president's ear and was using that access to commend Wilson on his "serene and tactful handling of the recent 'picket crisis.'"[96] She was also keeping keep him abreast of developments in the state referendum campaign in New York. They discussed the possibility that a backlash against the picketers would defeat the New York referendum, and Wilson issued a public statement of support for the New York referendum. But he privately expressed to Catt his confidence that "so small a fraction of women" could not "prejudice the cause itself."[97]

Once again, Wilson called the election correctly. Woman suffrage, in fact, made huge gains in the states in 1917, winning not only in New York but in North Dakota, Nebraska, Rhode Island, and Arkansas. Woman now voted in sixteen of the forty-eight states. Catt kept up a low, steady drumbeat about support for the federal amendment as a war measure, arguing that if women did not have to work for "their own liberty and independence," they could throw their "entire energy into work for their country and for humanity." But despite claims of "sincere friendship" with NAWSA, Wilson resisted the entreaties coming at him from all sides, including from members of Congress, to give up his stubborn insistence on the state method, support a federal amendment, and let the states weigh in during the ratification process.[98]

Dramatic accounts of Wilson's conversion to a federal amendment approach to woman suffrage typically credit the White House pickets with forcing him to acquiesce. But in Wilson's own reflections on how the suffrage story would be told, he noted that "historians are very dull persons and do not accept ingenious explanations." He predicted that "history will deal very candidly with the circumstances" surrounding the suffrage denouement.[99] Those circumstances certainly included the White House pickets, but had they been operating alone—without NAWSA's access to the president, without the state referenda victories, without a Congress whose members increasingly represented woman suffrage states, without a war in which women's service was evident to all—the NWP's pickets would not have won the day. In the absence of other forces acting on him, Wilson might well have resisted the pickets. As it was, the pressure of the pickets gave NAWSA, as well as prosuffrage representatives and senators, the leverage they needed to approach the president as problem solvers and mediators. He was, after all, an advocate of suffrage. That was not the issue in 1917. However bitter his conduct toward the picketers, that conduct was not about women's right to vote. It was about Wilson's inability to rise above anger and live by the liberal principles he espoused.

The House of Representatives, led by its new Committee on Woman Suffrage, was scheduled to vote on the federal amendment on January 10, 1918. On January 8, Elizabeth Bass, the head of the Democratic National Committee's Women's Division, wrote to the president pleading for a public endorsement of the amendment lest the Republicans use his intransigence against the Democrats in the midterm elections. Wilson had heard those threats before, of course, and had always brushed them off. But wartime and electoral influences now opened him to Bass's argument that it was more important to become "the second Great Emancipator" by enfranchising women than to stand on the rigid principle of states' rights or party leadership. "In these days," sighed a war-weary Bass, "when all foundations are shifting, methods do not seem to matter very much."[100]

Wilson met with the House Committee on Woman Suffrage the next day and, still clinging to protocol, allowed the committee to issue a brief typewritten statement to the effect that the president had not felt "at liberty to volunteer his advice to members of Congress in this important matter, but when we sought his advice, he very frankly and earnestly advised us to vote for the amendment as an act of right and justice to the women of the country and of the world."[101] Three years earlier, the House of Representatives had defeated the woman suffrage amendment, 204 to 174, but five states had enfranchised women in the interim, and this time the vote went in favor of the amendment, 274 to 136. The president's endorsement may have emboldened a few members of Congress, but the results in the Senate the following October suggest that Wilson's word alone was not enough.

On the eve of the Senate vote on the amendment, Wilson answered a plea from Catt, "written in sheer desperation."[102] The next day, September 30, he went to the floor of the Senate and delivered an "appeal for woman suffrage," using every argument he could muster. Some in the audience must have been thrilled to hear the president say all the things they had waited for him to say; others were likely furious to hear him make arguments he could have made months earlier. He admitted, for example, that "no disputable principle is involved, . . . only a question of method" and "the method of state action proposed in the party platforms of 1916 is impracticable within any reasonable length of time, if practicable at all." He announced, in high tones, that "we must either conform" to the suffrage demand or reject it and "resign the leadership of liberal minds to others." He not only claimed that female enfranchisement was "vital to the winning of the war," finally using the argument Catt had proposed months earlier, he also claimed that "we shall need [women's] moral sense" when the war was over "to preserve what is right and fine and worthy. . . .Without their counselings, we shall be only half wise."[103]

Despite Wilson's fine rhetoric, victory in the Senate was, Catt reported, a "miracle . . . beyond the President's power to achieve"; passage of the amendment fell two votes short, with the Democrats splitting twenty-six "yea" and twenty-one "nay" and the Republicans splitting twenty-seven "yea" and ten "nay."[104] Woman suffragists had to fight four more senatorial campaigns, against two antisuffragist Democrats and two antisuffragist Republicans, and face one more rejection by the Senate in February 1919, before the amendment passed in June 1919. That victory, like the earlier victory in the House, rested not on the president's influence but on the political networks forged at the state level.[105] At the time of the congressional victory, Wilson rejoiced but could not take credit. And though he did what he could, from his perch at Versailles, to encourage state ratification of the amendment, that, too, was a state-by-state effort, reliant on the electoral infrastructure woman suffragists had themselves created.

Conclusions: Gender Politics Mattered

Woodrow Wilson's gender politics and his stand on suffrage mattered, but not because his endorsement spelled instant success. Certainly, his endorsement of state-sponsored enfranchisement in 1915 legitimized the women's cause, as did his frequent, if awkward, meetings with suffrage delegates during his tenure in the White House. But all the effort that the suffragists expended to win his support for a federal amendment bore greater fruit in publicity and lobbying experience than in his actual influence over Congress. Arguably, for both NAWSA and NWP members, his stubborn states' rights suffrage stance mattered because it demanded constant tending and strategizing. His support for a state approach represented sincere support, but it was tactically incomplete. As the first president to endorse the concept of woman suffrage at all, he loomed large in the suffragists' victory plan; his conversion to a federal amendment represented the prize to be won—and, therefore, the prize to be constantly sought. As the pages and pages on Wilson in the suffrage literature testify, he was at the center of the suffragists' screen because he was theoretically on their side—but he still required their time and attention.

For Wilson scholars, there is more to this story than has been appreciated or integrated into the larger picture of his presidency. The failure to examine woman suffrage as an example of his idealistic notions of party leadership or as a clue to his evolving relationship with southern Democrats and social justice progressivism suggests that Wilson scholars have been embarrassed by his suffrage history, as if it were an unseemly affair of the heart, not an example of serious politics. So, too, those interested in Wilson's racism and his civil liberties failures have not yet exploited the suffrage story's potential to shed light on these unsavory aspects of his administration. If scholars are to make profitable use of woman suffrage in analyzing Wilson, they will have to set aside the naive assumption that his persistent romanticism about women and his vengeful anger when women violated that romantic image means he was not a sincere suffragist. They will also have to drop the notion that his political maneuverings meant that he did not favor white women's enfranchisement. Those political maneuverings are, in fact, strong evidence that he embraced the fact of white female suffrage and moved on to treat it like every other political fact: something to be leveraged, controlled, and exploited. His paternal romanticism about women is a factor in this story, but not the only factor—and not proof of his opposition to woman suffrage.

The history of gender in Wilson's day makes clear that many men, most men, and probably most women embraced woman suffrage when they figured out how to incorporate it into their existing views on gender, the family, and sex. As the most famous and most important male convert to woman suffrage, Woodrow Wilson represents an attitude that shaped women's lives after winning the vote: the belief that women voters would watch over all that was "right and fine and worthy" in America. Wilson was willing to grant women the vote, but not their independence from the duties he romantically assigned to them. There is more of a story there than has yet been told.

Notes

1. Stockton Axson, *"Brother Woodrow": A Memoir of Woodrow Wilson* (Princeton, N.J.: Princeton University Press, 1993); John Morton Blum, *Woodrow Wilson and the Politics of Morality* (Boston: Little, Brown, 1956); Kendrick A. Clements, *The Presidency of Woodrow Wilson* (Lawrence: University Press of Kansas, 1992); Kendrick A. Clements and Eric A. Cheezum, *Woodrow Wilson* (Washington, D.C.: CQ Press, 2003); John Milton Cooper Jr., *The Warrior and the Priest* (Cambridge, Mass.: Harvard University Press, 1983); August Heckscher, *Woodrow Wilson* (New York: Charles Scribner's Sons, 1991); Thomas J. Knock, *To End All Wars: Woodrow Wilson and the Quest for a New World Order* (New York: Oxford University Press, 1992); Earl Latham, ed., *The Philosophy and Policies of Woodrow Wilson* (Chicago: University of Chicago Press, 1958); Arthur C. Link, *Woodrow Wilson: A Profile* (New York: Hill & Wang, 1968); Arthur S. Link, *Wilson: The New Freedom* (Princeton, N.J.: Princeton University Press, 1956); Arthur C. Link, *Wilson, Confusions and Crises* (Princeton, N.J.: Princeton University Press, 1964); Arthur Link, *The Higher Realism of Woodrow Wilson and Other Essays* (Nashville: Vanderbilt University Press, 1971); Robert M. Saunders, *In Search of Woodrow Wilson: Beliefs and Behavior* (Westport, Conn.: Greenwood Press, 1998); Daniel Stid, *The President as Statesman: Woodrow Wilson and the Constitution* (Lawrence: University Press of Kansas, 1998); John A. Thompson, *Woodrow Wilson: Profiles in Power* (London: Pearson Education, 2002); Niels Aage Thorsen, *The Political Thought of Woodrow Wilson* (Princeton, N.J.: Princeton University Press, 1988); Joseph Tumulty, *Woodrow Wilson As I Know Him* (New York: Doubleday, Page, 1921).

2. Christine A. Lunardini and Thomas J. Knock, "Woodrow Wilson and Woman Suffrage: A New Look," *Political Science Quarterly* 95 (Winter 1980–81): 655–71.

3. Progressive Party Platform, adopted in Chicago, August 7, 1912; http://www.pbs .org/wgbh/amex/presidents/26_t_roosevelt/psources/ps_trprogress.html.

4. For a useful analysis of the various political factors that aligned to produce victory in the woman suffrage campaign, see Alana S. Jeydel, *Political Women: The Women's Movement, Political Institutions, the Battle for Woman Suffrage and the ERA* (New York: Routledge, 2004), chap. 5.

5. Clements and Cheezum, *Woodrow Wilson*, 120.

6. Clements, *Presidency of Woodrow Wilson*, x.

7. Blum, *Woodrow Wilson and the Politics of Morality*, 118; David Morgan, *Suffragists and Democrats: The Politics of Woman Suffrage in America* (East Lansing: Michigan State University Press, 1972), 8; Link, *Higher Realism of Woodrow Wilson*, 305.

8. Lunardini and Knock, "Woodrow Wilson and Woman Suffrage," 670–71.

9. Christine Lunardini, *From Equal Suffrage to Equal Rights: Alice Paul and the National Woman's Party, 1910–1928* (New York: New York University Press, 1986), 139.

10. Sally Hunter Graham, "Woodrow Wilson, Alice Paul, and the Woman Suffrage Movement," *Political Science Quarterly* 98 (Winter 1983–84): 665–66; Cooper, *Warrior and the Priest*, 210; John Milton Cooper Jr., *Pivotal Decades: The United States, 1900–1920* (New York: W. W. Norton, 1990), 218.

11. Lunardini, *From Equal Suffrage to Equal Rights*, 139.

12. Wilson Shorthand Diary entry, in *The Papers of Woodrow Wilson*, 69 vols., ed. Arthur S. Link et al. (Princeton, N.J.: Princeton University Press, 1966–94) (hereafter, *PWW*), vol. 1, 143.

13. Woodrow Wilson to Ellen Axson, October 31, 1884, in ibid., 389.

14. Woodrow Wilson to Ellen Axson, March 1, 1885, in ibid., 316–19.

15. Wilson's Confidential Journal, October 20, 1887, in ibid., 619.

16. Diary of Colonel Edward House, July 26, 1917, in ibid., vol. 40, 290.

17. Woodrow Wilson to Frederic Yates, September 5, 1908, in ibid., vol. 18, 417.

18. Woodrow Wilson interview, *Royal Gazette*, March 3, 1908, in ibid., 3–4.

19. Woodrow Wilson to Witter Bynner, June 20, 1911, in ibid., vol. 23, 160.

20. "Governor Wilson Pledges Aid to the Consumers' League," Trenton, N.J., *True American*, February 25, 1911, in *PWW*, vol. 22, 453.

21. Ibid., 452.

22. Progressive Party Platform, 1912, "Equal Suffrage" plank. For a discussion of Roosevelt and woman suffrage, see Kathleen Dalton, *Theodore Roosevelt: A Strenuous Life* (New York: Alfred A. Knopf, 2002), chap. 12.

23. "Sussex Society Tenders Wilson Hearty Greeting," *Newark Evening News*, February 19, 1912, in *PWW*, vol. 24, 180.

24. Oswald Garrison Villard Diary entry, August 14, 1912, in ibid., vol. 25, 26; Oswald Garrison Villard to Susan Walker FitzGerald, August 14, 1912, in ibid., 29.

25. "Wilson's Friends Very Confident," *Pittsburgh Post*, April 11, 1912, in ibid., vol. 24, 315; Woodrow Wilson to Governor Eugene Noble Foss, August 17, 1912, in ibid., vol. 25.

On January 31, 1912, Edith M. Whitmore, chair of the Richmond Borough of the Woman Suffrage Party in Staten Island, New York, wrote to Wilson asking him if he favored woman suffrage and, "if elected will you openly do so?" Wilson's reply, a week later, was similar to his answer to Mary Bakewell. Describing suffrage as "a very difficult question," Wilson could "only say that my own mind is in the midst of the debate which it involves. I do not feel that I am ready to utter any confident judgment as yet about it. I am honestly trying to work my way toward a just conclusion." Woodrow Wilson to Edith M. Whitmore, February 8, 1912, in ibid., vol. 24, 140. In his 1948 memoir, *Enjoyment of Living*, Max Eastman claimed that when he and Wilson shared the dais at a Syracuse, New York, banquet on April 9, 1912, Wilson asked the prosuffrage Eastman for a tutorial on the woman suffrage question. Whether Eastman was embellishing to please readers in 1948 or Wilson was disarming to get information in 1912 is not clear, but Eastman said that Wilson confessed to ignorance on the matter of female enfranchisement. Eastman's memory may have been shaped by the general view among suffragists that Wilson was in need of education on their issue. Max Eastman, *Enjoyment of Living* (New York: Harper & Brothers, 1948), 385.

26. "A Campaign Address at the Academy of Music in Brooklyn," October 19, 1912, in ibid., vol. 25, 438.

27. Eleanor Flexner, *Century of Struggle: The Woman's Rights Movement in the United States* (Cambridge, Mass.: Harvard University Press, 1959), 262–65; Ellen Carol Du Bois, *Harriot Stanton Blatch and the Winning of Woman Suffrage* (New Haven, Conn.: Yale University Press),182–89; Lunardini, *From Equal Suffrage to Equal Rights*, chaps. 3–6.

28. Jeydel, *Political Women*, 123.

29. Inez Haynes Irwin, *The Story of Alice Paul and the National Woman's Party* (Fairfax, Va.: Denlinger's Publishers, 1964), 32–33; Lunardini, *From Equal Suffrage to Equal Rights*, 38.

30. Irwin, *Story of Alice Paul and the National Woman's Party*, 34–35, 43, 45–46, 58–64, 192–95.

31. Ibid., 34.

32. "The President and the Suffragists," *Literary Digest*, December 20, 1913, 1209–10.

33. Irwin, *Story of Alice Paul and the National Woman's Party*, 59.

34. "Suffragists Snub President When He Refuses Them Aid," *New York World*, February 3, 1914, in *PWW*, vol. 30, 214.

35. Irwin, *The Story of Alice Paul and the National Woman's Party*, 61–64; Remarks to Woman Suffrage Delegation, June 30, 1914, in *PWW*, vol. 31, 226–28; "Wilson Won't Let Women Heckle Him," *New York Times*, July 1, 1914.

36. Cited in "The President and the Suffragists," 1210. Wilson also argued that he was not "free" to lobby Congress on legislative matters. On this point, Lunardini and

Knock note that Wilson was "disingenuous," for he was a notably effective lobbyist with Congress on matters such as the Underwood Tariff and the Federal Reserve Act. Lunardini and Knock, "Woodrow Wilson and Woman Suffrage," 659.

37. Jane Addams to Woodrow Wilson, January 29, 1915, in *PWW*, vol. 42, 162.

38. Remarks to a Delegation from the National Woman Suffrage Convention, December 8, 1913, in ibid., vol. 30, 21–22.

39. "The President and the Suffragists."

40. Remarks to a Woman Suffrage Delegation, June 30, 1914, in *PWW*, vol. 31, 227.

41. Jeydel, *Political Women*, 99.

42. "Suffrage Loses in Senate Vote," *New York Times*, March 20, 1914.

43. For discussion of the relationship between suffrage, gender, and race, see Glenda Gilmore, *Gender and Jim Crow: Women and the Politics of White Supremacy in North Carolina, 1896–1920* (Chapel Hill: University of North Carolina Press, 1996); and Marjorie Spruill Wheeler, "The Woman Suffrage Movement in the Inhospitable South," in *Votes for Women! The Woman Suffrage Movement in Tennessee, the South, and the Nation*, ed. Marjorie Spruill Wheeler (Knoxville: University of Tennessee Press, 1995), 25–52.

44. Anne Firor Scott and Andrew MacKay Scott, *One Half the People: The Fight for Woman Suffrage* (Urbana: University of Illinois Press, 1982), 161–63. Scott and Scott list as the "southern" states: Virginia, Alabama, Arkansas, Florida, Georgia, Louisiana, Mississippi, North Carolina, South Carolina, and Texas.

45. Flexner, *Century of Struggle*, 278; Robert Booth Fowler, *Carrie Catt: Feminist Politician* (Boston: Northeastern University Press), 145–49; Lunardini, *From Equal Suffrage to Equal Rights*, 44–45, 77.

46. Margaret M. Finnegan, *Selling Suffrage: Consumer Culture and Votes for Women* (New York: Columbia University Press, 1999).

47. Diary of Colonel Edward House, December 15, 1915, in *PWW*, vol. 35, 360. See, too, Cooper, *Warrior and the Priest*, 210; and Clements, *Presidency of Woodrow Wilson*, 159.

48. Irwin, *Story of Alice Paul and the National Woman's Party*, 109–10, 116–18; "Wilson Hears Pleas of Pros and Antis," *New York Times*, December 15, 1915. According to the *Times*, Wilson shook hands with 1,000 women that day; 200 of them represented the National Association Opposed to Woman Suffrage, while 800 represented members of the National American Woman Suffrage Association, including Alice Paul's Congressional Union, which had organized the motor tour and collected the petition signatures.

49. Irwin, *Story of Alice Paul and the National Woman's Party*, 65; Remarks to a Delegation of Democratic Women, January 6, 1915, in *PWW*, vol. 33, 22.

50. Diary of Nancy Saunders Toy, January 5, 1915, in *PWW*, vol. 33, 21–22.

51. Irwin, *Story of Alice Paul and the National Woman's Party*, 65; Remarks to a Delegation of Democratic Women, January 6, 1915, in *PWW*, vol. 33, 22.

52. Lunardini and Knock, "Woodrow Wilson and Woman Suffrage," 660–61; Arthur Link, *Wilson: Confusions and Crises* (Princeton, N.J.: Princeton University Press, 1965), 1–14.

53. "Wilson Hears Pleas of Pros and Antis," *New York Times*, December 15, 1915. Just weeks after the president voted for woman suffrage in New Jersey, antisuffragists publicly thanked him for continuing to oppose a federal amendment, deftly ignoring the fact that he was now aligned with the principle of female enfranchisement. Six months later, the antisuffragist wife of a colleague of Wilson's wrote him a letter that defined Wilson as an antisuffrage ally as long as he continued to oppose a federal amendment. His noncommittal reply thanked Thompson for her confidence that he would not change his position merely to gain votes. Mary Wilson Thompson to Woodrow Wilson, July 30, 1916, and Woodrow Wilson to Mary Wilson Thompson, August 3, 1916, in *PWW*, vol. 38, 502–4, 518. In her 1939 recollection, "My Story: Of How and Why I Became an Antisuffrage Leader," Josephine Anderson Pearson of Tennessee ignored Wilson's New Jersey vote and charged him with "perfidy" and a "face about" when supported the federal amendment. *Votes for Women!* ed. Wheeler, 225, 241.

54. Woodrow Wilson to Leona Laura Larrabee, September 27, 1916, in ibid., vol. 39, 281.

55. Democratic Party Platform, 1916, Section XX, "Woman Suffrage." For the text of the whole platform, see http://www.presidency.ucsb.edu/showplatforms.php?plat index=D1916.

56. Du Bois, *Harriot Stanton Blatch and the Winning of Woman Suffrage*, 197; Woodrow Wilson to Ellen Duane Davis, August 5, 1916, in *PWW*, vol. 38, 529. Wilson's forces had held off an attempt by the governor of Texas to substitute the plank recommending state enfranchisement of women with a plank simply reaffirming the party's respect for states' rights in suffrage matters. See ibid., 237.

57. John Humphrey Small to Woodrow Wilson, August 2, 1916, in ibid., 513–14; Charles Spalding Thomas Memorandum for the President, August 7, 1916, and Woodrow Wilson to Senator Charles Spalding Thomas, August 8, 1916, in ibid., vol. 39, 4–5, 9.

58. Lunardini, *From Equal Suffrage to Equal Rights*, chap. 6.

59. Republican Party Platform, 1916, "Suffrage." The entire plank read: "The Republican Party, reaffirming its faith in government of the people, by the people, for the people as a measure of justice to one-half the adult people of this country, favors the extension of the suffrage to women, but recognizes the right of each state to settle this question for itself." See http://www.presidency.ucsb.edu/showplatforms.php?plat index=R1916.

Wilson regarded Hughes's support for a federal amendment as a "misinterpretation of his party platform" and an act that revealed the Republican nominee to be a "special pleader" whose willingness to trade party loyalty for votes "is winning a great deal of ridicule and distrust." Woodrow Wilson to Ellen Duane Davis, August 5, 1916, in *PWW*, vol. 38, 529.

60. Lunardini, *From Equal Suffrage to Equal Rights*, 82; Carrie Chapman Catt to Woodrow Wilson, August 7, 1916, in *PWW*, vol. 38, 539–40. This invitation to Wilson to address the NAWSA convention in September handed him an excellent opportunity to align himself with the principle of woman suffrage.

61. Lunardini, *From Equal Suffrage to Equal Rights*, 84; Jeydel, *Political Women*, 98–102.

62. Joseph Tumulty to Woodrow Wilson, July 27, 1916, in *PWW*, vol. 38, 491.

63. "The President and the Suffragists"; Norman Hapgood to Woodrow Wilson, August 28, 1916, in *PWW*, vol. 39, 87.

64. Carrie Catt to WW, August 7, 1916, in ibid., vol. 38, 539–40, Woodrow Wilson to Carrie Catt, August 10, 1916, in ibid., vol. 39, 19–20; "Wilson Pledges His Aid to Women in Fight for Vote," *New York Times*, September 9, 1916; Address in Atlantic City to the National American Woman Suffrage Association, September 8, 1916, in *PWW*, vol. 39, 163.

65. Woodrow Wilson, Address in Atlantic City to the National American Woman Suffrage Association, September 8, 1916, in ibid., 163.

66. Woodrow Wilson, Address in Atlantic City to the National American Woman Suffrage Association, September 8, 1916, in ibid., 161, 163, 164.

67. "Wilson Pledges His Aid to Women in Fight for Vote," *New York Times*, September 9, 1916.

68. Ellen Duane Davis to Woodrow Wilson, August 3, 1916, and Woodrow Wilson to Ellen Duane Davis, August 5, 1916, in *PWW*, vol. 38, 522–23, 529; Woodrow Wilson to Frederic C. Howe, August 23, 1916, in ibid., vol. 39, 78.

69. A Memorandum by Homer S. Cummings, August 7, 1916, in ibid., 6.

70. Cooper, *Warrior and the Priest*, 250.

71. Lunardini, *From Equal Suffrage to Equal Rights*, 101–2.

72. Irwin, *Story of Alice Paul and the National Woman's Party*, 183–86.

73. Alice Paul to Woodrow Wilson, January 1, 1917; Thomas Brahany Memorandum for the President, January 6, 1917; and Woodrow Wilson to Thomas Brahany, January 8, 1917—in *PWW*, vol. 41, 379, 420–21, 423. Irwin, *Story of Alice Paul and the National Woman's Party*, 192, 194.

74. "Suffragists Will Picket the White House," *New York Times*, January 9, 1917.

75. Irwin, *Story of Alice Paul and the National Woman's Party*, 192–95; Du Bois, *Harriot Stanton Blatch and the Winning of Woman Suffrage*, 202; Lunardini, *From Equal Suffrage to Equal Rights*, 104–6.

76. Lunardini, *From Equal Suffrage to Equal Rights*, chap. 7.

77. Fowler, *Carrie Catt*, chapter 9; see 139 on Catt's ejection from the Woman's Peace Party.

78. Carrie Catt to Woodrow Wilson, May 7, 1917, in *PWW*, vol. 43, 237; Wilson responded with gratitude for Catt's "generous attitude" and agreed that this was not "the opportune time to press the claims of our women upon the Congress." Woodrow Wilson to Carrie Catt, May 8, 1917, in ibid., 241.

79. Link, *Wilson: The New Freedom*, 69.

80. Carrie Catt to Woodrow Wilson, May 7, 1917, in *PWW*, vol. 43, 237.

81. Helen Hamilton Gardener to Woodrow Wilson, May 10, 1917, in ibid., 269–70; "The President and the Suffragists," 1209.

82. Woodrow Wilson to Rep. Edward W. Pou, May 14, 1917, in *PWW*, vol. 43, 293.

83. Irwin, *Story of Alice Paul and the National Woman's Party*, 198–226; Lunardini, *From Equal Suffrage to Equal Rights*, 104–15; Edith Bolling Wilson, *My Memoir* (New York: Bobbs-Merrill, 1938), 125.

84. Link, *Woodrow Wilson: A Profile*, "Introduction: In Search of Woodrow Wilson's Personality," xi.

85. Irwin, *Story of Alice Paul and the National Woman's Party*, 198–266; Woodrow Wilson to Dee Richardson, July 25, 1917, in *PWW*, vol. 44, 273. For additional descriptions of the White House pickets, see Doris Stevens, *Jailed for Freedom: American Women Win the Vote*, ed. Carol O'Hare (Troutdale, Ore.: New Sage Press, 1995); Lunardini, *From Equal Suffrage to Equal Rights*, chaps. 7 and 8; Flexner, *Century of Struggle*, chap. 21.

86. Anna Howard Shaw to Alice B. Warren, March 9, 1917, enclosed in letter from Alice B. Warren to Woodrow Wilson, March 13, 1917, in *PWW*, vol. 42, 399–400; Lunardini, *From Equal Suffrage to Equal Rights*, 127; Graham, "Woodrow Wilson, Alice Paul, and the Woman Suffrage Movement," 669–79.

87. Woodrow Wilson to Jessie Wilson Sayre, June 22, 1917, in *PWW*, vol. 43, 560. Wilson commented to his prosuffrage daughter, Jessie, that "the representatives of the Woman's Party here at the gates of the White House . . . certainly seem bent upon making their cause as obnoxious as possible." Writing at the end of five months of violence against the picketers, and ignoring the fact that Paul's Congressional Union had become the National Woman's Party in 1916, Creel advised the president to refuse a request to see "the militant suffragettes," insisting that "Mrs. Catt and Dr. Shaw speak for equal suffrage in the nation, and the Congressional Union is without standing and deserves no recognition." George Creel to Woodrow Wilson, November 9, 1917, in ibid., vol. 45, 551.

88. Louis Brownlow, *A Passion for Anonymity: The Autobiography of Louis Brownlow, Second Half* (Chicago: University of Chicago Press, 1958), 78.

89. Alison Low Turnbull Hopkins to Woodrow Wilson, July 20, 1917, in *PWW*, XLIV, 235. Hopkins, the wife of J. A. H. Hopkins, a Progressive Party committeeman from Morristown, N.J., wrote a sharp letter to Wilson. Noting that the presidential pardon was unaccompanied by any explanation, Hopkins said she was left with two possible explanations: Either the president agreed that no laws had been violated or he was seeking to save himself "the embarrassment of an acute and distressing political situation." Because Hopkins had no desire to save Wilson any embarrassment and believed it her right to challenge the police powers "despotically" wielded against her, Hopkins chose to decline the pardon. Her defiant stance and tone are representative of picketers who confronted Wilson in 1917.

90. See, e.g., *Washington Post*, July 15, 18, 19, and 20, 1917; and *New York Times*, July 17 and 19, 1917. Gilson Gardner Memorandum to Woodrow Wilson, July 17, 1917, in *PWW*, vol. 44, 201–2. Gardner was the Washington correspondent for the Scripps newspapers and his wife was among the suffragists arrested and put in

Occoquan prison. Lunardini, *From Equal Suffrage to Equal Rights*, 197–99, documents the regular reports on prison conditions appearing in *The Suffragist*.

91. Diary of Colonel Edward House, July 26, 1917, in *PWW*, vol. 44, 291–92; Dudley Field Malone to Woodrow Wilson, September 7, 1917, in ibid., vol. 45, 167–69; Diary of Colonel Edward House, September 10, 1917, in ibid., 185. "Malone Resigns as Collector to Aid Suffrage: Dissatisfied with Treatment by Administration of White House Pickets," *New York Times*, September 8, 1917.

92. Charles A. Lindbergh to Woodrow Wilson, August 27, 1917, in *PWW*, vol. 45, 108–16; Woodrow Wilson to Newton Baker, September 1, 1917, in ibid., 108.

93. Woodrow Wilson to William Gwynn Gardiner, November 10, 1917, in ibid., 562.

94. William Gwynn Gardiner to Woodrow Wilson, November 9, 1917, in ibid., 559–61. Three days after the receipt of Gardiner's report, Wilson advised Joseph Tumulty on how to respond to a set of suffrage resolutions from a committee representing 1,000 New York working women, which included claims to mistreatment at Occoquan. Wilson said, "I think it would be worthwhile adding that the treatment of the women picketers has been grossly exaggerated and misrepresented." Woodrow Wilson to Joseph Tumulty, November 13, 1917, in ibid., vol. 46, 40.

95. Irwin, *Story of Alice Paul and the National Woman's Party*, 291.

96. Helen Hamilton Gardener to Thomas W. Brahany, July 26, 1917, in *PWW*, vol. 44, 284–85.

97. Woodrow Wilson to Carrie Catt, October 13, 1917, and Carrie Catt to Woodrow Wilson, October 16, 1917, in ibid., vol. 45, 372, 391.

98. Helen Gardener on behalf of Carrie Catt, July 19, 1917, in ibid., vol. 44, 214–15; "Wilson Unshaken in Suffrage View," *New York Times*, November 10, 1917.

99. Woodrow Wilson, Remarks to a Group of Suffragists, in ibid., vol. 52, 190.

100. Elizabeth Merrill Bass, January 8, 1918, in ibid., vol. 46, 542.

101. "Wilson Backs Amendment for Woman Suffrage," *New York Times*, January 10, 1918. Wilson Statement, January 9, 1918, in *PWW*, vol. 46, 545.

102. Carrie Catt to Woodrow Wilson, September 29, 1918, in ibid., vol. 52, 155–57.

103. Woodrow Wilson, An Address to the Senate, September 30, 1918, in ibid., 158–60.

104. Carrie Chapman Catt, *Woman Suffrage and Politics: The Inner Story of the Suffrage Movement* (New York: Charles Scribner's Sons, 1923), 325–26; Scott and Scott, *One Half the People*, 161–63; "Suffrage Beaten by the Senate," *New York Times*, October 2, 1918. In the *New York Times* article, Senator John S. Williams was quoted as saying, "I love the President of the United States more than any other man here in this Senate," but Williams could not support a measure that would enfranchise "Chinese, Japanese, and nigger women."

105. Eileen McDonagh, "Issues and Constituencies in the Progressive Era: House Roll Call Voting on the Nineteenth Amendment, 1913–1919," *Journal of Politics* 51 (February 1989): 119–36. McDonagh found that the single best predictor of a member of Congress's

vote on woman suffrage was not party or region or issues such as prohibition or immigration but whether women had already been enfranchised in his state. Ironically, insistence on a state approach and NAWSA's determined campaigns to win state referenda proved to be more decisive than Woodrow Wilson's endorsement in gaining passage of the federal amendment in the House of Representatives if not in the Senate.

Part III
The Seeds of Wilsonianism

6. Revolution, War, and Expansion: Woodrow Wilson in Latin America

Mark T. Gilderhus

Francisco Madero's revolt in 1910 against President Porfirio Díaz in Mexico signaled the onset of a tumultuous age. During the second decade of the twentieth century, great revolutions in Mexico, China, and Russia overturned established orders and elicited violence and instability as consequences running parallel with those of World War I. In each instance, the effects challenged prevailing beliefs and institutions. In response, President Woodrow Wilson articulated an ambitious vision of a new world system, the workability of which depended on two stipulations. The Great Powers must cooperate in defense of stability and peace, and the United States should accept a larger role in international affairs than ever before.

For Latin America, meanwhile, an assortment of significant changes altered traditional relations with the outside world. As a consequence of the Great War, the United States displaced the European powers as the dominant economic presence. In efforts to consolidate the U.S. advantage, Wilson experimented with various methods of imperial control, including coercion in the form of military intervention and cajolery based on notions of Pan Americanism. His tactical shifts implied some innovations but also served the traditional strategic goals of reducing European influence in the Western Hemisphere, securing access to markets and raw materials, and maintaining the peace when possible.

Latin America and the Outside World

For fifty years after gaining their independence in the 1820s, the Latin American countries failed to count for much in the international arena. Self-

This chapter has been adapted and updated from "Revolution, War, and Expansion, 1913–1929," chapter 2 in *The Second Century: U.S.–Latin American Relations since 1889*, by Mark T. Gilderhus (Wilmington, Del.: SR Books, 2000).

contained and self-absorbed, they experienced the disorganizing effects of political turmoil, economic stagnation, and complex diplomatic quarrels over boundaries and territories. Such conditions became less pervasive following the establishment of more stable, oligarchic, and usually authoritarian regimes in many of the region's countries. During the 1870s and after, such governments endorsed an export-led model of economic development. Seeking trade and investment, Latin American leaders opened their countries to foreign goods and capital and embraced the Europeans in a kind of neocolonial economic relationship. Unlike the colonized regions of Asia and Africa, Latin America required no formal devices of imperial subjugation. Performing much like colonies, Latin Americans produced raw materials and agricultural commodities for the industrializing Europeans in return for capital and finished goods, thereby obtaining integration into the world market system.[1]

Among the largest countries, Argentina featured livestock and cereal products for export, especially wheat, maize, beef, wool, hides, and linseed. Between 1875 and 1914, Argentine exports expanded impressively at an estimated rate of 5 percent a year. By 1914, the 7.8 million Argentines relied more heavily on overseas sales than any other Latin Americans and enjoyed the region's highest living standards. Their capital, Buenos Aires, stood out as a testimony. Affluent, cosmopolitan, and European in appearance, style, and taste, the city symbolized Argentina as the embodiment of wealth, culture, and promise for the future.

Exports similarly served Brazil. A functioning monarchy until 1889–90, then a republic after a virtually bloodless revolution, Brazil relied upon coffee as the mainstay of profit. Indeed, in the years before World War I, coffee often accounted for more than half its overseas sales and made its economy vulnerable to cyclical tendencies within the world market. Periodic, often abrupt contractions in demand led to oversupply and low prices. In response, Brazilians experimented with "valorization" plans to restore higher prices by holding coffee off the market. Brazil, a nation of 25 million people in 1914, also sold tobacco and cotton in foreign markets and for a time experienced a rubber boom in the Amazon River Basin. Overall, the export trade affected different parts of this vast country unevenly, with most of the benefits accruing to the coastal regions and the capital city, Rio de Janeiro.

Chile, inhabited by 3 million people in 1914, relied on copper exports. At the same time, the country avoided some of the dangers of monoculture—that is, undue dependence on one product—by promoting the sale of wheat, wool, and nitrates. The last item, especially important in balancing shifting demands for copper, counted heavily in trade with Europe and the United States. During the early twentieth century, the proceeds from nitrate sales totaled around 14 percent of the nation's gross national product and provided the government in Santiago with more than 50 percent of its operating revenues.[2]

In Mexico, too, a country of 12 million people in 1910, economic dependencies characterized links with the outside world. During the so-called Porfiriato, the era dominated by President Porfirio Díaz from 1876 to 1910, foreign investments centered on such crucial sectors as transportation, mining, and petroleum. Meanwhile, growth patterns typified Mexican overseas sales of silver, gold, rubber, hides, coffee, minerals, vegetables, and oil. The oil industry, controlled by British and U.S. companies, assumed special significance during the first decade of the twentieth century. In Mexico as elsewhere, bad effects occurred when declining demand within the world economy reduced export prices and income from exports.[3]

In the other countries of Central and South America, export economies typically featured monocultures. Colombia depended upon coffee, as did Venezuela, until the petroleum boom beginning in the 1920s. In Central America and the Caribbean, tropical agriculture produced bananas, coffee, sugar, and tobacco. Everywhere in Latin America, the export trade rendered the participants susceptible to downward shifts in demand and price, underscoring unmistakably the risks of involvement in an unstable international economic environment.[4]

Financial relations, another form of dependency, also entailed a mixture of advantages and risks. In the view of many historians, "the era of high capitalism" before World War I constituted "a golden age for foreign investment in Latin America." Britain was the largest investor, followed by Germany and France. Until the 1890s, small-scale U.S. investments centered on rails and mines in Mexico, sugar plantations in Cuba, and a few railroads and landed estates in Central America. During the early years of the twentieth century, U.S. investors also acquired a stake in Chilean and Peruvian mining. By 1914, some 87 percent of direct U.S. overseas investments were concentrated in Mexico, Cuba, Chile, and Peru. From about $300 million in 1897, the total increased to almost $1.6 billion in 1914, including direct investments of nearly $1.3 billion.

European investments, estimated at $7 billion in 1914, differed in some respects. More dispersed, they affected every country. In addition, a larger portion appeared in the construction of infrastructure, such as railways, ports, power companies, and utilities. Also, about a third went into government bonds. British investments of nearly $5 billion touched every country but had the greatest significance in Argentina, where they amounted to a third of the total foreign investment; in Brazil, they accounted for about a quarter; and in Mexico, about a fifth. French and German investors favored the same three countries.

These estimates suggest orders of magnitude and degrees of integration into the world system. The transfer of investment capital into regions without financial resources advanced the European interest in gaining access to Latin American markets and raw materials. The process also enabled Latin Americans to respond to overseas demands with the construction of necessary facilities— railroads, shipping services, and communication systems—without which the region's producers could not have supplied consumers. Consequently, more efficient modern technologies came into existence in the export sectors, including mining, ranching, farming, and milling, and also complex networks of economic dependency. Throughout Latin America, foreign-owned mercantile houses played crucial roles in organizing the export and import trade, and foreign-owned banks provided the financial means.[5]

Some modern scholars, especially proponents of dependency theory, depict these arrangements as economically debilitating, more attuned to foreign needs than to Latin American interests, amounting actually to a form of exploitation. Not all contemporaries would have agreed with this assessment. According to the historian William Glade, most members of the Latin American elites at the end of the nineteenth century exhibited enthusiasm for "the benefits of what they perceived to be modernization" through engagement with the world economy. Nonetheless, exceptions stood out. In Mexico after 1910, revolutionary leaders erected barriers to safeguard their country against the influence of foreign economic power.[6]

Mexico and Other Matters

The role of foreign interests in Mexico took on critical importance during the revolutionary era. Indeed, according to one view, the integration of Mexico into the world economy contributed to political destabilization in 1910 by making the country more vulnerable to cyclical tendencies and economic downturns.[7] The revolution, sometimes understood in the present day historiography more as a struggle among rival elites than as a popular uprising by the people, successfully ousted the dictator Porfirio Díaz in 1911 and then assumed many implications. During the ensuing factional strife, foreign interests, economic and other, came under threat both from the ongoing violence and the emerging processes of reconstruction. The Constitution of 1917 specifically introduced new dangers by incorporating the principles of nationalization and expropriation, thereby in theory providing Mexican leaders with new instruments of control over the resources of their nation.[8]

On the basis of a political call for free elections and no-boss rule, the revolt against Díaz mobilized a broad but unstable constituency, which subsequently was incapable of sustaining President Francisco Madero's reformist regime. A series of insurrections culminated in a military takeover on February 19, 1913, in the course of which assassins killed Madero. General Victoriano Huerta, the army chief of staff and a principal instigator, then sought to impose order by authoritarian means and provoked an uprising among dissidents in the northern states. Led by Venustiano Carranza, the governor of Coahuila, the so-called Constitutionalists denounced Huerta as a usurper and demanded his removal from power.[9]

Shocked by these events, Woodrow Wilson, the new president of the United States, reacted with moralistic righteousness and committed determination. He had been a university professor of political science and had served as the president of Princeton University and as a one-term governor of New Jersey. As a scholar and a devout Presbyterian—indeed, the son of a clergyman—he preferred the high moral ground, prized the constraints of constitutional provision, and regarded Huerta's methods while seizing power as illegitimate and unacceptable. Unlike the leaders of Britain and the other European powers, he withheld diplomatic recognition from Huerta's regime and tried to encourage mediation as the means to establish a legal government.[10] He wanted Huerta to stand aside, and when Huerta refused, Wilson resorted to military intervention.

Meanwhile, U.S. secretary of state William Jennings Bryan, a Democrat from Nebraska and a three-time loser as a presidential candidate, launched his own initiatives. Though lacking experience in foreign affairs, he had high ambitions, some of them a bit unconventional. As a peace advocate, he urged the negotiation of "cooling off" treaties with every country in the world. These conciliation agreements required a nonpartisan investigation of the causes of a dispute before a resort to war. Most Latin American governments consented, except Mexico, still unrecognized under Huerta, and Colombia, still aggrieved over the loss of Panama. Bryan also envisioned a reduction of Latin American financial dependence on European bankers. He reasoned that cheap loans from the U.S government would permit "our country" to acquire "such an increased influence . . . that we could prevent revolution, promote education, and advance stable and just governments." His projects stirred some interest within the administration, but Wilson, unconvinced, preferred to rely on conventional means and private bankers.[11]

Another issue, the unilateral practice of military intervention by the United States in Latin America, also pressed upon the new administration. A number of critics raised questions about the exercise of an international police power while lambasting Theodore Roosevelt's Corollary to the Monroe Doctrine as a hegemonic pretension. According to them, TR had inverted Monroe's original intent by taking a prohibition on European intervention in the Western Hemisphere and making it a justification for U.S. intervention. Other observers wanted to apply a multilateral definition so that joint measures with other nations could, if necessary, provide the means for safeguarding peace and order. A leader among them, Hiram Bingham of Yale University, the discoverer of the Inca ruins at Machu Picchu in Peru, described the Monroe Doctrine as "an obsolete shibboleth." For him, it typified paternalistic condescension toward Latin Americans. As a better approach, he proposed some kind of collective action. In the event of trouble, the United States should call together "a family meeting" among Western Hemisphere nations and "see what if anything needs to be done."[12]

These ideas won support from Progressive Era reformers and radicals, including leaders in the peace movement, the labor unions, the churches, the universities, and among the international lawyers. For many, the development of a collective security system ranked high as a guarantee of national sovereignty. Similarly, Wilson, a committed reformer with messianic instincts, favored exalted purposes among nations by seeking to advance mutual ideals and interests. He was sometimes described as "a liberal-capitalist internationalist," and he subsequently aspired to the creation of a world system based on a League of Nations for the purpose of defending and extending representative democracy and economic capitalism all around the globe. While presuming universal applicability, the president hoped to serve humankind by extending U.S. values and institutions everywhere.[13]

Though it was sometimes flawed by arrogance and delusion, Wilson's emerging vision of international order drew inspiration from his experiences with Latin America. On March 11, 1913, in his first statement on foreign affairs, he set forth basic principles and expectations; central among them was his profound belief that mutual respect for national rights and obligations could achieve international harmony. To such ends, he invited "the friendship and . . . the confidence of our sister republics" and "the most cordial understanding and cooperation" in relations with them. With General Huerta presumably in mind, Wilson also insisted on the rule of law. Accordingly, he affirmed his opposition to "those who seek to seize the power of government to advance their own personal interests or ambition" and his support for "those who act in the interest of peace and honor, who protect private rights, and respect the restraint of constitutional provision."

In Mexico, such pronouncements appeared confusing and contradictory. On October 10, 1913, Huerta dashed the U.S. hope for mediation by dissolving the Chamber of Deputies and declaring himself a candidate for the presidency. On the following day, Sir Lionel Carden, the new British minister, presented his credentials at the Foreign Office in Mexico City. His arrival impressed U.S. leaders as a conscious and deliberate affront. To them, Huerta now appeared both as an illicit tyrant and a creature of British imperialism.

Wilson discussed this issue on October 27, 1913, in his celebrated address before the Southern Commercial Congress at Mobile. Stating his concern over European economic domination in Latin America, he warned that foreign concessions and special privileges threatened self-determination; Mexico, in his view, already had fallen victim. Nevertheless, he promised "emancipation" if Latin Americans would assist in the promotion of "true constitutional liberty" through the world. As a pledge of good faith, he affirmed, the United States "never again" would seek "one additional foot of territory by conquest."

Wilson's Mobile address, which has sometimes been regarded by historians as a promise of nonintervention, actually anticipated broader U.S. involvement in Latin American affairs. In what verged on a declaration of economic war, Wilson wanted Latin American support in rolling back European presences. Colonel Edward M. House, Wilson's trusted friend and adviser, understood the intent. For him, the speech established "a new interpretation of the Monroe Doctrine." For almost a century, the United States had tried "to keep Europe from securing political control of any state in the Western Hemisphere." Now the Wilson administration had taken a position that it is "just as reprehensible to permit foreign states to secure financial control of those weak unfortunate republics." Similarly, John Lind, a special diplomatic emissary to Mexico, expressed his belief that Huerta's continuation in power would make the country "a European annex, industrially, financially, politically."

Mounting suspicions had the effect of producing a chill in U.S. relations with Britain. Although British leaders disparaged Wilson's claim as a consequence of bewildered hypocrisy, the historian Friedrich Katz credits the president with a correct understanding of British aims. As Katz shows, the British government consistently opposed revolutionary factions and supported counter-revolutionary groups. Such positions, in his view, accurately reflected British concerns for economic stakes and petroleum interests.[14]

The Wilson administration, meanwhile, adopted other ambitious plans. To advance various forms of political and economic integration, the leaders focused attention on Argentina, Brazil, and Chile—the so-called ABC countries. As the most populous and influential nations in South America, the ABC countries also contained prospective customers. Close relations already existed in relations with Brazil. As a matter of conscious design, Brazilians had forged "an unwritten alliance" with the United States early in the twentieth century through the policies of Foreign Minister José Maria da Silva Paranhos, also known as the Baron de Rio Branco. He wanted to enlist the United States as a trading partner and political counterweight against Argentina. For the United States, Brazil's diplomatic status ranked high. Before Wilson, only Brazil had qualified for an ambassadorial appointment; the other South American countries received ministers, a lesser diplomatic designation. Seeking more cordial ties during the summer of 1914, the Wilson administration established diplomatic parity by exchanging ambassadors with Argentina and Chile.[15]

Because the Wilson administration was troubled by trade deficits in South America, it also promoted commercial expansion. The Panama Canal, scheduled for completion soon, amplified high expectations. U.S. leaders intended to take advantage by renovating the Merchant Marines and developing regular steamship routes to South America. The Federal Reserve Act of December 1913 rectified another shortcoming by authorizing national banks of the United States to create branches in other countries. The establishment in Latin America of such facilities would free U.S. commerce from dependencies on British banking institutions.[16] But then new difficulties resulted in obstruction.

An incident at Tampico, a Mexican port city on the Caribbean coast, set the trouble in motion. On April 9, 1914, General Huerta's troops arrested some U.S. sailors who had wandered into a restricted zone. In response, U.S. admiral Henry T. Mayo demanded a formal apology and obtained President Wilson's support. At the same time, another problem impended. The *Ypiranga*, a German commercial vessel carrying weapons for Huerta, would soon arrive in Veracruz, the principal eastern port. Adjuring diplomacy, Wilson obtained authorization from Congress to force a showdown. On April 21, 1914, he seized Veracruz by sending in U.S. Marines. In this way, he intended to block the arms shipment, cut off customs revenues to Huerta, and safeguard petroleum installations near the two cities. He erred by anticipating only light resistance. The Veracruz defenders lost over two hundred soldiers, and war subsequently threatened. Not only Huerta but also his enemies, the Constitutionalists, condemned the invasion as an unacceptable violation of Mexican sovereignty.

At the very least, this episode revealed limitations in Wilson's understanding of harmony among nations. Paradoxically, he conceived of the intervention as a defense of Mexican self-determination against an illegitimate tyrant backed by unscrupulous British imperialists, but in doing so he underestimated Mexican nationalist reactions. Fortunately, his courtship of Argentina, Brazil, and Chile paid off when their mediation offer enabled him to avoid an unwanted conflict. An international conference at Niagara Falls, Canada, facilitated face-saving devices, achieved cosmetic effects, and provided a way out of war. In Mexico, meanwhile, General Alvaro Obregón's marched into the capital city during the summer of 1914 and forced Huerta into exile.[17]

The leaders in the Wilson administration subsequently rejoiced that multilateral measures had assisted in keeping the peace. Colonel House indulged in high praise, comparing the actions of the ABC countries with the efforts of friends and neighbors who in times of crisis banded together to fight house fires. Similarly, Robert Lansing, the counselor of the State Department, called for efforts to build on this achievement. In a June 1914 memorandum, "The Present Nature and Extent of the Monroe Doctrine and Its Need for Restatement," he presented a case against unilateral intervention by the United States and in favor of multilateral approaches to advance "fraternal responsibility" with Latin Americans.

Much like Bryan earlier, Lansing also worried about European encroachments on the Western Hemisphere by means of loans and investments. Specifically, he warned against the "European acquisition of political control through the agency of financial control over an American republic." Similarly concerned, Colonel House addressed the same issue during a European visit in July 1914. In conversations with British, French, and German leaders, he inquired whether they would join with the United States in an agreement to reduce the costs of international borrowing. At the same time in his private diary, he expressed misgivings, accusing the Europeans of subverting weak, debt-ridden Latin American states through demands for "concessions" and "usurious interest." He wanted to find a better way, but his timing was all wrong. During the summer of 1914, the Great Powers of Europe embarked upon a world war.[18]

Pan American Initiatives

The consequences of the Great War extended into most inhabited regions of the globe. In the Western Hemisphere, the initial impact injured Latin American economies by obstructing the flow of capital and goods. In response, the United

States assumed a larger role as the prime purchaser of raw materials and the main supplier of finished products. During the three years from July 1, 1914, and June 30, 1917, trade between the United States and Latin America increased by more than 100 percent. In contrast, ambitious U.S. political initiatives accomplished much less. For the Wilson administration, the war occasioned both opportunities and rebuffs.

As a neutral country until the spring of 1917, the United States responded to the war by attempting to insulate the Western Hemisphere against it. As part of this endeavor, U.S. leaders also courted Latin American governments, seeking more intimate political and economic ties. The opening of the Panama Canal in August 1914 served as a powerful symbol. This grand event, knitting the Western Hemisphere more closely together, reduced the distance from Colón on the Atlantic to Balboa on the Pacific from 10,500 nautical miles, the distance around South America, to 45, the actual length of the new passage. The Western Hemisphere had become a much smaller place.[19]

The prospect of commercial opportunity encouraged a variety of promotional activities sponsored by the Wilson administration. On September 10, 1914, a Latin American Trade Conference assembled in Washington, at the invitation of Secretary of State William Jennings Bryan and Secretary of Commerce William C. Redfield. Delegates from the U.S. Chamber of Commerce, the Southern Commercial Congress, and the National Foreign Trade Council enthusiastically called for improved transportation and banking facilities and also for more effective sales techniques, conforming more closely to Latin American tastes and preferences. Elsewhere across the United States, the prospect of commercial expansion into Latin America stimulated growing interest among local chambers of commerce, boards of trade, and business associations. Even President Wilson became a booster. In his annual message to Congress on December 8, 1914, he urged the United States "as never before, to serve itself and to serve mankind with its resources, its forces of production, and its means of distribution."

Wilson also experimented with peacekeeping devices. Inspired mainly by Colonel House, these efforts eventuated in a proposed Pan American Treaty that, among other things, called for a regional collective security system, featuring compulsory arbitration and a multilateral definition of the Monroe Doctrine. House initiated the discussions late in November 1914 by urging Wilson to pay "greater attention" to issues in foreign affairs. Specifically, he wanted the president to devise "a constructive international policy" demonstrating "that friendship, justice, and kindliness were more potent than the mailed fist." House criticized the legacies of unilateral intervention. By "wielding the 'big stick' and dominating the two Continents," he averred, the United States had "lost the friendship and commerce of South and Central America and the European countries had profited from it." A better approach could have more desirable consequences by bringing "North and South American together in a closer union" and welding together . . . the two western continents."

Three weeks later, in December 1914, House again raised the issue, this time exhorting Wilson "to play a great and beneficent part in the European tragedy." While declaring that Wilson could do something at once, namely, establish a "model" for peace based on "a policy that would weld the Western Hemisphere together," House sketched out a draft proposal for collective security arrangements to guarantee territorial integrity, political independence, and republican forms of government. Much impressed, Wilson authorized House to engage the ambassadors of Argentina, Brazil, and Chile in conversations.

The discussions elicited favorable responses from Rómulo S. Naón of Argentina and Domicio de Gama of Brazil but not from Eduardo Suárez Mújica of Chile. For him, the implementation of such arrangements suggested the possibility of embarrassment over Tacna and Arica, the nitrate-rich provinces taken from Peru in the War of the Pacific. According to the Treaty of Ancón in 1884, a plebiscite should decide the question of ownership, but none had ever taken place. Chileans also described the proposed commitment in defense of republican institutions as a limitation on national sovereignty and possibly an invitation for U.S. intervention. Undeterred, House pressed on, including in later drafts other requirements for arbitration of territorial and boundary disputes and endorsing Bryan's "cooling off" formula.[20]

Meanwhile, a new civil war in Mexico ravaged the country. After defeating Huerta, the victorious Constitutionalists dissolved into feuding factions, pitting Carranza and his ally Alvaro Obregón against Francisco Villa and Emiliano Zapata. Wilson again sought peace through reconciliation but without much positive effect. House proposed joint action with the ABC countries as the best solution. He also rejoiced when Secretary of State Bryan resigned his position in June 1915 as a protest against Wilson's handling of the *Lusitania* crisis. In House's view, Bryan, a fool and a bungler, had messed up wise and workable policies. In contrast, his successor, Lansing, the former State Department counselor and a renowned international lawyer, shared some of House's convictions and appeared more manageable. Lansing, too, believed that German plots endangered Mexico, Haiti, Santo Domingo, and other Latin American countries. As a counter to German designs, he favored "a Pan American doctrine" and "friendly relations with Mexico." To this end, he advocated the diplomatic recognition of Carranza, presumably "the stronger" contender among the rivals.

Beginning in August 1915, Secretary of State Lansing orchestrated moves in conjunction with six countries. Working in tandem with diplomatic representatives from Argentina, Brazil, Chile, Bolivia, Guatemala, and Uruguay, Lansing exhorted the various Mexican factions to settle their differences. In response, Villa and Zapata took conciliatory positions allowing for a compromise, but Carranza intransigently would not bend. He insisted that only his government possessed the attributes of sovereignty. Ultimately, Lansing and the others arrived at the same conclusion. On October 9, 1915, they extended diplomatic recognition on a de facto basis, in effect accepting Carranza's regime as stable and functioning.

Wilson construed the decision as a triumph of high principle. For him, Mexico's right to self-determination had survived the test. In a report to Congress on December 7, 1915, he claimed that "her [Mexico's] fortunes are in her own hands." He also applauded the good effects of his Pan American policy as vindication of international cooperation, having obtained "a full and honorable association as of partners." To build on this achievement, he publicly endorsed the proposed Pan American Treaty on January 6, 1916, at the Second Pan American Scientific Conference in Washington. If the others would ratify it, then the nations of the Western Hemisphere could uphold "the principles of absolute political equality among the states" and "the solid, eternal foundations of justice and humanity."[21]

Such expectations notwithstanding, Wilson's policies in the Western Hemisphere never really achieved much coherence. Instead, they abounded with inconsistency and contradictions as his subsequent interventions in the Caribbean confirmed. In a phrase, Wilson had difficulty reconciling his commitment to self-determination with other U.S. interests in promoting trade, security, and stability. In 1915, political turmoil caused violence and disorder in Haiti. Similarly in 1916, the Dominican Republic succumbed to riot and revolution. In each instance, the Wilson administration responded by sending in military forces. U.S. leaders justified such measures on grounds of wartime exigency, claiming that threats of German subversion and defense of the Panama Canal required them. Moreover, in each instance, derogatory racial stereotypes and condescending cultural assumptions provided additional incentives by disparaging the alleged incapacity of the inhabitants, especially those of African descent, to govern themselves. Once the Marines moved in, U.S. occupation authorities took charge of government functions and finances. In response,

Dominican and Haitian resistance movements precipitated hard-fought guerrilla conflicts. These so-called banana wars featured small-scale but brutal violence in which native contingents waged something like "wars of national liberation" against the U.S occupiers.[22]

Meanwhile, the Wilson administration launched other programs designed to win over Latin Americans. On May 24, 1915, the first Pan American Financial Conference in Washington attracted delegates from eighteen Latin American countries. The main organizer, Secretary of the Treasury William Gibbs McAdoo, focused attention on trade and finance. Specifically, he called for consideration of the principal economic problems emanating from the Great War. He anticipated that the United States would have to replace the Europeans as the main supplier of goods and capital. To coordinate the pursuit of practical solutions, those in attendance created a body known as the International High Commission. It consisted of finance ministers and other specialists from each country who in the future would meet periodically to issue advisements and recommendations, most of which never happened.

For leaders in the Wilson administration, commercial statistics bolstered high spirits. Between August 1914 and August 1915, U.S. trade with the region reached $3 billion, at the time the largest amount ever in a single year. Indeed, the United States surpassed Britain as the world leader in trade with the region. In South America, U.S. exports rose from $38.7 million during the first six months of 1914 to $60.6 million during the first six months of 1915, while South American sales in the United States expanded from $105.5 million to $153 million. Although these figures still marked an undesirable deficit in the balance of payments, they failed to dissipate the optimism over long-term prospects. The National City Bank of New York opened branches in Montevideo, Buenos Aires, Rio de Janeiro, Santos, São Paulo, and Havana; the Caribbean and Southern Steamship Company initiated regular voyages to Argentina and Brazil, and President Wilson accepted a commitment to build a modern merchant marine capable of carrying increased trade.

Though encouraged by such gains in Latin America, U.S. leaders still worried about resumed European competition after the war. They expected that especially Britain and France would not readily submit to a permanently weakened economic position in the New World. Indeed, British and French behavior at the Paris Economic Conference in June 1916 intensified such concerns, when the Allies established plans to punish their enemies, mainly the Germans, through the establishment of a mercantilist, state-directed system. The main features included a variety of restrictive devices such as trade preferences, state subsidies, government protection of foreign markets, pooling agreements, and cooperative purchases of raw materials. In 1915, the Central Powers had devised their own Mitteleuropa plan, intended to promote economic consolidation through the exclusion of the British, the French, and the Russians. To officials in the Wilson administration, all of this portended ill, and they anticipated the possibility of drastic steps. Secretary of State Lansing, for example, reasoned that "the best way to fight combination is by combination." He wanted "some definite plan to meet the proposed measures of the allies" in conjunction with the Latin Americans. Similarly, Henry P. Fletcher, then U.S. ambassador to Chile and later to Mexico, advised collective arrangements with the ABC countries to hold "our market position in South America." Somewhat fantastically, he also suggested the establishment of "an American economic League for mutual protection."[23]

Meanwhile, mounting political difficulties destroyed the negotiations over Wilson's proposed Pan American treaty. At first, Chilean opposition accounted for delays. Later, the U.S. punitive expedition into Mexico in 1916 ruined the plan completely by calling Wilson's good faith into question. Villa precipitated the crisis on March 9, 1916, by attacking the border town of Columbus, New Mexico, probably in an effort to demonstrate Carranza's incapacity to safeguard the international frontier. In response, the Wilson administration sent in military forces commanded by General John J. Pershing. By insisting on the right of "hot pursuit," Wilson created an impasse. Carranza, for his own political reasons, could not sanction the presence of U.S soldiers in his country and wanted them out as soon as possible; Wilson, in turn, insisted upon guarantees against future border violations. Subsequent armed clashes between Mexican and U.S. troops near the northern towns of Parral and Carrizal caused more trouble, even a likelihood of war. Argentina's offer of mediation presented the Wilson administration with a dilemma bearing directly on the president's credibility in the rest of Latin America. Lansing understood the issue and dreaded the prospect of a full-scale intervention in Mexico. Any such action would have "a very bad effect on our Pan-American program." Indeed, all of Latin America would regard it as "extremely distasteful." Yet border security also had importance, especially in 1916, a presidential election year. Even suggestions of weakness along the border could demolish Wilson as a viable candidate.[24]

Thus constrained by political imperatives, U.S. leaders spurned the Argentine offer and kept the punitive expedition in Mexico. At the same time, they sought direct negotiations. In this way, the Wilson administration retained a free hand but simultaneously wrecked the Pan American part. During the summer and fall of 1916, while the United States maintained the pressure by refusing to withdraw and insisting upon Carranza's responsibility for border defense, a joint Mexican-American commission sought solutions. The United States also tried to broaden the scope by including discussions of foreign property rights in Mexico, an issue with growing importance during the latter part of 1916 during the proceedings of the Mexican Constitutional Convention.

This assembly promulgated the Mexican Constitution of 1917 on February 5 and sanctioned radical provisions. From the U.S. viewpoint, article 27 of the Constitution became an object of special concern. It allowed for the expropriation of privately owned property and for the nationalization of mineral resources. To Mexican leaders, these claims affirmed the prerogatives of national sovereignty and permitted no complaint from other countries through the agencies of international diplomacy. Among outraged U.S. critics, this expression of hyperinflated nationalism aroused fears over the sanctity of foreign property rights in Mexico, and in response U.S. property holders demanded protection from their government. Unable to reconcile competing interests, Wilson simply withdrew the punitive force on February 5, 1917—coincidentally, the same day the Constitution took effect.[25] Soon afterward, the United States became a participant in World War I.

Waging War, Making Peace

In 1917–18, the Wilson administration entered World War I, cultivated cordial connections with Latin Americans, and envisioned an independent role in shaping the postwar world. As a safeguard against subsequent European competition, U.S. leaders still advocated Pan American solidarity but elicited centrifugal tendencies. Notably, Mexico and Argentina espoused Pan Hispanic alternatives, calling for Latin American unity against the United States, while Brazil remained the centerpiece of Wilson's policy in South America.

The German resumption of unrestricted submarine warfare on February 1, 1917, precipitated the U.S. entry into World War I. Seeking a quick decision through decisive boldness, German leaders revoked the *Sussex* pledge of May 1916, making Allied merchant ships and passenger liners once again the objects of attack and endangering vessels in the war zone around the British Isles. For the Germans, loans from U.S. banks to the Allies already had created an informal alliance, and they gambled on a British collapse before an American military presence could make a difference. Hoping to force the Germans to reconsider, Wilson severed diplomatic relations on February 3, 1917.

The German U-Boat offensive compelled Latin American governments to decide whether to follow the U.S. lead. The first reactions predictably affirmed support from Cuba, Panama, Haiti, Nicaragua, and Brazil. Chile, in contrast, wanted no trouble with any of the belligerents, while Mexico and Argentina remained aloof as neutrals. Indeed, the Argentines under President Hipólito Yrigoyen endorsed a call for ending the war through neutral mediation. The Wilson administration responded with expressions of suspicion about German intrigue in each country.

Though probably inflated, U.S. apprehensions over German activities in Latin America had some basis in fact. In the summer of 1915, German agents had supported General Huerta's bid to regain power in Mexico. Though frustrated by U.S. Department of Justice agents who arrested the deposed dictator as he moved toward the border, the scheme implied a German interest in diverting the United States from Europe by provoking trouble with Mexico. For similar reasons, Villa's raid on Columbus, New Mexico, encouraged unproven but much-discussed allegations of German incitement. For Germany, Foreign Minister Arthur Zimmermann's clandestine courtship of Carranza resulted in a disaster. The details appear most fully and accurately in Friedrich Katz's *The Secret War in Mexico*.

In broad outline, the scheme unfolded this way. Zimmermann sent coded messages to Heinrich von Eckhardt, the German minister in Mexico City, on January 15, 1917, informing him of plans to resume unrestricted submarine warfare. Zimmermann also authorized discussions with Carranza over the possibility of an alliance. Under the terms, the two countries would make war and peace together, and as a reward Mexico would recover its lost provinces of Texas, New Mexico, and Arizona. The plan went awry when British intelligence, already in possession of the German code, intercepted the transmissions and then, after the requisite deceptions, turned the information over to the United States. When published in the newspapers on March 1, the revelation appeared as proof positive of German duplicity. Meanwhile, the German refusal to rescind the U-Boat decision moved Wilson ever closer to war. Convinced that only his vision of harmony among nations contained the mechanism for peace in the future, Wilson asked Congress for a declaration of war on April 2, 1917, paradoxically believing that only by taking part in the fighting could he have a substantial voice in shaping the terms of peace.

The U.S. entry into the conflict elicited sympathetic but diverse responses in Latin America. Most governments applauded Wilson's defense of neutral rights but otherwise reacted according to their own interests. Within two weeks, ten countries affirmed neutrality: Argentina, Chile, Colombia, Costa Rica, Mexico, Paraguay, Peru, El Salvador, Uruguay, and Venezuela. Seven others broke relations: Bolivia, Brazil, the Dominican Republic, Ecuador, Guatemala, Haiti, and Honduras. Two declared war: Cuba and Panama. Later in 1917, Brazil, Costa Rica, Guatemala, Haiti, Honduras, and Nicaragua also followed with war declarations. These countries went along with the United States in large part because of the expected rewards. Cut off from European markets and capital, Brazil supported the United States with a war declaration in October 1917 after a series of submarine attacks on Brazilian ships; its actual participation consisted of naval deployments in the South Atlantic. The others played no part at all. As neutral countries, Mexico and Argentina urged mediation to stop the fighting. Such efforts failed but encouraged U.S. observers to look for signs of pro-German sympathies. In Mexico, the already-suspect Carranza produced more irritation by upholding antiforeign provisions in the Constitution of 1917. In Argentina, Yrigoyen similarly aroused mistrust because of his allegedly pro-German nationalism. Nicknamed "El Peludo" after "a hairy kind of subterranean armadillo," which was also secretive and reclusive, Yrigoyen pugnaciously pursued his own course independently of the United States.[26]

While preparing for war, the Wilson administration also got ready for peace. To establish a planning agency, early in September 1917 the president created the Inquiry. Consisting of experts, mainly professors and journalists, the members formulated peace terms based upon their understanding of history, geography, economics, and ethnography. With regard to Latin America, the recommendations typically incorporated hegemonic and paternalistic assumptions. One report, for example, assigned to the United States "a dominating influence in peace discussions as far as the Americas and Mexico are concerned." The reason was obvious: a simple acknowledgement of the U.S. "historic position" and "special relation to all the nations of the Western Hemisphere."[27]

After the fighting, the planners expected a resumption of "economic warfare." Consequently, the Wilson administration perceived the British mission to South America in the spring of 1918 as an alarming portent. The mission delegates, headed by Maurice de Bunsen, a special ambassador, had instructions to promote British commerce and goodwill for the future. U.S. observers viewed such initiatives as dangerous. To counter them, Colonel House called for international commitments in support of free trade, nonaggression, and representative democracy. In other words, he wanted to adopt a set of rules favorable to the United States.

The Mexican Constitution of 1917 remained a source of ongoing difficulty. On June 6, 1918, in an address before a group of visiting Mexican journalists, President Wilson ill-advisedly spoke of his "sincere friendship" for their country and then compounded the error by recalling the provisions of the failed Pan American Treaty. According to him, the proposed agreement had placed a laudable emphasis on multilateral endeavors so that "if any one of us . . . violates the political independence or the territorial integrity of any of the others, all the others will jump on her." Mexican critics immediately spotted the inconsistency, and newspaper editorials in Mexico City attacked U.S. opposition of article 27 of the new Constitution. A couple of months earlier, on April 2, the State Department had filed an official protest, warning against the infringement of U.S. property rights. Mexican officials regarded the act as a threat of intervention and devised an ideological defense under the terms of the so-called Carranza Doctrine. Consistent with the nationalistic requirements of the Mexican Revolution, Carranza depicted article 27 as an affirmation of Mexican sovereignty that took precedence over foreign conceptions of property rights. He also invoked nonintervention as an absolute principle and exhorted the rest of Latin America to join with him in repudiating the Monroe Doctrine.

These responses unsettled U.S. officials. The ambassador to Mexico, Henry P. Fletcher, warned of dire consequences. In his alarmist view, Carranza wanted to eliminate "the financial, economic, and political influence of the United States in Mexico" and "to isolate the United States and destroy its influence in this hemisphere." As Fletcher cautioned, "under the shibboleth of this Carranza Doctrine, Mexico would enforce Article 27 . . . and justify its disregard of the elemental principles of justice and fair dealings in treatment of foreigners."[28] Big trouble was brewing. However overblown, Fletcher's perceptions expressed the fears of oilmen and politicians who opposed the Mexican Constitution and were spoiling for a showdown at the end of World War I.

At the Paris Peace Conference, Wilson assumed the statesman's role. In pursuit of peace, he called for a purge to rid the European system of autocracy, colonialism, and militarism, that is, those practices and conditions he regarded as the causes of the war in the first place. According to his plan, the Central Powers, perceived as the aggressors, unquestionably required an array of changes to bring about reform and rehabilitation. But the same held true for the Allies. Wilson had never identified very closely with Allied war aims and opposed the division of the spoils among the victors as envisioned in the so-called secret treaties. He preferred "a peace among equals." His Fourteen Points statement of January 8, 1918, established his principal goals. He was appropriately described by some historians as "liberal-capitalist international-ist," and he thus regarded representative democracy, free trade, and interna-tional cooperation as essential parts of a durable peace. Other points centered on specific territorial issues while emphasizing the right of national self-deter-minations for white people. The fourteenth point, his most cherished, called for the creation of a League of Nations.[29]

Wilson's plan for world peace incorporated devices with which he had already experimented in Latin America. The proposal for defense of national self-determination through collective security drew on many of the same assumptions as the Pan American Treaty. Latin American critics immediately identified discrepancies. They described Wilson's hegemonic practices in the Western Hemisphere as contradictions of high-blown principles. How could the Monroe Doctrine coexist with the Fourteen Points? Was not the exercise of a self-proclaimed hemispheric politic power by the United States inconsistent with conceptions of self-determination and international responsibility?

Latin American issues possessed only peripheral importance at the Paris con-ference. Dominated by European concerns, the peacemaking centered on the consequences of the Great War; the collapse of the Russian, Turkish, and Austro-Hungarian empires; and the communist threat posed by the Russian Revolution. Latin Americans, nevertheless, wanted to play a part, and eleven nations sent delegations: Bolivia, Brazil, Cuba, Ecuador, Guatemala, Haiti, Honduras, Nicaragua, Panama, Peru, and Uruguay. Mexico contributed an unofficial envoy, Alberto J. Pani, who lobbied against the influence of the big oil companies and the possibility of U.S. intervention in his country.

The official proceedings began on January 12, 1919. Because various com-mittees and commissions exercised authority over routine matters by conduct-ing investigations, assembling information, and devising recommendations, competition for representation produced high levels of rivalry among the small-er states. The big decisions came about in other ways. Wielding primary author-ity at first, the Supreme Council, or the Council of Ten, comprised the heads of state and the foreign ministers of the five Great Powers: Britain, France, Italy, Japan, and the United States. Later, the Council of Four functioned as the power center, featuring Prime Minister David Lloyd of Britain, Premier Georges Clemenceau of France, Premier Vittorio Orlando of Italy, and President Woodrow Wilson of the United States.

For the Europeans, the restoration of stable and functioning political and economic systems in their domains assumed the top priority. For them, the menace of Russian Bolshevism required immediate attention, together with the definition of German peace terms, the disposition of German colonies, the settlement of territorial issues in Central and Eastern Europe, and the restoration of continental security. For Wilson, in contrast, the creation of the League of Nations became the first obligation, transcending all others. Upon completion of the League of Nations Covenant, he presented the provisions to the assembled delegates on February 14, 1919, while exclaiming, "A living thing is born." For Latin Americans, Great Power dominance over the proceedings meant mistrust and bitterness. Although most favored a League of Nations as a means of keeping the United States under control in their part of the world, they disliked the insignificance of the roles assigned to them. Their principal concerns, mainly trade issues and border disputes, figured only tangentially in the peacemaking process, and then usually as diversions.

Such was the case with the Monroe Doctrine. At the peace conference, U.S. leaders insisted upon formal international recognition of the hallowed creed. Consequently, under the authority of article 21, the treaty endorsed the doctrine by upholding "the validity of international engagements, such as treaties of arbitration or regional understandings . . . for securing the maintenance of peace." Pani, the Mexican observer, sounded warnings, cautioning that such a stipulation might serve the United States as a justification for military intervention in his country. For the same reason, Carranza repudiated the Monroe Doctrine altogether, calling it a "species of tutelage" unacceptable to Latin Americans.

During 1919, difficulties with Mexico provoked growing criticism in the United States. Ambassador Fletcher played a leading role by complaining repeatedly of the mistreatment of foreigners and came close to advocating the transformation of Mexico into a U.S. protectorate, something like Cuba. In his words, he would issue a "call upon the recognized Government of Mexico to perform its duties as a government" or else "accept disinterested assistance from the United States." His hard-line position won support from such powerful interests groups as the Oil Producers Association and the National Association for the Protection of American Rights and from many Republicans. Senator Albert Bacon Fall of New Mexico, a border-state politician with long-standing interests in Mexican affairs, abominated Carranza's regime and regarded Wilson's policies as contemptible. To force a change, he proposed measures that included the withdrawal of diplomatic recognition, the encouragement of a military revolt, and the installation of a new government more friendly to the United States. On August 8, 1919, he instigated a Senate investigation into Mexican affairs by means of which he intended to bring both Wilson and Carranza into disrepute.

By the end of the Paris conference, Wilson's foreign policies had run into big trouble. For reasons of politics, personality, and principle, Republicans in the Senate spurned collective security by rejecting the Versailles Treaty and the League of Nations. Wilson responded to these partisan attacks by undertaking an exhausting speaking tour in an effort to mobilize public opinion, but instead he suffered a personal catastrophe. On September 25, 1919, he collapsed after a speech in Pueblo, Colorado, and then experienced a cerebral thrombosis. The illness forced him out of action for two months and deprived his pro-League supporters of leadership at a critical time. The effects also may have made him more intransigent. He ruled out compromise with his opponents when three votes went against him and thereby doomed the larger endeavor.

The crisis in Mexican affairs took place during a showdown early in December 1919. Using the Senate investigation as a forum, Senator Fall introduced a resolution calling for a break in diplomatic relations. From his sickbed in the White House, Wilson managed to thwart the plan by affirming his absolute opposition to it. He then moved to rebuild his shattered administration by naming a new secretary of state. Lansing resigned early in 1920 after losing Wilson's confidence, presumably for acts construed as insubordination. The president saw him as a usurper of presidential prerogatives because he acted independently in dealing with the Versailles Treaty and Mexico.

Lansing's successor, Bainbridge Colby, a New York lawyer and former Progressive Party member, had no diplomatic experience but nevertheless creditably served out the term. Among other things, he tried to improve relations with Latin America, mainly by speaking against U.S. intervention. For that reasons, some historians have characterized him as a precursor of the Good Neighbor Policy, a less direct, more accommodating approach favored by President Franklin D. Roosevelt in the 1930s. Though probably somewhat exaggerated, this view correctly underscores Colby's more discerning approach to Latin American affairs. Notably, he questioned the wisdom of sustaining Caribbean protectorates and undertook a goodwill tour into South America in 1920. His voyage, a symbolic gesture, signified the president's ongoing but unfulfilled efforts in the Western Hemisphere.

Overall, Wilson's policies in Mexico, the Caribbean, and South America had failed to elicit the desired results. True, his attempts to expand commerce had some good effects, mainly as a consequence of propitious circumstances created by World War I. But in other areas, he had little to show for his various political initiatives, and a reputation for arrogance, hypocrisy, and contradiction will probably persist as stains on his legacy as a policymaker. His efforts to give the

Monroe Doctrine a multilateral definition merit commendation, but his various military interventions in Mexico and the Caribbean suggest the impact of condescension, paternalism, and racism, characteristics that, alas, are all too frequently present in U.S. policy toward Latin America.[30]

Notes

1. See Victor Bulmer-Thomas, *The Economic History of Latin American since Independence* (New York: Cambridge University Press, 1994), chaps. 1–3; and William Glade, "Latin America and the International Economy, 1879–1914," in *The Cambridge History of Latin America, Volume 4, c. 1870 to 1914*, ed. Leslie Bethell (New York: Cambridge University Press, 1986), chap. 1.

2. Glade, "Latin America," 10–16; Bill Albert, *South America and the First World War: The Impact on Brazil, Argentina, Peru, and Chile* (New York: Cambridge University Press, 1988), chap. 1.

3. Friedrich Katz, "Mexico: Restored Republic and Porfiriato, 1867–1910," in *The Cambridge History of Latin America, Volume 5, c. 1870 to 1930*, ed. Leslie Bethell (New York: Cambridge University Press, 1986), chap. 4; Glade, "Latin America," 16–17.

4. Bulmer-Thomas, *Economic History*, chap. 3.

5. Glade, "Latin America," 39–41; Bulmer-Thomas, *Economic History*, 161.

6. Glade, "Latin America," 47. Ronald H. Chilcote and Joel C. Edelstein, eds., *Latin America: Capitalist and Socialist Perspectives of Development and Underdevelopment* (Boulder, Colo.: Westview Press. 1986), provides an introduction to dependency theory.

7. John Mason Hart, *Revolutionary Mexico: The Coming and Process of the Mexican Revolution* (Berkeley: University of California Press, 1987), chaps. 6–7.

8. See ibid.; John Mason Hart, *Empire and Revolution: The Americans in Mexico since the Civil War* (Berkeley: University of California Press, 2002); Ramón Eduardo Ruiz, *The Great Rebellion: Mexico, 1905–1924* (New York: W. W. Norton, 1980); Friedrich Katz, *The Secret War in Mexico: Europe, the United States, and the Mexican Revolution* (Chicago: University of Chicago Press, 1981); Friedrich Katz, *The Life and Times of Pancho Villa* (Stanford, Calif.: Stanford University Press, 1998); and Allan Knight, *The Mexican Revolution*, 2 vols. (New York: Cambridge University Press, 1986).

9. Mark T. Gilderhus, "Carranza and the Decision to Revolt, 1913: A Problem in Historical Interpretation," *Americas* 33 (October 1976): 298–310; Kenneth J. Grieb, *The United States and Huerta* (Lincoln: University of Nebraska Press, 1969), chap. 4; Michael C. Meyer, *Huerta: A Political Portrait* (Lincoln: University of Nebraska Press, 1972), chaps. 4–5; Douglas A. Richmond, *Venustiano Carranza's Nationalist Struggle, 1893–1920* (Lincoln: University of Nebraska Press, 1983), chap. 3.

10. Mark T. Gilderhus, *Diplomacy and Revolution: U.S.–Mexican Relations under Wilson and Carranza* (Tucson: University of Arizona Press, 1977), 3.

11. Mark T. Gilderhus, *Pan American Visions: Woodrow Wilson in the Western Hemisphere* (Tucson: University of Arizona Press, 1986), 14–16.

12. Thomas L. Karnes, "Hiram Bingham and his Obsolete Shibboleth," *Diplomatic History* 3 (Winter 1979): 39–57; the quotation is on 45.

13. N. Gordon Levin Jr., *Woodrow Wilson and World Politics: America's Response to War and Revolution* (Oxford: Oxford University Press, 1968), chap. 1;

14. Gilderhus, *Pan American Visions*, 7–19; Katz, *Secret War*, chap. 5.

15. Gilderhus, *Pan American Visions*, 28–29; Albert, *South America and the First World War*, chap. 1; E. Bradford Burns, *The Unwritten Alliance: Rio Branco and Brazilian-American Relations* (New York: Columbia University Press, 1966); Joseph Smith, *Unequal Giants: Diplomatic Relations between the United States and Brazil, 1889–1930* (Pittsburgh: University of Pittsburgh Press, 1991), chaps. 2–3.

16. Gilderhus, *Pan American Visions*, 20, 28–29; Burton I. Kaufman, *Expansion and Efficiency: Foreign Trade Organization in the Wilson Administration, 1913–1921* (Westport, Conn.: Greenwood Press, 1974), chaps. 1–2; Jeffrey J. Safford, *Wilsonian Maritime Policy, 1913–1921* (New Brunswick, N.J.: Rutgers University Press, 1978), chaps. 1–2.

17. Gilderhus, *Diplomacy and Revolution*, chap. 1; Hart, *Revolutionary Mexico*, chaps. 8–9; Robert E. Quirk. *An Affair of Honor: Woodrow Wilson and the Occupation of Veracruz* (New York: McGraw-Hill, 1964).

18. Gilderhus, *Pan American Visions*, 33–45.

19. Albert, *South America and the First World War*, chap. 2.

20. Gilderhus, *Pan American Visions*, 44–52; William F. Sater, *Chile and the United States: Empires in Conflict* (Athens: University of Georgia Press, 1990), 75.

21. Gilderhus, *Pan American Visions*, 64, 67–70; Gilderhus, *Diplomacy and Revolution*, chap. 2.

22. Bruce J. Calder, *The Impact of Intervention: The Dominican Republic during the U.S. Occupation of 1916-1924* (Austin: University of Texas Press, 1984); Hans Schmidt, *The United States Occupation of Haiti, 1914–1934* (New Brunswick, N.J.: Rutgers University Press, 1971); Frederick S. Calhoun, *Uses of Force and Wilsonian Foreign Policy* (Kent, Ohio: Kent State University Press, 1993), chap. 4; Brenda Gayle Plummer, *Haiti and the United States: The Psychological Moment* (Athens: University of Georgia Press, 1992), chaps. 5–6; Gayle Plummer, *Haiti and the Great Powers, 1902–1915* (Baton Rouge: Louisiana State University Press, 1988); G. Pope Atkins and Larman C. Wilson, *The Dominican Republic and the United States: From Imperialism to Transnationalism* (Athens: University of Georgia Press, 1998), chap. 2; Lester D. Langley, *The Banana Wars: An Inner History of American Empire, 1900–1934* (Lexington: University of Kentucky Press, 1983).

23. Gilderhus, *Pan American Visions*, 61, 70–74, 77–80; Kaufman, *Expansion and Efficiency*, 165–75; Carl Parrini, *Heir to Empire: United States Economic Diplomacy, 1916–1923* (Pittsburgh: University of Pittsburgh Press, 1969), chap. 2.

24. Gilderhus, *Diplomacy and Revolution*, chap. 3; Linda B. Hall and Don M. Coerver, *Revolution on the Border: The United States and Mexico, 1910–1920* (Albuquerque: University of New Mexico Press, 1988), chap. 5.

25. Gilderhus, *Diplomacy and Revolution*, chap. 3.

26. Ernest R. May, *The World and American Isolation, 1914–1917* (Cambridge, Mass.: Harvard University Press, 1959); Gilderhus, *Pan American Visions*, chap. 3; Katz, *Secret War*, chaps. 9–10.

27. Lawrence E. Gelfand, *The Inquiry: American Preparations for Peace, 1917–1919* (New Haven, Conn.: Yale University Press, 1963).

28. Gilderhus, *Pan American Visions*, 113, 125–27; Gilderhus, *Diplomacy and Revolution*, 96.

29. Levin, *Wilson and World Politics*, chaps. 5–7.

30. Gilderhus, *Pan American Visions*, 142–56; Gilderhus, *Diplomacy and Revolution*, chap. 6; Dimitri D. Lazo, "Lansing, Wilson, and the Jenkins Incident," *Diplomatic History* 22 Spring 1998): 177–98; Daniel M. Smith, *Aftermath of War: Bainbridge Colby and Wilsonian Diplomacy, 1920–1921* (Philadelphia: American Philosophical Society, 1970), 10-31; Lars Schoulz, *Beneath the United States: A History of U.S. Policy toward Latin America* (Cambridge, Mass.: Harvard University Press, 1998), chap. 12.

7. Mr. Wilson's First Amendment

Geoffrey R. Stone

Between the outbreak of war in Europe and the decision of the United States to enter the conflict in the spring of 1917, there was continuing debate about the nation's best course of action. Most Americans believed that the war in Europe did not implicate the vital interests of the United States. President Woodrow Wilson's proclamation that America should remain neutral was greeted warmly throughout the nation. What finally drew the United States into the war was the German submarine blockade.[1]

Although Americans valued the "freedom of the seas," many did not find it a sufficiently compelling reason to spill American blood on the battlefields of Europe. The more sensible course, they argued, was simply to stand aside, forgo trade with the belligerents, and let the storm pass. Nonetheless, after Germany stepped up its submarine campaign against American vessels in early 1917, President Wilson, who had won reelection the preceding fall on the slogan that he had "kept America out of war," finally sought a declaration of war, declaring that Germany had thrown "to the winds all scruples of humanity." The United States, he explained, could not "choose the path of submission and suffer the most sacred rights of our nation and our people to be ignored or violated."[2]

The voices of dissent were immediate and sharp. Many Americans saw the conflict not as a war to make the world "safe for democracy" but as a war to protect the interests and investments of the wealthy. On April 4, 1917, during Congress's debate over the war resolution, Republican Senator George Norris of Nebraska stated that "we are about to put the dollar sign upon the American

This chapter is adapted from Geoffrey R. Stone, *Perilous Times: Free Speech in Wartime from the Sedition Act of 1798 to the War on Terrorism* (New York: W. W. Norton, 2004); and Geoffrey R. Stone, *War and Liberty: An American Dilemma* (New York: W. W. Norton, 2007).

flag" and that "we are committing a sin against humanity and against our countrymen."[3] The administration's proposal to reinstitute the draft triggered bitter attacks. Champ Clark, the Democratic speaker of the House, objected that "there is precious little difference between a conscript and a convict," and Senator James Reed, recalling the draft riots during the Civil War, warned that reinstitution of the draft "will have the streets of our American cities running red with blood."[4]

In seeking a declaration of war, President Wilson cautioned that "if there should be disloyalty, it will be dealt with with a firm hand of stern repression."[5] In proposing the Espionage Act of 1917, the first federal legislation against disloyal expression since the Sedition Act of 1798, Wilson insisted that those who refused to support the nation in time of war surrendered their right to civil liberties.[6] In these and similar pronouncements, he set the tone for what was to follow.[7]

"We Are So Accustomed to Agitation"

Because the United States had not been directly attacked, there was no event like Pearl Harbor to unite the American people. Even after the declaration of war, many individuals were unenthusiastic about the enterprise, and dissent was particularly sharp among German Americans, pacifists, internationalists, socialists, and anarchists. Among the most effective critics of the war were Eugene V. Debs, the national leader of the Socialist Party, who had received a million votes for president in the 1912 election, and Emma Goldman, who was known in the press as Red Emma and was the most prominent anarchist of the era. In a blistering speech in Ohio, Debs condemned the war:[8]

> Wars throughout history have been waged for conquest and plunder. . . . The master class has always declared the wars; the subject class has always fought the battles. The master class has had all to gain and nothing to lose, while the subject class has had nothing to gain and all to lose—especially their lives.

Goldman's essay "The Promoters of the War Mania," published in *Mother Earth* in March 1917, just three months before she was arrested for obstructing the draft, is illustrative of her response to the call for American involvement:

> At this critical moment it becomes imperative for every liberty-loving person to voice a fiery protest against the participation of this country in the European mass murder. [It] is unthinkable that the American people should

really want war. During the last thirty months they have had ample opportunity to watch the frightful carnage in the warring countries. . . . We are told that the "freedom of the seas" is at stake and that "American honor" demands that we protect that precious freedom. What a farce! . . . The only ones that have benefited by the "freedom of the seas" are the exploiters, the dealers in munition and food supplies. . . . Out of international carnage they have made billions. . . . Militarism and reaction are now more rampant in Europe than ever before. Conscription and censorship have destroyed every vestige of liberty. . . . The same is bound to take place in America should the dogs of war be let loose here.[9]

Wilson understood that, if allowed to fester, such antiwar dissent could undermine morale and make it more difficult for the nation to prosecute the war successfully. If citizens become disillusioned with a war, they will inevitably be more reluctant to serve in the military, commit their financial resources, and support the effort politically. War is not merely a battle of armies but also a contest of wills. Defeat can come from collapse of the home front as well as from failure in the trenches. Wilson knew that the resilience of a nation's determination to fight is as important to military success as its capacity to train and equip its army.

When questioned about "tolerance" at a Flag Day event, Wilson proclaimed that there should be no tolerance for those who "inject the poison of disloyalty into our most critical affairs." Americans, he declared, should teach such people "once and for all that loyalty to this flag is the first test of tolerance." As the nation moved closer to war, administration officials increasingly expressed concern that the government needed new ways to restrict "warfare by propaganda."[10] It is ironic that Wilson took so strident a position on this issue. Only four years before his election to the U.S. presidency, while serving as president of Princeton University, he published his influential *Constitutional Government in the United States*, in which he stated what might be taken as quite a different view:

We are so accustomed to agitation, to absolutely free, outspoken argument for change, to an unrestrained criticism of men and measures carried almost to the point of license, that to us it seems a normal, harmless part of the familiar processes of popular government. We have learned that it is pent-up feelings that are dangerous, whispered purposes that are revolutionary, covert follies that warp and poison the mind; that the wisest thing to do with a fool is to encourage him to hire a hall and discourse to his fellow citizens. . . . Agitation is certainly of the essence of a constitutional system, but those who exercise authority under a non-constitutional system fear its impact with a constant dread and try by every possible means to check and kill it, partly no doubt because they know that agitation is dangerous to arrangements which are unreasonable.[11]

Wilson's view of the respect due "agitation" in a democracy changed dramatically after he assumed the presidency. Indeed, the day after his 1916 address to Congress, the Cabinet asked Attorney General Thomas Gregory to prepare legislation to deal with disloyalty. The proposed legislation was presented to Congress in mid-1916 but not acted upon until Congress declared war a year later. Wilson's approach to dissent in World War I was very much a product of his own character. As his biographer Arthur Link observed, Wilson had a "temperamental inability to cooperate with men who were not willing to following his lead completely." He had a habit, reflected throughout his academic and political career, "of making his political enemies also his personal enemies, whom he despised and loathed. He had to hold the reins and do the driving alone. It was the only kind of leadership he knew."[12]

The Espionage Act of 1917

Less than three weeks after Congress voted a declaration of war, it began debate on what would become the Espionage Act of 1917. Although directed primarily at such matters as espionage and the protection of military secrets, the original bill included three sections directly relevant to the freedom of speech. For the sake of convenience, I refer to them here as the "press censorship" provision, the "disaffection" provision, and the "nonmailability" provision. An understanding of the debate over these three provisions is essential to understanding what went wrong in the United States over the next eighteen months.

As presented to Congress, the press censorship provision would have declared it unlawful for any person in time of war to publish any information that the president had declared to be "of such character that it is or might be useful to the enemy." The provision added that "nothing in this section shall be construed to limit or restrict any discussion, comment, or criticism of the acts or policies of the Government."[13]

The disaffection provision would have declared it unlawful for any person in time of war (1) willfully to "make or convey false reports or false statements with intent to interfere with the operation or success" of the military forces of the United States or "to promote the success of its enemies," or (2) willfully to "cause or attempt to cause disaffection in the military or naval forces of the United States."[14]

The nonmailability provision would have granted the postmaster general authority to exclude from the mails any writing or publication that violates "any of the provisions of this act" or is otherwise "of a treasonable or anarchistic character."[15]

The press censorship provision provoked the most heated discussion. The Wilson administration's support of this provision triggered a firestorm of protest from the press, which objected that it would give the president the final authority to determine whether the press could publish information about the conduct of the war. The American Newspaper Publishers' Association protested that this provision "strikes at the fundamental rights of the people, not only assailing their freedom of speech, but also seeking to deprive them of the means of forming intelligent opinion." The association added that "in war, especially, the press should be free, vigilant, and unfettered."[16]

Individual newspapers were equally critical. The *New York Times* assailed the provision as "high-handed," asserting that "the newspaper or the individual who criticizes or points out defects in policies . . . with the honest purpose of promoting remedial action . . . is not a public enemy."[17] The *Milwaukee News* characterized the press censorship provision as a "glaring attempt . . . to muzzle the press,"[18] and the *Philadelphia Evening Telegraph* declared that there should be no "power in this country . . . to control the voice of the press, or of the people, in honest judgment of the acts of public servants."[19]

When the press censorship provision was first presented to the House on April 30, 1917, Representative Edwin Webb of North Carolina, the chairman of the House Judiciary Committee, initiated the debate by reminding the press that, "in time of war, while men are giving up their sons and while people are giving up their money," the press should be willing to give up its right to publish what the president "thinks would be hurtful to the United States and helpful to the enemy."[20] Webb added that we are in "one of those situations where we have to trust somebody." Just as we trust the president, as commander in chief, with the fate of our boys in uniform, so too must we trust him to prescribe what information "would be useful to the enemy."[21]

Opposition to the provision was fierce. Representative Simeon Fess of Ohio warned that "in time of war we are very apt to do things" that we should not do.[22] Senator Hiram Johnson of California reminded his colleagues that "the preservation of free speech" is of "transcendent importance" and that in times of stress "we lose our judgment."[23] Representative Fiorello La Guardia of New York characterized the provision as a "vicious precedent,"[24] and Representative William Wood of Indiana warned that it could become "an instrument of tyranny."[25]

When it began to appear that the press censorship provision would go down to defeat, President Wilson made a direct appeal to Congress, stating that the "authority to exercise censorship over the press . . . is absolutely necessary to the public safety."[26] Members of Congress were unmoved. Representative Ira Hersey of Maine complained that "we, the Congress of the United States," are now "importuned by the executive . . . to enact unconstitutional laws, to place in the hands of the President unlawful powers, to grant to him the . . . authority to take away from the citizen the protection of the Constitution."[27]

On May 31, the House defeated the press censorship provision by a vote of 184 to 144, with 36 Democrats joining the Republican opposition.[28] This effectively ended consideration of the provision for the duration of the war.[29]

The nonmailability provision also generated controversy. Several members of Congress objected to granting the postmaster general such broad authority to exclude political material from the mails. Senator Charles Thomas of Colorado, for example, argued that this provision would enable postmasters to exclude "legitimate" as well as illegitimate publications and would produce "a far greater evil than the evil which is sought to be prevented."[30] There was particular concern about the words "treasonable" and "anarchistic," which led to a lengthy debate over their meaning.[31] Representative Johnson objected that this provision would be subject to the whim of whoever "happens to be high in the Post Office Department."[32]

After vigorous debate, Congress amended the nonmailability provision to replace the phrase "treasonable or anarchistic character" with the much narrower phrase "containing any matter advocating or urging treason, insurrection or forcible resistance to any law of the United States."[33] As a result of this amendment, only *express advocacy* of unlawful conduct could fall within the catchall clause of this provision. Statements that were "treasonable" or "anarchistic" but did not *expressly advocate* "treason, insurrection or forcible resistance" were excluded from the clause.

The disaffection provision, which turned out to be the most important provision of the bill, received less attention. But even this provision was amended in a significant manner. The Judiciary Committee found the term "disaffection" to be "too broad," "too elastic," and "too indefinite."[34] To narrow and clarify the provision, it replaced the phrase "cause or attempt to cause disaffection" with "cause or attempt to cause insubordination, disloyalty, mutiny, or refusal of duty."[35] Representative Webb explained that "to make it a crime to create disaffection" in the military "might subject a perfectly innocent person to punishment." A mother, for example, might write her son to "tell him the sad conditions back home." Webb insisted that this amendment would "protect the honest man" but "get the dishonest fellow who deliberately undertakes to spread disloyalty."[36]

After nine weeks of grueling debate, Congress enacted the Espionage Act of 1917. With the various emendations, including the elimination of the press censorship provision and the narrowing amendments to the disaffection and non-mailability provisions, the relevant part of the act made it a crime when the nation is at war for any person (1) willfully to "make or convey false reports or false statements with intent to interfere" with the military success of the United States or "to promote the success of its enemies"; (2) willfully to "cause or attempt to cause insubordination, disloyalty, mutiny, or refusal of duty, in the military or naval forces of the United States"; or (3) willfully to "obstruct the recruiting or enlistment service of the United States." Violations were punishable by prison sentences of up to twenty years.[37] The act also authorized the postmaster general to exclude from the mails any writing or publication that is "in violation of any of the provisions of this act" or that contains "any matter advocating or urging treason, insurrection or forcible resistance to any law of the United States."[38]

"An Avenging Government"

As the congressional debate suggests, the Espionage Act of 1917, as enacted, was not a broadside attack on all criticism of the war. It was, rather, a carefully considered enactment designed to deal with specific military concerns. Although Congress's stance in enacting the Espionage Act could hardly be characterized as civil libertarian, its elimination of the press censorship provision (over the strong objections of Wilson) and its significant amendments to both the disaffection and nonmailability provisions reflected a genuine concern for the potential impact of the legislation on "the freedom of speech, or of the press."

But what would the act mean in practice? Would passing out antiwar leaflets be regarded as a willful "attempt to cause insubordination" in the armed forces? Would a public speech denouncing the draft be deemed a willful obstruction of "the recruiting or enlistment service of the United States"?

In the first instance, much would depend on the attitude and approach of the Wilson Justice Department. The administration was clearly disappointed in the legislation. Not only had Wilson's personal appeal to Congress been rebuffed, but a year later Attorney General Thomas Gregory expressed the administration's frustration in a statement to the American Bar Association. Gregory complained that when war broke out the administration had "secured the passage of the Espionage Act, but most of the teeth which we tried to put in it were taken out."[39]

In light of the president's often caustic statements about disloyalty, and the attorney general's evident disappointment in the legislation, there was little reason to expect much prosecutorial restraint. Any doubt on this score was erased when Attorney General Gregory, referring to war dissenters, declared in November 1917, "May God have mercy on them, for they need expect none from an outraged people and an avenging government."[40]

Because there had been no direct attack on the United States, and no direct threat to America's national security, the Wilson administration needed to create an "outraged public" to arouse Americans to enlist, contribute money, and make the many other sacrifices war demands. This was the first and perhaps the greatest challenge to the administration. To excite the public to a state of "outrage," Wilson decried the "sinister intrigue" that was being "actively conducted in this country" by "dupes of the Imperial German Government," and he warned that the German government had agents in the United States "in places high and low."[41]

To build public support and patriotic fervor, Wilson established the Committee on Public Information (CPI)[42] under the direction of George Creel, a progressive journalist and public relations expert. Creel's goal was to generate enthusiasm for the war.[43] Under his direction, the CPI produced a flood of pamphlets, news releases, speeches, newspaper editorials, political cartoons, and even motion pictures. As Frank Cobb, editor of the *New York World*, observed, the government "conscripted public opinion" as it "conscripted men and money and materials" and, having conscripted it, then "mobilized it" and "taught it to stand at attention and salute."[44] As the conflict wore on and American casualties mounted, the need to instill a sense of national purpose and dampen criticism became ever more critical.

Creel's efforts concentrated on two main themes: feeding hatred of the enemy and promoting loyalty to the nation.[45] The CPI produced war movies, such as *The Kaiser: The Beast of Berlin*, that depicted unspeakable German atrocities. Its pamphlets, speeches, and editorials included vitriolic attacks on German culture, false charges that Germans and German Americans were orchestrating criticism of the Wilson administration, and incendiary attacks on the loyalty of those who questioned the war.

Creel's propaganda campaign intensified divisions that had been building within American society for decades. Over the past quarter century, with new waves of immigration, divisive issues of national identity had begun to surface. By the early years of the twentieth century, many "established" Americans, fearing that the nation had been inundated by an alien tide, were hostile to the claims of these newer, often eastern European arrivals.[46] Many of the most radical opponents of the war, especially anarchists like Goldman, were seen as interlopers who had no loyalty to the United States and should simply go back where they belong.

When the war came, it—and the CPI—unleashed new demands for conformity and allegiance. Although hatred of the enemy proved a powerful force, even more potent was the demand that every person prove his or her loyalty. As the nation was whipped into a fury of patriotism, many citizens looked askance at "strangers," and many communities went so far as to ban German-language teaching and to burn German-language books.

Over the next year, a torrent of mistrust and hysteria burst across the nation. Government propaganda united most of the public in common cause and common hatred. There was widespread and unfounded fear that swarms of German spies and saboteurs roamed the country. A frightful and crusading spirit settled upon the land. One patriot warned that "if Germany wins the war, . . . German soldiers will be bayoneting American girls and women . . . rather than take the trouble to shoot them."[47]

In the first month of the war, Attorney General Gregory asked loyal Americans to act as voluntary detectives and to report their suspicions directly to the Department of Justice.[48] The results were staggering. Each day, thousands of accusations of disloyalty flooded into the department. Adding to the furor, the CPI encouraged citizens to form voluntary associations dedicated to informing the authorities of possible disloyalty.

The largest of these citizen groups, the American Protective League (APL), quickly enlisted more than 200,000 members.[49] APL members ferreted out disloyalty wherever they could find it. They reported thousands of individuals to the authorities on the basis of hearsay, gossip, and slander. The leadership of the APL consisted primarily of conservative men of means—bankers, insurance executives, factory owners. Other similar volunteer organizations included the Knights of Liberty, the Boy Spies of America, the Sedition Slammers, and the Terrible Threateners.[50]

In April 1918, Attorney General Gregory boasted that the assistance of these volunteer organizations "enables us . . . to investigate hundreds of thousands of complaints and to keep scores of thousands of persons under observation. We have representatives at all meetings of any importance."[51] H. L. Mencken observed that "between Wilson and his brigades of informers, spies, volunteer detectives, perjurers and complaisant judges, . . . the liberty of the citizens has pretty well vanished in America."[52]

The activities of these organizations went well beyond the reporting of alleged disloyalty. With implicit immunity, they engaged in wiretaps, breaking and entering, bugging offices and examining bank accounts and medical records. Vigilantes ransacked the homes of German Americans. In Oklahoma, a former minister who opposed the sale of Liberty bonds was tarred and feathered. In California, a brewery worker who had made pro-German remarks was tarred and feathered and then chained to a brass cannon in a city park. In Texas, six farmers were horsewhipped because they declined to contribute to the Red Cross. In Illinois, an angry mob wrapped an individual suspected of disloyalty in an American flag and then murdered him on a public street.[53]

After the war ended, Assistant Attorney General John Lord O'Brian conceded that these associations were one of the "chief embarrassments" generated by the "war mania." Because of their excessive zeal, they "interfered with the civil rights of many people" and contributed greatly "to the oppression of innocent men." In this respect, O'Brian observed, "the systematic and indiscriminate agitation against what was claimed to be an all-pervasive system" of disloyalty did serious damage to the American people. Even Creel, writing years later, agreed that these associations were "hysteria manufacturing bodies, whose patriotism was, at the time, a thing of screams, violence and extremes."[54]

Wilson, Gregory, and Creel had helped create not only an "outraged public" but also "a divided, fearful, and intolerant nation."[55] It was in this atmosphere of accusation and suspicion that federal judges were called upon to interpret and apply the Espionage Act of 1917.

The Federal Judiciary

Faced with a frustrated and aggressive Justice Department and an increasingly hysterical public, how would courts construe the Espionage Act of 1917? The federal judiciary was, of course, a product of its times. The predominant view during this era was that civil liberties were intended for respectable, law-abiding citizens. This did not bode well for those whose views could readily be labeled "disloyal," "radical," or "seditious." Moreover, the legal profession of the era was both politically and jurisprudentially conservative. Bar associations tended to embrace the fierce patriotism of the war effort, and lawyers who criticized the war—or even defended war critics—were subject to ostracism and occasionally even formal discipline.[56] Judges who bucked the dominant attitudes of their profession could expect to be treated no less harshly.[57]

Moreover, there was as yet no deeply rooted commitment to civil liberties within the legal profession, and no well-developed understanding of the freedom of speech. Before the Espionage Act, there was scant judicial precedent on the meaning of the First Amendment.[58] State and lower federal courts had occasionally interpreted the First Amendment (or a state constitutional equivalent), but free speech claims had not fared very well.

Most judges assumed that speech could be restricted if its natural and probable effect was "destructive of the ends of society."[59] Courts following this approach rarely held government restrictions of speech unconstitutional.[60] This approach to the First Amendment was roundly criticized in the scholarly commentary.[61] Professor Thomas Cooley of the University of Michigan, for example, reasoned that although publications could be punished under English common law because of their "tendency . . . to excite disaffection with the government," this principle was wholly "unsuited" to the "people of America," for the "repression of full and free discussion is dangerous in any government resting upon the will of the people." Cooley argued that political expression must be protected from restriction unless it is made with the "evident intent and purpose . . . to excite rebellion and civil war." Moreover, because the danger of repression is especially great "in times of high party excitement," even "violent discussion" of public issues must be protected.[62]

It was an open question whether federal judges would follow the more restrictive lower-court judicial precedents or the more protective approach of the legal scholars. As it turned out, without firm precedent unambiguously protecting the freedom of speech, few federal judges had either the inclination or the fortitude to withstand the mounting pressure for suppression. They, and the First Amendment, were swept away in the tide of patriotic fervor.

A few particularly courageous judges did take a clear stand in favor of free speech, however. By far the most important decision in which a federal district judge held fast against a broad construction of the Espionage Act was *Masses Publishing Co. v. Patten*.[63] *The Masses* was a monthly "revolutionary" journal that regularly featured a remarkable collection of writers, poets, playwrights, and philosophers, including Max Eastman, John Reed, Vachel Lindsay, Carl Sandburg, Bertrand Russell, Louis Untermeyer, and Sherwood Anderson. In the summer of 1917, Postmaster General Albert Burleson ordered the August issue of *The Masses* excluded from the mail, exercising his authority under the Espionage Act. The *Masses* sought an injunction to prohibit the local postmaster from refusing to accept the August issue for mailing.[64] The postmaster argued that four cartoons and four pieces of text violated the Espionage Act, thus justifying the order of exclusion.[65]

Illustrative of these were a cartoon drawn by Henry J. Glintenkamp titled "Conscription" and a poem by Josephine Bell titled "A Tribute." The poem, a "tribute" to Emma Goldman and Alexander Berkman, who were then in jail for opposing the war and the draft, included this illustrative verse:[66]

> Emma Goldman and Alexander Berkman
> Are in prison tonight.
> But they have made themselves elemental forces
> Like the water that climbs down the rocks:
> Like the wind in the leaves;
> Like the gentle night that holds us;
> They are working on our destinies;
> They are forging the love of the nations; . . .
> Tonight they lie in prison.

The postmaster argued that the cartoons and text violated the Espionage Act in that they willfully caused or attempted "to cause insubordination, disloyalty, mutiny or refusal of duty in the military or naval forces" and obstructed "the recruiting or enlistment service of the United States."[67] Judge Learned Hand granted the injunction and thus prohibited the postmaster from excluding the *Masses* from the mail.

Judge Hand conceded the postmaster's claim that "to arouse discontent and disaffection among the people with the prosecution of the war and with the draft tends to promote a mutinous and insubordinate temper among the troops." But he argued that to read the word "cause" so broadly would involve "necessarily as a consequence the suppression of all . . . opinion except what encouraged and supported the existing policies."[68] Hand reasoned that because such an approach "would contradict the normal assumption of democratic government," the exercise of that power "is so contrary to the use and wont of our people that only the clearest expression of such a power justifies the conclusion that it was intended." He held that the actual language of the statute did not require such an understanding of its scope.[69]

The challenge for Judge Hand, then, was to separate "legitimate" from "illegitimate" speech under the act. He asserted that it "has always" been recognized that "one may not counsel or advise others to violate the law as it stands." Words, he observed, "are not only the keys of persuasion, but the triggers of action, and those which have *no purport but to counsel the violation of law* cannot by any latitude of interpretation be a part of that public opinion which is the final source of government in a democratic state."[70]

Hand readily conceded that speech falling short of express advocacy of unlawful conduct could have negative consequences. "Political agitation," he admitted, "may . . . stimulate men to the violation of law." But "to assimilate agitation, legitimate as such," with express advocacy of "violent resistance, is to disregard the tolerance of all methods of political agitation which in normal times is a safeguard of free government." This "distinction," he emphasized, "is not a scholastic subterfuge, but a hard-bought acquisition in the fight for freedom."[71]

Hand thus concluded that "if one stops short of urging" others to violate the law, "one should not be held to have attempted to cause its violation." "If that not be the test," he cautioned, "I can see no escape from the conclusion that under this [act] every political agitation which can be shown to be apt to create a seditious temper is illegal." He declared his confidence that "Congress had no such revolutionary purpose in view."[72] Applying this approach to the facts of the *Masses*, Judge Hand held that neither the cartoons nor the text crossed the line of *express advocacy* of unlawful conduct.

Attorney General Gregory charged that Hand had gutted the Espionage Act,[73] and Hand's opinion in the *Masses* decision was promptly and emphatically reversed by the court of appeals.[74] The circulation of the *Masses* dropped sharply because of its inability to move through the mails. Only a few days after the decision of the court of appeals upholding the order of the postmaster, seven of its editors and staff were indicted for conspiracy to violate the Espionage Act. By the end of the year, the *Masses* was out of business.[75]

Unlike Learned Hand, most judges during the war were determined to impose severe sentences on those charged with disloyalty, and no details of legislative interpretation or appeals to the First Amendment were likely to stand in the way. These judges were operating in a feverish atmosphere not conducive to careful judicial reflection.[76]

John Lord O'Brian, the head of the War Emergency Division of the Department of Justice, observed shortly after the war that "immense pressure" had been brought to bear on the department "for indiscriminate prosecution" and for "wholesale repression and restraint of public opinion." In this setting, the Department of Justice invoked the Espionage Act of 1917 to prosecute more than two thousand dissenters during the war for allegedly disloyal, seditious, or incendiary speech.[77]

The prevailing approach in the lower federal courts is well illustrated by the decision of the U.S. Court of Appeals in *Shaffer v. United States*.[78] In *Shaffer*, the defendant was charged with mailing copies of a book *The Finished Mystery* in violation of the Espionage Act. The book contained the following passage, which was specified in the indictment:[79]

Standing opposite to these Satan has placed . . . a certain delusion which is
best described by the word patriotism, but which is in reality murder, the
spirit of the very devil. If you say it is a war of defense against wanton and
intolerable aggression, I must reply that . . . it has yet to be proved that
Germany has any intention or desire of attacking us. . . . The war itself is
wrong. Its prosecution will be a crime. There is not a question raised, an issue
involved, a cause at stake, which is worth the life of one blue-jacket on the
sea or one khaki-coat in the trenches.

Shaffer was convicted, and the court of appeals affirmed, with the following
reasoning:[80]

It is true that disapproval of the war and the advocacy of peace are not
crimes under the Espionage Act; but the question here . . . is whether the
natural and probable tendency and effect of the words . . . are such as are
calculated to produce the result condemned by the statute. . . . Printed
matter may tend to obstruct the . . . service even if it contains no mention
of recruiting or enlistment, and no reference to the military service of the
United States. . . . The service may be obstructed by attacking the justice
of the cause for which the war is waged, and by undermining the spirit of
loyalty which inspires men to enlist or to register for conscription in the
service of their country. . . . It is argued that the evidence fails to show that
[Shaffer] committed the act willfully and intentionally. But . . . he must be
presumed to have intended the natural and probable consequences of what
he knowingly did.

This "bad tendency" approach was embraced by almost every federal court
that interpreted and applied the Espionage Act during World War I.[81] As critics
of the act had warned, these judges and juries were "swayed by wartime hysteria."[82] Consider the following:

• Rose Pastor Stokes, a Russian immigrant who had worked as a cigar maker for
twelve years before becoming editor of the socialist *Jewish Daily News*, was
convicted under the act for saying, "I am for the people and the government
is for the profiteers," during an antiwar statement to the Women's Dining
Club of Kansas City. Her speech was later published in the *Kansas City Star*.
Although there were no soldiers—indeed, no men—in her intended audience,
the government nonetheless argued that she had violated the act because "our

armies . . . can operate and succeed only so far as they are supported and maintained by the folks at home," and Stokes's statement had the tendency to "chill
enthusiasm, extinguish confidence, and retard cooperation" of mothers, sis-
ters, and sweethearts. She was sentenced to ten years in prison.[83]

• J. P. Doe, the son of a chief justice of the Supreme Court of New Hampshire,
was convicted for mailing a "chain" letter to "friends of immediate peace," stating that Germany had not broken a promise to end submarine warfare.
Although this was clearly a matter of historical interpretation, the government
argued that this statement "would have a direct tendency to obstruct the
recruiting and enlistment service."[84]

• The Reverend Clarence H. Waldron was convicted for distributing a pamphlet
stating that "if Christians [are] forbidden to fight to preserve the Person of their
Lord and Master, they may not fight to preserve themselves, or any city they
should happen to dwell in." The government charged that in distributing this
pamphlet Waldron had attempted to cause insubordination and to obstruct the
recruiting service. He was sentenced to fifteen years in prison.

• Robert Goldstein was convicted under the Espionage Act for producing and
exhibiting a motion picture about the American Revolution. *The Spirit of '76*
depicted Paul Revere's ride, the signing of the Declaration of Independence,
and General George Washington at Valley Forge. But it also included a scene
portraying the Wyoming Valley Massacre, in which British soldiers bayoneted
women and children. The government charged that this was an attempt to
promote insubordination because it negatively portrayed America's ally in the
war against Germany. In upholding the seizure of the film, the trial judge
explained, "History is history, and fact is fact. There is no doubt about that."
But, he added, "this is no time" for "those things that may have the tendency
or effect of sowing . . . animosity or want of confidence between us and our
allies." Goldstein was sentenced to ten years in prison.[85]

In 1919, Assistant Attorney General O'Brian explained that the Espionage
Act "was not directed against disloyal utterances." Rather, it was intended "to
protect the process of raising and maintaining our armed forces from the dangers of disloyal propaganda."[86] But in the hands of the Justice Department and
the federal judiciary, the act became an efficient tool for the blanket suppression
of all "disloyal utterances."

None of these defendants expressly advocated insubordination, refusal of service, or any other unlawful conduct. But by questioning the legality, morality, or conduct of the war, each of their statements increased the likelihood of unlawful conduct. As these cases illustrate, under the "bad tendency" interpretation of the act, it was impossible to oppose the war without running the risk of being accused of attempting to obstruct the war effort. Against the background of these convictions, and the severity of these sentences, no sensible person would dare publicly to criticize the Wilson administration's policies. As the Harvard law professor Zechariah Chafee concluded, under the bad tendency test, "all genuine discussion" of the justice and wisdom of continuing the war became "perilous."[87]

Criminal prosecution under the Espionage Act was only one of several tools used to suppress dissent during World War I. As we have seen, the act's "nonmailability" provision gave the postmaster general authority to exclude from the mail any publication that violated the substantive provisions of the act or that advocated "treason, insurrection or forcible resistance to any law of the United States."

As evidenced by the *Masses* case, Postmaster General Burleson construed this provision broadly, and the courts granted him a high level of deference. He announced that newspapers "cannot say that this Government is the tool of Wall Street or of munitions makers" and that nothing can be mailed that might "interfere with enlistments . . . or the sale of authorized bonds."[88] He ordered not only the *Masses* excluded from the mail but also the *Internationalist Socialist Review*, the *Milwaukee Leader*, the *Gaelic American*, the *Irish World*, Thorstein Veblen's *Imperial Germany and the Industrial Revolution*, Lenin's *Soviets at Work*, the *Nation*, and scores of other books, magazines, and newspapers.[89]

Efforts to suppress disloyalty were not confined to the federal government. State and local officials aggressively punished dissent. Eleven states enacted new sedition statutes, and dozens of cities passed laws prohibiting disloyal expression.[90] Most states established "councils of defense" to generate enthusiasm for the war and ferret out disloyalty. These councils pressured individuals to buy Liberty bonds. If they failed to do so, their names were publicly posted, they were threatened with revocation of their licenses to do business, and, in some instances, their property was seized and sold at auction to buy bonds.[91] The Pittsburgh Symphony was forbidden to perform Beethoven, and the Los Angeles public schools prohibited any discussion of the virtues of peace. In such an oppressive climate, "antiwar expression . . . had little chance" to survive.[92]

The Sedition Act of 1918

Even with the "bad tendency" test well entrenched and the number of prosecutions of dissenters climbing daily, the Department of Justice sought to amend the Espionage Act to close what it described as a few loopholes in the original legislation. In the spring of 1918, Attorney General Gregory asked Congress to amend the act to prohibit any person from interfering with the government's efforts to borrow funds for the war and to clarify that the act prohibited attempts to obstruct recruiting and enlistment, as well as the actual obstruction of such activities.[93]

In April, the attorney general urged the American Bar Association to support these amendments. Pointing to the recent lynching of a German American suspected of disloyalty, Gregory argued that such incidents occurred because otherwise law-abiding citizens believed that existing laws were inadequate to deal effectively with disloyalty and therefore felt justified in taking the law into their own hands. He complained that Congress had taken the "teeth" out of what the administration had proposed a year earlier. "We got what we could," he explained, but it was not enough. He advocated greater "protection of the nation against the insidious propaganda of the pacifist." He insisted that Congress had to make the Espionage Act "more drastic." Unless citizens are satisfied that disloyal individuals will not be allowed to roam free, he warned, and "unless the hysteria, which results in the lynching of men, is checked, it will create a condition of lawlessness from which we will suffer for a hundred years."[94]

Still, the amendments to the 1917 act proposed by the attorney general were relatively narrow. Although some members of the House complained that the Espionage Act was already too broad,[95] the House adopted Gregory's proposed changes with almost no debate. The Senate Judiciary Committee, however, took it upon itself to go far beyond Gregory's recommendations, creating the most repressive legislation in American history.

The new amendment, which became known as the Sedition Act of 1918, forbade any person, "when the United States is in war,"

- to willfully utter, print, write, or publish any disloyal, profane, scurrilous, or abusive language about the form of government of the United States, or the Constitution of the United States, or the military or naval forces of the United States, or the flag of the United States, or the uniform of the Army or Navy of the United States,

• or to use any language intended to bring the form of government of the United States, or the Constitution of the United States, or the military or naval forces of the United States, or the flag of the United States, or the uniform of the Army or Navy of the United States into contempt, scorn, contumely or disrepute, . . .[96]

The debate in Congress over the Sedition Act of 1918 was striking. Almost every member of Congress found it necessary to proclaim his loyalty to the nation and his disdain for anyone who might harbor doubts about the justness of the American cause. There was a strong undercurrent of repression even within Congress. At one point, Senator Henry Cabot Lodge of Massachusetts complained, "I have become a little weary of having Senators get up here and say to those of us who happen to think a word had better be changed" that we "are trying to shelter treason."[97] After declaring his opposition to the Sedition Act, Senator Hiram Johnson of California observed that what "has transpired again and again," both "in this Chamber" and "all over this land," is that any person who does "not subscribe *instanter*" to every effort to suppress dissent has by "that very token" been deemed "an enemy of his country."[98]

Attorney General Gregory's claim that the new legislation was necessary to curb mob violence echoed throughout the debates. Senator Lee Overman of North Carolina argued that "the people of this country are taking the law in their own hands" because "Congress is not doing its duty."[99] Anyone listening to the debate might have concluded that "the best of all possible ways to protect freedom of speech was to abridge it."[100] To be sure, there had been several vicious beatings and even one lynching, but there was no persuasive evidence linking these acts to the government's failure to indict people for seditious speech. Certainly, passage of the Sedition Act would discourage some inflammatory utterances, but the more basic reason for the legislation was simply to squelch dissent that others found offensive.

The fundamental question, of course, was whether the Sedition Act was consistent with the Constitution. In support of the legislation, Senator William E. Borah of Idaho argued that if our soldiers can risk their lives to protect "our form of government, our Constitution and our flag," then is it not "too much to ask complete devotion upon the part of those who remain at home to the things for which our boys are fighting and dying upon the western front."[101] Senator Miles Poindexter of Washington expressed exasperation that, "regardless of its effect upon the war," some people attached so much importance to the right of free speech, "while at the same time we take men's bodies, conscript them into the Army" and "subject them to the dangers of the firing line." "I should like to know," he asked, "what distinction there is, . . . while we are taking their bodies, . . . if we also take away from them somewhat of this license of speech which is so much defended?"[102]

Senator Thomas Hardwick of Georgia offered a reply:[103]

> We are in this war. We ought to prosecute it vigorously. . . . But it is by no means necessary . . . in the prosecution of that war to . . . sacrifice . . . American liberties. . . . In times of war people grow hysterical, and when people grow hysterical even executives, even legislative bodies, are not exempt from the contagion of hysteria. It is better to move along slowly; it is better . . . not to confer powers that are so broad that they are not only capable of abuse but liable to abuse; that are so broad that . . . honest, loyal American citizens may be persecuted.

John Lord O'Brian acknowledged the "sweeping character" of the new legislation and declined to defend its constitutionality.[104] Attorney General Gregory, concerned about the potential impact of the Sedition Act, immediately issued a circular to all U.S. attorneys, warning that the new law "should not be permitted to become the medium whereby efforts are made to suppress honest, legitimate criticism of the administration or discussion of Government policies."[105]

A few months later, Gregory issued another circular, declaring that no additional cases should be submitted to grand juries under the Sedition Act without the prior approval of the attorney general. According to O'Brian, however, "the general publicity given the statute . . . fanned animosities into flame, vastly increasing the amount of suspicion and complaints throughout the country." This led to "a large increase" in the number of prosecutions.[106] With passage of the Sedition Act in the summer of 1918, the government had put in place the perfect instrument to suppress dissent.

The Supreme Court

In 1919, the Supreme Court was in firmly conservative hands. The values and experiences of the justices led most of them to hold anarchists, socialists, and other "radical" dissenters in contempt. This was not a Court likely to take a bold stand in favor of those who condemned capitalism and denounced the established order.[107]

Schenck v. United States was the Supreme Court's first significant decision interpreting the First Amendment and its first decision in an Espionage Act prosecution.[108] *Schenck* was decided in March 1919, after the signing of the armistice ending World War I. The defendants had been charged with conspiring to obstruct the recruiting and enlistment service by circulating a pamphlet to men who had been called and accepted for military service.

The pamphlet argued that the draft was unconstitutional, described a conscript as "little better than a convict," and intimated that conscription was a "monstrous wrong" designed to further the interests of Wall Street. It urged readers to "assert . . . your rights" and to join the Socialist Party, write their representatives to protest conscription, and "petition for the repeal of the act." The defendants were convicted at trial because the "natural and probable tendency" of the pamphlet was to dampen the willingness of men to serve in the armed forces and because the jury could reasonably infer that the defendants intended to cause the natural and probable consequences of their actions.[109] It was, all in all, an unexceptional case under the Espionage Act.

Justice Oliver Wendell Holmes wrote the opinion for a unanimous Court—upholding the conviction. He addressed the First Amendment in the following passage, one of the most famous in the annals of American legal history:

> We admit that in many places and in ordinary times the defendants, in saying all that was said in the circular, would have been within their constitutional rights. But the character of every act depends upon the circumstances in which it is done. The most stringent protection of free speech would not protect a man in falsely shouting fire in a theater, and causing a panic. . . . The question in every case is whether the words used are used in such circumstances and are of such a nature as to create a clear and present danger that they will bring about the substantive evils that Congress has a right to prevent. It is a question of proximity and degree. When a nation is at war many things that might be said in time of peace are such a hindrance to its effort that their utterance will not be endured so long as men fight and no Court could regard them as protected by any constitutional right.[110]

At first blush, Holmes's standard seems more speech protective than the "bad tendency" test. Whereas the latter required only a remote connection between the speech and the harm, Holmes's "clear and present danger" test (as illustrated by the "false cry of fire" hypothetical) implied an immediate and reflexive connection between the speech and the harm. This is promising. But it is unclear whether

Holmes applied the "clear and present danger" standard in *Schenck*. If that test, as elucidated by the "false cry of fire" example, had been applied in *Schenck*, it would have led the Supreme Court to *reverse* the conviction. Although the circulation of the pamphlet certainly satisfied the "bad tendency" test, it did not pose a clear and present danger in any way analogous to Holmes's "causing a panic" paradigm. Unlike the danger created by the false cry of fire, the danger in *Schenck* has nothing "clear" or "present" about it.

Strange as it may seem, the most reasonable inference is that Holmes did not intend the phrase "clear and present danger" to reflect a change in the "bad tendency" test.[111] More likely, he simply approved that test under a different name.[112] Any doubt on this score was erased only a week later, when the Court handed down its decisions in *Frohwerk v. United States*[113] and *Debs v. United States*.[114]

Jacob Frohwerk was a copy editor who helped prepare and publish a series of antiwar, antidraft articles in the *Missouri Staats Zeitung*, a German-language newspaper. He was convicted under the Espionage Act of conspiring to cause disloyalty, mutiny, and refusal of duty in the military and naval forces of the United States. He was sentenced to ten years in prison. The Supreme Court, again in an opinion by Justice Holmes, unanimously affirmed the conviction. One of the articles stated that our participation in the war "appears to be outright murder without serving anything practical," and another suggested that those who resist the draft are "more sinned against than sinning."[115] Holmes gave short shrift to the First Amendment issue, holding that the speech could be punished because "the circulation of the paper was in quarters where a little breath would be enough to kindle a flame."[116] Thus, only a week after *Schenck*, Holmes made no reference to clear and present danger. Instead, he appeared to invoke a new "little breath that could kindle" standard.

Debs v. United States, of course, involved Eugene Debs, the national leader and spiritual father of the Socialist Party. A major national figure, Debs strongly opposed both conscription and the U.S. intervention in the war. On June 16, 1918, to demonstrate his support of those who had been jailed for their opposition to the federal government, he visited three Socialists who were then in prison in Canton, Ohio, for violating the Espionage Act. Only a short distance from the prison, he made a bold and provocative speech to a crowd of some twelve hundred listeners. Although his address dealt mainly with the history and ideals of socialism, he also spoke directly about the three "martyrs for freedom," noting that they "are simply paying the penalty, that all men have paid in all the ages of history for standing erect, and for seeking to pave the way to better conditions for mankind."[117] For this speech, he was arrested, tried, and convicted under the

Espionage Act for obstructing the recruiting and enlistment service of the United States.[118] He was sentenced to a prison term of ten years.[119] The Supreme Court, speaking once again through Justice Holmes, unanimously rejected Debs's claim that his conviction violated the First Amendment. According to Holmes, Debs's First Amendment claim had in practical effect been "disposed of" in *Schenck*.[120] As in *Frohwerk*, Justice Holmes made no reference to clear and present danger.[121]

The University of Chicago law professor Harry Kalven has aptly observed that "although the American traditions of political and intellectual tolerance are enormously indebted to Justice Holmes for the contributions his pen and prestige are to make during the next decade, the awkward fact is that the legal tradition gets off to a limping start" with his opinions in *Schenck*, *Frohwerk*, and *Debs*.[122]

The following fall, the Supreme Court decided *Abrams v. United States*.[123] The defendants in *Abrams*, a group of young Russian-Jewish emigrants, had fled Russia between 1908 and 1913 to escape the tsar's harsh, anti-Semitic policies. They were self-proclaimed socialists and anarchists who had been deeply moved by the Bolshevik overthrow of the tsar. They distributed several thousand copies of each of two leaflets, one of which was written in English, the other in Yiddish. The leaflets, which were circulated secretly and thrown from a window, called for a general strike to protest "the hypocrisy of the plutocratic gang in Washington."[124] After a highly public and very controversial trial that was tainted by the judge's anti-alien, anti-Semitic, and anti-Bolshevik sentiments,[125] the defendants were convicted of conspiring to violate the Sedition Act of 1918 and sentenced to prison terms ranging from three to twenty years.[126]

The Supreme Court affirmed the convictions on the grounds that the defendants had conspired "to incite, provoke or encourage resistance to the United States" and to urge curtailment of the production of war materials with intent to "cripple or hinder the United States in the prosecution of the war." Speaking for the Court, Justice John H. Clarke summarily rejected the defendants' First Amendment argument, noting simply that "this contention is sufficiently discussed and is definitely negatived" in *Schenck* and *Frohwerk*.[127] Indeed, this seemed unassailable.

Surprisingly, Justice Holmes, joined by Justice Louis D. Brandeis, dissented. Holmes declared that it is "only the present danger of immediate evil or an intent to bring it about that warrants Congress in setting a limit to the expression of opinion."[128] Turning to the defendants, Holmes explained that "nobody can suppose that the surreptitious publishing of a silly leaflet by an unknown man, without more, would present any immediate danger that its opinions would hinder the success of the government arms or have any appreciable tendency to do so."[129]

Holmes maintained that in this case "sentences of twenty years imprisonment have been imposed for the publishing of two leaflets that I believe the defendants had as much right to publish as the Government has to publish the Constitution of the United States now vainly invoked by them." Holmes added that "we should be eternally vigilant against attempts to check the expression of opinions that we loathe and believe to be fraught with death, unless they so imminently threaten immediate interference with the lawful and pressing purposes of the law that an immediate check is required to save the country."[130]

Although the explanation for Holmes's sudden passion for the freedom of speech remains a wonderful mystery, there can be little doubt that his reading in the summer of 1919 and his discussions with Learned Hand, Zechariah Chafee, and Harold Laski sparked a change in his thinking. In this sense, the shift in Holmes's views on the First Amendment was itself a splendid illustration of the philosophy of free speech in action.

With Holmes's dissent in *Abrams*, "the free speech tradition divides sharply."[131] Both Justice Holmes and the majority appealed to *Schenck* as the critical precedent. Holmes read his *Abrams* version of the "clear and present danger" test back into *Schenck*, claiming it was there all along and that the majority had irresponsibly departed from settled precedent. The majority emphasized the outcome in *Schenck*, arguing that the phrase "clear and present danger" had never meant anything more than "bad tendency." This division within the Court was evident in several post-*Abrams* decisions in which the Court, over the dissents of Justices Holmes and Brandeis, consistently upheld further World War I convictions under the Espionage and Sedition acts.

Conclusion

Many themes played out in the actions taken by the Woodrow Wilson administration during World War I. The government found it necessary to balance a broad range of conflicting interests. It needed to rally the people and sustain public morale; channel nativist fears of aliens, socialists, and anarchists; "Americanize" a new generation of immigrants during a period of intense political and social turmoil;[132] restrain vigilante "justice" and mob violence; deflect demands that the nation intern all enemy aliens and establish military tribunals to prosecute persons charged with disloyalty; cabin powerful conservative forces that sought to manipulate charges of disloyalty to destroy the critics of capitalism; assuage the incessant demands of "superpatriots" for ever more repressive government action; and, of course, win the war.[133]

The challenge proved daunting. But even before the war, President Wilson set the tone for an era of repression. He did not use the loyalty issue in a cynical effort to destroy his political opponents, but he did squelch disharmony that might have impeded his mission of making "the world safe for democracy."[134] Moreover, he too often overlooked the heavy-handed behavior of federal officials who acted in his name. He allowed his subordinates to inflame public hysteria, which he did little to control, and he permitted his administration to support private groups that intimidated and harassed war critics.[135] When individuals raised concerns about the suppression of civil liberties, his administration resorted to invocations of patriotism and accusations of disloyalty to stifle those concerns. The nation, after all, was at war, and Wilson took the position that it was not asking too much for people to put aside their criticisms so that the war could be prosecuted successfully.

The responsibility for what occurred during World War I rests less with the Congress that enacted the Espionage Act of 1917 than with the Wilson administration, which sought to exploit and manipulate public opinion; the Department of Justice, which may have meant well, but too often lacked the authority and the discipline to fulfill its aspirations; the postmaster general, who abused his authority; the federal judiciary, which rashly interpreted and applied the law, routinely meting out unconscionably harsh sentences of ten, fifteen, and twenty years' imprisonment to individuals who did nothing more than distribute seditious leaflets or make "disloyal" speeches;[136] the state and local officials who failed to protect dissenters; the Congress that enacted the Sedition Act of 1918; and the Supreme Court justices, who strained to excuse the government's actions. Kalven has rightly described the Court's performance in this era as "simply wretched."[137]

In the fall of 1919, Alfred Bettman, John Lord O'Brian's colleague in the Department of Justice, who was in charge of enforcement of the Espionage Act, defended the wartime performance of the Department of Justice. Like O'Brian, he argued that the department had spent much of its energy during the war subduing lynch mobs and "stemming the tide of intolerance." He privately conceded, however, that the general "atmosphere of intolerance" had led to serious constitutional violations and that this "was one of the shadows in our conduct of the war."[138]

The government's extensive repression of dissent during World War I and its conduct in the immediate aftermath of the war had a significant impact on American society. It was at this moment, in a reaction to the country's excesses, that the modern civil liberties movement truly began.[139] With the benefit of hindsight, many supporters of the Wilson administration were shocked by what the nation had done.

Before the war, the philosopher-educator John Dewey, one of the leading intellectuals of his day, argued that the government's suppression of dissent was justified on grounds of pragmatism.[140] After the war, however, he wrote in the *New Republic* that "the increase of intolerance of discussion to the point of religious bigotry" had led the nation to condemn as seditious "every opinion and belief which irritates the majority of loyal citizens."[141] Like many of his contemporaries, Dewey came to understand as a result of his experiences during World War I that civil liberties "go into the discard when a nation is engaged in war."[142] In 1920, Dewey helped found the American Civil Liberties Union.

On December 13, 1920, Congress quietly repealed the Sedition Act of 1918 (but the Espionage Act of 1917 remains in effect to this day).[143] Shortly after becoming attorney general in 1924, Harlan Fiske Stone ordered an end to the Bureau of Investigation's surveillance of political radicals, explaining that "a secret police may become a menace to free government and free institutions because it carries with it the possibility of abuses of power which are not always quickly apprehended or understood." "It is important," he said, that the bureau's activities be "strictly limited to the performance of those functions for which it was created" and that this would no longer include investigations of the "political or other opinions of individuals."[144]

After the war, the question arose of amnesty for those who had been convicted under the Espionage and Sedition Acts.[145] Before leaving office in March 1919, Attorney General Gregory, on the advice of O'Brian and Bettman, recommended to President Wilson the release or reduction in sentence of two hundred prisoners then in jail for Espionage Act or Sedition Act convictions.[146] Gregory explained that in many of these cases injustices had been done because of the "intense patriotism" of the jurors. In other instances, he said, the sentences had been clearly "out of proportion to the offense."[147] The president accepted these recommendations. On February 1, 1921, however, without stating his reasons, Wilson rejected the recommendation of the Department of Justice that he commute Eugene Debs's sentence.[148]

Over the next several years, sustained efforts were made, both back-channel and in public demonstrations, to secure the release of Debs and the remaining "political prisoners."[149] On Christmas Day 1921, President Warren Harding pardoned Debs and twenty-four others. In December 1923, President Calvin Coolidge ordered the release of the remaining prisoners.[150] In 1933, President Franklin Delano Roosevelt granted an amnesty to all individuals convicted under the Espionage Act and the Sedition Act, restoring their full political and civil rights.[151]

Notes

1. See Edward M. Coffman, *The War to End All Wars: The American Military Experience in World War I* (Oxford: Oxford University Press, 1968), 1–25; William H. Rehnquist, *All the Laws But One: Civil Liberties in Wartime* (New York: Alfred A. Knopf, 1998), 171–72; and Harry N. Scheiber, *The Wilson Administration and Civil Liberties, 1917–1921* (Ithaca, N.Y.: Cornell University Press, 1960), 2–3.

2. Woodrow Wilson, Address to Joint Session of Congress, April 2, 1917, in *The Papers of Woodrow Wilson*, 69 vols., ed. Arthur S. Link et al. (Princeton, N.J.: Princeton University Press, 1966–94) (hereafter, *PWW*), vol. 41, 520, 521.

3. 65th Cong., 1st Sess., in 55 *Cong. Rec.* S 214 (April 4, 1917).

4. See Coffman, *The War to End All Wars*, 25; Robert J. Goldstein, *Political Repression in Modern America: From 1870 to the Present* (Cambridge, Mass.: Schenkman, 1978), 105–7.

5. Woodrow Wilson, Address to Joint Session of Congress, April 2, 1917, in *PWW*, vol. 41, 526.

6. See Paul L. Murphy, *World War I and the Origin of Civil Liberties in the United States* (New York: W. W. Norton, 1979), 53.

7. In his speech requesting a declaration of war, Wilson also observed that Germany "has filled our unsuspecting communities and even our offices of government with spies and set criminal intrigues everywhere afoot against our national unity of counsel, our peace within and without, our industries and our commerce." Woodrow Wilson, Address to Joint Session of Congress, April 2, 1917, in *PWW*, vol. 41, 524. Six members of the Senate and fifty members of the House voted against the declaration of war. 65th Cong, Spec. Sess., in 55 *Cong. Rec.* S 104 (April 2, 1917).

8. Eugene V. Debs, Speech in Canton, Ohio, June 16, 1918, in *Writings and Speeches of Eugene V. Debs*, ed. Arthur M. Schlesinger Jr. (Tenafly, N.J.: Hermitage, 1948), 425.

9. Emma Goldman, "The Promoters of War Mania," *Mother Earth*, March 1917.

10. See U.S. Department of Justice, *Annual Report of the Attorney General of the United States for the Year 1918* (Washington, D.C.: U.S. Government Printing Office, 1918), 16–17.

11. Woodrow Wilson, *Constitutional Government in the United States*, March 24, 1908, in *PWW*, vol. 18, 94.

12. See Arthur S. Link, *Wilson: The Road to the White House* (Princeton, N.J.: Princeton University Press, 1947), 307. Also see James Chace, *1912: Wilson, Roosevelt, Taft & Debs—The Election That Changed the Country* (New York: Simon & Schuster, 2004); and Murphy, *World War I and the Origin of Civil Liberties*, 54–55. The Supreme Court unanimously upheld the constitutionality of the conscription law in January 1918. See *Selective Draft Law Cases*, 245 U.S. 366 (1918).

Shortly before seeking a declaration of war, Wilson told the journalist Frank Cobb that he had no illusions about what would happen in the United States. According to Cobb, Wilson said that war "would require illiberalism at home to reinforce the men at the front." Although expressing the hope that the United States could "maintain the ideas of

Government that all thinking men shared," he doubted it was possible. Wilson predicted that the people would "forget there ever was such a thing as tolerance" and that "the spirit of ruthless brutality will enter into the very fibre of our national life, infecting Congress, the courts, the policeman on the beat, the man in the street." He warned that "conformity would be the only virtue," that "every man who refused to conform would have to pay the penalty," and that "free speech and the right of assembly would go." John L. Heaton, *Cobb of "The World": A Leader in Liberalism* (New York: E. P. Dutton, 1924), 269–70.

13. HR 291 tit I § 4, 65th Cong., 1st Sess., in 55 *Cong. Rec.* H 1695 (May 2, 1917).

14. Report of the Committee on the Judiciary, HR Report No. 30, 65th Cong., 1st Sess. 9 (1917). See 54 *Cong. Rec.* S 3606–7 (February 19, 1917) (discussing the use of the word "disaffection"). Violations were punishable by fines of up to $10,000 and prison sentences of up to twenty years, or both.

15. HR 291 § 1100, 65th Cong., 1st Sess., in 55 *Cong. Rec.* H 1595 (April 30, 1917).

16. Resolutions of the American Newspaper Publishers' Association, 65th Cong., 1st Sess. (April 25, 1917), in 55 *Cong. Rec.* S 1861 (May 5, 1917).

17. "The Espionage Bill," *New York Times*, April 13, 1917.

18. *Milwaukee News*, April 30, 1917, excerpted by Thomas F. Carroll, "Freedom of Speech and of the Press in War Time: The Espionage Act," 17 *Mich. L. Rev.* 621, 624 (1919).

19. *Philadelphia Evening Telegraph*, excerpted in "Oppose Censorship as Now Proposed," *New York Times*, April 22, 1917). See also 65th Cong., 1st Sess., in 55 *Cong. Rec.* H 1709–10 (May 2, 1917) (there were similar editorials in the *New York American*, the *Philadelphia Inquirer*, and the *Washington Times*).

20. 65th Cong., 1st Sess., in 55 *Cong. Rec.* H 1590–91 (April 30, 1917). See also ibid., 1695 (May 2, 1917) (Representative Morgan's observation that "in time of great national peril, it is necessary sometimes that individual citizens shall be willing to surrender some of the privileges which they have for the sake of the greater good").

21. Ibid., 1590–91 (April 30, 1917). See also Carroll, 17 *Mich. L .Rev.* at 627 (noting that an important defense of the provision was the argument that "the President, as Commander-in-Chief of the military forces, is the best judge" of whether such control of the press is "necessary to carry the war to a successful conclusion").

22. Ibid., 1591 (April 30, 1917).

23. 65th Cong., 1st Sess., in 55 *Cong. Rec.* S 2097 (May 11, 1917).

24. 65th Cong., 1st Sess., in 55 *Cong. Rec.* H 1594 (Apr 30, 1917).

25. Ibid., 1773 (May 3, 1917).

26. Letter from Woodrow Wilson to Representative Webb, May 22, 1917, in *PWW*, vol. 42, 369–70. The administration offered a "compromise" version of the press censorship provision, which failed of passage. See Conf. Rep. No. 65, on HR 291, 65th Cong., 1st Sess., in 55 *Cong. Rec.* H 3124, 3125 (May 31, 1917) (amended press censorship provision in title I, section 4).

27. 65th Cong., 1st Sess., in 55 *Cong. Rec.* H 3134 (May 31, 1917).

28. See "House Defeats Censorship Law by 184 to 144," *New York Times*, June 1, 1917 (stating that party lines were "shattered" in defeating the bill).

29. The House instructed the conferees to strike the press censorship provision from the bill. See House of Representatives Report No. 69, 65th Cong., 1st Sess. 19 (1917). The defeat of this part of the bill had unintended consequences, for once Wilson was "defeated on the censorship, press criticism and, indeed, press notice of the Espionage Act suddenly ceased. If it is true that 'after its elimination, a majority of the national lawmakers apparently believed that the bill could not be used to suppress critical opinion,' then these Congressmen were mistaken." Scheiber, *Wilson Administration*, 18–19, quoting Horace C. Peterson and Gilbert C. Fite, *Opponents of War, 1917–1918* (Madison: University of Wisconsin Press, 1957), 16.

30. 65th Cong., 1st Sess., in 55 *Cong. Rec.* S 2062 (May 10, 1917).

31. 65th Cong., 1st Sess., in 55 *Cong. Rec.* H 1595–97 (April 30, 1917). The debate also touched upon "nihilism" and the views of Tolstoy and Emerson.

32. Ibid., 1604 (noting that the opinion of the solicitor of the Post Office Department would "prevail without a trial").

33. Conf. Rep. No. 65, on HR 291, 65th Cong., 1st Sess., in 55 *Cong. Rec.* H 3124, 3129 (May 29, 1917); 65th Cong., 1st Sess., in 55 *Cong. Rec.* H 3306 (June 7, 1917).

34. 65th Cong., 1st Sess., in 55 *Cong. Rec.* H 1594 (April 30, 1917) (Representative Webb).

35. See Espionage Act of 1917, 40 Stat at 219.

36. 65th Cong., 1st Sess., in 55 *Cong. Rec.* H 1594–95 (April 30, 1917).

37. Espionage Act of 1917, 40 Stat 217, 219.

38. Ibid., 230–31.

39. Thomas Gregory, "Suggestions of Attorney General Gregory to Executive Committee in Relation to the Department of Justice," *ABA Journal* 4 (1918): 305, 306.

40. *New York Times*, November 21, 1917.

41. Woodrow Wilson, Flag Day Address, June 14, 1917, in *PWW*, vol. 42, 503. See Roy S. Baker and William E. Dodd, eds., *The Public Papers of Woodrow Wilson: The New Democracy* (New York: Harper & Brothers, 1927), vol. 5, 60, 66.

42. The situation became especially acute after the 1918 midterm elections, when Wilson appealed personally for a vote of confidence from the electorate but the voters instead elected Republican majorities in both houses of Congress.

43. Creel described his mission as one of "driving home to the people the causes behind the war, and the great fundamental necessities that compelled a peace-loving nation to take up arms to protect free institutions and preserve our liberties." George Creel, "Public Opinion in War Time," *Annals of the American Academy of Political and Social Science* 78 (1918): 185–86.

44. Frank Cobb, "The Press and Public Opinion," *New Republic*, December 31, 1919.

45. Creel was successful on both counts. The CPI succeeded in building a spirit of confidence and public support for the war, but its aggressive campaigning caused the loyalty of many innocent people to be impugned. At times, the CPI drowned "out the voices of those who took a more balanced and judicious view." Scheiber, *Wilson Administration*, 17.

46. For a review of the nation's increasingly hostile treatment of immigrants in the years leading up to World War I, see William Preston Jr., *Aliens and Dissenters: Federal Suppression of Radicals, 1903–1933* (Cambridge, Mass.: Harvard University Press, 1963), 2–10.

47. See Meirion Harries and Susie Harries, *Last Days of Innocence: America at War, 1917–1918* (New York: Vintage Books, 1997), 296; Peterson and Fite, *Opponents of War*, 194–207. Also see *Meyer v. Nebraska*, 255 U.S. 390 (1923) (invalidating a law prohibiting the teaching of German); and O. A. Hilton, "Public Opinion and Civil Liberties in Wartime, 1917–1919," *Southwestern Social Science Quarterly* 28 (1947): 201, 208–12.

48. Murphy, *World War I and the Origin of Civil Liberties*, 94–95. Also see Harries and Harries, *Last Days of Innocence*, 307.

49. To his credit, President Wilson was uneasy about this effort. In June 1917, he told Gregory that "it seems to me that it would be very dangerous to have such an organization operating in the United States." Gregory insisted, however, that the Justice Department needed the assistance of such organizations, and Wilson relented. Letter from Woodrow Wilson to Thomas W. Gregory, June 4, 1917, in *PWW*, vol. 42, 446.

50. See Peterson and Fite, *Opponents of War*, 18; Goldstein, *Political Repression*, 111. On the American Patriot League, see, generally, Joan M. Jensen, *The Price of Vigilance* (Chicago: Rand McNally, 1968). On the effectiveness of government propaganda during World War I, see Hilton, "Public Opinion and Civil Liberties," 201.

51. Gregory, "Suggestions of Attorney General Gregory," 309. Gregory authorized the American Protective League, in its efforts to recruit members, to state on its letterhead, "Organized with the Approval, and Operating under the Direction of the United States Department of Justice, Bureau of Investigation." See Murphy, *World War I and the Origin of Civil Liberties*, 89–90.

52. Terry Teachout, *The Skeptic: A Life of H. L. Mencken* (New York: HarperCollins, 2002), 144–45.

53. See Harries and Harries, *Last Days of Innocence*, 282–308; Murphy, *World War I and the Origin of Civil Liberties*, 94–95; and Hilton, "Public Opinion and Civil Liberties," 202–12.

54. See John Lord O'Brian, "Civil Liberty in War Time," *Report of the New York State Bar Association* 42 (1919): 275, 299–300; and George Creel, *Rebel at Large: Recollections of Fifty Crowded Years* (New York: Putnam, 1947), 196. Creel attempted to maintain some measure of judgment in running his program. As a result, he was often harshly attacked by less tolerant members of Congress for not going even farther in his defense of the war effort. See 65th Cong., 2d Sess., in 56 *Cong. Rec.* S 4763–64, 4827–32 (April 8–9, 1918); and Murphy, *World War I and the Origin of Civil Liberties*, 107–16.

55. Harries and Harries, *Last Days of Innocence*, 308.

56. E.g., the Illinois Bar Association adopted a resolution declaring that it would be unpatriotic and unprofessional for a lawyer to defend an alleged draft evader, a resolution for which Attorney General Thomas Gregory stated his admiration. In Texas, a

German-born lawyer was disbarred for saying that "Germany is going to win this war, and . . . I hope she will." A Chicago attorney was accused on subversion when, acting on behalf of his client, he challenged the constitutionality of the draft law. See Gregory, "Suggestions of Attorney General Gregory," 314.

57. See Jerold S. Auerbach, *Unequal Justice: Lawyers and Social Change in Modern America* (Oxford: Oxford University Press, 1976), 104–5; and Murphy, *World War I and the Origin of Civil Liberties*, 179–211.

58. The Court did decide several pre–World War I cases involving the First Amendment. See, e.g., *Patterson v. Colorado*, 205 U.S. 454 (1907) (contempt of court); *Turner v. Williams*, 194 U.S. 279 (1904) (deportation); and *Ex Parte Jackson*, 96 U.S. 727 (1877) (lottery tickets). Also see, generally, David M. Rabban, *Free Speech in Its Forgotten Years* (New York: Cambridge University Press, 1997), 132–41.

59. William Blackstone, *Commentaries on the Laws of England* (Chicago: University of Chicago Press, 1979), vol. 4, 151–52.

60. For illustrative decisions, see *Commonwealth v. Karvonen*, 219 Mass. 30, 32, 106 NE 556, 557 (1914) (a law prohibiting the display of a red flag "cannot be stricken down as unconstitutional unless [it has] no tendency" to endanger public safety); *State v. Pioneer Press Co*, 100 Minn. 173, 177, 110 NW 867, 868 (1907) (speech may be restricted if it "naturally tends to excite the public mind and thus indirectly affect the public good."); *State v. McKee*, 73 Conn. 18, 46 A 409, 412 (1900) (speech may be restricted if it tends "to public demoralization"); and *People v. Most*, 128 N.Y. 108, 115-16, 27 N.E. 970 (1891) (an "incendiary" speech may be restricted where "dangerous . . . consequences . . . may result from [the] speech"). Also see Rabban, *Free Speech*, 129–76.

61. See ibid., 177–210.

62. Thomas M. Cooley, *A Treatise on the Constitutional Limitations*, 4th ed. (Boston: Little, Brown, 1878), 534–37.

63. *Masses Publishing Co. v. Patten*, 244 F 535 (S.D. N.Y. 1917).

64. Murphy, *World War I and the Origin of Civil Liberties*, 196.

65. See *Masses*, 244 F at 542–43.

66. The verse is reprinted in *Masses*, 244 F at 544.

67. Ibid., 536–37. In July 1917, Amos Pinchot wrote President Wilson to protest Burleson's decision to exclude the *Masses* from the mails. Wilson's reply indicated that Burleson had "made it clear to the President that he would enforce the Espionage Act . . . as he saw fit and that his resignation might follow any attempt at interference." Scheiber, *Wilson Administration*, 36–37.

68. *Masses*, 244 F at 539.

69. Ibid., 540.

70. *Masses*, 244 F at 540; italics added.

71. Ibid.

72. Ibid.

73. See Gregory, "Suggestions of Attorney General Gregory," 305–7.

74. *Masses Publishing Co v. Patten*, 246 F 24 (2nd Cir. 1917).

75. Among those indicted were Max Eastman, John Reed, Josephine Bell, and Henry Glintenkamp. The *Masses* defendants were tried twice. Each trial ended in a hung jury. A successor publication, the *New Masses*, appeared from 1927 to 1947.

76. See Thomas A. Lawrence, "Eclipse of Liberty: Civil Liberties in the United States during the First World War," *Wayne State University Law Review* 21 (1974): 33, 70.

77. See Murphy, *World War I and the Origin of Civil Liberties*, 80; Rabban, *Free Speech*, 256; Department of Justice, *Annual Report of the Attorney General*, 47. More precisely, 2,168 individuals were prosecuted and 1,055 were convicted. See Scheiber, *Wilson Administration*, 46–47.

78. 255 F 886 (9th Cir 1919).

79. Ibid., 887.

80. Ibid., 887–89.

81. See, e.g., *Goldstein v. United States*, 258 F 908 (9th Cir 1919); *Coldwell v. United States*, 256 F 805 (1st Cir 1919); *Kirchner v. United States*, 255 F 301 (4th Cir 1918); *Deason v. United States*, 254 F 259 (5th Cir 1918); *Doe v. United States*, 253 F 903 (8th Cir 1918); *O'Hare v. United States*, 253 F 538 (8th Cir 1918); *Masses Publishing Co v. Patten*, 246 F 24 (2d Cir 1917) (reversing Judge Hand's opinion); *United States v. Nagler*, 252 F 217 (WD Wis 1918); and *United States v. Motion Picture Film "The Spirit of '76,"* 252 F 946 (SD Cal 1917). For additional citations, see Rabban, *Free Speech*, 256–59.

82. Murphy, *World War I and the Origin of Civil Liberties*, 190.

83. See *United States v. Stokes* (unreported) (D. Mo. 1918), revd 264 F 18 (8th Cir. 1920), quoted by Zechariah Chafee, *Free Speech in the United States* (Cambridge, Mass.: Harvard University Press, 1941), 52–53; and Peterson and Fite, *Opponents of War*, 185–86. See "Mrs. Stokes Denies Assailing Red Cross," *New York Times*, May 22, 1918 (reporting Stokes's statements during her trial); "Mrs. Stokes Denies Disloyal Intent," *New York Times*, May 23, 1918 (reporting the conclusion of Stokes's trial and summation arguments by both attorneys); and "Mrs. Rose R. Stokes Convicted of Disloyalty; Illegal to Impair National Morale, Says Judge," *New York Times*, May 24, 1918. On March 9, 1920, a federal court of appeals overturned Stokes's conviction, ruling that that district judge had placed "too heavy a burden" on the defendant because of his inappropriate "partisan zeal." *Stokes*, 264 F at 26. See also "Ten-Year Sentence of Mrs. Rose Stokes Overruled by Federal Court in St. Louis," *New York Times*, March 10, 1920. On November 15, 1921, the government finally dismissed the charges against Stokes; "Mrs. Stokes Freed; Debs May Soon Be," *New York Times*, November 16, 1921.

84. *United States v. Doe* (unreported) (D. Colo. 1918), affd., 253 F 903 (8th Cir 1918), excerpted in Chafee, *Free Speech*, 54–55.

85. *"Spirit of '76,"* 252 F at 947–48 (confiscating the film and prohibiting its presentation without modification). See Peterson and Fite, *Opponents of War*, 185–86. The movie was finally screened at Town Hall in New York City in July of 1921. See "Revive 'Spirit of '76,' Film Barred in 1917," *New York Times*, July 14, 1921. After Goldstein's conviction, moviemakers quietly toed "the war-party line."

86. John Lord O'Brian, "Civil Liberty in War Time," 299–300.

87. Chafee, *Free Speech*, 52.

88. Espionage Act of 1917, 40 Stat at 230; "Burleson to Editor and Publisher," *New York World*, October 31, 1917.

89. See Chafee, *Free Speech*, 97–100. It is difficult to measure the impact of Burleson's policies because the number of publications actually banned from the mails substantially understates the amount of expression suppressed. Faced with Burleson's policies, many publications moderated their editorial comment. E.g., "after a hearing before Burleson in October, 1917, Abraham Cahan, the distinguished editor of the Yiddish *Daily Forward*, announced that 'the paper will henceforth publish war news without comment and will not criticize the allies, in order to avoid suspension of mailing privileges.'" *New York Times*, October 7, 1917, excerpted in Scheiber, *Wilson Administration*, 34.

Wilson now and then made suggestions to Burleson, such as the admonition that he use "the utmost caution and liberality in all our censorship." Letter from Woodrow Wilson to Albert Burleson, Oct 11, 1917, in *PWW*, vol. 44, 358. But "the Postmaster General usually had the last word in censorship matters." On two occasions, one involving an issue of the *Nation* and another involving an issue of Norman Thomas's pacifist *World Tomorrow*, Wilson did override Burleson's orders of exclusion. More often, though, Burleson simply ignored Wilson's reservations and persisted in his campaign to cleanse the mails of all "disloyal" publications. The responsibility for restraining the postmaster general rested "squarely upon Woodrow Wilson." That Wilson realized this but generally did nothing was deeply troubling. See Murphy, *World War I and the Origin of Civil Liberties*, 96–103; and Scheiber, *Wilson Administration*, 30–31, 36–37, 39.

90. For examples of such legislation, see Murphy, *World War I and the Origin of Civil Liberties*, 86 n. 42.

91. See Peterson and Fite, *Opponents of War*, 141–46.

92. Murphy, *World War I and the Origin of Civil Liberties*, 118. See also Robert K. Murray, *Red Scare: A Study in National Hysteria, 1919–1920* (Minneapolis: University of Minnesota Press, 1955), 13 (individuals and even towns with Germanic names changed them in "self-defense").

93. See O'Brian, "Civil Liberty in War Time," 275.

94. Gregory, "Suggestions of Attorney General Gregory," 313, 316.

95. 65th Cong., 2d Sess., in 56 *Cong. Rec.* H 3003 (March 4, 1918) (Reprentative Gard). See also ibid. ("It strikes me that . . . we have plenty of law now.") (Reprentative Cox).

96. 40 Stat 553.

97. 65th Cong., 2d Sess., in 56 *Cong. Rec.* S 4783 (April 8, 1918).

98. Ibid., 4566 (April 4, 1918). In announcing that he would vote against the Sedition Act, Senator Hardwick of Georgia stated, "In taking this position, I am well aware that I will subject myself to bitter . . . criticism. It will be contended . . . that I am disloyal to the country." Ibid., 5940 (May 2, 1918).

99. Ibid., 4562 (April 4, 1918). See also ibid., 4764 (April 8, 1918) ("The object of this proposed law is to prevent violence. . . . It is for the sake of keeping the peace of this country, to prevent a breach of the peace, that it is necessary.") (Senator Nelson); ibid., 4714 (April 6, 1918) ("The principal object of this bill . . . is to prevent mob law.")

(Senator Myers); ibid., 4633 (April 5, 1918) ("If we do not do our duty here, the impulses of loyal men and women will seek justice in rougher ways. . . . I shudder at the thought that this proud Republic is about to resort to the law of riot and disorder.") (Senator Borah).

100. Richard Polenberg, *Fighting Faiths: The Abrams Case, the Supreme Court, and Free Speech* (New York: Viking Press, 1987), 31.

101. Ibid., 4633.

102. Ibid., 4637.

103. Ibid.

104. O'Brian, "Civil Liberty in War Time," 304.

105. Memo from Attorney General Thomas Gregory to All United States Attorneys, May 23, 1918, excerpted by Murphy, *World War I and the Origin of Civil Liberties*, 94. See also O'Brian, "Civil Liberty in War Time," 305.

106. Ibid., 305–6.

107. See Polenberg, *Fighting Faiths*, 198; David P. Currie, *The Constitution in the Supreme Court: The Second Century, 1886–1986* (Chicago: University of Chicago Press, 1990), 126–30; Murphy, *World War I and the Origin of Civil Liberties*, 182–83; and Robert Cover, "The Left, The Right and the First Amendment: 1918–1928," *Maryland Law Review* 40 (1981): 349.

108. *Schenck v. United States*, 249 U.S. 47 (1919).

109. *Schenck*, 249 U.S. at 50–51 (the Court describing the contents of the pamphlet).

110. Ibid., 52.

111. Indeed, if Holmes had intended to adopt a standard different from the one under which the defendants had been tried and convicted, he would not have *affirmed* the convictions. Clearly, the defendants had not been tried under the "clear and present danger" standard, which did not yet exist. Thus, if Holmes had intended to adopt a new standard, he would have remanded the case to the federal district court for a new trial, which would then have applied the *correct* constitutional standard. But Holmes did not do remand; he simply affirmed the convictions.

112. The Court had arguably applied some version of the "bad tendency" test (without an independent requirement of specific intent) in several pre-*Schenck* decisions. See, e.g., *Toledo Newspaper Co v. United States*, 247 U.S. 402, 420 (1918) (the freedom of the press, "as every other right enjoyed in human society, is subject to the restraints which separate right from wrongdoing"); *Fox v. Washington*, 236 U.S. 273 (1915) (upholding a conviction for encouraging the commission of a crime); *Patterson v. Colorado*, 205 U.S. 454 (1907) (upholding a contempt citation for criticizing judicial conduct in a pending case); *Turner v. Williams*, 194 U.S. 279 (1904) (upholding the deportation of an alien for advocating anarchism); and *Ex Parte Jackson*, 96 U.S. 727 (1877) (upholding a federal statute prohibiting the use of the mails for lottery advertisements). None of these decisions was cited in *Schenck*, however. For a full discussion of these decisions, see Rabban, *Free Speech*, 132–41.

113. *Frohwerk v. United States*, 249 U.S. 204 (1919).

114. *Debs v. United States*, 249 U.S. 211 (1919).

115. Ibid., 207–8.

116. Ibid., 208–9.

117. Debs, Speech in Canton, Ohio, June 16, 1918, in *Writings and Speeches of Eugene V. Debs*, ed. Schlesinger, 417–22 (parentheticals in original).

118. The U.S. attorney for northern Ohio, E. S. Wertz, sent a copy of Debs's speech to the Justice Department in Washington to get advice about whether to prosecute him. Attorney General Gregory discouraged the proposed prosecution because the government did not want to make a martyr of Debs and because the case for conviction was not clear. Wertz disregarded this advice and initated the prosecution. See Nick Salvatore, *Eugene V. Debs: Citizen and Socialist* (Urbana: University of Illinois Press,1982), 294–96.

119. See, e.g., "Debs Arrested; Sedition Charged," *New York Times*, July 1, 1918; "Swears Debs Upheld Anti-War Program," *New York Times*, September 11, 1918; "E. V. Debs Declines to Offer Defense," *New York Times*, September 12, 1918; "Find Debs Guilty of Disloyal Act," *New York Times*, September 13, 1918; and "Debs Case in High Court," *New York Times*, January 28, 1919.

120. 249 U.S. at 212–15. In the 1920 presidential campaign, Debs again received almost 1 million votes, even though he ran the campaign from his prison cell. A popular campaign button showed Debs in prison garb, standing outside the prison gates, with the caption "For President—Convict No. 9653."

121. Ibid., 215–16.

122. Harry Kalven Jr., *A Worthy Tradition: Freedom of Speech in America* (New York: Harper & Row, 1988), 135.

123. *Abrams v. United States*, 250 U.S. 616 (1919).

124. Ibid., 620–22.

125. Murphy, *World War I and the Origin of Civil Liberties*, 234. For a fuller account of the judge and the trial, see Polenberg, *Fighting Faiths*, 95–153.

126. On the trial, see, generally, ibid., 10840; and Lawrence, "Eclipse of Liberty," 33.

127. *Schenck*; and *Frohwerk*, 250 U.S. at 617–19.

128. *Frohwerk*, 250 U.S. at 627–28.

129. Ibid., 628.

130. Ibid., 629.

131. Kalven, *Worthy Tradition*, 146–47.

132. See Lawrence, "Eclipse of Liberty," 33–43. See also John P. Roche, *The Quest for the Dream* (New York: Macmillan, 1963) (suggesting that wartime repression reflected an effort to Americanize a set of pluralistic communities through enforced patriotism).

133. See Harold M. Hyman, *To Try Men's Souls: Loyalty Tests in American History* (Berkeley: University of California Press, 1959), 267–315 (recognizing the pressures placed on the Wilson administration by influential "superpatriots" to move against disloyalty).

134. Murphy, *World War I and the Origin of Civil Liberties*, 252–53.

135. See Hyman, *To Try Men's Souls*, 267–315; and Scheiber, *Wilson Administration*, 60 (Wilson's "abdication of personal responsibility left the fate of civil liberties to subordinate officials . . . at a time when few were inclined to be moderate").

136. According to the Department of Justice, many federal judges "imposed severe sentences as a means of fostering unity and bolstering morale." Scheiber, *Wilson Administration*, 43 n. 7.

137. See Kalven, *Worthy Tradition*, 147. See also Currie, *Constitution in the Supreme Court*, 127. (The Court's performance in these cases reflected "an extreme insensitivity to the values" of the First Amendment.)

138. Letter from Alfred Bettman to Zechariah Chafee Jr., September 20, 1919, excerpted by Rabban, *Free Speech*, 327.

139. See Rabban, *Free Speech*, 299.

140. See John Dewey, "Conscription of Thought," *New Republic*, September 1, 1917, 128–30; Henry F. May, *The End of American Innocence: A Study of the First Years of Our Own Time, 1912–1917* (New York: Alfred A. Knopf, 1959), 373; and John C. Farrell, *John Dewey and World War I: Armageddon Tests a Liberal's Faith*, Perspectives in American History 9 (Cambridge, Mass.: Harvard University Press, 1975), 299–340.

141. John Dewey, "In Explanation of Our Lapse," *New Republic* 13 (1917), reprinted in *John Dewey: The Middle Works, 1899-1924*, ed. Jo Ann Boydston (Carbondale: Southern Illinois University Press, 1980), vol. 10, 292.

142. John Dewey, "Liberalism and Civil Liberties," in *John Dewey: The Later Works, 1925–1953*, ed. Jo Ann Boydston (Carbondale: Southern Illinois University Press, 1987), vol. 2, 374.

143. See 66th Cong., 3d Sess., in 60 *Cong. Rec.* H 293-94 (December 13, 1920).

144. Max Lowenthal, *The Federal Bureau of Investigation* (New York: William Sloane Associates, 1950), 298.

145. See "March in Manacles, Plan of Radicals, *New York Times*, December 16, 1919 (2,000 people marched in New York City in manacles to protest the imprisonment of "political prisoners").

146. See "Wilson Commutes Espionage Terms," *New York Times*, March 6, 1919; "Palmer Request Clemency for 52," *New York Times*, April 12, 1919.

147. Letter from Thomas Gregory to Woodrow Wilson, March 1, 1919, quoted by Scheiber, *Wilson Administration*, 46.

148. See Letter from Alexander Mitchell Palmer, In the Matter of the Application for Pardon, In Behalf of Eugene V. Debs, January 29, 1921, in *PWW*, vol. 67, 102 n. 8 ("Wilson filled in the date of the application for executive clemency in behalf of Debs and wrote: "Denied. W. W."; emphasis in original). Letter to George Creel, March 2, 1921, in *PWW*, vol. 67, 186 n. 1; "Wilson Refuses to Pardon Debs," *New York Times*, February 1, 1921. Debs was then sixty-five years old and in failing health. The *New York Times* applauded Wilson's decision. See "Debs," *New York Times*, March 26, 1921 ("Debs 'deserved ten years' imprisonment if any man ever deserved it. . . . This man tried to assassinate the United States Government").

149. See "Nearing Attacks Holding Prisoners," *New York Times*, February 23, 1922 (the "joint amnesty committee" charged that the 112 individuals still in prison for Espionage Act violations were being held because of their efforts before the war "to attack the established industrial order"); "Urge House to Ask Pardons by Harding," *New York Times*, March 17, 1922 (in the face of "outspoken opposition," representatives of various "liberal organizations pleaded with the House Judiciary Committee" to ask the president to give "careful consideration to the propriety of giving immediate amnesty to 113 political prisoners serving long terms for violation of the Espionage Act"); "50 Congressmen Ask Harding for Amnesty," *New York Times*, March 22, 1922 (fifty representatives from twenty-one states signed a petition asking President Harding to release all remaining prisoners convicted under the Espionage Act); "Convicts' Children Picket White House," *New York Times*, April 30, 1922 (a group of thirty-five women and children picketed the White House in support of amnesty for their still imprisoned husbands and fathers); "Clash with Parade of Amnesty Seekers," New York Times, November 12, 1922 (more than two hundred demonstrators carrying American flags marched on Armistice Day in Lafayette Square across from the White House in support of amnesty for the sixty-four remaining prisoners. When a small group of anti-amnesty protestors entered Lafayette Square carrying banners bearing such messages as "We Want Out, Too-Chicken Thieves Society," a ruckus broke out and the police had to restore order); and "Wrangle in House on Amnesty Plea," *New York Times*, December 12, 1922 (a group of representatives assailed other representatives who had supported amnesty for individuals still imprisoned under the Espionage Act).

150. See "Coolidge Releases All War Offenders as Christmas Gift," *New York Times*, December 16, 1923.

151. See Jerold S. Auerbach, "The Depression Decade," in *The Pulse of Freedom: American Liberties, 1920-1970s*, ed. Alan Reitman (New York: W. W. Norton, 1975), 67–68.

8. Democracy, Peace, and World Order

Lloyd E. Ambrosius

Peacemaking has been a central concern in modern world history. Michael Eliot Howard, in *The Invention of Peace* (2000), noted that the idea of peace—the ordering of society to create a positive peace, not just a negative peace as a pause between wars—originated with the European Enlightenment.[1] That hope for enduring peace has shaped statecraft and intellectual inquiries in Western history ever since. In this modern tradition, President Woodrow Wilson attempted to create a new world order after World War I. His approach—known as Wilsonianism—called for peacemaking on the basis of collective security, national self-determination, and "open door" globalization. It expressed his belief in progress, which undergirded the promise that history would culminate in a new era of world peace.

Wilson's Vision of Peacemaking

Over the centuries, as political scientists have emphasized, different worldviews have shaped alternative approaches to peacemaking. Michael W. Doyle, in *Ways of War and Peace* (1997), identified three international relations theories from the ancient Greeks to contemporary Americans: Realism, Liberalism, and Socialism.[2] These three traditions have characterized European and American thinking about war and peace throughout modern world history. All three defined the choices for peacemakers after World War I. Some Western Europeans, such as French premier Georges Clemenceau, and some Americans, such as Senator Henry Cabot Lodge, accepted Realism as their primary worldview. Liberalism found its leading advocate in Wilson, but British prime minister David Lloyd George also embraced this tradition. Although not at the Paris Peace Conference of 1919, the new Bolshevik leader in revolutionary Russia, V. I. Lenin, proclaimed a radical version of Socialism. Leaders expressed

and epitomized the different alternatives, or variations of them. These competing traditions mixed together in the internal politics of each country as well as
the international politics of peacemaking. Statesmen in Paris and critics of the
Versailles peace treaty with Germany struggled over the ideological alternatives
of Realism, Liberalism, and Socialism.

Wilson's liberal vision did not prevail in 1919. After World War I, communism
and fascism presented even greater challenges to his legacy of Wilsonianism. Over
the long run, however, American foreign policy leaders and pundits continued to
believe in the Wilsonian way of peacemaking. Typical of this perspective, Michael
Mandelbaum argued that, by the twenty-first century, the "Wilsonian triad" of
peace, liberal democracy, and free markets had become—as the title of his book
announced—*The Ideas That Conquered the World* (2002).[3]

Wilson used his liberal vision of peace to justify American entry into the
Great War against Imperial Germany. On April 2, 1917, in his war message to
Congress, he called for a democratic partnership. "A steadfast concert for peace
can never be maintained except by a partnership of democratic nations," he
asserted. "No autocratic government could be trusted to keep faith within it or
observe its covenants." Democracy was the key to peace. He wanted the United
States to participate in the eventual postwar peacemaking to create "a league of
honor, a partnership of opinion. . . . Only free peoples can hold their purposes
and their honor steady to a common end and prefer the interests of mankind to
any narrow interest of their own." The recent Russian Revolution, in Wilson's
view, promised to give rise to a new liberal democratic state in place of the tsarist
regime. He welcomed the new Russia as "a fit partner for a League of Honor."
He also wanted Imperial Germany to undergo a similar transformation from
autocratic to democratic government. "The world must be made safe for
democracy," he proclaimed. "Its peace must be planted upon the tested foundations of political liberty." That was the high ideal for which the United States
would enter the European war. Wilson denied that Americans had any "selfish
ends to serve." They desired "no conquest, no dominion" and "no indemnities
for ourselves, no material compensation for the sacrifices we shall freely make."
The United States, he told Congress, would become "one of the champions of
the rights of mankind. We shall be satisfied when those rights have been made
as secure as the faith and the freedom of nations can make them." In this new
democratic world order, Wilson promised that the United States would join its
European partners to guarantee the postwar peace.[4]

Wilson outlined this new vision in his Fourteen Points of January 8, 1918.
This blueprint for peace called for a world more open to international travel,

shipping, commerce, and finance. His plan anticipated a peace settlement that would allow new European states to enjoy national self-determination. The last point called for a league of nations "under specific covenants for the purpose of affording mutual guarantees of political independence and territorial integrity to great and small states alike."[5] Quite different from traditional European alliances, this new league would unite the world rather than divide it. It would forsake old balances of power and guarantee peace by a community of nations, making it unnecessary for them to prepare for or fight another war. It would enable them to reduce military preparedness to the level required for internal and collective security, and thereby avoid another arms race. This new world order would allow the United States to participate in international affairs without entangling itself in Europe's wars. It would combine American unilateralism with a new multilateralism. Thus, it would permit the United States to reform European international politics yet preserve its own independence.

Wilson's approach to peacemaking expressed his American exceptionalism. The new partnership of democratic nations that he envisaged would be profoundly different from the Old World's traditional diplomacy and wars. He did not want the United States to join any alliance to restore or preserve Europe's balance of power. He had determined in 1917 that the United States would not join the Western alliance. This nation only associated itself with the Allies in the military coalition of the Allied and Associated Powers. As an "associated" power, the United States preserved its independence, thus affirming its unique character and place in world history. American exceptionalism shaped Wilson's distinction between the Old World and the New World, and his commitment to replace the old diplomacy, which the Allies as well as the Central Powers had practiced, with his new diplomacy. He had attempted to protect America's neutrality and keep out of the war. After 1917, he sought to transform European international relations into a new world order. The United States, he promised, would provide a different kind of global leadership in a league of nations—or actually hegemony, although he never used such language.

What Wilson wanted was a *new world* order, not just a new *world order*. His liberal internationalism embraced the essence of traditional American isolationism. He emphasized his commitment to unilateralism on September 27, 1918, when he reconciled his proposal for a new league of nations with traditional American avoidance of European entanglements. He denied that U.S. involvement in this new league would violate the diplomatic tradition that President George Washington had advised in his Farewell Address in 1796, when he urged Americans to protect their independence by avoiding unnecessary alliances.

Wilson explained: "We still read Washington's immortal warning against 'entangling alliances' with full comprehension and an answering purpose. But only special and limited alliances entangle; and we recognize and accept the duty of a new day in which we are permitted to hope for a general alliance which will avoid entanglements and clear the air of the world for common understandings and the maintenance of common rights."[6] He reconciled the essential core of isolationism with the global role that he foresaw for the United States in a new league of democratic states. He promised multilateral cooperation to implement America's universal principles, but without sacrificing its unilateral decision-making. His vision of a postwar league of nations thus conformed to historic American aloofness from the Old World.

The League of Nations

Wilson's advocacy of the League of Nations as the alternative to traditional alliances and balances of power emphasized the importance of external relations in peacemaking and peacekeeping. The organization of international relations was the key to a new world order. On May 27, 1916, when Wilson had first announced his commitment to the idea of a postwar league, he made a sharp distinction between old, entangling alliances, which he strongly condemned, and a new association of nations, which he began to advocate.[7] In his "peace without victory" address on January 22, 1917, he emphasized the difference between a world community and a balance of power. The best way to keep the peace, he proclaimed, would be a league for peace that the United States would help create after the two sets of belligerents, the Allies and the Central Powers, resolved their conflicts over competing war aims and negotiated a "peace without victory." He called for a new international partnership. "There must be," Wilson told the U.S. Senate, "not a balance of power, but a community of power; not organized rivalries, but an organized common peace." Identifying this vision with the Monroe Doctrine, he offered this American doctrine as the framework for world peace. "I am proposing," he affirmed, "that all nations henceforth avoid entangling alliances which would draw them into competitions of power; catch them in a net of intrigue and selfish rivalry, and disturb their own affairs with influences intruded from without. When all unite to act in the same sense and with the same purpose all act in the common interest and are free to live their own lives under a common protection."[8]

Wilson imagined an international society in which a league of nations could mobilize world public opinion—or the moral force of humanity—to preserve peace. On December 21, 1918, he shared his vision with the French people, telling his Paris audience how the proposed league would function. "My conception of the League of Nations is just this," he explained, "that it shall operate as the organized moral force of men throughout the world, and that whenever or wherever wrong and aggression are planned or contemplated, this searching light of conscience will be turned upon them and men everywhere will ask, 'What are the purposes that you hold in your heart against the fortunes of the world?' Just a little exposure will settle most questions."[9] Wilson claimed that, if there had been such a league in 1914, it could have prevented the war by rallying public opinion against the Central Powers, thereby using moral suasion to force them to choose peace over war. To remedy this problem, he advocated a league to organize international society. This vision expressed his liberal faith in the power of public opinion.

At the peace conference, Wilson gave top priority to creating the League of Nations. This international institution, he anticipated, would enable the United States to participate in world affairs without becoming entangled. He wanted peace and justice without war. On January 25, 1919, he reiterated his paradoxical vision of the proposed league. Americans, he said, had never regarded their entry into the war as "intervening in the politics of Europe or the politics of Asia or the politics of any part of the world." They had only joined "the cause of justice and of liberty for men of every kind and place." He still hoped to avoid entangling alliances while creating a league. "Therefore," he continued, "the United States should feel that its part in this war had been played in vain if there ensued upon it merely a body of European settlements. It would feel that it could not take part in guaranteeing those European settlements unless that guarantee involved the continuous superintendence of the peace of the world by the associated nations of the world."[10] He devoted his time during the first weeks of the peace conference primarily to drafting the Covenant for the League of Nations. Presenting it to a plenary session on February 14, 1919, he stressed its moral commitment. He said: "Throughout this instrument we are depending primarily and chiefly upon one great force, and that is the moral force of the public opinion of the world." Exposing sinister intrigues of states that might start wars to "the cleansing and clarifying and compelling influences of publicity" would be the League's way to maintain peace. Using military force to stop aggression would be only a last resort—and quite rare.[11]

Dubious about the League's reliance on world public opinion, French leaders at the peace conference sought a traditional alliance to protect their country against Germany. Clemenceau, who wanted to restore Europe's balance of power, eventually extracted commitments from Wilson and Lloyd George to a tripartite alliance. Under separate Franco-American and Anglo-French treaties, the American and British governments promised to guarantee French security against a potentially revengeful Germany. Wilson was never enthusiastic about the French security treaty, which might entangle the United States in Europe. He accepted it, however, as part of a compromise to settle disputes among the victors over the separation and occupation of the Rhineland, only by viewing this treaty's commitment as an example of what the League might do in the event of German aggression. After returning to the United States, he focused on the League and did not attempt to win approval for the French security treaty by the Senate.[12] He did not want the United States entangled in an alliance to preserve Europe's balance of power.

Although emphasizing the League's moral character, Wilson recognized its importance for international law. The Covenant was a legal document. Yet, unlike Secretary of State Robert Lansing, he did not regard legal precedents as particularly relevant in international relations. He was interested instead in infusing a new morality into international law. On May 9, 1919, he explained this different focus to the International Law Society in Paris. "If we can now give to international law the kind of vitality which it can have only if it is a real expression of our moral judgment," he said, "we shall have completed in some sense the work which this war was intended to emphasize."[13]

Some scholars have exaggerated Wilson's legal contribution to international relations. Frances Anthony Boyle, who credited Wilson with successfully fusing the "legalistic" and "moralistic" approaches to American foreign relations, regarded his role in creating the League of Nations as a major step toward establishing the legal foundations of world order.[14] However, the League was not viewed by Wilson as primarily an instrument of international law. Rather, it promised a new morality. It was "a league of right."[15] After the peace treaty was signed at Versailles on June 28, 1919, he emphasized the League's moral function to the American people: "It makes international law a reality supported by imperative sanctions."[16] Far more than Wilson, Republicans adopted the legalistic approach to U.S. foreign policy. Among these advocates were previous secretaries of state Elihu Root and Philander Knox, and their successors Charles Evans Hughes, Frank Kellogg, and Henry Stimson. All were lawyers. After the war, moreover, Root helped establish the World Court at The Hague, while Wilson remained largely indifferent toward this new legal institution.[17]

Although his advocacy of the League of Nations as the alternative to alliances and balances of power emphasized external relations, Wilson also stressed internal affairs. Democratic governments, he believed, were inherently more peaceful. Accordingly, he wanted a democratic partnership to preserve world peace. The modern democratic state, in his view, represented the ultimate end of political history, which was a long and slow process. In his early writings, he traced the origins of American democracy back to the Anglo-Saxons. At Johns Hopkins, where he had earned his PhD, professors Herbert Baxter Adams and Richard Ely introduced him to German historicism. According to this Hegelian theory of history, modern nations grew like biological organisms from primordial racial roots. Thus the essential character of the American people, including their democratic institutions, had come from their ancient ancestors. In *The State* (1889), Wilson identified American politics with "the first Teutons" who had gone to England. "The history of government in England, as in Germany, begins with the primitive politics of the Teutonic races," he wrote, adding that these ancestors had "a very fierce democratic temper." He believed that American liberty and democracy had originated from them.[18]

At this time, Wilson identified the United States and its democracy with the Anglo-Saxon race. His liberalism was intertwined with a particular racial nationalism. In 1885, he viewed the modern democratic state as "the result of history, not of theory, a creation of experience rather than speculation." He saw American democracy as "a truly organic growth" that originated "in our history, in our experiences as a Teutonic race set apart to make a special English character." His adaptation of German historicism made him confident that the world was progressing toward greater freedom and democracy. "The present trend of all political development the world over towards democracy is no mere episode in history," he rejoiced. Liberal democracy in a nation required "several all-important conditions," including the "homogeneity of race and community of thought and purpose among the people." He conceived of the democratic state as "the rule of the *whole*" or the organic nation. He expected minorities to acquiesce in this common will. Only when nations reached this stage of development would they be ready for democratic government. At the end of this history, democratic nations would enjoy "the most humane results of the world's peace and progress."[19]

In Wilson's interpretation of modern history, democracy and nationalism had emerged together. At first, he traced the origins of these two trends in the United States back to Anglo-Saxon or Teutonic ancestors, thus affirming racial nationalism. In the 1890s, however, he shifted his focus from European origins to the American West. This new perspective emphasized civic nationalism. He returned to Johns Hopkins in 1889 to deliver a series of lectures. There he met Frederick

Jackson Turner, a current graduate student. Turner persuaded him to study west-ern America. While writing *Division and Reunion* (1893), Wilson asked the young historian for information about the West's contributions to "the growth of the national idea, and of nationality, in our history." Turner sent him a copy of "Problems in American History," but he had already finished writing his book. Before reading Turner's first publication of his famous frontier thesis, Wilson con-cluded that the American West had produced "a new epoch" in the nation's histo-ry by 1829. He offered his own frontier thesis. Turner praised him for emphasiz-ing "the doctrine of American *development*, in contrast to Germanic *germs*."[20]

Shifting his focus from the Anglo-Saxon or Teutonic roots of the United States to the origins of American democracy on the western frontier, Wilson largely replaced the language of racial nationalism with the civic nationalist ideals of lib-erty and democracy. Yet white Anglo-Saxon racial prejudice still influenced his thinking. He still expected African Americans to accommodate themselves to the emerging Jim Crow system of racial segregation.[21] He also applied the hierarchy of race to U.S. foreign policy when he approved the American war with Spain in 1898 and the subsequent overseas empire. The closing of the continental frontier in 1890, he thought, required Americans to look abroad. "This great pressure of a people moving always to new frontiers in search of new lands, new power, the full freedom of a virgin world, has ruled our course and formed our policies like a Fate," he affirmed. This search for "new frontiers for ourselves beyond the seas" had led to the war with Spain and to the acquisition of colonies. Americans had become "apostles of liberty and of self-government," he believed. "We have given pledges to the world and must redeem them as we can."[22] The United States was now ready to bring the blessings of liberty and democracy to other races and nations, provided they first acquiesced in the required American tutelage.

This Wilsonian vision of America's global mission for the twentieth century promised a new world order. Paradoxically, it affirmed a European intellectual tradition with biblical and classical roots. It had not originated on the American frontier. As Jan Willem Schulte Nordholt observed, "the myth of the West" had come from the Old World. Yet this myth undergirded the American mission as Wilson understood it. It depicted the United States as the "last empire" or the culmination of world history, and it gave Americans confidence in their future. Their new land represented a "city on a hill" or "last frontier" or "end of histo-ry." Their incomparable empire was not really like those of other Great Powers that had risen and fallen. The myth promised the United States a happier des-tiny with unending progress. Wilson embraced this mythic American exception-alism in his understanding of world history.[23]

Wilson applied this nationalist perspective to peacemaking after World War I. Within the framework of American exceptionalism, the United States offered the world its best hope for enduring peace. The League of Nations, which he saw as the centerpiece of the Versailles Treaty, promised a new era of international relations. It would protect modern civilization against barbarism. After returning home from Paris, Wilson reiterated these themes when he submitted the treaty to the Senate on July 10, 1919. Creating the new world order had not been easy, he said, because "old entanglements of every kind stood in the way." But he had succeeded. The League, he claimed, would be "an indispensable instrumentality for the maintenance of the new order" in "the world of civilized men." This new institution would convert "the accepted principles of international law" into "the actual rule of conduct among the governments of the world." It would replace old rivalries with "the united power of free nations" to keep the peace. The Paris peacemaking had established the United States as the world's preeminent leader. He welcomed this global role. The League, he believed, would enable the American nation to provide worldwide leadership largely through its moral influence over public opinion, and thus fulfill its God-given destiny. "The stage is set, the destiny disclosed," the president concluded. "It has come about by no plan of our conceiving, but by the hand of God who led us into this way. We cannot turn back. We can only go forward, with lifted eyes and freshened spirit, to follow the vision. It was of this that we dreamed at our birth. America shall in truth show the way."[24] At stake was nothing less than the defense of civilization against the barbarism of another world war.

Wilson's belief in the God-given destiny of the United States and in progressive history blinded him from seeing what Wolfgang Schivelbusch called "the culture of defeat" in other countries. Having been born and raised in the American South, the president had experienced the trauma of defeat after the Civil War. This experience profoundly influenced him. Yet he found it very difficult to empathize with foreigners who suffered from similar military defeat. Schivelbusch compared the American South after the Civil War, France after the Franco-Prussian War of 1870–71, and Germany after World War I. The losers in all three wars claimed moral superiority over their conquerors. They saw themselves as true defenders of civilization against barbaric victors. Wilson's claim to have created a new world order of "civilized men" at the peace conference did not appear that way to most Germans in the Weimar Republic. Nor did it look that way to Clemenceau, who had experienced military defeat in the Franco-Prussian War. Wilson shared the white South's trauma after the American Civil War, but he did not understand either Clemenceau's fixation on French security or

Weimar Germany's almost universal rejection of the Versailles Treaty. Turning defeat into eventual victory had been the purpose of the South's Lost Cause and of France's Third Republic. This resolve profoundly influenced Wilson's and Clemenceau's statecraft. The culture of defeat would also quickly shape postwar politics in Weimar Germany.[25] Unfortunately, Wilson's new world order fell short of French and German expectations, and those of other nations that had anticipated more from the peacemaking in 1919. Belligerent nationalism that resulted from this widespread disillusionment, which manifested the culture of defeat, contributed to the failure of democracy and peace after World War I. Wilson's concept of a world community offered no solution to this postwar problem.

National Self-Determination

Both internal affairs and external relations intersected in Wilson's principle of national self-determination. Conflicting definitions of self-determination depended on whether race and ethnicity or liberal civic ideals were given primacy. New nations adopted different identities in accordance with their cultural values. A new state might affirm liberal ideals, avowing civic nationalism. Alternatively, its people might identify with their ancestral roots, emphasizing exclusive racial nationalism. The choice between these two substantially influenced a nation's understanding of the principle. Although different advocates might concur on its importance in the peacemaking, they often disagreed over its meaning and application in particular instances. The principle combined the earlier concepts of state sovereignty and democracy. Its pioneering historian, Alfred Cobban, defined it as "the right of a nation to constitute an independent state and determine its own government for itself."[26] Affirming both a state's sovereignty over certain territory and a people's right to self-government, the principle justified popular sovereignty within nation-states. But its meaning in practice was often in dispute. As both civic and racial nationalism had competed throughout American history, the United States itself had experienced ongoing tensions between the liberal inclusiveness of multicultural assimilation and the racial exclusiveness of white Anglo-Saxon Americanism.[27] These two traditions of civic and racial nationalism had influenced Wilson's thinking, and consequently his definition of national self-determination.

During World War I, Wilson made national self-determination a guiding principle of American foreign policy. On May 27, 1916, he declared that "every people has a right to choose the sovereignty under which they shall live." He thought that "small states" as well as "great and powerful nations" should enjoy sovereignty and

territorial integrity free from aggression.[28] He embraced nationalism as the dominant force in the modern world but expected democratic values and institutions to
prevent one nation's claims from endangering another's sovereign rights.
Democratic nations, he hoped, would join together for mutual security, thereby
creating a new world order that accommodated both nationalism and peace.

Daniel Patrick Moynihan credited Wilson with placing national self-determination at the top of the international agenda. "Wilson did not create nationalism,"
Moynihan noted in *Pandaemonium* (1993), "nothing of the sort. But he did
respond to it with the doctrine of self-determination."[29] This contribution to international law was a typically American amalgam of idealism and self-interest.
Moynihan criticized Henry Kissinger's "realist" perspective for exaggerating the
geopolitical or military aspects of international politics and ignoring ethnicity, or
what Walker Connor called "ethnonationalism."[30] Moynihan attributed the president's decision to intervene in 1917 to his pro-British bias. He concluded that
"Woodrow Wilson, Scotch-Irish that he was, believed that Americans were of the
'Anglo-Saxon race' and need come to the rescue of their brethren in Britain."[31]
Moynihan's conclusion ignored Wilson's independent Americanism and his shift
to civic nationalism after meeting Turner. Although the president identified with
his Scots-Irish and English ancestry, and with the Anglo-Saxon race, Moynihan
greatly exaggerated these ethnic influences on his diplomacy. British officials in
Washington and London clearly recognized the limits. They understood that,
despite his racial and ethnic prejudices, he would not follow British wartime leadership. He pursued his own nationalist perspective in international politics.[32]

American history shaped Wilson's understanding of national self-determination. During the Civil War, President Abraham Lincoln had denied self-determination to the South to save the Union. After the Spanish-American War of 1898,
the United States had annexed the Philippines, postponing the right of its inhabitants to self-determination as an independent nation. At the Paris Peace
Conference in 1919, Wilson followed these precedents in his reluctance to foster
self-determination for new nation-states throughout the world. He never challenged British rule in Ireland, Egypt, and India, or French control in Indochina,
and he approved the transfer to the empires of Britain, France, Belgium, and Japan
of Germany's African and Pacific island colonies in the form of mandates under
the League of Nations. He recognized only those new nations that emerged from
the Russian, German, Austro-Hungarian, and Ottoman empires. He limited
national self-determination to a few new states in Europe.[33]

Wilson's concept of national self-determination helped Germany by limiting
its postwar territorial losses. He opposed its dismemberment while favoring the

transformation of its government into a democratic republic. At Paris in 1919, he sought to restrict Germany's territorial losses to what he had outlined in his Fourteen Points. He approved both the French annexation of Alsace-Lorraine and the Polish corridor to the Baltic sea. But he opposed most other extensive alterations in Germany's historical boundaries. On March 27, 1919, the president reiterated his antipathy toward redrawing the map of Europe. "Everywhere we are compelled to change boundaries and national sovereignties," he warned. "Nothing involves greater danger, for these changes run contrary to long-established customs and change the very life of populations whilst, at the same time, they affect their feelings. We must avoid giving our enemies even the impression of injustice."[34] He resisted adjustments that the Allies wanted in Germany's historical borders when he did not regard these as essential to the peace settlement.

When Clemenceau advanced historical and economic claims to the Saar region of Germany, Wilson rejected the historical argument. Sympathetic toward the French claims for economic compensation from the coal mines, he nevertheless opposed all efforts to take this territory from Germany. "The annexation of these regions to France," he told Clemenceau, "does not have a sufficient historical foundation." Lloyd George suggested the alternative of detaching the Saar from Germany and establishing it as a separate state. Wilson rejected that compromise as well, explaining that "I believe that we violate the principle of self-determination as much by giving one people an independence it does not request as by making them pass under the sovereignty of another. The sole principle I recognize is the one of the consent of the governed."[35] These statesmen finally settled their differences by placing the Saar under the League of Nations for fifteen years. The French would administer this region for the League. Then a plebiscite would allow the local people to choose their national affiliation. Meanwhile, the Saar would remain nominally under German sovereignty.[36]

Wilson resisted Germany's dismemberment even for the sake of European security. He refused to consider French plans for separating the Rhineland from Germany because this would violate its right of national self-determination. French strategic arguments did not persuade him to sacrifice his principle. He also rejected Clemenceau's appeal for permanent occupation of the Rhineland, although he eventually acquiesced in its temporary occupation by U.S. and Allied troops for fifteen years. He said, "I insist on maintaining the right of self-determination."[37] The president resisted substantial adjustments in Germany's historical boundaries beyond what he had called for in his Fourteen Points, even to prevent future German aggression.

On Germany's eastern frontier, Wilson approved extensive changes to accommodate the new nation of Poland. He agreed with the Allied premiers to give Poland access to the sea, as he had promised in the Fourteen Points, and to establish Danzig as a free city. He also endorsed the Polish claim to the rich industrial area of Upper Silesia. He regarded these changes as essential to Poland's restoration. In drawing the new German-Polish borders, while giving Poland access to the sea, he wanted to "respect ethnographic lines as much as possible." In the East Prussian provinces of Marienwerder and Allenstein, he thought the people should decide by plebiscite whether to remain German or become Polish.[38] Yet he concurred in the transfer of Upper Silesia to Poland without a plebiscite, not viewing this territorial change as a violation of his Fourteen Points. Because of the dominant influence of German capitalists and civil servants in Upper Silesia, he did not believe that a plebiscite could fairly determine the will of the local population, which he thought was largely Polish. When the German delegation at Versailles later protested against the loss of Upper Silesia, Lloyd George advocated a plebiscite, suggesting that the principle of national self-determination required it. Wilson retorted: "I cannot allow you to say that I am not for the right of self-determination. That is absurd. What I want is the true expression of popular sentiment." However, he eventually agreed to a plebiscite in Upper Silesia to allow its inhabitants to decide their national identity.[39]

Seeking to draft the peace treaty in accordance with national self-determination, Wilson preferred historical boundaries. This approach, while often favoring Germany by minimizing its territorial losses, sometimes worked against it. He never believed that all Germans had a right to live in the same nation-state. He did not share Germany's ethnonationalist interpretation of self-determination. He approved the historic frontier between the German and Austro-Hungarian empires as the new border between Germany and Czechoslovakia.[40] He also readily agreed to forbid Germany from annexing what remained of Austria. Denying this possibility to Germany, he sought to protect Austria's self-determination by recognizing its right to unite with Germany, subject to approval by the League of Nations.[41]

Wilson clarified his principle of national self-determination while dealing with problems of national and religious minorities in postwar Europe. The Versailles Treaty would leave some Germans in Austria, Czechoslovakia, and Poland. Jews also lived as outsiders in the new states of Central and Eastern Europe. The mixture of different nationalities already produced serious ethnocultural conflict, posing the question of the rights of ethnic and religious minorities.[42] It was impossible to draw borders along either historic or ethnographic lines that would satisfy all the nationalities. In accordance with civic nationalism, Wilson hoped that the historical process of nation building would resolve these ethnic problems by integrating minorities into the new nations. His attitude toward minority rights expressed his liberal view of assimilation. The melting pot might solve ethnocultural problems in Europe, as he thought it had in the United States. The president and Allied premiers agonized particularly over the rights of minorities in Poland, where anti-Semitism was rampant. Yet Wilson rejected the idea of autonomy for the Jewish community, hoping instead that the Poles would assimilate the Jews into their nation. He expressed this same idea toward the Germans in postwar Poland. He hoped they would transfer their loyalty to Poland, along with their land, affirming that "we don't want them to remain German forever."[43]

For racial or ethnic nationalists, this made no sense. But it seemed realistic to Wilson in the framework of civic nationalism. Although desiring to protect the rights of Jews and Germans, he did not want to interfere with Poland's internal affairs. At his insistence, however, the United States and the Allies required Poland to sign a treaty for the protection of ethnic and religious minorities. Yet it gave no right to the Jews or other minority communities to appeal for protection directly to the League of Nations. Wilson insisted on keeping decisions about intervention in the internal affairs of a member state exclusively under the control of the League's Council. Unless the Great Powers themselves decided to protect minorities, he did not want the League to violate Poland's sovereign right of self-determination.[44] This restriction would also prevent the League from hearing an appeal from African Americans or other minorities in the United States.

Wilson emphasized historical continuity and liberal civic ideals in his advocacy of national self-determination. On May 26, 1919, he reminded the Allied premiers that the United States had entered the war in 1917 because Imperial Germany had threatened the "political liberty and national independence of all the countries of the world." He explained that "nations completely disinterested in European territorial questions" had participated "as in a crusade, not for territorial changes, but for the destruction of the intolerable danger of a political and ethnic tyranny which would have held back the progress of the world for a century or more." In the peacemaking, Wilson told them, he had opposed territorial changes that violated the principle of national self-determination, affirming that "it is impossible for me to agree that a people can be handed over to foreign domination without their consent."[45]

Only where the collapse of empires had required the drawing of new borders to replace historical boundaries did Wilson give primacy to ethnicity, despite his belief that "ethnographic affinities" were more important than either strategic or economic considerations. In general, he subordinated ethnic factors as well as strategic and economic considerations to the higher priority of maintaining historical boundaries. Only if it was necessary to delineate new borders for new nation-states did he focus on ethnic identity. Even in those cases, there were some exclusions, including "nearly impassible frontiers, . . . such as the one drawn by the crests of the Alps." But when redrawing the map of Europe was unavoidable, he affirmed, "we have followed the boundaries traced by ethnographic affinities, according to the right to self-determination."[46]

Still, Wilson never thought that each racial, ethnic, or language group was entitled to its own nation-state. He had not promised that kind of peace in his Fourteen Points, and he did not attempt to achieve it at the peace conference. Again, he hoped that the historical process of nation building would overcome divisive ethnocultural factors with a new civic consciousness, thereby creating homogeneous nations. It was therefore acceptable to him that Poland, Czechoslovakia, and Yugoslavia, all included various nationalities, as did the United States. He hoped these peoples would assimilate into good citizens in the new nations.

The Limits of Wilson's New World Order

Wilson's own racism shaped his approach to international relations, however. His idea of democracy did not affirm racial equality. On the contrary, this southern-born president believed in white supremacy. His attitude toward African Americans at home had its counterpart in his foreign policy. He used the hierarchy of race to define the stages of development that would characterize the various types of League of Nations mandates (A, B, and C) for the former empires of the defeated Central Powers. In his judgment, Europeans were ready for self-government but the peoples of color were not. In the Near East, A mandates would be established for some people who were regarded as fairly advanced, replacing the former Ottoman Empire. B and C mandates would be created for so-called less developed peoples of Germany's former African and Pacific island colonies. In his view, Africans were the least developed people of color. This hierarchy of race allowed him to accommodate traditional European colonialism in the new guise of the League mandates. He limited the application of the principle of national self-determination to Europe. During the drafting of the Covenant for the League, he also rejected the Japanese amendment affirming the equality of all races or nations. His liberal internationalism, which generally emphasized civic ideals, thus also expressed his white racism.[47]

Wilson's vision of the new world order did not guarantee universal human rights. Race was not the only limitation. The Armenian genocide of 1915 illustrated this point. Although he clearly understood that the Armenian people were suffering from genocide, he restricted his actions on their behalf. They were white Christians, and therefore high on his racial hierarchy, but he still did not think the United States could or should intervene with military force to protect them against the Turks or later the Bolsheviks. He did not want the United States to bear this burden. Both Republicans and Democrats gave bipartisan support for U.S. involvement to help the Armenians. The Allies at the peace conference also endeavored to convince him that the United States should accept a League of Nations mandate for this Caucasian nation. Nevertheless, he declined to take any significant action. While touting the League as the defender of all nations against external aggression, he eschewed this responsibility on behalf of the Armenians. He made a realistic assessment that military intervention in Armenia would be too costly, although this decision contradicted his supposedly universal promise. He unilaterally decided not to accept a mandate for Armenia, despite his idealistic rhetoric that promised self-determination and collective security for all nations. Committing U.S. troops for that purpose in the Near East looked too much like an entangling alliance in the Old World. His response to Armenian genocide revealed the limits of his ideology and of American power to transform or redeem the Old World.[48]

While seeking to avoid military obligations, Wilson wanted to make the world safe for progressive capitalism as well as democracy. These were closely linked in his understanding of liberalism. American-style "open door" economic globalization should replace the old European colonial empires. The League of Nations mandates, in his view, were a step in this direction. He envisaged a world order that was even more open to international travel, shipping, commerce, and finance. In effect, he wanted an informal American empire with extensive political and economic control but without formal colonies or even a League mandate for the United States. He expected other democratic and capitalist nations to help achieve the goal, which he had outlined in his Fourteen Points, of creating an international society that would promote global economic modernization as he had done at home with his New Freedom reforms.

The Great War devastated Europe and its empires and opened a new era in world history. The geographer Isaiah Bowman, who advised the American peace delegation, noted this historic transition. In *The New World* (1921), he emphasized that the war's effects were "so far-reaching that we shall have henceforth a new world." As a consequence, he noted, "people everywhere have created or adopted new ideas and new material arrangements." Jolted from their past routines, they were creating a different future for themselves. "This new era will date from the years of the World War just as medieval Europe dates from the fall of Rome, or as the modern democratic era dates from the Declaration of Independence." Both integration and fragmentation shaped the contemporary world in this global era. Although the war had its greatest impact on Europe, "even in the United States, remote though it be, the evil effects are manifold." Global interdependence prevented even the United States from escaping the war's fragmenting influence on economic as well as political relationships. "No American, however secluded his life, however distant his home from the big cities and the coasts, is free from the consequences of the World War. The world is broken; its international life is disrupted; it is in a state of general economic disorder."[49]

Given this reality, peace depended on establishing a new international economic order. To do so, Wilson rejected the option of socialism, whether Lenin's radical Bolshevism or more moderate variations. His strong preference for progressive capitalism, no less than his commitment to democracy, expressed his liberal values. Thus he believed that peace depended on "open door" economic globalization, not just on the League of Nations or national self-determination. Later, in his last article in *The Atlantic* (1923), titled "The Road Away from Revolution," he reiterated that the future progress or development of modern civilization required both capitalism and democracy.[50]

Wilson's Legacy

Woodrow Wilson's legacy endured into the twenty-first century. To liberal Americans, he still appeared as the champion of anticolonialism against traditional European empires. Identification of Europe with imperialism and of the United States with anti-imperialism seemed to confirm America's exceptional virtue, even when it sought to enhance its own global power by opening the colonial empires of European nations to economic opportunities for itself. The senior editor of *The New Republic*, John B. Judis, used an idealized view of Wilson, which expressed this exceptionalist perspective, to criticize President George W. Bush. In *The Folly of Empire* (2004), Judis condemned Bush for ignoring the lessons of history that the Progressive presidents Theodore Roosevelt and Wilson had learned from the American imperial experience at the turn of the twentieth century. Learning from that aberration in America's history, those two presidents had rejected the pursuit of an empire and exemplified a prudence in their statecraft that was lacking in Bush's new imperialism. "The end of the Cold War," Judis argued, "created the conditions for finally realizing the promise of Wilson's foreign policy." Peace with collective security among nations and prosperity with "open door" globalization were again within reach. But Bush chose "the folly of empire" instead. Thus he squandered this opportunity to achieve what Wilson had attempted but failed to accomplish after World War I.[51]

As a liberal, Judis used American exceptionalism to criticize Bush, who, ironically, also operated within that same ideological tradition. Judis believed the United States had not created an empire except for its momentary aberration after the Spanish-American War. It had shunned colonialism and championed anti-imperialism, making America's experience quite different from Europe's. Its nineteenth-century territorial expansion across North America and its status as the world's preeminent twentieth-century power did not appear to him as evidence that this nation had become a global empire. He credited Wilson instead with establishing the ideal of "a world of democracies."[52] Nor did Judis recognize what the British historian Niall Ferguson, himself an advocate of a liberal American empire, called "the imperialism of anti-imperialism."[53] Wilson called for a new international order to make the world safe for democracy and capitalism, but Judis did not identify his search for hegemony—or what Wilson's contemporaries called "international social control"—with the pursuit of an American empire.[54] Thus, "the myth of the West" still shaped Judis's interpretation of American history, as it did Wilson's a century earlier. They both affirmed America's uniqueness as an anti-imperial power unlike the Old World.

Some scholars have escaped the categories of the Wilsonian worldview, derived from American exceptionalism, in their assessments of the president's ideology and statecraft. In *Promised Land, Crusader State* (1997), Walter A. McDougall recognized inherent weaknesses in Wilson's liberal internationalism and criticized its false promise of enduring peace through the reform or redemption of the Old World—a greatly exaggerated promise it could not possibly fulfill after World War I. "As a blueprint for world order," McDougall argued, "Wilsonianism has always been a chimera, but as an ideological weapon against 'every arbitrary power anywhere,' it has proved mighty indeed. And that, in the end, is how Wilson did truly imitate Jesus. He brought not peace but a sword."[55]

After World War I, Wilsonianism failed to create conditions favorable either to democracy in Weimar Germany or to a new world order of peace. In *After Victory* (2001), a comparative study of peacemaking in 1815, 1919,

1945, and 1989, G. John Ikenberry developed a persuasive argument that combined insights from the realist and liberal traditions of international relations theories. He emphasized the contributions of international institutions to peace. He recognized, moreover, that these institutions depended on a postwar strategic balance among the victorious and defeated Great Powers. Only with such a balance of power could an international society become viable. Wilson's peacemaking after World War I, which sought to avoid a new balance, contrasted with the earlier statecraft of European diplomats at the Congress of Vienna after the Napoleonic Wars and with the later diplomacy of American and European leaders who constructed the "long peace" after World War II. Like Wilson, they sought to build new international institutions to preserve peace among the Great Powers. But unlike him, they formed alliances with firm commitments to deter potential aggressors and protect possible victims, thereby stabilizing the balance of power. With alliances and regular forums for ongoing diplomatic consultation, and with a realistic appreciation of the existing strategic balance and of the importance of sustaining it, they managed to create stable and peaceful international orders that survived for decades. As a result, the prolonged nineteenth century (1815–1914) and the Cold War era (1945–89) escaped major wars. Long periods of peace characterized Europe's international history after the Napoleonic Wars and after World War II. The same experience occurred as well during the first decade after the Cold War.[56] In contrast to these achievements, Wilsonian peacemaking failed after World War I. His unrealistic vision of a new world order did not provide the foundation for postwar peace among democratic nations in the way he had hoped.

Despite Wilson's unsuccessful peacemaking after World War I, Wilsonianism continued to flourish as an ideology. At the end of the Cold War, triumphal Americans affirmed that world history was moving toward the culmination of Wilsonian ideals. On the basis of the Hegalian philosophy that had earlier influenced Wilson's historicism, Francis Fukuyama proclaimed the "end of history." He asserted that "the fact that there will be setbacks and disappointments in the process of democratization, or that not every market economy will prosper, should not distract us from the larger pattern that is emerging in world history." He thought the range of "choices that countries face in determining how they will organize themselves politically and economically has been *diminishing* over time." Although human history had witnessed various types of regimes in the past, "the only form of government that has survived intact to the end of the twentieth century has been liberal democracy."[57] Mandelbaum fully agreed.

Although Wilson himself had failed to create a new world order based on his ideas of peace, democracy, and free markets, this "Wilsonian triad" had apparently conquered the world by the twenty-first century. "Wilson's ideas did not take hold [after World War I], another terrible war erupted two decades later, and his career came to be regarded as a failure, its details forgotten by all but historians," Mandelbaum noted. "At the outset of the twenty-first century, however, these ideas had come to dominate the world. His prescription for organizing political and economic life and for conducting foreign policy are the keys to understanding the new world that emerged when the great global conflict of the second half of the twentieth century, the Cold War, came to an end."[58] World history seemed to be progressing toward the final triumph of Wilsonianism.

In President George W. Bush's foreign policy, neoconservative Wilsonianism became the dominant ideology. Like Wilson earlier, he felt confident that he could create a new world order of democracy and peace. After September 11, 2001, however, he believed that the United States needed first to fight a global war on terrorism. John Lewis Gaddis applauded Bush's decision to use aggressive or preemptive military force to implement Wilsonian ideals. "So the formula," Gaddis explained, "is Fukuyama plus force: the United States must finish the job that Woodrow Wilson started. The world, quite literally, is to be made safe for democracy, even those parts of it, like the Muslim Middle East, that have so far resisted that tendency. Terrorism—and by implication the authoritarianism that breeds it—must become as obsolete as slavery, piracy, or genocide: 'behavior that no respectable government can condone or support and that all must oppose.' Otherwise democracy, in this new age of vulnerability, will never be safe in the world."[59] Thus, making the world safe for democracy and peace required perpetual war.[60]

Yet world history still did not conform to the pattern that Bush and his intellectual cheerleaders prescribed. Given the increasingly obvious disparity between ideals and results, Fukuyama searched for an alternative way to reach the same end. Instead of reconsidering the philosophical assumptions and cultural values of the Wilsonian worldview that had led to false promises and expectations during World War I and again during Bush's global war on terrorism, Fukuyama proposed the oxymoronic concept of "realistic Wilsonianism."[61] In the twenty-first century, true believers still could not bring themselves to reexamine their erroneous premises about the presumably progressive direction of world history toward democracy and peace. For the sake of democracy, peace, and world order, it is time for a fundamental reconsideration of the Wilsonian worldview and legacy in U.S. foreign relations.

Notes

1. Michael Eliot Howard, *The Invention of Peace: Reflections on War and International Order* (New Haven, Conn.: Yale University Press, 2000).

2. Michael W. Doyle, *Ways of War and Peace: Realism, Liberalism, and Socialism* (New York: W. W. Norton, 1997).

3. Michael Mandelbaum, *The Ideas That Conquered the World: Peace, Democracy, and Free Markets in the Twenty-First Century* (New York: PublicAffairs, 2002), 6. See also Tony Smith, *America's Mission: The United States and the Worldwide Struggle for Democracy in the Twentieth Century* (Princeton, N.J.: Princeton University Press, 1994); Amos Perlmutter, *Making the World Safe for Democracy: A Century of Wilsonianism and Its Totalitarian Challengers* (Chapel Hill: University of North Carolina Press, 1997); Frank Ninkovich, *The Wilsonian Century: U.S. Foreign Relations since 1900* (Chicago: University of Chicago Press, 2000); Robert S. McNamara and James G. Blight, *Wilson's Ghost: Reducing the Risk of Conflict, Killing, and Catastrophe in the Twenty-First Century* (New York: PublicAffairs, 2001); and Akira Iriye, *Global Community: The Role of International Organizations in the Making of the Contemporary World* (Berkeley: University of California Press, 2002).

4. Woodrow Wilson, "Address to Congress," April 2, 1917, in *The Public Papers of Woodrow Wilson*, ed. Ray Stannard Baker and William E. Dodd, 6 vols. (New York: Harper & Brothers, 1925–27), vol. 5, 6–16, and in *The Papers of Woodrow Wilson*, ed. Arthur S. Link, 69 vols. (Princeton, N.J.: Princeton University Press, 1966–94) (hereafter, *PWW*), vol. 41, 519–27; the quotations here are on 524–25.

5. Woodrow Wilson, "Address to Congress," January 8, 1918, in *Public Papers of Woodrow Wilson*, vol. 5, 155–62, and in *PWW*, vol. 45, 534–39; the quotation is on 538.

6. Woodrow Wilson, "Address," September 27, 1918, in *Public Papers of Woodrow Wilson*, vol. 5, 253–61, and in *PWW*, vol. 51, 127–33; the quotation is on 131.

7. Woodrow Wilson, "Address to the League to Enforce Peace," May 27, 1916, in *Public Papers of Woodrow Wilson*, vol. 4, 184–88, and in *PWW*, vol. 37, 113–17.

8. Woodrow Wilson, "Address to the Senate," January 22, 1917, in *Public Papers of Woodrow Wilson*, vol. 4, 407–14, and in *PWW*, vol. 40, 533–39; the quotation is on 536, 539. For the scholarly debate over the balance of power and hegemony, see G. John Ikenberry, *America Unrivaled: The Future of the Balance of Power* (Ithaca, N.Y.: Cornell University Press, 2002).

9. Woodrow Wilson, "Address at University of Paris," December 21, 1918, in *Public Papers of Woodrow Wilson*, vol. 5, 329–31, and in *PWW*, vol. 53, 461–63; the quotation is on 462.

10. Woodrow Wilson, "Address to Peace Conference," January 25, 1919, in *Public Papers of Woodrow Wilson*, vol. 5, 395–400, and in *PWW*, vol. 54, 265–69; the quotation is on 266.

11. Woodrow Wilson, "Address to Peace Conference," February 14, 1919, in *Public Papers of Woodrow Wilson*, vol. 5, 413–29, and in *PWW*, vol. 55, 154–78; the quotations here are on 175.

12. Lloyd E. Ambrosius, "Wilson, the Republicans, and French Security after World War I," *Journal of American History* 59 (September 1972): 341–52.

13. Woodrow Wilson, "Address to International Law Society," May 9, 1919, in *Public Papers of Woodrow Wilson*, vol. 5, 478–81, and in *PWW*, vol. 58, 598–600; the quotation is on 599.

14. Francis Anthony Boyle, *Foundations of World Order: The Legalist Approach to International Relations, 1898–1922* (Durham, N.C.: Duke University Press, 1999).

15. Woodrow Wilson, "Address at Brussels," June 19, 1919, in *Public Papers of Woodrow Wilson*, vol. 5, 509–15, and in *PWW*, vol. 61, 16–20; the quotation is on 18.

16. Woodrow Wilson, "Cablegram to the American People," June 28, 1919, in *Public Papers of Woodrow Wilson*, vol. 5, 523–24; the quotation is on 523.

17. Jonathan Zasloff, "Law and the Shaping of American Foreign Policy: From the Gilded Age to the New Era," *New York University Law Review* 20 (2001): 1–128; Jonathan Zasloff, "Law and the Shaping of American Foreign Policy: The Twenty Years' Crisis," *New York University Law Review* 20 (2002): 1–100.

18. Woodrow Wilson, *The State: Elements of Historical and Practical Politics* (Boston: D. C. Heath, 1889), 366–67, 469; the quotation is on 366–67. See also Ronald J. Pestritto, *Woodrow Wilson and the Roots of Modern Liberalism* (Lanham, Md.: Rowman & Littlefield, 2005), 33–65.

19. Woodrow Wilson, "The Modern Democratic State," in *PWW*, vol. 5, 58–92; the quotations here are on 64–65, 67, 69–70, 74, 76, 90.

20. Wilson to Turner, August 23, 1889, and Turner to Wilson, August 31, 1889, and January 23, 1890, in *PWW*, vol. 6, 368–71, 381–84, 478–79 (the quotation is on 369); Turner to Wilson, July 16, 1893, and December 20, 1893, in *PWW*, vol. 8, 278–79, 417; Fulmer Mood, "Turner's Formative Period," in *The Early Writings of Frederick Jackson Turner*, ed.. Louise P. Kellogg (Madison: Wisconsin State Historical Society, 1938), 36–38; Woodrow Wilson, *Division and Reunion: 1829–1899* (New York: Longmans, Green, 1893).

21. Woodrow Wilson, "The Making of the Nation," *Atlantic Monthly* 80 (July 1897): 1–14, in *Public Papers of Woodrow Wilson*, vol. 1, 310–35, and in *PWW*, vol. 10, 217–36.

22. Woodrow Wilson, "The Ideals of America," *Atlantic Monthly* 90 (December 1902): 721–34, in *Public Papers of Woodrow Wilson*, vol. 1, 416–42, and in *PWW*, vol. 12, 208–27; the quotations here are on 215 and 217, respectively.

23. Jan Willem Schulte Nordholt, *The Myth of the West: America as the Last Empire* (Grand Rapids: William B. Eerdmans, 1995). See also C. Vann Woodward, *The Old World's New World* (New York: Oxford University Press, 1991).

24. Woodrow Wilson, "Address to the Senate," July 10, 1919, in *Public Papers of Woodrow Wilson*, vol. 5, 537–52, and in *PWW*, vol. 61, 426–36; the quotations here are on 429, 432, 434, 436.

25. Wolfgang Schivelbusch, *The Culture of Defeat: On National Trauma, Mourning, and Recovery* (New York: Picador, 2004).

26. See Alfred Cobban, *The Nation State and National Self-Determination* (London: Collins, 1969), 104. See also Derek Heater, *National Self-Determination: Woodrow Wilson and His Legacy* (New York: St. Martin's Press, 1994).

27. Rogers M. Smith, *Civic Ideals: Conflicting Visions of Citizenship in U.S. History* (New Haven, Conn.: Yale University Press, 1997); Robert H. Wiebe, *Who We Are: A History of Popular Nationalism* (Princeton, N.J.: Princeton University Press, 2002); Gary Gerstle, *American Crucible: Race and Nation in the Twentieth Century* (Princeton, N.J.: Princeton University Press, 2002).

28. Wilson, "Address to the League to Enforce Peace," in *Public Papers of Woodrow Wilson*, vol. 4, 187, and in *PWW*, vol. 37, 113–17; the quotation is on 115.

29. Daniel Patrick Moynihan, *Pandaemonium: Ethnicity in International Politics* (New York: Oxford University Press, 1993), 81.

30. Walker Connor, *Ethnonationalism: The Quest for Understanding* (Princeton, N.J.: Princeton University Press, 1994).

31. Moynihan, *Pandaemonium*, 14.

32. G. R. Conyne, *Woodrow Wilson: British Perspectives, 1912–21* (London: Macmillan, 1992).

33. Lloyd E. Ambrosius, "Dilemmas of National Self-Determination: Woodrow Wilson's Legacy," in *The Establishment of European Frontiers after the Two World Wars*, ed. Christian Baechler and Carole Fink (Bern: Peter Lang, 1996), 21–36; Lloyd E. Ambrosius, *Wilsonianism: Woodrow Wilson and His Legacy in American Foreign Relations* (New York: Palgrave Macmillan, 2002), 21–29, 125–34; Erez Manela, *The Wilsonian Moment: Self-Determination and the International Origins of Anticolonial Nationalism* (New York: Oxford University Press, 2007).

34. Paul Mantoux, *The Deliberations of the Council of Four (March 24–June 28, 1929)*, ed. Arthur S. Link, 2 vols. (Princeton, N.J.: Princeton University Press, 1992), vol. 1, 31.

35. Ibid., vol. 1, 55–68, 83–85; the quotations here are on 62, 67.

36. Ibid., vol. 1, 185–86, 195–99, 204–8, 210–17.

37. Ibid., vol. 1, 459.

38. Ibid., vol. 1, 106–9, 123–24 (the quotation is on 109); vol. 2, 282.

39. Ibid., vol. 2, 269–86, 307–14, 352–53, 388–93, 452–55; the quotation is on 281–82.

40. Ibid., vol. 1, 144–45, 234; vol. 2, 392, 422.

41. Ibid., vol. 1, 458–60.

42. Carole Fink, "The Minorities Question at the Paris Peace Conference: The Polish Minority Treaty, June 28, 1919," in *The Treaty of Versailles: A Reassessment after 75 Years*, ed. Manfred F. Boemeke, Gerald D. Feldman, and Elisabeth Glaser (Cambridge: Cambridge University Press, 1998), 249–74.

43. Mantoux, *Deliberations*, vol. 2, 527.

44. Ibid., vol. 1, 439–41, 472–73; vol. 2, 88–91, 330–33, 341, 481–83, 524–27, 578–81.

45. Ibid., vol. 2, 222–24; the quotations here are on 222–23.

46. Ibid., vol. 2, 226.

47. Ambrosius, *Wilsonianism*, 21–29; Joseph A. Fry, *Dixie Looks Abroad: The South and U.S. Foreign Relations, 1789–1973* (Baton Rouge: Louisiana State University Press,

2002), 139–74; Margaret MacMillan, *Paris 1919: Six Months That Changed the World* (New York: Random House, 2001), 98–106, 306–21; Lloyd E. Ambrosius, "Woodrow Wilson and *The Birth of a Nation*: American Democracy and International Relations," *Diplomacy and Statecraft* 18 (December 2007): 689–718.

48. Lloyd E. Ambrosius, "Wilsonian Diplomacy and Armenia: The Limits of Power and Ideology," in *America and the Armenian Genocide of 1915*, ed. Jay Winter (Cambridge: Cambridge University Press, 2003), 113–45; Samantha Power, *"A Problem From Hell": America and the Age of Genocide* (New York: Basic Books, 2002), 1–16; Peter Balakian, *The Burning Tigris: The Armenian Genocide and America's Response* (New York: HarperCollins, 2003); Simon Payaslian, *United States Policy Toward the Armenian Question and the Armenian Genocide* (New York: Palgrave Macmillan, 2005).

49. Isaiah Bowman, *The New World: Problems in Political Geography* (Yonkers-on-Hudson, N.Y.: World Book Company, 1921), 2–3.

50. Woodrow Wilson, "The Road Away from Revolution," *Atlantic Monthly* 132 (August 1923): 145–46, reproduced in *Public Papers of Woodrow Wilson*, vol. 6, 536–39, and in *PWW*, vol. 68, 393–95.

51. John B. Judis, *The Folly of Empire: What George W. Bush Could Learn from Theodore Roosevelt and Woodrow Wilson* (New York: Charles Scribner's Sons, 2004), 7–9; John B. Judis, "What Woodrow Wilson Can Teach Today's Imperialists," *New Republic*, June 9, 2003, 19–23.

52. Judis, *Folly of Empire*, 116–17. For a more persuasive interpretation, see Andrew J. Bacevich, *American Empire: The Realities & Consequences of U.S. Diplomacy* (Cambridge, Mass.: Harvard University Press, 2002).

53. Niall Ferguson, *Colossus: The Price of America's Empire* (New York: Penguin Press, 2004), 61–104; the quotation here is actually a heading for this section of the book.

54. For my interpretation, see Lloyd E. Ambrosius, *Woodrow Wilson and the American Diplomatic Tradition: The Treaty Fight in Perspective* (Cambridge: Cambridge University Press, 1987); and Lloyd E. Ambrosius, "Woodrow Wilson, Alliances, and the League of Nations," *Journal of the Gilded Age and Progressive Era* 5 (April 2006): 139–65.

55. Walter A. McDougall, *Promised Land, Crusader State: The American Encounter with the World Since 1776* (Boston: Houghton Mifflin, 1997), 122–46; the quotation is on 146.

56. G. John Ikenberry, *After Victory: Institutions, Strategic Restraint, and the Rebuilding of Order after Major Wars* (Princeton, N.J.: Princeton University Press, 2001). See also Paul Kennedy and William I. Hitchcock, eds., *From War to Peace: Altered Strategic Landscapes in the Twentieth Century* (New Haven, Conn.: Yale University Press, 2000).

57. Francis Fukuyama, *The End of History and the Last Man* (New York: Free Press, 1992), 45; Francis Fukuyama, "Beyond Our Shores," *Wall Street Journal*, December 24, 2002.

58. Mandelbaum, *Ideas That Conquered the World*, 6, 17.

59. John Lewis Gaddis, *Surprise, Security, and the American Experience* (Cambridge, Mass.: Harvard University Press, 2004), 90.

60. For an excellent critique of this perspective, see Robert A. Divine, *Perpetual War for Perpetual Peace* (College Station: Texas A&M University Press, 2000).

61. Francis Fukuyama, *America at the Crossroads: Democracy, Power, and the Neoconservative Legacy* (New Haven, Conn.: Yale University Press, 2006), 9. For my critique, see Lloyd E. Ambrosius, "Woodrow Wilson and George W. Bush: Historical Comparisons of Ends and Means in Their Foreign Policies," *Diplomatic History* 30 (June 2006): 509–43.

Part IV
Post-Wilsonian Wilsonianism

9. Progressive Internationalism and Reformed Capitalism: New Freedom to New Deal

Emily S. Rosenberg

Franklin Delano Roosevelt often cast himself as a successor to Woodrow Wilson. On a policy level, both Democratic presidents saw themselves as reformers; both served during a world war; and both claimed to seize unique opportunities to turn world crisis into a reworked international order. On a personal level, of course, there were also strong connections: Roosevelt had served in the Wilson administration as assistant secretary of the Navy. In 1920 he ran as vice president on the Democratic ticket and campaigned on behalf of U.S. entry into the controversial League of Nations. Many of Roosevelt's advisers, likewise, had gained experience in the Wilson administration and hoped to build on its vision while learning from its mistakes. As World War II proceeded, the Roosevelt administration and its supporters insisted that FDR was assuming the mantle of a revitalized Wilsonian internationalism and fighting against a willful group of shortsighted isolationists who should shoulder the blame for the appeasement that had led to Pearl Harbor.

Because the foreign policies of these two presidents lend themselves to comparison, there is a large historical literature that addresses the Wilsonian legacy in the Roosevelt administration. Most of the standard histories adopt the view that Roosevelt reanimated Wilson's approach to the world, providing a "second chance" for Wilsonian internationalism. Lloyd E. Ambrosius, for example, identifies four attributes of Wilson's vision: national self-determination, open door economic globalization, collective security, and a vision of progressive history. These, in Ambrosius's view, "provided the dominant ideology for the United States during this so-called American Century." N. Gordon Levin's influential book on Wilson's foreign policy concluded that Wilsonianism, "even while losing the battle over the League of Nations, eventually triumphed in the more long-term struggle over the ultimate definition of the nature of twentieth-century American foreign policy.[1]

This chapter supports the claim that the Wilsonian legacy loomed large in Roosevelt's approach to foreign policy, but it shifts the focus of the argument. The proposition that FDR brought a "second chance" for Wilsonian internationalism usually centers on the narrative that Wilson's ideas for a League of Nations mutated into proposals for a United Nations, which ultimately triumphed over the forces of the "isolationism" that had contributed to the Depression and then war.[2] Looking away from this well-explored theme, I wish instead to advance a slightly different frame for viewing Wilson's and Roosevelt's commitments to internationalism: their approaches to creating an international financial umbrella under which a liberal capitalist system could function and thrive. This chapter focuses on Wilsonianism and its legacy in the arena of international economic policymaking.

As participants in the early-twentieth-century movement called Progressivism, both Wilson and Roosevelt envisioned a "reformed capitalist" order. Both were convinced that capitalism provided the only system that would create wealth and, broadly, lift living standards at home and around the globe. In their views, however, businesses that abused their marketplace power undermined the capitalist order, and capitalism therefore needed some public-sector regulation to work properly. Corporations could be constructive when they contributed to general prosperity and progress but destructive when, in a greedy pursuit of profits, they sought monopoly and engaged in exploitative, disruptive practices. The tasks of government, in the progressive vision of both Wilson and Roosevelt, involved aiding responsible businesses, curbing corruption and the power of monopolies, and marshalling the economic expertise that would help organize a rational and predictable system.

This superficially ambiguous relationship between government and private capital—with government cast as partner and as discipliner—helps explain why the Wilson and Roosevelt administrations have been represented in scholarship both as architects of an American corporatism and as antibusiness progressives who sought to curb monopolistic abuses. Reformed capitalism simultaneously sought both ends.

A distrust of particularistic business interests and a faith in the application of public-sector expertise characterized many of the interwar anti-interventionists as well. This chapter, therefore, endorses those historians who have advanced an extended critique of the familiar "internationalist versus isolationist" dichotomy that has generally structured the story of the League of Nations proposal, its repudiation, and the revived proposal for the UN.[3] Some anti-interventionists of the 1930s, when their views are framed in terms of reformed capitalism, emerge less as an anti-internationalist opposition to two internationalist presidencies than as a bridge that helped link the reformed capitalist ideas of the New Freedom to those of the New Deal.

This examination of the Wilson and Roosevelt administrations' commitments to reformed capitalism in the international realm proceeds in three sections. The first concentrates on the Wilson administration. The second assesses the interwar opposition to foreign lending and military interventionism, challenging the framework that has, too simplistically, placed "Republican isolationists" in opposition to a Wilson-Roosevelt "internationalism." The third section examines how FDR built upon, but updated, Wilson's notion of a reformed capitalist order. In each section, the chapter deliberately shifts away from the usual concentration on collective security-style institutions, an emphasis that I argue has abetted the creation in historiography of the misleading category called "isolationists" and has thus marginalized the economic critique that so many progressive anti-interventionists shared with Wilson and Roosevelt. The New Freedom, the New Deal, and many of the interwar anti-interventionists *all* stressed the dangers that unregulated capitalism posed to the international order and advocated state intervention to discipline capitalists and save global capitalism from instabilities aggravated by its own excesses.

Wilson's International Vision of Reformed Capitalism

Woodrow Wilson's policies aimed to promote a reformed capitalism in the world at large—through means far less formal than FDR would pursue but with similar goals. Throughout his administration, Wilson worked energetically to expand the nation's commercial and financial networks, yet he stood opposed to businesses that violated his notion of progress toward an open, liberal, and democratic world.

As scholars have long noted, Wilson shared the view, often associated with progressives, that capitalism, if left unregulated, could generate its own undoing. Greed and widening social distinctions, he feared, could lead to disorder and revolution. Various turn-of-the-century progressive measures aimed to employ government to marshal the specialized expertise that might ameliorate late-nineteenth-century capitalism's booms and busts, growing inequalities, and resulting social turmoil. Curbing exploitative business practices would reduce the appeal of social revolutionary ideologies, allow a liberal order to flourish, and enrich the prosperity of all.

Wilson's election in 1912 coincided with an upsurge in popular denunciations of a so-called money trust. After the financial panic of 1907, which demonstrated the enormous power of J. P. Morgan, concern about the power of private capital had become widespread. Muckraking journalists, such as Lincoln Steffens, and populist members of Congress, such as Robert La Follette of Wisconsin and Charles A. Lindbergh Sr. of Minnesota, among others, demanded inquiries and reform. In 1912, Representative Arsene P. Pujo from Louisiana presided over a House investigation into the power of monopolistic banking combinations. The Pujo committee's charge that the country was experiencing an alarming concentration of wealth and resources because of a dangerous "money trust" found wide dissemination through the popularity of Louis D. Brandeis's book *Other People's Money* (1914).[4]

During the election campaign of 1912, which came during a break in the Pujo inquiry, Wilson picked up on the popularity of antimonopoly themes and, with Brandeis as a close adviser, promised a "New Freedom" that would bring monopolistic abuses under control.

Once elected, Wilson showed that he could both denounce the exploitation by "trusts" but still work closely with economic experts and responsible business leaders to reform capitalism into a fairer and more robust system. The Federal Reserve Act aimed to create a central banking system that could provide both stability and liquidity among the nation's still fairly regionalized economies. Its goal was not to make profits for bankers in any direct sense but to build general prosperity by improving the currency and credit system upon which the smooth production and distribution of goods relied. As James Livingston argues, the Federal Reserve Act represented an effort to remake capitalism in such a way as to limit the potential for destabilizing factors such as irrational speculation, exploitation, and class conflict.[5]

Wilson tried to apply a similar vision of reformed capitalism internationally, even though such a task carried obvious jurisdictional challenges. He, for example, had little use for businesses that undermined stability and democracy in other countries and then called on the U.S. government to support them.

Throughout his administration, he refused to assist most oil and mining interests that he believed were feeding instability in Mexico. When these interests helped overthrow the Francisco Madero government, which was not to their liking, Wilson intervened militarily against the new government of Victoriano Huerta, whose coup he regarded as illegitimate. Seizing and occupying Mexico's major seaport, Veracruz, in 1914, Wilson refused to take American-owned oil fields north of the port into protective custody and denounced the Huerta government that oil interests supported. This military intervention, he hoped, would teach both the Mexicans and foreign businesses to abide by constitutional processes. In 1919, when the U.S. oil companies operating in Mexico requested military intervention to secure their holdings against possible nationalization under Mexico's new Constitution of 1917, Wilson refused the companies' requests and undertook what became a lengthy negotiation to both prevent another U.S. military intervention and to secure property guarantees from Mexico. Oil companies and their allies condemned Wilson for what they saw as his temporizing over threats of revolutionary nationalism and for his reluctance to follow the war in France with a "stronger" policy in a country that appeared to threaten significant American investments. But Wilson chastised these oil companies for confusing their private profits with the national interest and for undermining stability on the U.S. border.[6]

In Costa Rica, Wilson similarly denied a request by United Fruit Company to recognize a government that the company had apparently sponsored in a military coup. Again, Wilson lectured both the new Costa Rican government and United Fruit officials on abiding by constitutional and electoral rules. Using wartime economic controls to embargo exports to Costa Rica, the Wilson administration induced such economic distress in the country that the regime fell. United Fruit energetically lobbied the administration, to no avail.[7]

These policies provided warnings to individual U.S. businesses that they should be good citizens and promote, rather than undermine, democratic processes and constitutional stability. Far from being antibusiness, such policies represented Wilson's larger efforts to tame the excesses of capitalism.

For those businesses that behaved responsibly, in Wilson's view, his administration created a wide range of new services. The Cabinet departments of Commerce, Treasury, and State each developed specialized bureaucracies and policies to promote trade and investment abroad. New agencies such as the Federal Trade Commission, the Federal Reserve, and the War Trade Board also conducted studies and developed initiatives aimed at enhancing U.S. exports and foreign investment.[8] To broaden access to strategic materials, such as oil, Wilson took a strong stand in favor of the "open door." At the Paris Peace Conference, he advocated that the open door be honored in former colonies designated as League of Nations mandates. Moreover, although he resisted specific oil company pressures in Mexico after World War I, his administration nonetheless strongly promoted U.S. oil interests in broader ways. It endorsed the General Leasing Law of 1920, which prohibited companies domiciled in countries discriminating against U.S. oil firms from leasing fields in the public domain, and it worked closely with oil companies during the war to establish the basis for expanding oil production into new territories, especially in Colombia and the Middle East.[9]

Wilson also developed a strong working relationship with America's large bankers. Although he had denounced the "money trust" in 1912, Wilson had then worked with bankers to fashion the Federal Reserve Act, which provided a public-private hybrid structure within which currency expertise, rather than individual private profits, would presumably guide action. World War I brought Wilson and large banking houses, especially J. P. Morgan, closer together. Wilson came to support the Allied cause, in which U.S. bankers had heavily invested. Moreover, once the United States entered the war, bankers helped supervise the stock exchanges, stabilize exchange rates, underwrite wartime trade in essential commodities, and publicize Liberty Loan bond drives.

The Wilson administration's policies increasingly reflected a view that U.S. banking consortia, working in partnership with government agencies, could provide the stabilizing financial architecture for the postwar world. As the war drew to a close, the Wilson administration worked especially with Thomas Lamont of the J. P. Morgan interests to develop plans for using America's now-gigantic capital resources to reconstruct and expand the gold standard internationally, to regularize currency convertibility among nations, to safeguard property from threats of revolutionary nationalism and of inflation, and to expand international trade by encouraging governments to shift pubic revenue sources away from customs duties and toward other forms of taxation.[10]

As part of this attempt to work with U.S. banks toward a stable postwar order, officials in the Wilson administration sought to use the leverage of private bank loans to enlarge the number of countries whose public finances would be directly supervised by American experts vetted or even appointed by the U.S. government. In this effort, Wilson built upon the very formula that he had denounced as William Howard Taft's "dollar diplomacy" in the campaign of 1912. During and after the war, Wilson's State Department worked with U.S. bankers and banking consortia to devise plans whereby bankers would offer loans to countries in return for their consent to various sorts of financial supervision and reform. Such loan-for-supervision contracts brought Haiti, the Dominican Republic, Nicaragua, and Liberia all into the kind of quasi-colonial arrangement that Britain had used in Egypt—exercising power through a strong financial adviser and a vigorous program of constabulary training. Officials hoped, and expected, that similar arrangements would be worked out for other countries, especially those in Latin America, at the end of the war. Concrete plans, drawn up by U.S. officials and bankers, aimed to bring postwar "stabilization" to Mexico and China (two areas of crucial concern because of their revolutionary disorder), but negotiations broke down when the governments of both countries decided that loans were less attractive than limits on their sovereignty.[11]

In these efforts, President Wilson and his advisers envisioned a postwar world in which an American, or in some cases Anglo-American, financial umbrella provided the stabilizing economic counterpart to the League of Nations' collective security plan. Private bank loans to various governments, arranged with the assistance of the State Department and sometimes in conjunction with international banking consortia, would leverage compliance with "sound" financial practice and thereby spread a predictable infrastructure in which trade and private investment could flourish. In this view, American bankers and their international loans could structure gold standard stability and convertibility; open door policies could boost international trade; and American investments in foreign bonds and enterprises would recycle America's vast postwar wealth, lifting all boats. Government, responsible bankers, and experts would all work together in an international effort to reform and regularize economic (especially currency and exchange) rules and procedures. Although Wilson never proposed any Bretton Woods–style institutions to formalize international economic rules, many of the goals he pursued in cooperation with bankers at the end of the war were broadly similar to those of the New Dealers who later crafted the Bretton Woods settlements.

Historical discussions of Wilson's postwar economic policy have too often focused mainly on Versailles and the controversies raised in John Maynard Keynes's *Economic Consequences of the Peace* (1920).[12] Keynes's book criticized President Wilson for allowing a postwar settlement that subsequently levied ruinous reparations on Germany and thereby set the stage for interwar financial instabilities and resentments. Keynes's thesis, of course, spawned a cottage industry of studies by those who accept, amend, or wholly reject his interpretation. Regardless of the position one adopts on this reparations controversy, however, the debate itself has helped overshadow other elements of Wilson's global economic vision.

Judging Wilson's international economic policies only in the context of the machinations at Paris is far too narrow. The ambiguity of the Versailles settlement with regard to German reparations grew out of Wilson's larger expectation that government would continue to work closely with responsible bankers to use the power of loans to spread financial expertise internationally in the postwar world, and that the expansion of internationally standardized economic practices would not be driven simply by immediate self-interest (of either countries or companies) but by governmental involvement on behalf of a broad assessment of systemic stability.

Wilson's "reformed capitalism," in short, mixed hostility to monopolistic, disruptive corporate actions with strong support for an open access world in which U.S. companies could flourish as long as they enforced, rather than undermined, consistent rules of the game. Government would (and should) lend assistance to businesses only if their actions spread liberal capitalism, encouraged republican forms of government, and contributed to the long-term stability of the system. The approach taken by the New Freedom at home—punishing and regulating exploitative capital interests while working closely with others to create consistent rules—thus had a counterpart in foreign economic policy. Wilson pursued an American capitalism that, purged of destabilizing tendencies and excessive greed, he hoped would become a "moral force" in the world.[13]

Interwar Politics: International Loans, Interventionism, and Foreign Policy

A focus on government's relationship to large capital interests in the international arena complicates the common narrative about the interwar backlash against Wilsonian internationalism. This section avoids the term "isolationist" in order to emphasize the diversity of those who opposed U.S. foreign interventions during the 1920s and 1930s.

Both Wilson and Roosevelt entered the White House in the midst of public concern and congressional hearings over the power of bankers, and both pledged to take action against unscrupulous practices. Many interwar anti-interventionists shared these concerns, fearing that narrow profit seeking might undermine domestic social stability and a well-functioning system of international trade and investment. A closer look at political coalitions and debates will illustrate the strength of progressive internationalist traditions during the interwar period.

Drawing support from the widespread public disillusionment over World War I, the Republican administrations of the 1920s constructed an alternative to Wilsonianism: a unilateralist and "nationalist" foreign policy that emphasized private-sector, rather than government-to-government, relationships. In their view, the supposedly peaceful and constructive sinews of private capital and cultural associations, not states or collective bodies that represented states, should organize global networks. Under their leadership, the United States veered in a nationalistic direction, refusing to work with the United Nations, join the World Court, or cancel World War I war debts to allies. They sponsored immigrant restriction acts; undertook interventions in what nationalists considered the U.S. sphere of interest near the Caribbean, and generally pressed a nationalist view of international economic policy.

Republicans built on Wilsonian policies that had favored economic integration of the world economy. They continued to push open door and most-favored-nation policies, global radio-communication agreements, gold-standard-based currency convertibility, and private bank financial supervision of countries need-ing "stabilization." Although such policies had emerged from Wilson's vision of the need for government-business cooperation in the postwar era, Wilson had emphasized a guiding role for professionalized government bureaus and econom-ic experts, while his Republican successors emphasized a less constrained role for private businesses. Many Republicans saw little problem with providing energetic governmental assistance to various private interests without interfering much in their practices—as the unhealthy binge of private bank lending that presaged the Depression would show.

Left to themselves, markets produce cycles of boom and bust. The boom side of the lending cycle, which gained momentum during the 1920s, accompanied an exuberant globalization. Exports, investments, and cultural products flowed out from the United States. Indeed, the 1920s seems a prelude to the outpour-ing of American goods, dollars, and ideas (and to the contentious debates in many countries over "Americanization") that would also characterize the post–World War II era. Neither the government's unilateralist policies nor pri-vate-sector arrangements, however, proved capable of counteracting the lending cycle bust that followed. The banking crisis of the late 1920s touched off a spi-ral of ever-more-massive defaults, shrinking trade, currency devaluations, eco-nomic depression, and political instability. There existed no national or interna-tional authority powerful enough to step in and short-circuit the declines that ravaged the capitalist world.

With the Depression, America generally turned inward. The works of promi-nent historians and congressional investigations advanced the view that U.S. involvement in World War I had grown out of the pressures on Wilson from bankers who had lent money to Britain and from munitions makers and suppli-ers eager to fatten their wallets by war. During the 1930s, the contention that the United States should never have entered World War I enjoyed widespread cultural currency throughout the country (70 percent in 1937), and the pop-ulist-progressive distrust of business elites fanned this pervasive antiwar senti-ment. From this perspective, Wilson was to blame for conceding too much influence over policy formation to Anglo-American capital interests.

Criticism of the privatized and unilateralist policies of the Republican administrations of the 1920s augmented this increasingly critical perspective on U.S. involvement in World War I, especially in the farm states of the Midwest. As the farm depression spread during the 1920s, resentment against bankers and global companies grew. Many farm-state politicians, for example, opposed the 1924 Dawes Plan loans to Germany. They feared that Germany might absorb

U.S. private investment capital and thus contribute to higher loan rates for domestic farmers. Farm-state legislators also led a coalition that promoted congressional hearings in the mid-1920s intended to reveal how American private bank loans had sparked U.S. military occupations, and then wars, in the Dominican Republic, Haiti, and Nicaragua.

From this perspective, during the first two decades of the twentieth century, American international loans had produced costly (in both lives and dollars) military involvements in World War I and in the three occupied Latin American dependencies. None of these interventions had produced a beneficial end. Both political parties, it seemed, followed the bidding of a banking establishment based in New York, while outlying and rural areas paid the bill through "ruinous" interest rates and taxes. Third-party efforts—such as the Farmer-Labor movement in Minnesota, the Progressive ticket that ran Robert La Follette of Wisconsin for president in 1924, and the neopopulists in North Dakota who had established the only state-owned bank in the country—all stemmed from discontents that rippled through both major parties and spread into other parts of the country. Farm-state progressives and their allies distrusted the influence of economic elites, who could, in their view, call up the power of the state and define "national interest" on their own behalf.

The arguments of farm-state progressives during the 1920s and 1930s often resonated with urban allies: Irish, Italian, and German ethnics, especially opposed to close ties with imperialist Britain; union movements that were influenced by anti-British, anti-imperialist ethnic politics; localistic business interests; leaders of the National Association for the Advancement of Colored People (particularly outspoken on issues related to the lengthy U.S. occupation and military dictatorship in Haiti); antiwar right-wing "mothers' movements"; and left-leaning women's groups, pacifists, and socialists. The leaders of all these groups worked together (and separately) not as "isolationists" but as a coalition opposed to military interventionism as a consequence of what they variously termed "dollar diplomacy" and "imperialism." Many were outspoken internationalists, if that meant building transnational coalitions to oppose, for example, the U.S. banking, railroad, and fruit company interests that were being backed up by U.S. military force in Nicaragua. The war in Nicaragua in the late 1920s, one of the most prominent foreign policy controversies of the interwar era, became so unpopular domestically that President Calvin Coolidge removed U.S. troops after Congress threatened to cut off military funding. It would be misleading to label this broad opposition to U.S. military force in Nicaragua "isolationist."[14]

The critique of "dollar diplomacy," which overlapped with a more general popular distrust of "imperialism," found additional vindication during the early years of the Great Depression. In two spectacular efforts to expose corporate corruption and manipulation, a congressional committee headed by Ferdinand Pecora hauled the country's leading international bankers before public hearings focused on their lending practices, and another committee headed by Gerald P. Nye investigated the nefarious pre–World War I influence of bankers and munitions makers.[15]

In this context, reminiscent of Wilson's campaign of 1912 and the Pujo hearings, Franklin Roosevelt, elected in 1932, promised to chase the "moneylenders out of the temple" of government. His early New Deal was reticent to assist holders of defaulting foreign bonds, and it carried out an abrupt currency devaluation, giving the amelioration of domestic hardship priority over adherence to gold standard rules and rejecting banker-led cooperation on international remedies. In a fireside chat of September 1934, FDR emphasized government's role both to help and to regulate businesses: "Private enterprise in times such as these cannot be left without assistance and without reasonable safeguards lest it destroy not only itself but also our processes of civilization."[16] In 1936 FDR again campaigned by invoking the old progressive antimonopoly themes. In a speech in New York, he thundered that

> we had to struggle with the old enemies of peace—business and financial monopoly, speculation, reckless banking, class antagonism, sectionalism, war profiteering. They had begun to consider the Government of the United States as a mere appendage to their own affairs. We know now that government by organized money is just as dangerous as government by organized mob.

Everywhere he spoke, he promised that his goal was to save the political and economic system by protecting it from the "concentration of economic power."[17]

Both Democrats and Republicans felt pressure from those who warned that economic elites would engineer international involvements against the interests of ordinary Americans. Both parties also had business-internationalist wings. As the world crisis mounted, both were consequently split on foreign policy.

The Republican Party, of course, still had its anti-Wilsonian unilateralists who had opposed the League of Nations and championed the nationalist approach of the 1920s. The Republican Party also had a "progressive" wing of determined anti-interventionists. In addition, however, it had an internationalist wing, often connected to the Northeast and to international banking establishments and other global businesses. This wing was exemplified in leaders such as Wendell Willkie, Harold Stassen, and later Dwight Eisenhower.[18]

The Democratic Party was similarly split. During the 1920s and 1930s, some Democrats continued to uphold the vision of Wilson and worked for international courts, for collective security, and ultimately for intervention against the spread of fascism. Others, particularly in the South, were Democrats by tradition. They had been Wilsonians partly by virtue of their alliance with the southern-born president's racial policies. Others who had denounced the privatized unilateralism and the "dollar diplomacy" of the Republican 1920s feared that international involvements would just be a cover for a new order run by and for economic elites.

As FDR moved toward favoring military intervention on behalf of the Allies during the late 1930s, the interwar progressive coalitions fractured (analogous to how antiwar progressives had split over Wilson's policies in 1917). Groups realigned especially over what policy the United States should take toward the Spanish Civil War. Some emphasized the threat of fascism and hoped that intervention might help bring a New Deal to the world. Others remained opposed to any involvement in foreign conflicts.

Opposition to war, even—or especially—by some internationalists, becomes more explicable when seen forward from the 1920s than viewed backward from the 1940s. Many of Roosevelt's critics after 1937, although often derided then and by later historians as slightly hysterical, backward-looking provincials and anti-Semites (to be sure, anti-Semitism often did find fertile ground within the antibanking discourses of some), sounded the themes of reformed capitalism that had circulated widely within early-twentieth-century politics. Concerned, above all, over unchecked concentrations of political and economic power, they warned against a governing elite that consorted with internationally extended capital interests and had lost touch with the needs of ordinary Americans. They also feared that international investments (loans to foreign governments and enterprises, branch plants, and acquisition of raw materials such as petroleum) would stretch the definition of national interest globally and thereby necessitate an enormous military establishment at the beck and call of special interests. America's long tradition of civilian rule stood under threat.

These themes, it should again be stressed, played particularly prominently in the West and Midwest but were not rooted in any single political party, region, religion, class, or position on the ideological spectrum. They came from socialists, such as Norman Thomas; the *Nation*'s publisher (until 1935), Oswald Garrison Villard; nonsocialist Republican progressives, such as the historian

Charles Beard; progressive-eventually-turned-libertarian politicians, such as Henrik Shipstead (a Farmer-Labor Party and then Republican senator from 1923 to 1947); antiwar luminaries, such as Dorothy Detzer; America's most influential advertising man, Bruce Barton; nationalistic businessmen, such as Robert E. Wood of Sears Roebuck; cosmopolitan Republicans, such as Harvard-educated Senator Robert Taft; old progressive Republicans, such as Gerald P. Nye and Hiram Johnson; and Democrats, such as Burton K. Wheeler and Bennett Clark. Thus, as Justus Doenecke has argued at greater length, the interwar noninterventionists represented no single ideological position. Some emphasized a "fortress America" vision of foreign policy. Some, however, were avowed internationalists but distrusted war or military interventionism as effective tools of policy. Most feared that economic elites could duplicitously construe threats to private profits as threats to the nation.[19]

After Pearl Harbor, the Roosevelt administration pressed a simplified interpretation of history. Lumping together its diverse opponents as "isolationists," New Dealers increasingly tried to pin this disapproving label on the Republican opposition to Franklin Roosevelt.

To blame the Republican Party for the "isolationism" that had caught the U.S. "asleep" at Pearl Harbor, the Roosevelt administration sought to revive the reputation of Woodrow Wilson and Wilsonian internationalism. In May 1942, with the war going badly, the president's popular approval in decline, and congressional elections looming, the publicity director of the Democratic Party, Charles Michelson, published a column called "Dispelling the Fog," which blamed the Republicans for the trouble in the world. The Republican repudiation of Wilsonian internationalism in the form of the League of Nations, Michelson avowed, had set the stage for international instability and the rise of an aggressive Germany and Japan. He urged voters not to make the mistake of 1918, when Republican majorities were elected in the House and Senate.[20] FDR's supporters had to revise the negative image of Wilsonianism to sell the war and pin "isolationism" solely on the Republicans.

In myriad ways during the war, FDR cast himself as the carrier of Wilsonian internationalism and the Republicans as the party of unpreparedness and weakness. The adoption of the terms "World War I" and "World War II" emphasized the continuities between Wilson and Roosevelt. Darryl F. Zanuck's film *Wilson* (1944), made with the encouragement of the Office of War Information, focused on the League of Nations controversy and ended with Wilson's prophesy that the Republican senators who blocked the League would be responsible, one day, for another world war. Popular magazines featured articles reviving a positive memory of President Wilson.[21] Prominent historians such as Thomas A. Bailey, writing during the war, lamented Wilson's "lost peace" and appealed for a restoration of the internationalism that had been "lost."[22] Other historians, many of whom began working for wartime agencies, embraced internationalism and presented the defeat of the League as the central mistake that policymaking in World War II should rectify. All these frameworks emphasized that Roosevelt's administration offered a "second chance" for Wilsonianism and cast interwar "isolationism" as an evil. On a popular level, the U.S. failure to join the League of Nations became the paramount "lesson" to be learned from Wilsonianism.[23]

Many New Dealers, however, also embraced a less visible "lesson" from the interwar era: An international economic system run primarily by private bankers would be unstable, and the state should exercise a stronger role in regulating capitalism. New Dealers approached substantially the same question that Wilson had tried to tackle. How could the state create an environment in which supposedly disinterested expertise, rather than narrow profit seeking, provided the framework for the international system? How could the state discipline private interests to benefit the system as a whole? The Bretton Woods agreements of 1944, especially, would draw from the Wilsonian vision of reformed capitalism, updated by the "lessons" about the failures of the interwar era.

FDR's Economic Internationalism and a New Financial Architecture

Just as the Franklin Delano Roosevelt administration denounced the "isolationism" that kept the United States out of the League of Nations, so it also repudiated the interwar Republican's reliance on private bankers and, instead, echoed the Wilsonian vision that expertise and some state involvement would be needed to tame private avarice. During the war, the Roosevelt administration fashioned a working relationship with business interests and also moved toward creating an international financial structure that would stand apart from them.[24] This approach epitomized the formula of Wilsonian progressivism: The state should play a strong role in forming the ground rules for a functioning international economic (especially monetary) order but, under that umbrella, the state would also help responsible businesses expand their trade and investment into the world.[25]

The early New Deal had been badly divided on the approach to take toward international economic recovery. Secretary of State Cordell Hull, a single-minded proponent of freer trade, devoted himself to promoting open door and tariff-lowering agreements. Nationalists such as George Peek, the State

Department's foreign trade adviser and head of the Export-Import Bank until his resignation in July 1935, favored a "nationalist" program, opposing most international economic, political, or disarmament agreements.[26] At the same time, officials in the Treasury Department advocated a mix of cooperative international agreements and of greater national flexibility, which they felt could preserve necessary social welfare spending in a crisis, on issues related to gold standard currency exchange. The Treasury's approach provided the basis for the Bretton Woods proposals.

Secretary of the Treasury Henry Morgenthau worked to shift international monetary policy away from the Federal Reserve Bank of New York, with its close ties to Anglo-American private banking interests, and into the hands of his own Cabinet department. Morgenthau—a progressive who had known Roosevelt in Democratic politics since 1915 and whose father had served as Wilson's ambassador to Turkey—brought to the Treasury a new generation of monetary experts who generally took what would become known as a Keynesian approach to the economy. In 1934 seven members of the Harvard University Economics Department had published *The Economics of the Recovery*, an attack on the New Deal's recovery programs. In response, six other young, untenured Harvard instructors, including Lauchlin Currie and his friend Harry Dexter White, signed a letter expressing strong support for Roosevelt's programs. After their forced departure from Harvard, Currie and White joined the Treasury Department and gradually became important voices in postwar planning. They promoted a more active role for national monetary authorities and international cooperative bodies.[27]

The New Dealers in the Treasury Department had their perspectives shaped by what they regarded as the failures of the interwar years: the practices of private bankers that contributed to instabilities leading to the Great Depression, the inability of either national governments or of international cooperative efforts in the 1930s to reverse the cycle of economic decline, the competitive devaluations of currency, and inflexibilities of gold standard rules. This new generation of economic experts sought to remedy these problems through a system in which currency experts from various countries would establish rules and run the postwar system— expertise wedded to internationalism. Generally, they sought greater flexibility for national monetary authorities who needed to keep in view the welfare of their citizens, a system of international coordination of exchange rates, and a subordinate role for private bankers in designing and running the new monetary system.

Roosevelt had long had support from some sectors of banking and industrial enterprises. Wilson's close adviser Colonel Edward House, whose daughter married Gordon Auchincloss, had become close to the Rockefeller interests, and

House became an adviser to Roosevelt before the 1932 presidential election. With House's help, some of the anti-Morgan interests, including Chase National Bank, backed Roosevelt in 1932, and they worked with him in pursuing the banking reform legislation of the early New Deal.[28] Like Wilson's Federal Reserve Act, Roosevelt's Glass-Steagall Act both responded to progressive demands that government needed to regulate the power of private banks and also reflected a pragmatic need to shape legislation in consultation with sympathetic business groups.

During the war Roosevelt, like Wilson before him, became ever friendlier to corporate interests. According to the journalist James Weschler, "the money changers who were driven from the temple are now quietly established in government offices." As the end of the war approached, many corporate leaders themselves acknowledged the value of Keynesian-style macroeconomic policies and the importance of the government's role in managing the transition from war to peace. A new Committee for Economic Development, based in Chicago with 50,000 business executives as members, endorsed a stronger role for government. American Keynsians, especially Alvin Hansen, had been stressing the use of fiscal policy to pump spending into the economy. Higher purchasing power and greater consumption would be the goal of the future—one that business could enthusiastically endorse. *Fortune* magazine became a powerful megaphone applauding the idea of greater government involvement and greater international cooperation in the regulation of postwar monetary affairs and reconstruction.[29]

The wartime conference held at Bretton Woods in New Hampshire during June and July of 1944 tried to tackle the problem of constructing such a postwar international economic order. The resulting blueprint for the International Monetary Fund and the World Bank represented an institutionalized approach to international economic adjustments. The Bretton Woods agreements, in which Keynes (for Britain) and White (for the United States) became dominant personalities, embodied the Roosevelt administration's commitment to exerting a strong governmental role in the economy and giving flexibility to national governments to retain a commitment to domestic welfare programs rather than to bow automatically to the rigidities of gold standard rules. They sought to ameliorate the destabilizing effects of short-term capital flows (hot money) by erecting some controls over capital movement. The new institutions, according to Secretary Morgenthau, aimed to be "instrumentalities of sovereign governments and not of private financial interests." Although Keynes, White, and many others involved in designing Bretton Woods advanced differing plans, all agreed on the need for an international framework of rules and an institution to enforce them.[30] The rhetoric of Bretton Woods promised that the new order would stand apart from the partisanship of economic interest and of nation and, instead, rely on economic experts, whom conference papers usually referred to as "technicians."[31]

The Bretton Woods agreements, however, went too far for some in the business community, especially bankers who feared the decline of their own power to organize the postwar financial system in line with "free market" principles. Winthrop Aldrich of Chase National Bank, Henry Hazlitt, economics journalist for the *New York Times*, and the editors of the *Wall Street Journal* led the public attack on Bretton Woods, arguing that it went too far in taking over the functions of private markets. Generally, they charged that the settlements were "too complex" and premature—that is, that political settlements should precede economic ones. They also suggested that bilateral arrangements with Britain, rather than a multilateral framework, would be more workable. Major banking interests wished to keep more of the basic building blocs of the prewar order: an international economic system run largely through central bank cooperation and without capital controls. They also favored a larger role for the Bank for International Settlements, a bastion of orthodox monetary thinking.[32]

The Department of the Treasury, however, mobilized supporters behind the new institutions. Randolph Feltus, a public relations expert, was hired to sell the Bretton Woods agreements to Congress and the public. The Treasury also mobilized bankers outside of New York, who were just as happy to see the power of the East Coast banking establishment curtailed. In addition, the Congress of Industrial Organizations (CIO) and other pro–New Deal organizations carried out a grassroots campaign on behalf of the Bretton Woods agreements. The CIO, for example, published *Bretton Woods Is No Mystery*, a pamphlet that countered the opponents' arguments. Claiming that the critics of Bretton Woods represented big bankers and reactionary members of Congress, labor's campaign argued that there was nothing "too complex" about Bretton Woods: "Bretton Woods" stood for "Bread and Wages"—more jobs and less control over international finance by greedy bankers.

The antimonopoly and proexpertise discourses of the first three decades of the twentieth century emerged full blown on behalf of this New Deal international economic order.[33] Roosevelt's public appeal for Congress to pass legislation enabling U.S. membership promised that the International Monetary Fund "would put an end to monetary chaos" by establishing a "code of agreed principles for the conduct of exchange and currency affairs." The president stated that "the Fund agreement spells the difference between a world caught again in the maelstrom of panic and economic warfare culminating in war—as in the

1930s—or a world in which the members strive for a better life through mutual trust, cooperation, and assistance."[34]

The international order envisioned by many New Dealers would see modification in practice. Signed in July 1944, the Bretton Woods agreements did not go to Congress for ratification until early 1945 because neither party wanted them to become an election issue. The Roosevelt administration was keenly aware of the consequences of Wilson's failure to compromise his postwar vision and reached out to form coalitions. As a result, during congressional debate, oppositional bankers and senators gained some concessions that curbed the international character of the decisionmaking and kept tighter control over the use of U.S. monetary contributions to the IMF.[35] In addition, President Roosevelt died in April, 1945, and Morgenthau and White had little influence in the new Harry Truman administration. By the time of the first meeting of the Board of Governors of the International Monetary Fund and the World Bank, Keynes detected a nationalistic American attempt to seize control of international economic matters. "The boys of the New Deal are now being eliminated," he wrote.[36] Instead, some of the very bankers who had opposed the agreement emerged as the guiding lights of U.S. policy.

The Bretton Woods system fell essentially inactive for a few years, while private bankers refused to help European governments control a disruptive capital flight that accompanied a major economic crisis in 1946–47. After 1947, the wartime vision of a system of political security, anchored by the United Nations, and a system of international economic security, anchored in the Bretton Woods institutions, became less and less central to postwar U.S. goals. During the early Cold War, key institutions became less international and more and more Americanized. A new president, distrustful of the left wing of the New Deal, promulgated the Truman Doctrine and developed the Marshall Plan, both expressions of U.S. power. The UN and Bretton Woods institutions themselves also became primarily responsive to U.S. policies. And all these postwar economic institutions, over time, became increasingly beholden to influential private interests, as had happened in the 1920s.[37]

Conclusion

This chapter has offered two interrelated arguments. First, the New Freedom and the New Deal, drawing from a critique of unregulated private power, both shared a vision of a reformed capitalism. They sought to create an international economic order in which the state, marshalling economic expertise, would curb abuses by large capital interests and, at the same time, assist those businesses who cooperated in promoting systemic stability. Both called upon corporate executives to serve the nation in wartime and worked to develop a cooperative relationship among government, military, and corporate sectors. The postwar future seemed to require not only new forms of international political cooperation to mitigate conflicts so that international commerce could flourish but also a structure that assured predictability in international exchange and lending. The Wilson and Roosevelt administrations thus exemplified what Daniel Yergin and Joseph Stanislaw describe as a long twentieth-century swing to give the state some control over what John Maynard Keynes called the "commanding heights."[38] The goals were to provide a better global distribution of goods, to promote rising standards of living for workers, and to prevent the dangerous spread of revolutionary ideologies.

The Wilson and Roosevelt administrations did not, of course, adopt the same approach to building this reformed capitalism internationally. Their eras were very different; the dominant economic theories changed; and the champions of a more assertive role for government became stronger with the New Deal.[39] Wilson's efforts were rather limited. His administration assumed that both government and business had reciprocal interests in encouraging an open door world and in applying expertise to regularize and spread gold standard currency systems and to stabilize international monetary exchange, but it sought an essentially informal cooperative relationship between government and business. In Wilson's view, the power of American capital, working together with governmental experts, could provide the "moral force" for a predictable and robust international economy, while the League of Nations would keep the peace by deterring aggression and helping settle disputes.

Roosevelt's efforts, in contrast, took shape out of the economic wreckage of the Great Depression. Paramount to New Dealers was the lesson that international bankers had not operated for the general good and that narrow profit seeking had undermined the larger economic system. They sought larger, more formalized, roles for governments; institutions to regularize and internationally coordinate policies on exchange rates; rules against competitive devaluation; and greater flexibility for national economic authorities—all so that the rigidity imposed by gold standard rules would not jeopardize important domestic programs and countercyclical interventions. International agencies such as those sketched at Bretton Woods—not private bankers—would organize and run the system. The close ties that the Roosevelt administration developed with sectors of corporate America during the war were not inconsistent with the creation of this new international economic architecture, although in time private interests came to be more dominant than progressives had envisioned.

Second, most traditional historiography of the Wilson-FDR continuum in foreign policy has focused on "internationalism" in the form of collective security-style arrangements. Looking away from the League of Nations and UN and into the realm of international economic policy, however, reframes the conventional view that has often presented two "internationalist" presidents who confronted the follies of "isolationism." The interwar anti-interventionists, who have misleadingly been conflated into "isolationists," were a diverse coalition that included many who came from the same internationalist political tradition as Wilson and Roosevelt. Fearing that wars were related to the unchecked power of a "money trust," this group of anti-interventionists advanced a critique of unregulated international capital that was prominent in American political culture during the first three-quarters of the twentieth century.

In short, the themes of the New Freedom (the need to reform capitalism through the application of expertise and the power of the state) echoed in the politics of many of the interwar anti-interventionist groups, whose members worried particularly about the power of international financiers and militarism. These same themes also could be heard in FDR's administration, particularly in its vision for the postwar Bretton Woods system. The equation of internationalism with collective security-style organizations, so common in histories of the Wilson-Roosevelt connection, has eclipsed the visibility of this economic critique and the calls for reformed capitalism. Wilson and Roosevelt both sought to establish checks on the excesses of capitalists to save the world for capitalism.[40]

Notes

1. Robert A. Divine, *Second Chance: The Triumph of Internationalism in America during World War II* (New York: Athenaeum, 1967); Lloyd E. Ambrosius, *Wilsonianism: Woodrow Wilson and His Legacy in American Foreign Relations* (New York: Palgrave Macmillan, 2002), 2; N. Gordon Levin, *Woodrow Wilson and World Politics: America's Response to War and Revolution* (New York: Oxford University Press, 1968), 260. Almost all other scholars of Wilsonianism (arguing from various interpretive persuasions) have also seen Wilson as a central presence in the shaping of U.S. foreign policy during World War II and after. Realists George Kennan and Henry Kissinger both lament the moralistic legacy of Wilsonianism but acknowledge its continuing power to shape the rhetoric and goals of diplomacy. Neo-Wilsonian Tony Smith lauds the Wilsonian legacy that linked the global expansion of democracy to national security. Frank Ninkovich and Akira Iriye stress how Wilsonian ideology worked to animate American power throughout the twentieth century. Thomas J. Knock sees the Franklin

Roosevelt administration as embracing Wilsonian internationalism during the war, although he views the Cold War "globalism" that followed as the antithesis of Wilson's "progressive internationalism," which was based on ideas of international cooperation and mediation of disputes rather than on a preponderance of U.S. power. See George F. Kennan, *American Diplomacy*, expanded edition (Chicago: University of Chicago Press, 1985); Henry Kissinger, *Diplomacy* (New York: Simon & Schuster,1994), 52–54; Tony Smith, *America's Mission: The United States and the Worldwide Struggle for Democracy in the Twentieth Century* (Princeton, N.J.: Princeton University Press, 1994); Frank Ninkovich, *The Wilsonian Century: U.S. Foreign Policy since 1900* (Chicago: University of Chicago Press, 2000); Akira Iriye, *The Globalizing of America, 1913–1945* (New York: Cambridge University Press, 1993); and Thomas J. Knock, *To End All Wars: Woodrow Wilson and the Quest for a New World Order* (New York: Oxford University Press, 1992), 273–74. With regard to domestic policy, Otis Graham, *An Encore for Reform: Old Progressives and the New Deal* (New York: Oxford University Press, 1967), provides an examination of the continuities and discontinuities between the Wilson and Roosevelt administrations.

2. Almost all standard works anchor discussion of Wilson's "internationalist" vision on the League of Nations with hardly any mention of an international economic dimension. These include Thomas A. Bailey, *Woodrow Wilson and the Lost Peace* (New York: Macmillan, 1944); Arthur S. Link, *Woodrow Wilson and the Progressive Era, 1910–1917* (New York: Harper & Brothers, 1954); Robert H. Ferrell, *Woodrow Wilson and World War I, 1917–1921* (New York: Harper & Row, 1985); John Milton Cooper Jr., *Vanity of Power American isolationism and the First World War, 1914–1917* (Westport, Conn.: Greenwood Press, 1969); and John Milton Cooper Jr., *Breaking the Heart of the World: Woodrow Wilson and the Fight for the League of Nations* (Cambridge: Cambridge University Press, 2001).

3. Justus D. Doenecke, *Storm on the Horizon: The Challenge of American Intervention, 1939–1941* (Lanham, Md.: Rowman & Littlefield, 2000).

4. Melvyn I. Urofsky, ed., *Other People's Money and How the Bankers Use It: by Louis D. Brandeis* (New York: Bedford, 1995).

5. James Livingston, *Origins of the Federal Reserve System: Money, Class, and Corporate Capitalism, 1890–1913* (Ithaca, N.Y.: Cornell University Press, 1986). See also chapter 3 in this volume by W. Elliot Brownlee.

6. Linda B. Hall, *Oil, Banks, and Politics: The United States and Postrevolutionary Mexico, 1917–1924* (Austin: University of Texas Press, 1995), 36–59, 84–103. Mark T. Gilderhus, *Diplomacy and Revolution: U.S.-Mexican Relations under Wilson and Carranza* (Tucson: University of Arizona Press, 1977).

7. This episode is documented in documents from 1917 in the National Archives, Department of State, Record Group 79, M-699, 818.00/64-385. Wilson conveyed, through William Gibbs McAdoo, the message to United Fruit that his government would withdraw diplomatic protection of the company in Central America unless its disruptions to Central American politics ceased. Robert Lansing to McAdoo, February 17, 1917, Papers of Robert Lansing, vol. 24, Library of Congress, Washington.

8. Emily S. Rosenberg, *Spreading the American Dream: American Economic and Cultural Expansion, 1890–1945* (New York: Hill and Wang, 1982), 65–75.

9. Joan Hoff Wilson, *American Business and Foreign Policy, 1920–1933* (Lexington: University Press of Kentucky, 1971), 87.

10. Emily S. Rosenberg, *Financial Missionaries to the World: The Politics and Culture of Dollar Diplomacy* (Durham, N.C.: Duke University Press, 2003), 79–96.

11. See Rosenberg, *Financial Missionaries*, 79–93; Joseph S. Tulchin, *The Aftermath of War: World War I and U.S. Policy toward Latin America* (New York: New York University Press,1971), 155–57, on bringing Latin American debt under the jurisdiction of American bankers; and Carl P. Parrini, *Heir to Empire: United States Economic Diplomacy, 1916–1923* (Pittsburgh: University of Pittsburgh Press, 1969).

12. John Maynard Keynes, *The Economic Consequences of the Peace* (New York: Harcourt, Brace, and Howe, 1920).

13. Memo, Edward Hurley, head of Shipping Board, to Bernard Baruch, head of War Industries Board, after a meeting with Wilson, May 21, 1918, National Archives, Department of State, Record Group 79, 6000.001/24.

14. Rosenberg, *Financial Missionaries*, 236–37; Robert David Johnson, *The Peace Progressives and American Foreign Relations* (Cambridge, Mass.: Harvard University Press, 1995), 132–38. On specific aspects of noninterventionist politics, see Elizabeth McKillan, *Chicago Labor and the Quest for a Democratic Diplomacy, 1914–1924* (Ithaca, N.Y.: Cornell University Press, 1995); Alan Dawley, *Changing the World: American Progressives in War and Revolution* (Princeton, N.J.: Princeton University Press, 2003); Scott H. Bennett, *Radical Pacifism: The War Resisters League and Gandhian Nonviolence in America, 1915–1963* (Syracuse: Syracuse University Press, 2003).

15. John Madden et al., *America's Experience as a Creditor Nation* (New York: Prentice Hall, 1937); Vincent P. Carosso, *Investment Banking in America: A History* (Cambridge, Mass.: Harvard University Press, 1970), 328–50; Wayne S. Cole, *Senator Gerald P. Nye and American Foreign Relations* (Minneapolis: University of Minnesota Press, 1962), 66–76.

16. Franklin Roosevelt, "Government and Modern Capitalism," Fireside Chat, September 30, 1934, in *FDR's Fireside Chats*, ed. Russell D. Buhite and David W. Levy (Norman: University of Oklahoma Press, 1992), 55.

17. Quoted by Nicholas Halasz, *Roosevelt through Foreign Eyes* (Princeton, N.J.: D. Van Nostrand, 1961), 73.

18. On the victory of Republican internationalists at the party convention in 1940, see Charles Peters, *Five Days in Philadelphia* (New York: PublicAffairs, 2005).

19. Doenecke, *Storm on the Horizon*; Thomas N. Guinsburg, *The Pursuit of Isolationism in the United States Senate from Versailles to Pearl Harbor* (New York: Garland, 1982); Johnson, *Peace Progressives*.

20. Thomas J. Fleming, *The New Dealers' War: Franklin D. Roosevelt and the War within World War II* (New York: Basic Books, 2001), 137–38.

21. Knock, *To End All Wars*, 272; Divine, *Second Chance*.

22. Bailey, *Woodrow Wilson and the Lost Peace*; Thomas A. Bailey, *Woodrow Wilson and the Great Betrayal* (New York: Macmillan, 1945).

23. See note 1 above.

24. Ellis W. Hawley, *The New Deal and the Problem of Monopoly* (Princeton, N.J.: Princeton University Press, 1966), which concerns itself only with domestic policy, argues that the New Deal had elements both of accepting monopoly, if controlled, and attacking it.

25. John Ikenberry, "The Political Origins of Bretton Woods," in *A Retrospective on the Bretton Woods System: Lessons for International Monetary Reform*, ed. Barry Eichengreen and Michael D. Bordo (Chicago: University of Chicago Press, 1993), 155–82.

26. Wayne S. Cole, *Roosevelt and the Isolationists, 1932–45* (Lincoln: University of Nebraska Press. 1983), 37–127.

27. Richard Parker, *John Kenneth Galbraith: His Life, His Politics, His Economics* (New York: Farrar, Straus and Giroux, 2005), 50–51. Alvin Hansen's Fiscal Policy Seminar at Harvard had provided the principal sounding board for the new Keynesian thought in the United States. On the growing influence of Keynes, see ibid., 68–91. Marriner Eccles, one of the main supporters of government as a "compensatory agent" in the economy, however, claimed that he had not heard of or read Keynes when he first advanced his views. "Keynesianism" seems to have been a set of approaches that apparently came from many sources and then took the name of the great British economist. William E. Leuchtenburg, *Franklin Roosevelt and the New Deal* (New York: Harper & Row, 1963), 244–47. Robert M. Collins, *The Business Response to Keynes in America* (New York: Columbia University Press, 1982), 23–112, traces the various reactions to Hansen/Keynesianism in the mid-1940s.

28. Thomas Ferguson, "Industrial Conflict and the Coming of the New Deal: The Triumph of Multinational Liberalism in America," in *The Rise and Fall of the New Deal Order, 1930–1980*, ed. Gary Gerstle and Steve Fraser (Princeton, N.J.: Princeton University Press, 1989), 3–31.

29. Parker, *John Kenneth Galbraith*, 166–69 (the quotation is on 166); Alan Brinkley, "The New Deal and the Idea of the State," in *Rise and Fall of the New Deal Order*, ed. Gerstle and Fraser, 85–121; and Alan Brinkley, *The End of Reform: New Deal Liberalism in Recession and War* (New York: Alfred A. Knopf, 1995), 217–52, traces FDR's measures aimed at raising purchasing power. For an extended treatment of the how the war helped create a military-corporate alliance that then came to dominate policymaking, both domestic and foreign, see Brian Waddell, "Corporate Influence and World War II: Resolving the New Deal Political Stalemate," *Journal of Policy History* 11, no. 3 (1999): 223–56; and Paul A. C. Koistinen, *Arsenal of World War II: The Political Economy of American Warfare, 1940–1945* (Lawrence: University Press of Kansas, 2004).

30. Richard N. Gardner, *Sterling-Dollar Diplomacy: The Origins and the Prospects of Our International Economic Order* (New York: McGraw-Hill, 1969), 71–77 (the quotation is on 76); Harold James, *International Monetary Cooperation since Bretton Woods* (New York: Oxford University Press, 1996), 1–57.

31. Elizabeth Borgwardt, *A New Deal for the World: America's Vision for Human Rights* (Cambridge, Mass.: Harvard University Press, 2005), 88–140, esp. 91; Robert Skidelsky, *John Maynard Keynes: Fighting for Freedom, 1937–1946* (New York: Viking

Press, 2000), 182. Accounts and interpretations of details of the Bretton Woods plan and negotiation include Gardner, *Sterling-Dollar Diplomacy*; R. Bruce Craig, *Treasonable Doubt: The Harry Dexter White Spy Case* (Lawrence: University of Kansas Press, 2004), 135–55 (on White); and Anne-Marie Burley (Slaughter), "Regulating the World: Multilateralism, International Law, and the Projection of the New Deal Regulatory State," in *Multilateralism Matters: The Theory and Praxis of an Institutional Form*, ed. John Ruggie (New York: Columbia University Press, 1993).

32. Eric Helleiner, *States and the Reemergence of Global Finance: From Bretton Woods to the 1990s* (Ithaca, N.Y.: Cornell University Press, 1994).

33. On the selling of Bretton Woods at home, see George Fujii, "*Bretton Woods Is No Mystery?* Translating Complex International Financial Policy to Domestic Audiences," paper presented at Society for Historians of American Foreign Relations conference, Lawrence, Kan., June 24, 2006; Randall Bennett Woods, *A Changing of the Guard: Anglo-American Relations, 1941–1946* (Chapel Hill: University of North Carolina Press, 1990), 228–32; and Alfred E. Eckes, *A Search for Solvency: Bretton Woods and the International Monetary System, 1941–1971* (Austin: University of Texas Press, 1975), 35–46, 168–69.

34. "The President Urges Immediate Adoption of the Bretton Woods Agreements, Feb. 12, 1945," in *The Public Papers and Addresses of Franklin D. Roosevelt, 1944–45*, ed. Samuel I. Rosenman (New York: Harper & Brothers, 1950), 552–53.

35. On the political struggles and compromises, see especially Woods, *A Changing of the Guard*, 232–43; and Gardner, *Sterling-Dollar Diplomacy*, 129–44.

36. Quoted in James, *International Monetary Cooperation*, 72.

37. Michael J. Hogan, *The Marshall Plan: America, Britain, and the Reconstruction of Western Europe, 1947–1952* (Cambridge: Cambridge University Press, 1987), sees both Bretton Woods and the Marshall Plan as an expression of the "New Deal coalition" that united the American government, big labor, and international-oriented businesses behind global economic growth. Helleiner, *States and the Reemergence of Global Finance*, and James, *International Monetary Cooperation*, stress how the Marshall Plan veered slightly away from the New Dealers' initial goals at Bretton Woods in what groups (more American and more private interests) would ultimately be in control of the "rules of the game." On Truman's national security policy generally, see, especially, Melvyn P. Leffler, *A Preponderance of Power: National Security, the Truman Administration, and the Cold War* (Palo Alto, Calif.: Stanford University Press, 1992).

38. Daniel Yergin and Joseph Stanislaw, *The Commanding Heights: The Battle between Government and the Marketplace That Is Remaking the Modern World* (New York: Simon & Schuster, 1998).

39. For scholarly debates over whether the New Deal's legacy in the domestic arena represented "statism" or a continuation and intensification of the "New Liberalism" of the early twentieth century, see the forum "Liberalism and the Liberal State," *Law and History Review* 24 (Spring 2006): 115–213. This forum contains an essay by James A. Henretta, "Charles Evans Hughes and the Strange Death of Liberal America," with comments by Daniel T. Rodgers, William Forbath, William J. Novak, and Risa

Goluboff. Rodgers presents an especially cogent attack on the use of labels such as "statism" and "New Liberalism" (and I would, in the foreign policy area, add "isolationism") to try to make sense of the messy and contradictory past.

40. David Ciepley, *Liberalism in the Shadow of Totalitarianism* (Cambridge, Mass.: Harvard University Press, 2006), charts how U.S. elites, in opposition to totalitarian regimes during the Cold War, began to rethink the use of state power to pursue economic and social ends.

10. Woodrow Wilson and the Cold War: "Tear Down This Wall, Mr. Gorbachev"

Martin Walker

On January 16, 1991, President George H. W. Bush announced the launch of the air war against Iraq with the pledge that this campaign would bring "a new world order, a world where the rule of law, not the rule of the jungle, governs the conduct of nations—an order in which a credible United Nations can use its peacekeeping role to fulfill the promise and vision of the UN's founders."

Sources of Wilson's Ideals

The lofty goals set by President Bush, and the thinking behind them, both the phrases and the inspiration, echo and spring clearly from the legacy of Woodrow Wilson. Here, shortly after the end of what the British and Marxist historian Eric Hobsbawm dubbed "the short twentieth century," as at its beginning, is that authentic voice of American idealism, determined in the most high-minded way to inscribe, as Americans had done on their own new world, the American principles of freedom and law and representative government on the fresh page of history. As Henry Kissinger noted in his book *Diplomacy*: "Woodrow Wilson's principles have remained the bedrock of American policy thinking. . . . Wilson's intellectual victory proved more seminal any political triumph could have been. For, whenever America faced the task of constructing a new world order, it has returned in one way or another to Woodrow Wilson's precepts. . . . It is above all to the drumbeat of American idealism that American foreign policy has marched since his watershed Presidency and continues to march to this day."[1]

This is true up to a point, if we allow Kissinger the latitude sought in his telling phrase "one way or another." For Wilson has not been the sole guide of American foreign policy in the eight decades since his death. Kissinger has also suggested that the policymakers of Washington have followed two stars rather than one, and that the tough-minded realism of Teddy Roosevelt, committed to national self-interest and ambition, has proved as enduring and influential a presence as the ideals of Woodrow Wilson, or "Woody," as the future President Harry Truman affectionately dubbed him, writing letters home from his artillery battery on the Western front in 1918, in the closing stages of Woody's "war to end all wars."

In his memoirs, Truman described with some precision his own debt to Wilson, and his own conviction that at the close of World War II and at the start of the new Cold War, he was aware that he was part of an American foreign policy tradition that he traced back through his predecessor Franklin Roosevelt to Woodrow Wilson. Conscious of his own youthful enthusiasm for Wilson and the cause for which the young artillery officer from Missouri believed he had had been fighting, Truman said that that he determined to steer his course by Wilsonian precepts: "I hoped that we would come out of this war with a going world organization for peace, and at the same time, that we could help our friends and allies get back on their own feet."[2]

Tellingly, however, as a practical politician who had learned his vote-counting trade in the shadow of the legendary Boss Prendergast and had then gone to the graduate school of hard politics in the U.S. Senate, Truman stressed that there was another aspect of Wilson's legacy that he kept close to mind: "I was trying to profit by the mistakes of Woodrow Wilson."[3]

Truman was determined to learn from Wilson's example what *not* to do:

I had read carefully all of Woodrow Wilson's writings and speeches on the League of Nations. I followed closely the debate in the Senate on the Versailles Treaty and saw how a small group of what Woodrow Wilson called "willful men" in the Senate had managed to prevent American participation in the League of Nations. President Roosevelt had shared with me his determination to avoid the experience of Wilson by getting in advance the participation and consent of leaders of both parties, and include Republicans and Democrats in the delegation to San Francisco. . . . We did not want to run the risk of another League of Nations tragedy, with the United States standing in isolation on the sidelines.[4]

This was to become the orthodoxy of Wilsonian studies at the presidential level. Truman's successors all admired Wilson, cited him as inspiration and quoted his speeches, and saw in him some essential component of the American spirit and the guiding spirit of a singular continuity in its foreign policies, its concern for the security and stability of Europe. More than forty years after Wilson had left the White House, President John F. Kennedy declared in Paris that "I have come on the same mission which occupied many of my predecessors, stretching all the way back to President Woodrow Wilson at the conclusion of the First World War, and that is how it is possible to bind more intimately for the common interest France and the United States, Europe and the United States."[5]

President Dwight Eisenhower, who had marched as a young West Point cadet of the U.S. Army in Wilson's Inaugural parade, confessed himself at the end of his known second term to be still moved by Wilson's legacy: "Wilson said that what we seek is 'the reign of law, based upon the consent of the governed and sustained by the urgent opinion of mankind.' Today we have a second chance to win through to that goal. And we dare not fail. If we heed Wilson, we shall never hesitate to pay for freedom whatever price may be required."[6]

President Lyndon Johnson thought Wilson's defeat when the U.S. Senate refused to ratify the Treaty of Versailles to be a national tragedy, and he said so in characteristically pungent terms: "Worst thing that ever happened to this country was those sixty-year-old senators, smelling of rat piss, doing Number One on Wilson's Fourteen Points."[7] LBJ put the point rather more delicately in a speech in his 1964 election campaign against the Republican conservative Barry Goldwater, as he warned voters to go to the polling booth with Goldwater's warlike rhetoric in mind. "Don't wait like they did with Woodrow Wilson, Johnson said. "He envisioned a peace. He was almost in reach of it. Then he lost it and we went to World War II."[8] At the same time, like Johnson, most presidents and their advisers accepted the orthodox view that Wilson's ideals were considerably grander than his political skills, whether in dealing with foreigners or with the U.S. Congress, and that more than most, he fulfilled that haunting phrase of the British political intellectual and university professor Enoch Powell, that "all political careers are doomed to end in failure."

"Wilson was a truly great leader," Richard Nixon told his young political secretary. "His only fault was that he wasn't a realist enough to know that pragmatism had to be balanced with idealism. Idealism running rampant is impotent."[9]

One hesitates to correct Nixon, that classic exponent of realpolitik, and yet it must be said that a lack of political realism was not what many seasoned observers saw in Wilson. Watching him in action in the negotiations that led to the Treaty of Versailles, his own political confident Colonel Edward House confided dryly to the privacy of his diary that Wilson "talks like Jesus Christ but acts like Lloyd George."[10] In Central and Latin America, Wilson asserted that his policies were progressive and democratic. "I am going to teach the South American republics to elect good men," he maintained. To the ungrateful recipients of his teaching and the U.S. Marines he sent as forceful pedagogues, this seemed little different from the imperialism Wilson disdained. Facts were not always allowed to get in the way of Wilson's high-mindedness. His claim at the Paris peace conference that he had never seen the secret treaties promising large tracts of the Austro-Hungarian Empire to Italy startled British foreign secretary Arthur Balfour, who had himself shown them to Wilson in 1917. Wilson's own disillusioned (and sidelined) secretary of state, Robert Lansing, later said that Wilson even ignored established facts if they did not fit with Wilson's "intuitive sense," his "semi-divine power to select the right."

"There is such a thing as being too proud to fight," Wilson maintained, in defense of American neutrality. The British, pouring out their blood and treasure in a war that saw the United States make the dramatic transition from the world's leading debtor to its greatest creditor, had another explanation. Lord Bertie, the British ambassador to Paris, saw Wilson and his government as "a rotten lot of psalm-singing profit-mongering humbugs." The great liberal historian Sir George Trevelyan wrote of Wilson to his friend Lord Bryce in January 1917, "The man is surely the very quintessence of a prig."

In a burst of that secret diplomacy that Wilson's Fourteen Points were later to condemn, in 1916 Colonel House was empowered to negotiate an agreement with Britain's Lord Grey that, at a moment suitable to France and Britain, Wilson would propose an international conference to end the war. If Germany refused to attend, or were to reject terms that Wilson deemed reasonable (which were bound to include the return of the occupied territories of Belgium and northern France), then "the United States would enter the war against Germany." Wilson carefully inserted the word "probably" in his own hand, and given the dynamics of presidential and congressional powers over the making of war, there was nothing at all unrealistic about that.[11] And certainly there was some very tough-minded realism in Wilson's threats to outbuild Britain's Royal Navy, or in his blunt use of the U.S. financial power to browbeat Britain in the summer of 1916. When J. P. Morgan tried to raise a new loan in British bonds, the Federal Reserve, after checking the phrasing with Wilson, announced that it did "not regard it in the interest of the country at this time that they invest in foreign Treasury bills of that character."[12]

"Realism" and "idealism" are perilously simplistic terms, even when refined by scholars who recast them as Wilson's "higher realism," in the phrase of his biographer, Arthur S. Link, or the "meta-realism" of Francis Gavin. But it is fair to suggest that American foreign policy, like the minds of most voters in democratic states, has always contained varying measures of both realism and idealism.

American policy during the five decades of the Cold War illustrates the point. The strategic goal was grandly idealist, to manage this vast struggle between two fundamentally opposed systems in such a way that the devastation of nuclear war was avoided, that the physical security and financial health of the United States and its allies were undamaged, and that the formidable challenges of decolonization and emergent new nationalisms in Asia, Africa, Latin America, and the Middle East were resolved. The tactics applied were often crudely and even squalidly realist, in the raw Bismarckian sense. Ideals were sullied, in the support of French colonialism in Indochina, or even betrayed, in the murderously false encouragement of Hungarian freedom fighters in 1956. Gross mistakes of judgment were made, in the Vietnam War, but so was the coldly realistic decision to accept a bloody draw in the Korean War.

One lesson of the Cold War is that a stretch of history so prolonged is something of a palimpsest that can bear almost any interpretation., It is possible to write a history of the Cold War that portrays it as a triumph of the slow and patient application of Wilsonian ideals by his successors of both parties. It is equally possible to sketch such a history as a classic example of the coldest-eyed realism in American grand strategy. Neither such history would be wholly wrong; nor would it be wholly right.

Histories of the Cold War

A Wilsonian history of the Cold War would go like this. The United States established in the 1940s the global institutions that would protect and eventually enrich the free democracies, and it widened their ranks with a wise stewardship that guided the former enemies of Japan and West Germany firmly into the Western camp. These economic benefits were offered to the Soviet Union and its client states but were spurned. Not without some errors and missteps that were probably inevitable in a spirited democracy, the United States occupied and maintained the moral high ground throughout the Cold War. This was achieved on the domestic front by maintaining a high-growth and high-productivity economy that tamed the harshness of the capitalist system, provided for the poor and the elderly, and produced the world's first mass middle class. And despite intense domestic opposition, the United States dismantled the system of segregation that had been the weakest link in its moral armor and promoted the cause of civil rights, a domestic echo of its principled commitment to the cause of global freedom. While encouraging its allies to give independence to their colonies, and standing firm on the basis of international law against their French and British allies' neocolonial venture at Suez in 1956, the United States nurtured a free alliance of willing partners. This stood in stark contrast to the dragooned satellites of Moscow, and it developed a global economic system that benefited ever-wider reaches of the Earth and demonstrated the merits of the free and capitalist system over the sclerotic state-controlled Soviet economy. While keeping up its strategic guard, the United States chose to wait, rather than fight, in the justified belief that the Soviet Union would change or collapse from the burden of its own contradictions and failings. And while the Cold War was in its way a struggle to the death between two essentially irreconcilable systems, the United States maintained the diplomatic and economic connections with Moscow that eventually allowed the Cold War to end, in partnership with the enlightened leadership of Mikhail Gorbachev, without nuclear war and without major bloodshed.

A realist history of the Cold War might read as follows. The United States swiftly rallied the old enemies of World War II to its side as allies and subordinate partners in a global system of a robust defense against communist aggression, and if European electorates seemed reluctant to support this view, the American thumb could press the electoral scales, as in Italy in 1948, to win a suitable result. The United States—ready to wage limited wars to define and mark the boundaries of its strategic frontiers in Asia—astutely managed to achieve most of its goals with carefully husbanded means, and it used covert operations and armed allies, regardless of their lack of democratic credentials, to fight proxy wars to defend its interests in the Middle East, Latin America, and Africa. Along the way, America managed to replace Britain as the key Western power in the Middle East and thus to achieve an effective strategic dominance over the most important oil basins. This was achieved largely on the cheap, with a far smaller standing army than the Soviet Union and careful exploitation of the U.S. technological assets to stabilize the Cold War by nuclear deterrence. But this was a dynamic rather than stagnant stabilization. In the closing months of World War II, the United States was able to craft a postwar economic system uniquely favorable to American strengths and interests, promoting a series of tariff cuts and open door policies that dismantled the British and French system of colonial preferences and allowed the dollar to become the dominant world currency. While thoughtfully allowing others to share in the general prosperity, the United States became the linchpin and guarantor of a global economy of which it was the greatest beneficiary, and it was thus able to afford both guns and butter, aircraft carriers and private cars, and outspend, outproduce, and outlast the Soviet Union. The United States played the Cold War as a long game

with the economic odds stacked in its favor, and as the weaknesses of the Soviet system became apparent, the United States seized its opportunity in the 1980s at a point when the global oil price had sunk to a point that it could no longer bail out a limping Soviet economy, forcing a new high-technology arms race in which the Soviet Union was unable to compete.

Moreover, the United States' dominance of the global media and its mastery of public relations skills allowed it for most of the Cold War period to win enough of the arguments in the court of global public opinion to play the role of the good guy in the white hat, despite its cold-eyed support of a great many villainous allies in very black hats around the world. As a result, not only did the United States prevail in the Cold War, it was able to present this American victory as a universal human triumph, enabling its to dance on the grave of a defeated communist ideology, just as it had been able to consign fascism and Nazism to history by condemning them as eternally unacceptable and discredited.

The point is that either one of these competing narratives owes a great deal to the legacy of Woodrow Wilson, and doubtless as a result, historians have been arguing about his role in the Cold War ever since. Some of them have argued both sides. George F. Kennan, whose eminence owes as much to his professional diplomacy and strategic vision as it does to his role as historian, had it both ways. Kennan, as the archetypal realist, had set the terms of debate by arguing in *American Diplomacy* that Wilson had been "moralistic and legalistic" and had tried to build a world order for the ages by presenting the Americans as "more wise and noble than we really were."[13]

But then, in subsequent interviews, Kennan recanted: "I now view Wilson . . . as a man who like so many other people of broad vision and acute sensitivities, was ahead of his time, and did not live long enough to know what great and commanding relevance many of his ideas would acquire before this century was out. In this sense, I have to correct or modify, at this stage of my own life, many of the impressions I had about him at an earlier stage."[14]

This is confusing. Perhaps one way to clarify matters would be attempt to break down the cardinal features of American policy during the Cold War and see how far they made be said to demonstrate the Wilsonian legacy. There are perils here. Wilson's legacy is sufficiently broad, and his writings and speeches sufficiently copious, that some of the most unlikely characters have plundered his heritage with profit. President Ronald Reagan, not an obvious Wilsonian, repeatedly quoted his phrase that "liberty has never come from government. The history of liberty is the history of limitation of government's power, not the increase of it."

Scholarly Views

Scholars have categorized Wilson's legacy in various ways. Michael Mandelbaum has defined a "Wilsonian triad" of arms restraints, popular government, and free trade, adding that they were all wrapped into "international institutions to embody a rule of law." Walter Russell Mead defines Wilson's legacy as self-determination and national independence and democracy. Lloyd Ambrosius has defined four main currents of Wilsonianism: national self-determination, combing national sovereignty with democratic government; the open door policy of equal trading access, if not full free trade; collective security; and an essentially progressive view of history, that the lot of humanity as whole may be improved with wisdom and good governance. Joseph Nye has identified the preservation of the global commons, such as the freedom of the seas, and acting as the convener of conferences and the mediator of disputes as two other salient characteristics of the Wilsonian way. To all this we might an abiding concern for moral authority, rooted in a conviction of what Seymour Martin Lipset has called "American Exceptionalism."[15]

There is nothing unique in this. In the nineteenth century, British statesmen from Canning to Gladstone took pride in claiming to be representing concerns both grander and more noble than the traditional self-interest of nations. Like the United States—or indeed France, when it claimed its imperialism "*une mission civilisatrice*," and thus quite different from the money-grubbing British form—Gladstone has been accused of special pleading. As his great rival Benjamin Disraeli told the House of Commons: "It is not Mr. Gladstone's habit of producing the ace of trumps from up his sleeves that I deprecate, so much as his blithe assurance that God Almighty put it there." Other nations, as well as rival politicians, may question this assurance of probity. As Peter Rodman, the George W. Bush administration's assistant secretary of defense, has noted: "America is genuinely puzzled by the idea that American assertiveness in the name of universal principles could sometimes be seen by others as a form of American unilateralism." Indeed it is, and others do not always like it. "Wilsonian presidents drive them crazy," Rodman adds, "and have done so ever since the days of Woodrow Wilson."[16] This is the part of the legacy that includes a readiness to intervene militarily in the affairs of neighboring smaller states in the name of those supposedly universal principles.

There will be other features, but what follows—drawn from Wilson's Fourteen Points and main speeches, as well as a variety of other scholars—is a reasonably comprehensive list, although in no particular order and arbitrarily following the main lines of Wilson's foreign policy:

1. Arms control.
2. Popular and representative government, with an objective of democratic rule.
3. The open door, with an objective of free trade.
4. The building of international institutions.
5. The rule of law.
6. Transparency in international dealings ("open covenants, openly arrived at").
7. Self-determination and national independence.
8. Collective security, backed if necessary by force.
9. Freedom of the seas, and a care for the global commons.
10. The mediation of disputes and convening of conferences.
11. American moral authority, in pursuit of universal principles.
12. A readiness to intervene militarily.
13. A concern for the rights of colonial peoples.
14. Humanitarian concern.

The main features of the grand strategy of the United States in waging the Cold War may be presented as identical. But they deserve some elaboration and definition.

First, arms control. In the Cold War, this may be said to begin with the Acheson-Lilienthal proposals for the development of atomic materials to be the monopoly of a new international authority. But the first realization of arms controls in treaty form came with President John F. Kennedy's 1963 proposals for a ban on nuclear tests in outer space. Progress was measured, with the Anti–Ballistic Missile Treaty of 1972, followed by the Strategic Arms Limitation process, and then the Vienna conferences of confidence-building measures that sought to limit conventional forces in Europe.

Second, the promotion of democratic governments. West Germany and Japan were the first beneficiaries of what became a steady U.S. concern, which played an important symbolic role in the Cold War after the Soviet Union flouted the 1945 provisions of the Yalta agreement to "the earliest possible through free elections of governments responsive to the will of the people." The Helsinki Treaties of 1975, with the provisions for the recognition of human rights (including the UN covenants on civil and political rights) enshrined in the final basket of the Helsinki Accords inspired the Charter 77 movement in Czechoslovakia and other human rights activists throughout the Soviet bloc.

Third, the pursuit of free trade through the General Agreement on Tariffs and Trade (GATT). The GATT, which after forty-five years of tariff reductions grew into the World Trade Organization, became a key institution for the growth of world trade and the spread of prosperity. It was not, however, allowed to overrule the particular preferential tariff arrangements of the European Economic Community, given the wider strategic objective of maintaining the Atlantic alliance.

Fourth, the building of international institutions. The United Nations, as direct heir of Wilson's League of Nations, was the most prominent of these. But NATO and the World Bank, the GATT and the International Monetary Fund, were all to become important components of the U.S. grand strategy in the wake of the Marshall Plan that helped rebuilt the war-battered economies of Europe. It is significant that the aid of the Marshall Plan was also offered to the Soviet Union and its satellites. The Czech government announced its acceptance, before being reined in by Moscow.

Fifth, the rule of law. This was implicit in the terms of the United Nations and of the other institutions devised by British and American officials at the end of World War II.

Sixth, transparency in international dealings. There was no commitment to "open covenants, openly arrived at," but a concern for transparency was evident in Eisenhower's Open Skies proposals and in the strict verification and inspection terms built into the arms control treaties.

Seventh, self-determination and national independence. Although solemnly pledged at Yalta in 1945 by the Allied powers, the independence of the countries of Eastern Europe was achieved in form rather than in substance. The United States refused throughout the Cold War to recognize the incorporation of the three Baltic Sea states of Latvia, Lithuania, and Estonia into the Soviet Union. Though the United States paid lip service to the right of national self-determination in urging its Dutch, French, and British allies to grant self-rule and independence to their colonies, this was not taken to the extent of any breach of relations with its NATO allies.

Eighth, collective security, backed if necessary by force. This was explicit in chapter 7, article 42, of the UN Treaty but became a recurring feature of U.S. diplomacy with article 5 of the North Atlantic Treaty Organization, and similar undertakings of collective security with the CENTO and SEATO treaties. Indeed, in the Senate ratification hearings on the SEATO Treaty, it was said by Secretary of State John Foster Dulles that article IV of the treaty would explicitly include an attack on South Vietnam "by the regime of Ho Chi Minh."

Ninth, freedom of the seas, and a care for the global commons. The almost absolute dominance of the U.S. Navy, backed up by the Royal Navy and other NATO allies, did not hinder the use of the seas by the Soviet and Chinese navies. The concern for the global commons was rather more narrowly defined during the Cold War than it became after the Montreal agreement on environmental protection. But the restrictions on nuclear testing evince a clear commitment to protect the health of the planet.

Tenth, the mediation of disputes and the convening of conferences. Regular meetings of foreign ministers to resolve disputes was one of the postwar principles agreed on at Yalta, and it was further enshrined in the UN system, but this system was swiftly overtaken by summit meetings between U.S. and Soviet leaders.

Eleventh, American moral authority, in pursuit of universal principles. America's moral authority was repeatedly imperiled, at least in the eyes of many neutral and even allied observers, by the perpetuation of racial segregation in the American South; by the actions of Senator Joseph McCarthy and the House Un-American Activities Committee; by the urban and campus riots of the 1960s; by the Vietnam War; by covert operations to destabilize or overthrow foreign governments in Iran, Guatemala, and Chile; and by the alliances with highly unsavory and authoritarian regimes.

Twelfth, a readiness to intervene militarily. The United States repeatedly intervened covertly, and launched overt and major military operations, in Korea and in Vietnam, each time at the invitation of the recognized governments of those two divided countries, and in the case of Korea, with the support of a UN mandate. It did not intervene, despite some appeals to do so, in the prime theater of the Cold War, continental Europe, standing by as the Soviet army reimposed political control in Hungary in 1956 and Czechoslovakia in 1968. The United States also supported military interventions by proxies in Guatemala in 1954, in Cuba in 1961, and in Nicaragua and Afghanistan in the 1980s.

Thirteenth, a concern for the rights of colonial peoples. By the end of the Cold War, the European colonial empires had been reduced to handful of "statelets," most of which became recipients of U.S. foreign aid programs, with varying degrees of success. The United States promoted this process, without (with the exception of the Dutch East Indies) unduly forcing the pace. In the case of the NATO ally Portugal, this pace was glacial. And the decision by the British government in 1967 to withdraw from its commitments "east of Suez" was greeted with considerable alarm by the Johnson administration. By the end of the Cold War, "empire" had become a largely metaphorical term, used to describe the non-Russian republics of the Soviet Union and its Warsaw Pact allies. This terminology was then deployed against the United States, as the end of the Cold War left it the sole remaining superpower.

Fourteenth, humanitarian concern. Wilson insisted, at the end of World War I, that Herbert Hoover be put in charge of the Allied relief operations to tackle the food crisis in Germany, Belgium, and the former Austro-Hungarian Empire, and subsequently in Russia, over the objections of the other Allied leaders. With some delays, including the brief interruption of Lend-Lease shipments, the United States joined in similar efforts at the end of World War II, but not to the extent of the British, who introduced bread rationing in 1946 to feed the starving Germans, an extreme to which they had not been reduced in wartime in the teeth of German submarine warfare. Food Aid (which had to be shipped in United States–registered vessels) and other humanitarian efforts, often in association with the various UN agencies, thereafter became a fixture of postwar U.S. policies.

But there was a fifteenth feature of the Cold War strategy that Wilson ignored: a commitment to gaining bipartisan political support in the U.S. political system. This was the lesson that Wilson's successors had learned from his own defeat when the Senate refused to ratify the Treaty of Versailles. As Dean Acheson noted of President Roosevelt in *Present at the Creation*, FDR dreamed of being "the President who had succeeded where Woodrow Wilson had failed.[17]

The other reasons why Roosevelt and Truman succeeded where Wilson had failed may all be traced back to the lessons learned from Wilson's frustration. There was, for example, to be no repetition of the prolonged and deeply introspective peace conference of 1919, and there was to be no reenactment of the Treaty of Versailles. Roosevelt's demand for unconditional surrender at the Casablanca summit in effect made the armistice, conference, and treaty all redundant, and this spared a new American president the endless erosion of his goodwill and principles that had so exhausted Wilson in Paris. As the future ambassador Charles Bohlen noted of the Yalta agreement in February 1945, "The agreement meant that Roosevelt had apparently avoided President Wilson's mistake of waiting until after the war, when isolationist feelings returned, to solve the problems."[18] There are many criticisms that can be made about Roosevelt's insistence on unconditional surrender, but this was one substantial merit. The Germans would do what they were told by the Allied armies in place, and while there were to be substantial boundary changes, it is significant that the map of Europe at the end of 1945 looked very like the Europe of Woodrow Wilson's design, once the physical frontiers could be discerned beneath the massed ranks of the Red Army. Czechoslovakia, Austria, and Hungary were all recognizably intact, and though Poland had been shifted, it was still there and with Warsaw as its capital and Danzig, or Gdansk, as its port. Serbs, Croats, Slovenes, Montenegrins, and others had been bundled into Tito's Yugoslavia, and the Baltic states had been swallowed by Stalin, but Wilson's main outlines remained.

Another factor in the Roosevelt-Truman success was the grand revision of traditional and orthodox economics that had come with the Great Depression, the New Deal, and the work of John Maynard Keynes. His devastating attack on the financial provisions of the Versailles Treaties, *The Economic Consequences of the Peace*, had been a best seller in the United States as in Britain and Germany, although not, significantly, in France.[19] Wilson claimed to believe in free trade, which had been one of his Fourteen Points, and his first address to Congress after his inauguration as president in 1913 was to promote his Tariff Reform Bill, whose cuts meant $100 million lost in federal revenues that were to be made up by the new income tax. Wilson believed in trade as the path to greater prosperity, and that the United States needed more of it. "Our industries have expanded to such a point that they will burst their jackets if they cannot find a free outlet to the markets of the world," he told the Democratic convention in accepting the presidential nomination in 1912. But Keynes was to be dismayed by the failure of Wilson and the other Allied leaders to grasp the economic essentials, and above all by the ruinous terms of reparations that a defeated Germany would be unable to pay, and which would indeed ruin it in the attempt.

Keynes, as a senior economic adviser to the British delegation, drew up what he called (in a letter to his mother on April 17, 1919) his "grand scheme for the rehabilitation of Europe," which was based on the principle that the first priority should be the revival of economic and business life in Europe as a whole. This would be down by the issue of ?1,000 million in German government bonds, to be underwritten guaranteed by the Allied and associated governments, and the interest on these bonds would have priority over reparations payments. One-fifth of the bond receipts could be used for the purchase of food and materials, and the rest paid to the reparations accounts. (Other enemy counties would float similar bonds of lesser amounts.) This, and in Keynes's view only this, would finance not only the immediate payment of reparations by Germany but thus in turn the payment by the other Allies of the interest on their debts to the United States. As Keynes's biographer (and former pupil) Roy Harrod, put it, "It would prevent Germany being immediately stripped of all her working capital and would assist the European allies to carry their heavy burden. It was indeed a sort of Marshall plan, albeit on a smaller scale. Europe would be screened from the immediate catastrophe."[20]

When the Keynes plan was presented to him by Lloyd George, Wilson rejected the idea, and the U.S. Treasury said it was unthinkable that Congress would authorize any scheme that would involve the Federal Reserve making a loan of such a kind. In his reply to Lloyd George, Wilson wrote: "How can your experts or ours be expected to work out a new plan to furnish working capital to Germany when we deliberately start by taking away Germany's present capital? How can anyone expect America to turn over to Germany in any considerable measure new working capital to take the place of that which the European nations have determined to take from her?"[21]

These were reasonable questions, except that Wilson had already accepted the unhappy principle that war reparations would be paid, and he also insisted that America's war loans to its allies be repaid as soon as practicable. Moreover, the profits that the United States had made from the war meant that it was the prime available source of new capital, without which Europe's defeated powers and the victors alike would be hard pressed to rebuild their economies. In 1947, the United States of President Truman and Secretary of State George Marshall found the imagination to cut through the economic orthodoxies, to persuade Congress, and to fund the Marshall Plan. In 1919, Wilson failed to see, far less seize, the opportunity.

In a letter to Duncan Grant on May 14, 1919, Keynes wrote: "One most bitter disappointment was the collapse of my grand scheme for putting everyone on their legs. After getting it successfully through the Chancellor of the Exchequer and the Prime Minister and seeing it formally handed to Wilson and Clemenceau, the American Treasury (from whom no more was asked than anyone else) turns it formally down as a most immoral proposal which might cost them something and which senators from Illinois would not look at. They had a chance of taking a large, or at least a humane, view of the world, but unhesitatingly refused it. Wilson, of whom I have seen a good deal more lately, is the greatest fraud on earth."[22]

Conclusions

It would not be a bad defense of Wilson and Wilsonianism to say that whatever the failings of economic vision and political judgment that doomed his policies in 1919, he stood as a grim but extremely useful warning of what *not* to do for his successors faced with ever greater postwar challenges after 1945. Wilson faced a Europe dominated by his allies and incapable for the moment of mounting any serious threat to American interests. Truman and his successors faced a Europe in which America's allies needed propping up, in which Europe and Asia were at grave risk of communist domination, and in which the arrival of the atom bomb had rendered redundant most of what a generation of statesmen and generals thought they knew about strategy and war.

But a defense of Wilsonianism can go further than such an essentially negative role. The cardinal and singular merit of the Wilsonian vision was that he understood that the traditional calculations of the national interest, of wealth and weapons, threats and capabilities, were lacking in perspective. They failed to comprehend the difference between the short- and long-term interest, the immediate and the eventual, the temporary and the permanent. These were the terms that Wilson himself used in his address before the Second Plenary Session of the Paris Peace Conference, on January 25, 1919, in which he laid out his concept of the League of Nations:

> There are many complicated questions connected with the present settlements which perhaps cannot be successfully worked out to an ultimate issue by the decisions we shall arrive at here. I can easily conceive that many of these settlements will need subsequent reconsideration, but many of the decisions we make shall need subsequent alteration in some degree; for, if I may judge by my own study of some of these questions, they are not susceptible of confident judgments at present. It is therefore necessary that we should set up some machinery by which the work of this conference should be rendered complete. . . . It is a solemn obligation on our part, therefore, to make permanent arrangements that justice shall be rendered and peace maintained. This is the central object of our meeting. Settlements may be temporary, but the action of the nations in the interest of peace and justice must be permanent. We can set up permanent processes. We may not be able to set up permanent decisions.

The short-term interest of the United States, in 1919 and in 1945, was to achieve a stable and lasting peace that was reasonable enough to ensure and flexible enough to accommodate the inevitable changes of circumstance that peace would bring. In each case, some of the future strains were obvious enough: the status and restiveness of colonized peoples; the increasing articulate and organized demands of labor; the need to revive trade and economic health; the challenge of communism in Russia, and of nationalism elsewhere. So the long-term interest of the United States was to construct an international framework and an agreed-on organizing system that could cope with these foreseeable future challenges to peace and security, while also ensuring that it was sufficiently loose and capable of improvement to meet the challenges of the unforeseen and unforeseeable, whether the coming of an ideology like fascism or Nazism or a technology like the ballistic missile, the atom bomb, or in our own time the information revolution.

To Wilson must go the credit for the first working blueprint of such an international framework and organizing system, and had it worked as planned and included the United States, it might possibly have coped with the challenges hurled its way in the 1930s. We will never know. But there was sufficient sense and foresight in the Wilsonian vision for its main features—with suitable Keynesian amendments and made fit for the real world of American politics through the careful cultivation of bipartisan support—to be clearly discernible in the grand strategy of the United States during the Cold War.

A new generation of scholars, with the benefit of decades of hindsight and the sober new perspective given by the bloodshed and barbarism that have followed the end of the Cold War in the Balkans, the Middle East, and South Asia, has begun to build a new interpretation of Wilson along these lines. Francis Gavin, in an important review article in *Orbis*, described some of these new looks at Wilson in these terms:

> What if Wilson promoted democracy, determination, and the League of Nations, not out of ideological conviction, but out of a calculation that such a policy was really in America's long-term national interest? Perhaps Wilson was not inspired by messianic idealism, but a fear that a disordered world, absent massive U.S. intervention, would eventually become a geopolitical nightmare that America would be unprepared to meet, save by resorting to means (a garrison state) that would subvert core American values. Wilson, these works suggest, was the first modern statesman to understand that new means and new methods had to be used to secure the increasingly hard-to-define national interest.[23]

Tony Smith has seen the force of Wilson's legacy in an enduring American commitment to Wilsonian values and above all to the promotion of democracy abroad. He rightly suggests that the transformation of Germany and Japan from militarist autocracies into peaceful and prosperous democracies was a central event in the Cold War, demonstrating by deeds the essentially benign and even altruistic intentions of the American ally. And Smith relates this to the context of the shattered Europe of 1919, with Bolshevism seeking to consolidate power in Moscow and to export it to Germany and the other war-weary and hungry peoples of Europe, while fascism waited in the wings. At such a time, and in such a Europe, Wilson's espousal of liberal democracy appeared less as a high-minded recommendation than as a stout and assertive ideology of self-defense against the threat of extremism from left and right. In the same way, America's espousal of democracy during the Cold War became an aggressive defense against communism, supported by U.S. labor unions and social democrats, by the Central Intelligence Agency, and by the State Department. But whatever democracy's merits as a fighting ideology, Smith concludes that the American commitment to exporting democracy was a high-minded mission that contributed to "the surge in the number, the strength, and prestige of liberal democratic governments worldwide at the end of the twentieth century."[24] The Bush administration's interpretation of this tradition in its Iraq policy after 2003 may now make this contention appear a great deal more controversial than it did in the 1990s, in the immediate wake of the Cold War.

Frank Ninkovich, in his deconstruction and reconstruction of traditional U.S. foreign policy theory, has suggested that rather than idealism, fear and a sense of crisis and threat were the motors of Wilson's attempt to devise a liberal and cooperative internationalism, just as they spurred America's grand strategists of the late 1940s to meet the challenge of the Cold War with the Marshall Plan and the NATO alliance. This explains, Ninkovich suggests, why "in the Cold War, Wilsonianism was normalized as a way of dealing with a threat of infinite duration"[25] What Ninkovich calls "crisis internationalism" was the common factor in both the "idealism" of Wilson in 1919 and the "realism" of Dean Acheson and Paul Nitze in the late 1940s and early 1950s. "The rapid American response to Korea demonstrates that Wilsonianism, extremely controversial only ten years earlier, had been internalized by the policy elite," Ninkovich maintains.[26]

But while the new era spawned new threats to the U.S. national interest, it had also produced new tools that a visionary president could command. Wilson—aware as any elected president must be in the era of the Hearst and Pulitzer newspapers of the power of opinion, and deeply impressed by the extraordinary enthusiasm and crowds that greeted him in Europe—sought to mobilize public opinion in Europe and at home in defense of his policies. Even before his bid for the presidency, he had been thinking along these lines. And inspired by the effectiveness of Teddy Roosevelt's presidency, Wilson wrote the book *Constitutional Government in the United States*, which contains the following striking passage on the potential of a president who can effectively rally and deploy public opinion: "Let him once win the admiration and confidence of the country, and no other single force can withstand him, no combination of forces will easily overpower him. . . . If he rightly interpret the national thought and boldly insist upon it, he is irresistible; and the country never feels the zest of action so much as when its president is of such insight and caliber."[27]

Wilson's faith in this American version of what would come to be known in Germany as the *fuhrerprizip* proved, in the event, to be his undoing. He was unable to mobilize public opinion behind his League of Nations and win ratification of his treaty in the U.S. Senate. But whatever his skills in the grand design of American foreign policy, he failed in the essential task of a politician: to win the vote that mattered. But he can claim to have succeeded in the grander role of a statesman, in that his legacy proved enduring, even though scholars to this day can dispute what precisely that legacy is. However, his successors as U.S. presidents and as leaders of American foreign policy rarely bother with such quibbles. They have almost universally seen Wilson as a highly useful embodiment of a higher American purpose in the country's engagement with other countries and as a standing symbol of an America that seeks a just and fairer world. When an American politician reaches for ennobling rhetoric in addressing foreigners, almost instinctively Wilson becomes the man to be quoted, the idealist to be upheld, because his name is to this day so widely known, and his reputation as an idealist believer in an international rule of law ensuring a world at peace is so universally recognized.

"Woodrow Wilson's dream may not yet be universally realized, but it is engaged today by more people that at any other time in history," noted James A. Baker, one of the more realist-minded but admired secretaries of state in our times.[28] One of Baker's immediate successors at the State Department, Madeleine Albright, stressed the similarities between Wilson's day and her own period at the helm of U.S. foreign policy:

> We are wrestling with many of the same questions that bedeviled Woodrow Wilson. Is collective security the key to world peace, an illusion that could imperil our own security, or something in between? How do we accommodate the legitimate hope of nationalities without ensuring separatism and ethnic cleansing? How do we make economic sanctions a more effective way of isolating and influencing rogue regimes? How do we generate greater respect for international law? How do we forge a consensus in America that we can play the leading role we must play if international institutions are to be effective?[29]

Perhaps the most telling epitaph for the Cold War and for the inspiration of Wilson's ideals and his legacy came from a world statesman, and not an American, who can claim to have played a leading role in the end of the Cold War. In his address to the United Nations in 1988, seventy years almost to the day after Wilson's arrival in France to negotiate the Treaty of Versailles, Mikhail Gorbachev spoke in classically Wilsonian terms to announce that the Soviet Union, a state just being born amid bloodshed and terror as the Allied leaders gathered in Paris, was no longer dedicated to the global dictatorship of the proletariat. "Our ideal is a world community of states with political systems and foreign policies based in law," he said. The end of the Cold War, and the end of the Soviet Union, brought a measure of vindication to the scholar-president Woodrow Wilson, one of those rare prophets who found at least posthumous honor in his own land.

Notes

1. Henry Kissinger, *Diplomacy* (New York: Simon & Schuster, 1994), 30.

2. Harry S Truman, *Years of Decision* (Garden City, N.Y.: Doubleday, 1955), 373.

3. Ibid.

4. Ibid., 272.

5. Kennedy's speech was delivered on June 2, 1961.

6. This was an October 27, 1960, speech at Wilson's birthplace, Staunton, Va.

7. This was as cited by R. B. Woods, *LBJ: Architect of American Ambition* (New York: Free Press, 2006), 200.

8. Lyndon B. Johnson, Presidential Papers, October 27, 1964, Lyndon B. Johnson Presidential Library, University of Texas at Austin.

9. This is as quoted by Monica Crowley, *Nixon Off the Record* (New York: Random House, 1996), 10.

10. Cited by M. Walker, *Makers of the American Century* (London: Vintage, 2003), 73.

11. See G. Hodgson, *Woodrow Wilson's Right Hand* (New Haven, Conn.: Yale University Press, 2006), 169.

12. Walker, *Makers*, 62.

13. George F. Kennan, *American Diplomacy* (Chicago: University of Chicago Press, 1984), 169.

14. Cited by Tony Smith, *America's Mission: The United States and the Worldwide Struggle for Democracy in the Twentieth Century* (Princeton, N.J.: Princeton University Press, 1994), 379–80 n. 50.

15. Michael Mandelbaum, *The Ideas That Conquered the World: Peace, Democracy, and Free Markets in the Twenty-First Century* (New York: PublicAffairs, 2002); Walter Russell Mead, *Special Providence: American Foreign Policy and How It Changed the World* (New York: Alfred A. Knopf, 2001); Lloyd E. Ambrosius, *Wilsonianism: Woodrow Wilson and His Legacy in American Foreign Relations* (New York: Palgrave Macmillan, 2002); Joseph S. Nye Jr., *The Paradox of American Power: Why the World's Only Superpower Can't Go It Alone* (New York: Oxford University Press, 2002); Seymour Martin Lipset, *American Exceptionalism: A Double-Edged Sword* (New York: W. W. Norton, 1996).

16. This is as quoted by Bailey Morris-Eck, in a review of *Uneasy Giant: The Challenges to American Predominance*, by Peter W. Rodman, *European Affairs* (European Institute, Washington), Fall 2000, https://europeanaffairs.org/archive/2000_fall/2000_fall_108.php4.

17. Dean Acheson, *Present at the Creation: My Years in the State Department* (New York: W. W. Norton, 1969).

18. Charles Bohlen, *Witness to History* (New York: W. W. Norton, 1973), 20.

19. John Maynard Keynes, *The Economic Consequences of the Peace* (New York: Harcourt, Brace, 1920).

20. Roy Harrod, *Keynes* (New York: Harcourt, Brace, 1951), 246.

21. Ibid., 247.

22. Ibid., 250.

23. Francis Gavin, "The Legacy of Woodrow Wilson: American War Aims in World War I," *Orbis*, Fall 1997, http://findarticles.com/p/articles/mi_m0365/is_n4_v41/ai_20377525.

24. Smith, *America's Mission*, 379–80 n. 50.

25. Frank Ninkovich, *The Wilsonian Century: U.S. Foreign Policy since 1900* (Chicago: University of Chicago Press, 2000), 146.

26. Ibid., 177.

27. Cited by Walker, *Makers*, 67.

28. James A. Baker, "Is History Repeating Itself?" in *Legacies of Woodrow Wilson*, ed. James M. Morris (Washington, D.C.: Woodrow Wilson Center Press, 1995), 72.

29. Madeleine Albright, "America and the League of Nations: Lessons for Today," in *Legacies of Woodrow Wilson*, ed. Morris, 76.

11. Wilsonianism after the Cold War: "Words, Words, Mere Words"

Frank Ninkovich

What remains of Wilsonianism after the Cold War? Most scholars would agree that, for better or worse, Wilsonianism has had a great influence on American foreign policy in the twentieth century, and some believe that it continues to sway the thinking of policymakers to this very day. Michael Mandelbaum, for example, argues that Wilson's ideas "had come to dominate the world" by the beginning of the twenty-first century.[1] However, in this chapter I argue that Wilsonianism as an ideology is dead. My thesis is quite straightforward, but my way of supporting it is somewhat more complex. To make my case, I approach it from three different directions. First, I compare the world of 1919 with today's world with a view to suggesting that the structural differences between then and now are so great that to talk of applying Wilsonian policies in the present-day context makes little sense. Second, I take a brief look at the fifteen years following the end of the Cold War to suggest that Wilsonian ideas have been neither advocated nor pursued during this period—at least not in any substantive fashion. Third and finally, I argue that Wilsonianism as an ideology has been subject to a process of decay that is quite common to the historical careers of ideologies. Taken together, these approaches converge on the conclusion that while Woodrow Wilson the man remains a great historical figure whose achievements are well worth commemoration, Wilsonianism the ideology deserves a decent burial.

Structural Differences between Then and Now

Before embarking on a discussion of the state of Wilsonianism today, it would pay to spend some time reflecting on how today's international environment differs from the world inhabited by of Woodrow Wilson. The reason for doing so is simple: Any argument that seeks to make a case for a contemporary neo-Wilsonianism should be able to establish that international society is afflicted, in a general way at least, by the kinds of political ailments that Wilson wanted to treat; otherwise, it would be pointless to try to apply Wilsonian remedies. If we look closely, however, it becomes evident that the troubles that gave rise to Wilsonianism have pretty much disappeared. In other words, we no longer inhabit a recognizably Wilsonian world. A then-and-now comparison also calls to attention the fact that some of the themes most closely identified with Wilsonianism in the popular imagination actually had little or no pertinence for Wilson's diplomacy, thus raising the question whether contemporary policies that emphasize these themes can rightfully be sold under the Wilsonian label.

The League of Nations

The tendency to define Wilsonianism in excessively broad terms as a belief in international organization and international cooperation obscures how exceptional an international body the League of Nations was. To my mind, it was the most radical experiment in international organization ever, with the United Nations placing a distant second in breadth of ambition and endowed enforcement mechanisms. With desperate times calling for desperate measures, the League was created to solve what was then the central problem of international relations, the advent of catastrophic, self-defeating Great Power war, by creating diplomatic machinery that would make conflicts like the Great War impossible. And it is by this standard that it has, quite rightly, been judged. Virtually all discussions of the League's policies in the 1930s center on its failure to stop Great Power aggression and suggest that it was somehow impotent or, by its very nature, incompetent to deal with its great mission.

In its design, however, the League was far from being a toothless organization. The League's treatment of the veto power provides a good example of the lengths to which its architects were willing to go to constrain bad behavior by the Great Powers. It was not an absolute veto; indeed, it could not be if it the organization was to have any reasonable expectation of checking one of the heavyweights bent on aggressive expansion. According to article 5 of the Covenant, council decisions required unanimity, "except where otherwise expressly provided" in the Covenant. That express provision was located in article 15, which defined Council resolutions as authoritative if "unanimously agreed to by the members thereof other than the Representatives of one or more of the parties to the dispute," i.e., the votes of parties to the dispute would not be counted.[2] Thus, in the ballot condemning Italy's attack on Abyssinia, the

Italian vote against the resolution was disregarded. There was also an implicit threat of war in such a council recommendation, for the members promised *not* to go to war with a nation that abided by its recommendations. In certain cases, again according to article 15, a simple majority vote in the assembly, which had to include the unanimous council members, would be sufficient to express the League's will in a dispute. Sometimes the veto could be bypassed altogether, as in the case of sanctions against Italy in 1936, when creative lawyering in the Assembly allowed the resolution to pass by making the sanctions voluntary, by allowing what proved to be a coalition of the unwilling.[3]

The fact that nations like Japan and Germany felt compelled to withdraw suggests that continued League membership posed at least some inconveniences and perhaps some real dangers to those nations' plans for nationalist expansion. The League, after all, did vote sanctions against Italy and did accept and publish the Lytton Report condemning the invasion of Manchuria. It was not until the failure to effectively take punitive measures against Italy for its invasion of Ethiopia in 1935 that the League's shortcomings were plain for all to see. Also, mere membership in the League had important advantages and disadvantages. Under article 16 of the Covenant, a nation found guilty of violating the Covenant could be expelled by a vote of the council. The expulsion of the Soviet Union following its invasion of Finland in December 1939 is a case in point. From 1934 to 1939, the League had been valuable to the USSR as a forum for trumpeting the need for an antifascist coalition. Though the legality of the expulsion has since been questioned (the number of unanimous votes for expulsion was outnumbered by abstentions), it did not occur to the Soviets, who had taken Shakespeare's advice and killed all the lawyers, to challenge the action. No doubt the League had lost its utility for the Soviets by that time, but the excommunication contributed to a serious image problem that would be difficult to shake when the time came to reverse course once again and join hands with the western democracies in the war against Nazi Germany.[4]

The problem with the League of Nations was not that it was congenitally crippled by constitutional or procedural flaws. It was not. Rather, the difficulty was that its more powerful members, for fear of alienating other Great Powers, refused to exercise the powers and responsibilities that they possessed under the Covenant. The most powerful nations, most notably Britain, had no appetite for imposing sanctions and risking war. Thus, within the League, they practiced the appeasement that later became characteristic of their foreign policies outside the organization, thereby demonstrating the lack of precisely the kind of commitment to collective security that Wilson, in his 1919 speeches, had identified

as the quality indispensable to making the League a going concern. The enduring historical "What if?" is, of course, an unanswerable question: whether the
United States, had it joined, would have provided the necessary backbone. My
guess is that it would not have done so, for as we have seen, membership alone
could not provide the necessary will. The League's failure was due to a debility
of the spirit, not of the body, as the organization's advanced machinery proved
to be beyond the ability of nation states to operate successfully. That "debility,"
it should be noted, originated in the powerful hold of nationalism on the
human imagination, without which there would be no nations capable of creating an international society in the first place.

These kinds of questions are not even remotely at issue today. Most obviously,
the veto power within the UN Security Council makes impossible organization-
ally sanctioned punitive action against another Great Power.[5] As a result, from virtually the moment of its birth, the United Nations has been forced to sit on the
sidelines as the great problems of the day were settled by other means, principally
by alliances, multilateral organizations, and ad hoc groups created under
American leadership in what used to be called the "free world." To a large degree,
this pattern of behavior has continued since the end of Cold War. To be sure, the
United Nations has had its uses, but its ineffectualness in vital questions of international security is at least as much the consequence of deep-seated American
reluctance to cede power to an international organization on matters of deep
national interest as it is of external factors that have supposedly frustrated its more
successful functioning. Because the UN was designed to be powerless in such matters, adoption of current proposals for "reform" of the Security Council by adding
nations like India, Brazil, Japan, and Germany as permanent members would do
nothing to reverse its congenital impotence. Unsurprisingly, then, virtually no one
suggests that international terrorism, the problem that most preoccupies present-
day U.S. policymakers, can successfully be addressed by an international organization. Neither of the two contrasting approaches to terrorism—an American-led
military coalition against alleged state sponsors of terrorism, and international
police and intelligence cooperation—makes room for the United Nations to play
a significant role. Indeed, the organization's ability to conduct even minor peacekeeping missions has often been called into question.

More important, the kinds of concerns that preoccupied Wilson have been
rendered moot by history. Today there is little or no possibility of Great Power
war (a circumstance that owes absolutely nothing to collective security), though
there is no shortage of people who are willing to talk up the emergence of potential enemies like China. Despite the hegemonic status of the United States, one

sees no signs of a coalition being put together to challenge it, unless one imagines Hugo Chávez and Venezuela as the organizers of such a grouping. That is not to say that a serious "blowback" could not emerge—critics like Chalmers Johnson and John Grey insist that it will—but for the time being at least, classical balance-of-power diplomacy appears to be dead. If one looks to the future, the most likely challenger to that hegemony is the United States itself. Financial weakness, a limited supply of military manpower in the absence of conscription, a questionable ability to commit to far-sighted policies, political divisiveness, and an uncertain public opinion have made it impossible to pursue an effective hegemonic universalism, which helps to explain the one-legged reliance on diplomacy in dealing with "rogue states" like North Korea and Iran.[6] Even so, when the end of hegemony does come, barring a crash of globalization it seems more likely to be succeeded by more collegial Great Power cooperation than by rivalries conducted according to old balance-of-power rules.

The point of this is to suggest that the central elements of Wilsonianism— the danger of Great Power war and the resort to collective security as a solution—are missing from the contemporary scene. The major threats facing the world are far different from 1919, when the object was to prevent the kinds of increasingly destructive wars produced by the balance-of-power system. Not only were the ends of Wilsonianism different, so too were the means, for the Wilsonian version of international cooperation, later called collective security, had no room for coalitions of the willing. Even Theodore Roosevelt's decidedly less idealistic internationalism envisioned a more robust form of cooperation than the kind of watered-down coalition one finds in Iraq today.

There is a tendency when talking about Wilsonianism to ignore its central features while exaggerating the importance of the peripheral. But to call something Wilsonian without considering Wilson's ambitious program of collective security is like thinking about Einstein without relativity or John Coltrane without a saxophone. When set against today's views on the problems and prospects of international organization, it is not like comparing apples and oranges—it is more like apples and orangutans.

ECONOMIC INTERNATIONALISM

Free trade is another reputedly Wilsonian shibboleth whose contemporary meaning is far different from the significance it held following the Great War. The United States in 1919 was one of the most protectionist nations in the world, having been so successful in stimulating rapid industrialization under high-tariff Republican administrations after the Civil War that it had provided a model for European and other nations to emulate. With the emergence of free trade in the post–World War II era and its institutionalization, first in the General Agreement on Tariffs and Trade and later in the World Trade Organization, an increasingly integrated world economy was created that scarcely resembled the segmented economic habitats of the first half of the twentieth century. The emergence of China, Japan, India, Russia, the Asian "tigers," and the so-called emerging economies was still far beyond the horizon in Wilson's day, as were the international organizations and bilateral arrangements needed to manage a truly global market system organized according to liberal ground rules. To a large extent, the political benefits of economic interdependence have been realized in Thomas Friedman's "Golden arches theory of conflict prevention"—that two nations with McDonald's franchises cannot go to war.[7] People continue to worry about the fate of economic liberalization, but this concern centers on the possible revival of protectionism, a possibility that is not even a specter at this historical moment. In any event, there was nothing distinctively Wilsonian about economic internationalism, which was a widely shared liberal nostrum that was peddled long before Wilson's time, and long after, by people whom it would be difficult to characterize as Wilsonians.

NATIONAL SELF-DETERMINATION AND ANTI-IMPERIALISM

Another commonly accepted trademark feature of Wilsonianism was the advocacy of national self-determination. In practice, Wilson had a sorry record on this issue. It is common knowledge that he violated the principle in patching together the treaty's territorial settlement in Eastern Europe, in the Italian settlement, in China, and in the creation of the Kingdom of the Serbs, Croats, and Slovenes (later Yugoslavia). Though his actions in these cases are readily understandable as concessions to political reality at the peace conference, they were nevertheless blatant violations of the principle.

But how central a principle was it, really? One does not find it in Wilson's Fourteen Points, except by specific reference to the fate of Austria-Hungary and Russia. Czechoslovakia, which itself violated the principle in more than one way, owed its existence less to ideological conviction than to the charm and persuasiveness of Eduard Beneš and Tomáš Masaryk. One does not see it in the Five Particulars speech of September 1918, which is in some ways more revealing about Wilson's beliefs in a universal world order than his Fourteen Points address (democracy is not mentioned there, either). To be sure, he did mention national self-determination in a number of his speeches, but interestingly, Wilsonian rhetoric on this point had its greatest impact in the non-European world. In Egypt, India, Korea, China, and even Iraq, Wilsonian ideas had an electric political effect in stimulating demands for independence or the restoration of sovereignty.[8] But Wilson was not very enthusiastic about seeing his principles applied outside Europe. Indeed, so pronounced was his reluctance to pursue anti-imperialism and national self-determination that many of his left-liberal allies in the United States felt compelled to abandon him during the treaty fight.

Wilson's lack of enthusiasm is readily understandable. Though American liberals had been high on nationalism in general in the century preceding the Great War, they had not been very keen on applying the idea to Central and Eastern Europe, showing instead a surprising sympathy for the ramshackle, but somehow functional, autocracy known as Austria-Hungary. Wilson, like many other liberals, believed that nationalism required a degree of cultural maturity if it were to be a benign force, a level of advancement that many peoples of this region appeared to be lacking. The decision to impose limits in the peace treaties upon the rights of these new nations to deal with their minorities as they pleased was only one indicator of the low degree of confidence in their fitness to manage their affairs with which the powers viewed their forthcoming leap to sovereignty.[9]

If it was not fully applicable even in Europe, it is not surprising that national self-determination of colonized peoples should not have been high on Wilson's to-do list in Paris. The world of 1919 was a world of imperialism at high tide that Wilson, who expressed concern about imperialist competition and the injustices of colonial rule, hoped would recede in due course. One of his convictions, shared with many progressives of the day, was that the diplomacy of imperialism had contributed to an outbreak of the war. For that reason, if not necessarily out of human decency or a commitment to the idea of human equality across the world, it was necessary eventually to put a stop to imperialism. Wilson also took a significant step in the direction of exploding the old exploitative rationales for empire by advocating a mandate system that looked forward to the eventual independence of former German colonies and provinces of the Ottoman empire. But even had he wanted to Wilson was in no position to break up, at one fell swoop, the entrenched empires of the day because the politics of the peace conference, in which his closest allies were also the leading imperialist powers, forced him to approach the matter with a mixture of caution and contradiction. Thus while a strong case can be made that Wilsonian policies in Paris marked the beginning of the end of imperialism, his anti-imperialism was far from absolute and one can even understand why some might believe it was a sham.

The ideas of national self-determination and anti-imperialism only came fully to life in the post–World War II era. In 1919, the number of sovereign states was about one-fifth of today's total. The League of Nations had only 42 original members, of which some, like India, were not even sovereign. By the time of the founding of the United Nations in 1945, there were 51 original signatories, while today imperialism in its classical colonial guise is gone. One still hears much talk of empire and anti-imperialism, of course, but this is in a new post-Wilsonian and postmodern register. Today, with the United Nations counting 192 sovereign member states, it is difficult to see how much farther the principle of national self-determination can be taken; if anything, it is likely that the idea has been taken too far. But whatever one thinks of how Wilsonian these issues actually were, the undoubted political importance that they possessed in his time has been downgraded by events almost to the vanishing point.

DEMOCRACY

Unlike national self-determination and anti-imperialism, democracy was crucial to Wilson's "new diplomacy." To his mind, only democratic polities could generate the national public opinion that would make old-style cabinet wars impossible; only democracies could serve as the foundation for a world opinion that would make the League of Nations work and provide it with legitimacy. But in Wilson's time the number of democracies was few—14 to 21 in all, depending on how one counts.[10] In the course of the twentieth and early twenty-first centuries, the number of democracies has increased to around 120 in November 2003,[11] although that figure may be somewhat high inasmuch as the commitment to democracy in some cases may be only skin deep. This numerical explosion is a fairly recent development, for as late as the 1970s democratic states numbered only in the 40s.[12]

But we need to better understand Wilson's intent here. His oft-cited phrase "the world must be made safe for democracy" is certainly open to interpretation, but, as John Milton Cooper has pointed out, Wilson was quite careful with his language. My reading is that far from calling for the worldwide imposition of democracy by force, he was concerned instead to promote and preserve an open global environment in which liberal democracies could exist peacefully. To be sure, the League of Nations was originally conceived as a partnership of democratic nations, but it was not long before government of the people was dropped as a precondition of membership, and the League was never intended to be an instrument of coercion for creating new democracies. The absence of democratic exclusivity was by no means thought to be a fatal flaw, for it was well understood at the time (and often lamented) that democracy had taken root only in a relatively small number of nations and that the number of democratic states was not likely to explode in the near future. In the late nineteenth century and during the Theodore Roosevelt and William Howard Taft administrations, there had emerged the notion of a democratic core that included Britain and, more problematically, France. Wilson looked forward to expanding this core by incorporating a de-Kaiserized Germany and perhaps eventually China and Japan. In due course, Russia would become a member of the club, for as he said in his war address, Russia was "democratic at heart." Consequently, the United States would be fighting "for a universal dominion of right by such *a concert of free peoples as shall bring peace and safety to all nations and make the world itself at last free*" (emphasis added). The moral of the story? Making a neighborhood, even a global neighborhood, safe for its residents does not require making a democrat of everyone; it simply means providing law and order, for which a constabulary consisting of solid citizens will suffice.

On this issue of democracy, Wilson was a Burkean, an outlook that derived from his having grown up in a nineteenth century liberal milieu. In classical liberalism, democracy was an outcome of an organic process of growth, not something that could be instantly transplanted or magically conjured ex nihilo. Nineteenth-century liberals rejected the notion that democracy could be imposed in situations where there had been no substantial stretch of historical preparation and maturation. Instant democracy was, like instant coffee, a debased version of the real thing that was all too easily perverted by various elites for their own purposes—Napoleon III's plebiscitarian emperorship provides the classic example. Wilson made clear his views on this topic in some after-dinner remarks in Paris in May 1919. "You cannot throw off the habits of society that have bound us in the past," he said. "You cannot throw off the habits of society any more than you can throw off the habits of the individual immediately. They must be slowly got rid of, or, rather, they must be slowly altered."[13] Wilson's Burkean outlook can be overdone, for he was after all a progressive, but in general he did believe that you cannot make a silk purse out of a sow's ear.[14]

Regardless of how one interprets Wilson's words, his actual behavior suggests that he was in no hurry to embark upon democratizing crusades. The three chief instances were the impulse given to the creation of the Weimar Republic at the armistice negotiations and the attempts to impose democratic systems on the Dominican Republic and Haiti following the invasions and occupations of 1915 and 1916. The latter two adventures were not uniquely Wilsonian in provenance, for democratization had been U.S. policy in the newly acquired Philippines and in the two occupations of Cuba (1899–1902 and 1906–9). On a number of occasions, Wilson even showed a decided lack of enthusiasm for the idea. He did speak rashly about teaching the Mexicans how to elect good men, but after getting his fingers burned with the brief occupation of Tampico and Vera Cruz in the spring of 1914, he quickly backtracked from his desire to manipulate the course of the Mexican Revolution. The idea of using military power to reverse the Bolshevik Revolution also failed to rouse any democratizing fervor.

But it was not just a reluctance on Wilson's part, for the promotion of democracy failed to become part of U.S. foreign policy for Wilson's successors, too. Franklin D. Roosevelt's Four Freedoms—freedom of speech and expression, freedom of worship, freedom from want, and freedom from fear—did not include a freedom to vote. Democratization was pursued in Germany and Japan after World War II, but the installation of democracy in those nations was an effect of the war, not its cause. The commonly held notion that the United States has been eager to use its power to democratize the world is highly exaggerated, as other motives have tended to be far more prominent ingredients in the policy mixtures of various presidential administrations. For the most part, talk about spreading democracy has been empty, the political equivalent of talking about the weather. One needs only to begin counting the number of instances in which the U.S. has tolerated and openly supported authoritarian regimes to see that the strength of the so-called democratizing impulse is highly overrated.[15] It makes more sense to argue that the United States has been more interested in changing the international climate, that is, the international system, which would eventually have the effect of changing the weather. As a case in point, to the extent that democratization did explode in the 1980s, it was not because the United States imposed it upon peoples. It was in the air, and they breathed it in.

What are we to make of all this? Clearly, today's world faces problems of a kind that were not on Wilson's plate. Global society today differs structurally and culturally in so many respects that Wilson, were he to rise from the dead, would have such difficulty in getting his bearings that I doubt he would be able to find meaningful application for his ideas. So many of the preconditions of the Wilsonian dream—national self-determination, anti-imperialism, democratization, economic internationalism, and Americanization—have been realized that the need to focus on the prevention of Great Power war, which was the core element of Wilsonianism, has disappeared. Many liberals of Wilson's day believed globalization to be an all but accomplished fact, but the degree of economic, military, social, cultural, and ecological integration in today's world is unprecedented. While Wilson can legitimately be seen as a prophet of globalism, his ideas and policies offer little guidance in helping us to navigate the dangerous waters of today's world. He pointed the way—one way—to the promised land, but he had nothing to say about what to do once it had been reached.

Post–Cold War "Wilsonianism"

Daniel Moynihan used to say that although everyone is entitled to his own opinion, not everyone is entitled to his own facts. If one were to try to gauge the health of Wilsonianism on the basis of the contemporary public conversation, it would seem that the facts are against me, for Wilsonianism appears to have experienced something of a revival of late. Scholars and commentators differ on points of emphasis, but the general narrative appears to go something like this. After having failed in its first incarnation, Wilsonianism was given a "second chance" in World War II, only to be frustrated by the emergence of the Cold War and forty-five years of deadlock in the United Nations. With the collapse of the Soviet Union, "Wilsonianism 3.0" emerged in the 1990s. Thus John Judis, in a recent book, has argued that the Bush-Clinton years "represented a triumph of Wilsonianism."[16] Then, following an initial rejection of core Wilsonian ideas by the administration of George W. Bush, "Wilsonianism 3.5" was rolled out in the aftermath of the September 11, 2001, terrorist attacks and the invasion of Iraq when commentators in the press and in academia began to emphasize the Wilsonian inspiration behind neoconservative U.S. foreign policy.

A good starting point for a discussion of post–Cold War Wilsonianism—and, in some ways, a good ending point, as well—is the triumphal post–Gulf War address to Congress of George H. W. Bush of March 6, 1991. "Now, we can see a new world coming into view," said the president, "a world where the United Nations, freed from cold war stalemate, is poised to fulfill the historic vision of its founders. A world in which freedom and respect for human rights find a home among all nations."[17] Bush's speech was ironic, coming as it did from someone who was celebrated for mangling what he called "the vision thing." In one particularly incoherent response at a press conference in Egypt, the only insight that Bush managed to provide into the meaning of the new world order was that it had something to do with globality: "We're already seeing that "world order" means 'world,'" said he. It was ironic, also, because the Bush administration was notorious for its embrace of foreign policy realism, most conspicuously so in the president's "Chicken Kiev" speech, in which he had cautioned Ukraine, and by extension other secessionist Soviet states, against what he called "suicidal nationalism."

This was, in short, a false start for Wilsonianism. Some foreign policy analysts wrote suggestive articles like "The Triumph of Wilsonianism?" and "Third Try at World Order? America and Multilateralism after the Cold War,"[18] but these were rhetorical questions to which the clear answer was: Don't bet on it. Both Robert Tucker and John Ruggie suggested that the triumph of Wilsonianism was an illusion. "So dominant are the interest-driven discourse of realism and the triumphalist course of unilateralism," said Ruggie, "that even to raise [the idealistic element] risks being dismissed as a neo-Wilsonian idealist."[19]

Well, what about the Bill Clinton administration? With George H. W. Bush voted out of office not long after he had received unprecedented high ratings in public opinion polls, his successor Clinton opted for what Anthony Lake, his first national security adviser in an interview in the fall of 1993, called, rather mystifyingly, "pragmatic neo-Wilsonianism."[20] This term was not greeted, to say the least, with universal acclaim. Joe Klein, in *Newsweek*, wondered whether it was "a joke, perhaps? A bit of oxymoronic whimsy?"[21] The *New Republic* called it an "empty locution."[22] "Neo-Wilsonianism is an attitude, not a program" wrote the syndicated columnist William Pfaff.[23] It is hard to imagine what Lake might have meant. To my ear, neopragmatic Wilsonianism or neo-Wilsonian pragmatism sound nearly as good—or bad—depending on your point of view.

One doubts that President Clinton was seduced by this intellectual fancy footwork. He did confess on one occasion that "I'm frankly a fan of Woodrow Wilson's,"[24] but he was notably reluctant to go into specifics. Throughout his two terms, Clinton had little to say about Wilson, the most interesting aperçu being that Wilson had the biggest feet of any president—until Clinton's size 13Cs set foot inside the White House, that is. Clinton was famously preoccupied with domestic policy. Whenever Wilson was mentioned, it was almost always in a domestic context and more often than not in the same breath as Theodore Roosevelt. One gets the sense that these two exemplars of progressivism had merged in his mind into a single figure that could just as well have been named "Woodrow Roosevelt."

The few mentions of Wilson that touched on foreign affairs ranged from falsely attributed platitudes to outright heresy. On one occasion, for example, Clinton purported to quote Wilson: "Our security and prosperity depend upon our willingness to be involved in the world. Woodrow Wilson said that

Americans were participants in the life of the world, like it or not."[25] But that was not particularly Wilsonian. TR said something of the sort, as did many other presidents, before and after.[26] Some of Clinton's remarks, moreover, were distinctly anti-Wilsonian. "Ladies and gentlemen," he declared at a Veteran's Day ceremony, "we have learned that the world will never be completely safe for democracy, as President Woodrow Wilson hoped for on the eve of our entry into World War I. There will always be threats to our well-being, to the peaceful community of nations to which we belong."[27] In another speech, he was critical of national self-determination, arguing that federalism was the wave of the future.[28] Interventionism? Here is what Clinton had to say in Atlanta in April, 2000: "Somebody asked me the other day, 'What have you learned about foreign policy since you've been President?' And I said, 'I've learned it's a whole lot more like life than I thought it was.' What do I mean by that? That people everywhere, across all different cultures, are far more likely to respond to the outstretched hand than they are to respond to the clenched fist."[29] That notion may or may not be true, but it does not express an urgent need for collective security.

Whereas Wilson had seven interventions to his credit, Clinton was famously reluctant to intervene. As for other important members of the Clinton administration, they too showed an indifference to Wilson. Warren Christopher's memoirs cite Wilson on one occasion, as part of a discussion of human rights.[30] Madeleine Albright's contain only a few more mentions of Wilson, chiefly in connection with the formation of the new nation-states in Eastern Europe in the aftermath of World War I.[31] In international affairs, as in domestic, the refrain could well have been: "It's the economy, stupid!" David Marcus argued that "under Clinton, foreign policy has become almost synonymous with trade policy,"[32] while Lawrence Kaplan saw his policy more in the tradition of dollar diplomacy, in which trade would assure security, democracy, and other good things.[33]

This reference to dollar diplomacy is instructive, for the 1990s did in some ways resemble the 1920s. For a time in the 1990s, the world came to resemble a liberal utopia. It was a decade of astounding economic growth, during which the danger of Great Power war was virtually zero. There were, undeniably, serious problems, as emerging nationalisms caused chaos on the periphery of the former Soviet Union, leading some observers with fond memories of the Cold War to pine for the good old days of bipolar stability and predictability. There was also terrorism to contend with, but that was hardly a new problem. It had been contained in the past, and, in any event, it was a threat which to Americans seemed quite distant. Even as the World Trade Center buildings were bombed on two separate occasions, terrorism of the home-grown variety—the Oklahoma City explosion and the Unabomber's deadly parcels come to mind— seemed of greater moment to many. All in all, argued G. John Ikenberry in a notable piece, complaints about international instability were merely a "myth of post–cold war chaos."[34]

The rise of a "democratic peace" literature suggested that the turbulence of the century had finally been negotiated; and Francis Fukuyama's neo-Hegelian "end of history" implied that the end of ideological competition would cause international superstorms to abate for good. As substantive political differences diminished in domestic and foreign policy, the ferocity of the political infighting was inversely proportional to the decreasing ideological distance between the Republican and Democratic parties. In the absence of weighty issues to report, the news media tilted decidedly in the direction of infotainment. Those who wonder what the arrival of a domestic liberal utopia might look like were given a preview in the media frenzies created over O. J. Simpson's murder trial, the murder of Jon Benet Ramsey, and the athletic rivalry and its criminal subplot between the figure skaters Tonya Harding and Nancy Kerrigan.

In short, there was no *need* for Wilsonianism. The dangers that did exist were more in the nature of nuisances, eliminated with little sacrifice of life by the use of air power (the first Iraq war had fewer battle deaths than the Spanish-American War). Before Operation Desert Storm, Saddam Hussein had taunted the United States by predicting that Americans would not have the stomach for wars that produced large numbers of casualties. But the overwhelming use of airpower in the Gulf war, and then eight years later in the bombing of Serbia, suggested that the necessity of putting boots on the ground could be finessed.

Still, even though it was a far cry from Wilsonianism, Clintonian foreign policy came in for criticism in the 1990s as being too soft and idealistic. There was little enthusiasm on the domestic scene for the new internationalism, which was disparaged by conservatives and by the incoming George W. Bush administration. The preference was for a more manly, muscular, nationalist approach, one that was more willing to take advantage of America's seemingly overwhelming military power and less inclined to make the United States what one critic in *Foreign Affairs* called "the world's nanny." Michael Mandelbaum gave concise voice to this mood in his 1996 *Foreign Affairs* essay, in which he lit into the idea of "foreign policy as social work."[35] Often the preference was expressed that the historical guide to the nation's foreign policy should be not Wilson but Theodore Roosevelt, he of the squeaky voice and the big stick, who also had the good sense more often than not to mind his own business rather than meddle in the affairs of others.

That appeared to be the mindset of Clinton's successor, George W. Bush, at least at first. However, sometime after the 9/11 attacks, Wilsonianism was apparently rediscovered by the Bush administration. Supposedly its articulation can be found in, among other places, the 2002 National Security Strategy of the United States, Bush's speech to the National Endowment for Democracy, his address at Whitehall in November 2003, and his second inaugural address, in which promoting democracy abroad was declared to be 'the urgent requirement of our nation's security." In all these places, the connection between democracy and national security was elaborated, as was the willingness to use American power in pursuit of democratic regime change.[36]

According to a host of commentators who were attentive to the change, this was a new variety of Wilsonianism, a program in a new neoconservative build, that was as different from earlier varieties as the Microsoft Windows XP software was from MS-DOS. This was, according to various formulations, "muscular Wilsonianism," "Wilsonianism in boots," "hard Wilsonianism," "Wilsonianism with teeth," "Wilsonianism with fixed bayonets," and "Fukuyama plus force," to take some of the more striking descriptions. One commentator viewed the Bush administration as being Wilsonian in its ends but anti-Wilsonian in its methods.[37] This new appreciation of Wilsonianism, which centered on an understanding of the relationship between democracy and national security, left plenty of room for criticism of the shortcomings of previous versions of Wilsonianism that had been espoused by the Democratic Party. Depending on one's perspective—and the dividing line appeared to be the degree of commitment to multilateral cooperation—a face-off emerged between good and bad Wilsonianism.

Not all the remarks were laudatory. Sometimes the policies of the Bush administration and those of its two predecessors were lumped together under the heading of (neo-Wilsonian) idealism. From this perspective, Bush stood accused of being a Wilsonian for his failure to harmonize ends and means. Bush in Iraq "is continuing the tradition of articulating and pursuing a set of extremely ambitious and idealistic foreign policy goals," said one such critic. "In this sense, it must be said, George Bush is very much a Wilsonian."[38] More recently, the *New York Times* columnist John Tierney has suggested that "the Republicans have become Wilsonian idealists in foreign policy, the neoconservative innocents abroad who thought they could quickly transform the Middle East."[39]

With its Phoenix-like qualities, Wilsonianism, as one scholarly essay put it, was "the legacy that won't die."[40] It was the ideological counterpart to the endlessly resurrected Jason from the *Friday the Thirteenth* movies or Freddie Krueger from *Nightmare on Elm Street*. Frozen for a time like the corpse of Ted Williams, it was revived to become the dominant framework for understanding America's place in the world. Michael Sandel of Harvard in a Friedman column was quoted as noting ironically that Bush's emphasis on promoting democracy "puts him in the company of Wilson, the president who made liberal internationalism the core of his foreign policy." He added: "President Bush, who campaigned for the presidency as an ardent realist, scorning nation-building and idealism in foreign policy, is now quoting President Wilson and speaking about the need to make the Middle East safe for democracy."[41] Kaplan even had the Democratic Party surrendering the banner of liberal internationalism to the Republican Party.[42] In November 2003, William Safire described a major Bush address as one in which "he evoked Woodrow Wilson trying to make the world safe for democracy in 1918."[43] Even before the invasion of Iraq, Max Boot in the *Wall Street Journal* said of George W. Bush: "The 'W' Stands for Woodrow."[44]

But if one looks at these developments more closely, there is less than meets the eye—much less, for Bush's foreign policy had little or nothing to do with Wilsonianism. If one looks at the statements made by members of the administration, from the president on down, one will look in vain for admiring references to Wilson or the quotations that Sandel purported to find. Thus a search of the *Public Papers of the Presidents* through mid-2004, the most recently compiled volumes at the time of writing, uncovers only two presidential mentions of Wilson, both in 2003, neither of which comes close to making a case for resurrecting the Wilsonian world view.[45] Virtually all the attributions of Wilsonianism originated outside the administration in the writing of media pundits who seemed to know little about Wilson apart from the misconceptions that have been handed down in popular culture. On closer examination, the Wilsonian revival was largely a bundle of shopworn historical clichés that purported to connect contemporary problems to the very different world of 1919.

Still, some scholars seemed to believe that an intellectual makeover could demonstrate Wilsonianism's continuing attractiveness and relevance. One of the more serious efforts in this direction was made by Tony Smith, who boiled Wilsonianism down to four propositions. Wilsonianism, he argued, promoted democratization, emphasized open markets, sought to work through international organizations, and emphasized the indispensability of American leadership. "The Bush Doctrine may properly be called Wilsonian," he concluded, "for it embraces all but the third of these propositions. Because the fourth pillar may be seen as substituting for the third—that is, American leadership is a plausible alternative to collaboration in multilateral institutions on an equal basis—the *bona fides* of the Doctrine as Wilsonian are in order."[46] Wilsonianism is dead! Long live Wilsonianism!

This was a stunningly audacious attempt to redefine Wilsonianism by stripping it of its heart and soul—not unlike trying to sell a nuclear power plant without an atomic reactor. For if there is any feature of Wilsonianism that can be called a core principle, it is that of international cooperation and collaboration on vital questions of security. There was, for Wilson, no substitute for consensus of the world's leading powers. It was on that crucial point that he chose to take an all-or-nothing stand when he insisted on fidelity to the "all-for-one and one-for-all" pledge that was article 10 of the League Covenant. To be sure, this stand was not inconsistent with American leadership, something that Wilson consistently stated was essential, but it was poles apart from a hegemonic vision of the United States as an Atlas holding up the world. Nor did Wilson envision coalitions of the willing. On the contrary, it was the vow to participate in joint action even when national interests were not directly at risk that was supposed to make the League of Nations a genuinely internationalist body.

It may be useful to note that multilateralism as it was designed and practiced for many decades presupposed an ability to act on the basis of a consensus. It was a matter of principles and procedures. Multilateralism is a weapon of the weak, a process that privileges negotiation over the use of force. In its most prominent post-1945 form, it presumed self-restraint on the part of the hegemonic power. But the Bush administration's policies have stressed muscularity, a faith in military power to release underlying impulses to democracy, and leadership of the my-way-or-the-highway variety. As for international organization, the Bush administration's attitude toward the United Nations bears an uncomfortable resemblance to Groucho Marx's unwillingness to join an organization that would have him as a member.

But even if it is stipulated, despite my contention to the contrary, that Wilsonianism can be reduced to an aggressive promotion of democracy abroad, one has to wonder about the degree to which the Bush administration was truly committed to democratization. Fukuyama has suggested that the administration's advocacy of democracy and nation building in Iraq was a post facto rationalization adopted after the failure to discover weapons of mass destruction in Iraq.[47] But the concern for the democratization of Iraq was abandoned as quickly as it had been adopted. As the situation in Iraq deteriorated, a Reuters correspondent noted that "even the definition of victory has undergone a makeover, with Bush no longer focusing on the goal of transforming Iraq into a flourishing democracy in the Middle East."[48] To some extent, this reflects public opinion, in which polls suggest that support for the promotion of democracy is at its lowest point in three decades.[49]

If one asks how, specifically, despite the speech given by President Bush at the National Endowment for Democracy, policy changed toward the autocratic regimes of which the United States had been too tolerant in the past, it is difficult to come up with convincing evidence of a new evangelical enthusiasm for democracy. Did policy change toward Egypt? Syria? Pakistan? Saudi Arabia? The central Asian republics? Was Hamas legitimized? Though a good case could be made for the democratic bona fides of Hugo Chávez in Venezuela, one detected little enthusiasm in Washington for his leadership, nor was there much affection for Evo Morales in Bolivia. And how about the promotion of democracy in China? Or Russia? Clearly, the hope in these two cases was that economic growth and integration into the world economy would in due course produce democracy. Regarding China, the 2002 National Security Strategy stated: "Chinese leaders are discovering that economic freedom is the only source of national wealth. In time, they will find that social and political freedom is the only source of national greatness."[50] It's the economy, stupid!

One would think that, at a minimum, a significant expansion of informational and cultural programs would have been seized upon as a relatively inexpensive way of opening up Islamic societies to Western ideas, but here too there were no major initiatives. Apart from shifting some money around and placing his former PR guru Karen Hughes in charge of the U.S. Information Agency, the basic story remained one of *plus ça change, plus c'est la même chose*. Why no serious action? A cynical guess would be that major cultural and informational initiatives would have been truly upsetting to the status quo. The administration's admission that democratization was "the work of generations" suggested that this was more a fond wish than a policy,[51] which, after all, requires doing A with a causal expectation of arriving at result B. Ignoring the rhetoric, some critics have suggested that the Bush administration's policies have, if anything, undermined democracy, because the unwillingness to take serious steps toward reducing the nation's dependence on fossil fuels has resulted in the growing strength of petro-authoritarian regimes.

Given that the promotion of democracy has been rhetorical, and that there was nothing particularly Wilsonian about the rhetoric, it would require a wild stretch of the imagination to visualize George W. Bush, the current president, admitting, in the manner of Richard Nixon's surprise conversion to Keynesianism, that "I am a Wilsonian." One suspects that even a thorough regimen of waterboarding would not elicit such a confession. In part that is because there is no "there" there. Notwithstanding the numerous references to Wilsonianism, it is a poor conceptual tool for understanding developments in U.S. foreign relations over the past fifteen years. Beyond that, the Wilsonian pedigree is demonstrably bogus, for the Bush administration's unilateralist strain of thought is the product of an ideological lineage that can be traced back to isolationist times, and even to the "independent internationalism" of the 1920s.[52] The Republican administrations of that decade, let us recall, believed in economic internationalism, in international cooperation in Europe and in Asia, and in democratizing countries like Nicaragua through force. But pursuing that historical comparison would make for at least another chapter.

Wilsonianism as Ideology

Thus far, I have been treating Wilsonianism as an "-ism," that is, as an ideology. But did Wilson see himself as the founder of a creed? In a recent work, the historian Bruce Kuklick argues "no." "Woodrow Wilson could not see himself as initiating an American foreign policy impulse that would later have the doubtful connotation *Wilsonian,*" he writes.[53] I believe that elements of Wilson's thought were appropriated, transformed, and applied—though not the ideas that are most commonly associated with the man—in U.S. foreign policy from the time of World War II through the Cold War.[54] But not everyone agrees. I recall once asking the late Arthur Link, the leading Wilson scholar of the post–World War II years until his death in 1998, to comment on my thesis that neo-Wilsonian ideas had been crucial to the thinking of cold warriors. His response was to read me the riot act—in his unfailingly courteous way, I hasten to add. Wilson, Link replied, had nothing in common with the cold warriors.

It may be that Wilsonianism was a progressive approach to politics that, like the progressivism of the early twentieth century, is alien to our era. Wilsonianism was born of a particular time and place, and it could be argued that it was sui generis, unique, a one-time-only phenomenon, the product of a historical moment whose time has come and gone. Like Karl Marx, who said famously "Je ne suis pas Marxiste," Wilson, if questioned, might have denied being a Wilsonian for the simple reason that making such an admission would have been tantamount to a confession of failure for policies that were intended to solve urgent problems in the here-and-now—thus the more long-lived the ideology, the greater the failure. Although Wilson may not have had an interest in creating an ideology, subsequent generations, for their own reasons, have made Wilsonianism the paradigm of idealism in American foreign policy.

But as even a cursory review of U.S. foreign relations before and after Wilson would make clear, the Wilsonian moment, far from being the signature event of American exeptionalism, was quite exceptional for the United States, too. To the extent that Wilsonianism was the product of an extraordinary man and his charisma, everything that was important about it, save for its memory, may have died with him.

Nevertheless, ideologies do not always reflect the understandings of their founders, so let us assume for the sake of argument that Wilsonianism was and is an ideology. If so, it has suffered the fate of other ideologies like Fourierism, or anarcho-syndicalism, or Nazism. Like other belief systems that have not stood the test of time, it has perished. Ideologies, like everything in time, have histories. There is no uniform predetermined lifespan for an ideology. Cultures tend to be longer lived, though that is not always the case. The history of republicanism, for example, can be traced from the Greek city states, to Rome, to the Renaissance Italy of Machiavelli, and to Britain and America in the eighteenth and nineteenth centuries—and it is still not extinct. As a rule, however, ideologies have trajectories or careers, because to succeed they need to be embedded in or carried by social movements. Beginning in the 1920s, social scientists developed an ideal type that sought to explain the way in which social movements progress and decline. This conceptual scheme is equally applicable to organizations like business corporations (General Motors comes readily to mind), social movements, institutions in general, and ideologies. The sequence goes something like this: The prophet clears the ground; the founder occupies it; the institutionalizers who capitalize on the founder's charisma build on that ground; and, at some point, the ideological heirs, whose beliefs bear little resemblance to the original spirit of the founder, run down the estate and squander the legacy.

Within this overall trajectory, various causes—bureaucratization, the loss of charisma, and goal displacement, among other things—lead the organization or movement to a point that the political scientist Theodore Lowi once famously characterized as the "Jesus, don't come back" phase. His chief example was a Renaissance Roman Catholicism that had become so far removed from its founding principles that it would not have known what to do with Christ had he come back to Earth. According to Lowi, this was the stage at which "a Second Coming could be the worst thing that had ever happened to the Church."[55] There are ideological revivals, of course, but when we hear of "neo-this" or "neo-that," we can be sure that some pretty serious, perhaps even transformative, alterations have been made to the original, resulting in a gap between what the political scientist Martin Seliger called "fundamental ideology" and the very different "operative ideology."[56]

This typology presupposes that the original principles retain their relevance and are capable of being revitalized. In this case, that is not possible. The analogy to software releases with which I started this section suggests continuous improvement as the bugs are ironed out and new features are added. However, it seems to me that something like the reverse has occurred with Wilsonianism. With each new iteration, the creed has become more and more degraded so that it bears progressively less of a resemblance to the original. The ideological half-life of Wilsonianism, to change the metaphor, has passed the point at which it continues to radiate meaningful amounts of ideological energy. So: Would Wilson be a neoconservative if he returned today? Would neoconservatives know what to do with him if he made a miraculous appearance? Would Wilson be driving a sport-utility vehicle? I cannot prove it, because this is a counterfactual speculation, but I would like to think that Wilson is turning over in his grave at being identified with the Bush administration's policies.

It might be objected that not all of Wilsonianism has to survive in pure form to qualify as an ideology that continues to exert influence across the generations. As one blogger pus it, "After all, a great-granddaddy doesn't pass on all of his genes, but surely, Woodrow Wilson has seen to it that at least some of his genetic material has passed down to his foreign policy progeny that now run the White House."[57] According to this view, Wilsonianism has passed a cultural survival test, having been transmitted by a selfish cultural gene, as it were, that has assured its continuing existence. But the survival of genetic traits is trickier than that. A better way of describing Wilsonianism in evolutionary terms is that it was the *end* of one branching line of liberal ideological development. Better still as an evolutionary metaphor for what I have in mind is what biologists have called "genetic swamping," where a potentially adaptive genetic variation, through constant breeding with the general population, disappears, losing its distinctiveness or purity by reverting to the norm. And that is what I want to argue: that Wilsonianism stuck its head out and has since become swamped. Genetic swamping is a scientific version of the Japanese saying that the nail that sticks out will be hammered down. Wilsonianism was part of a larger liberal worldview whence it came and, after being hammered down, to which it has returned.[58]

Conclusion

In one sense, however, Wilsonianism is clearly not dead, for at times nothing seems to die in the postmodern world of mediated reality that is besotted with images. Like Elvis and Hitler, Wilson has been karmically recycled by a

Hinduized political discourse in which the past is absorbed and transformed as part of a living present. Because many scholars and social commentators continue to believe that Wilsonianism has ideological relevance and that it can be applied meaningfully in contemporary political debate, they continue without embarrassment to use the word. But Wilsonianism survives as a postmodern phenomenon that lacks any objective grounding either in verifiable history or in the actualities of the present-day world situation. Detached from historical context, it survives in free-floating pop cultural remnants, in halfbaked historical references, in voguish allusions thrown about by political spinmeisters with ulterior motives, and, alas, in bad scholarship. At best, this results in media dust devils that do no damage except to historical fidelity; at worst, in bad history putting a face on policy that otherwise might not withstand close inspection.

That is not to say that it does not have its uses, for that is why it continues to be used, but the politics of meaning that swirl around the term have been stripped of the clear policy implications that once were attached to it. Instead, Wilsonianism has become a rhetorical weapon intended, variously, to tug at the idealistic heart strings of audiences, to justify the use of force for noble purposes, or, conversely, to serve as a sort of rhetorical shorthand for those bent on criticizing a species of naïveté and silliness in the conduct of our foreign affairs. Most of all, its contemporary use is intended to evoke a sense that policies adopted in its name are deep-rooted and hence part of our identity, to rouse the feeling that it is OK to do this because we are doing nothing new—we have done this sort of thing in the past; this is part of our tradition; this is who we are. Politicians are notorious for selling new wine in old bottles because, at times, this is the only way it can be sold. But if, as I have argued, there is little in the way of a usable tradition to be found in Wilsonianism, if we are forced to strain to adapt Wilsonianism to our contemporary situation, to in effect adapt the unadaptable, this suggests to me a certain degree of disorientation in our political discourse born of an inability to recognize how far we have drifted from the shoreline of a tradition that, no longer visible to guide our course, has become imaginary. It is a depressing thought, but perhaps we need to believe that we believe, even if our faith is functionally dead.

The trade-off for being given a new life is that Wilsonianism has lost the vibrancy of its former existence. The Wilsonian impulse, however defined, and for good or ill, has mattered immensely in the past, for it reflected a coherent body of analysis and ideological conviction that was connected in a meaningful way to real-world problems. Whatever one thinks of it, Wilsonianism was able to generate an almost religious fervor among its believers during the Great War and during World War II, a sense of exaltation that was prompted by Wilson's imaginative ability to see the redemptive possibilities in what otherwise would have been an unspeakably bleak world situation. One detects neither that kind of deeply felt enthusiasm nor that kind of fear today—if anything, there is no shortage of critics who suspect that the fear has been largely manufactured and used as a device for selling a different agenda. If one adopts the quick-and-dirty definition of ideology as a secular religion, Wilsonianism today is to ideology what religion is to contemporary Europe: hollowed out and empty of meaning. Hence my chapter subtitle, which suggests the complete line from Shakespeare's *Troilus and Cressida*: "Words, words, mere words, no matter from the heart: the effect doth operate another way."[59]

Notes

1. Michael Mandelbaum, *The Ideas That Conquered the World: Peace, Democracy, and Free Markets in the Twenty-First Century* (New York, PublicAffairs, 2002), 17.

2. Alexandru Grigorescu, "Mapping the UN-League of Nations Analogy: Are There Still Lessons to Be Learned from the League?" *Global Governance* 11 (2005): 36; Roger Reed, *ONU : Droits pour tous ou loi du plus fort? Regards militants sur les Nations Unies* [What Is the United Nations?] (Paris: Éditions du CETIM, 2005).

3. Parenthetically, the veto as it was most commonly discussed in 1919 was in reference to America's responsibility to intervene on behalf of League under the terms of Article 10 in faraway lands where the United States did not have a direct interest. As Wilson put it, the League council could not make the United States intervene. "We have an absolute veto on the thing," he said, but then he added the important qualifier "unless we are parties to the dispute." Woodrow Wilson, "An Address in San Francisco," September 17, 1919, in *The Papers of Woodrow Wilson*, 69 vols., ed. Arthur S. Link et al. (Princeton, N.J.: Princeton University Press, 1966–94) (hereafter, *PWW*), vol. 63, 318.

4. League of Nations, *Official Journal 1939*, 506 (Council Resolution); 540 (Assembly Resolution); Leo Gross, "Was the Soviet Union Expelled From the League of Nations?" *American Journal of International Law* 39, no. 1 (January 1945): 35–44.

5. On some points of resemblance and difference between the UN and the League, see Leland Goodrich, "From League to United Nations," *International Organization* 1 (February 1947): 3–21. On the absence of the threat of sanctions against a Great Power in the UN system, see Pitman B. Potter, "The United Nations Charter and the Covenant of the League of Nations," *American Journal of International Law* 39, no. 3 (July 1945): 546–51; and John Fischer Williams, "The League of Nations and Unanimity," *American Journal of International Law* 19, no. 3 (July 1925): 475–88. On the unwillingness of the Great Powers to take action authorized by the League Covenant, see Raymond Leslie Buell, "The League of Nations' Record in the Sino-Japanese Conflict," *New York Times*, March 27, 1932.

6. For doubts about America's ability maintain its imperial status, see Niall Ferguson, *Colossus: The Price of America's Empire* (New York: Penguin, 2004), 267–302.

7. Thomas Friedman, *The Lexus and the Olive Tree: Understanding Globalization* (New York: Anchor Books, 2000), 249.

8. Erez Manela, "The Wilsonian Moment: Self-Determination and the International Origins of Anticolonial Nationalism, 1917–1920," PhD dissertation, Yale University, 2003.

9. Carole Fink, *Defending the Rights of Others: The Great Powers, The Jews, and International Minority Protection, 1878–1938* (New York: Cambridge University Press, 2004).

10. Tatu Vanhanen, *The Emergence of Democracy: A Comparative Study of 119 States, 1850–1979* (New York: Routledge, 1984), 70. Measured as a proportion of independent states, depending on the assumptions, the number in 1918 was between 25 and 4 percent. See Tatu Vanhanen, "New Dataset for Measuring Democracy," *Journal of Peace Research* 37 (March 2000): 259.

11. Öyvind Osterud, "The Narrow Gate: Entry to the Club of Sovereign States," *Review of International Studies* 23 (1997): 167–84.

12. Samuel Huntington, *The Third Wave: Democratization in the Late Twentieth Century* (Norman: University of Oklahoma Press, 1991), 13–26. See also Mandelbaum, *Ideas That Conquered the World*; and Seymour Martin Lipset and Jason Lakin, *The Democratic Century* (Norman: University of Oklahoma Press, 2004).

13. Quoted by George C. Osborn, *Woodrow Wilson: The Early Years* (Baton Rouge: Louisiana State University Press, 1968), 288. Also see a newspaper report of a lecture to the Sociological Institute, October 30, 1894, in *PWW*, vol. 10, 100; William Diamond, *The Economic Thought of Woodrow Wilson* (Baltimore: Johns Hopkins Press, 1943), 42–43; Woodrow Wilson, *The State: Elements of Historical and Practical Politics* (Boston: D. C. Heath, 1889), 635; and after-dinner remarks, Paris, May 9, 1919, in *PWW*, vol. 58, 598.

14. Niels Aage Thorsen, *The Political thought of Woodrow Wilson, 1875–1910* (Princeton, N.J.: Princeton University Press, 1988), 37–38, 158–60.

15. See., e.g., David F. Schmitz, *Thank God They're on Our Side: The United States and Right-Wing Dictatorships, 1921–1965* (Chapel Hill: University of North Carolina Press, 1999); and David F. Schmitz, *The United States and Right-Wing Dictatorships, 1965–1989* (New York: Cambridge University Press, 2006).

16. John B. Judis, *The Folly of Empire: What George W. Bush Could Learn from Theodore Roosevelt and Woodrow Wilson* (New York: Charles Scribner's Sons, 2004), p. 7 and chap. 8. The story of the Clinton administration in foreign affairs, according to one source, is continuity with the Bush administration. Gearoid O. Tuathail and Simon Dalby, eds., *The Geopolitics Reader* (New York: Routledge, 1998).

17. "Address Before a Joint Session of the Congress on the Cessation of the Persian Gulf Conflict," March 6, 1991, in *The American Presidency Project*, ed. John Woolley and Gerhard Peters, American Presidency Project, University of California, Santa Barbara, Gerhard Peters's database, http://www.presidency.ucsb.edu/ws/?pid=19364.

18. J. G. Ruggie, "Third Try at World Order? America and Multilateralism after the Cold War," *Political Science Quarterly* 109, no. 4 (Autumn 1994): 553–70.

19. Ruggie, "Third Try at World Order?" 560.

20. Anthony Lake, "From Containment to Enlargement," speech given at the School of Advanced International Studies, Johns Hopkins University, September 21, 1993, and reprinted in *The Clinton Foreign Policy Reader: Presidential Speeches with Commentary*, ed. Alvin Z. Rubinstein et al. (Armonk, N.Y.: M. E. Sharpe, 2000), 20–27.

21. Joe Klein, "Clinton's Caribbean Oxymoron," *Newsweek*, May 30, 1994, 54.

22. "The Abdication, Again," *New Republic*, June 19, 1995, 7–8.

23. William Pfaff, *Chicago Tribune,* November 21, 1993.

24. Remarks in a Town Meeting with Speaker of the House of Representatives Newt Gingrich in Claremont, New Hampshire, June 11, 1995, in *Public Papers of the Presidents* (Washington, D.C.: U.S. Government Printing Office, various years) (hereafter *PPP*), 856.

25. Remarks at the Dedication of the Ronald Reagan Building and International Trade Center, May 5, 1998, *PPP*, 1998, 691.

26. The TR statement reads: "We are participants, whether we would or not, in the life of the world. . . . What affects mankind is inevitably our affair." Shortly before his death in 1901, William McKinley said that "isolation is no longer possible or desirable." Pointing to the effective shrinkage of space and time brought about by rapid technological improvements in communication and transportation, he asserted that "no nation can any longer be indifferent to any other." Extracts from McKinley speech of September 5, 1901, in *The Diplomacy of World Power: The United States, 1889–1920*, ed. Arthur S. Link and William L. Leary Jr. (New York: St. Martin's Press, 1970), 39–41.

27. Remarks at a Veterans Day Ceremony in Arlington, Va., November 11, 1997, in *PPP*, 1997, 1540.

28. Remarks to the Forum of Federations Conference in Mont-Tremblant, Canada, October 8, 1999, in *PPP*, 1999, 1739.

29. Remarks at a Reception for Representative Cynthia A. McKinney in Atlanta, April 14, 2000, in *PPP*, 2000, 714.

30. Warren Christopher, *In the Stream of History: Shaping Foreign Policy for a New Era* (Stanford, Calif.: Stanford University Press, 1998), 45.

31. Madeleine Albright, *Madam Secretary: A Memoir* (New York: Hyperion, 2003), 5, 162.

32. David L. Marcus, "The New Diplomacy," *Boston Globe Magazine*, June 1, 1007, 17.

33. Lawrence F. Kaplan, "Dollar Diplomacy Returns," *Commentary*, February 1998, 52–54.

34. G. John Ikenberry, "The Myth of Post–Cold War Chaos," *Foreign Affairs*, May–June 1996, 75–91.

35. Michael Mandelbaum, "Foreign Policy as Social Work," *Foreign Affairs*, January–February 1996, 16–33. Walter A. McDougall, "Back to Bedrock: The Eight Traditions of American Statecraft," *Foreign Affairs*, March–April 1997, 134–46.

36. Tellingly, in the Whitehall speech, Bush mentions Wilson's fourteen points, only to immediately deflate their significance by juxtaposing them with Clemenceau's catty comeback that God only had ten commandments. And in an important address on the Iraq war delivered at the Woodrow Wilson Center in December 2005, Bush missed an obvious opportunity to make an explicit connection between the war and Wilsonian idealism,

37. Martin Wolf, "Bush Is All Big Stick and No Soft Speech," *Financial Times*, December 23–24, 2003.

38. Colin Dueck, "Hegemony on the Cheap: Liberal Internationalism from Wilson to Bush," *World Policy Journal*, Winter 2003–4, 8. For a review of the scholarly literature on this issue, written from the realist perspective, see Lloyd E. Ambrosius, "Woodrow Wilson and George W. Bush: Historical Comparisons of Ends and Means in Their Foreign Policies," *Diplomatic History* 30, no. 3 (June 2006): 508–43.

39. *New York Times*, October 10, 2006.

40. Paul Gottfried, "The Legacy That Won't Die," *Journal of Libertarian Studies* 9, no. 2 (Fall 1990): 177–26.

41. *New York Times*, December 7, 2003.

42. Lawrence F. Kaplan, *Wall Street Journal*, September 22, 2004.

43. *New York Times*, November 10, 2003.

44. Max Boot, *Wall Street Journal*, July 1, 2002.

45. Bush's widely cited Whitehall address of November 19, 2003, mentions Wilson only in passing, whereas in his discussion of international institutions he aligns himself with "11 presidents before me," i.e., the historical genealogy starts with FDR. In his speech at the Coast Guard Academy of May 21, Bush does laud Wilson's "spiritual energy," but the only concrete policy application of that energy was a projected doubling of the size of the Peace Corps. Finally, and quite curiously, Wilson is excluded from the subject and name indexes for that year. See "2003 Public Papers of the Presidents of the United States," books I and II, http://www.gpoaccess.gov/pubpapers/index.html.

46. Tony Smith, "The Bush Doctrine as Wilsonianism," in *Wilsonianism in Crisis?* ed. G. John Ikenberry (Princeton, N.J.: Princeton University Press, forthcoming), http://ase.tufts.edu/polsci/faculty/smith/wilsonianism.pdf.

47. Francis Fukuyama, "After Neoconservatism," *New York Times Magazine*, February 19, 2006, p. 62 ff; Joel Whitney, "A Darling of the Neocons Tells Why He Bailed Out," SFGate, http://www.sfgate.com/cgi-bin/article.cgi?file=/chronicle/archive/2006/05/07/INGRFIKUF81.DTL&type=printable.

48. Matt Spetalnuck, "Words Get in the Way for Bush in Iraq Debate," Reuters, October 24, 2006; http://news.yahoo.com/s/nm/20061024/pl_nm/iraq_bush_words_dc_2.

49. Chicago Council on Foreign Relations, "Americans on Promoting Democracy," September 29, 2005.

50. *The National Security Strategy of the United States of America*, September 2002, ii; http://www.globalsecurity.org/military/library/policy/national/nss-020920.pdf.

51. *The National Security Strategy of The United States*, March 2006, 1; http://www.whitehouse.gov/nsc/nss/2006/nss2006.pdf.

52. See Joan Hoff Wilson, *American Business & Foreign Policy, 1920–1933* (Lexington: University Press of Kentucky, 1971); and Joan Hoff Wilson, *Herbert Hoover: Forgotten Progressive* (Boston: Little, Brown, 1975).

53. Bruce Kuklick, *Blind Oracles: Intellectuals and War from Kennan to Kissinger* (Princeton, N.J.: Princeton University Press, 2006), 157.

54. I have argued in the past that Wilsonianism was a self-liquidating creed. Once the kinds of problems that Wilson encountered had been surmounted, the United States would resort to a default position, something that I called "normal internationalism." This is a term of art. No one else, to my knowledge, has used it and no policy maker in his right mind is likely ever to adopt this term. By this I meant that the United States would cycle out of crisis mode and revert, not to isolationism but to less sweeping degrees of international engagement, depending on the circumstances. That is what appeared to happen in the 1990s and in the early 2000s. Internationalism, in this argument, is a form of idealism, albeit an idealism that needs to be understood in a philosophical sense as a product of the interpretive necessities of the human condition, which is a far cry from viewing the world through rose-colored glasses. For the full argument, see Frank Ninkovich, *The Wilsonian Century: U.S. Foreign Relations since 1900* (Chicago: University of Chicago Press, 2000).

55. Theodore Lowi, *The Politics of Disorder* (New York: W. W. Norton, 1971), 49; Rosa Mayreder,*Der typischer Verlauf sozialer Bewegeungen* (Vienna: Anzenngruner Verlag, 1925).

56. Martin Seliger, *Ideology amd Politics* (New York: Free Press, 1976).

57. Karen De Coster, "Neo-Wilsonianism as a Great-Granddaddy of Neoconservatism," http://www.lewrockwell.com/decoster/decoster91.html.

58. If one Googles "Wilsonianism," one gets a sense of its subordinate status as an ideological subspecies. When I last checked, Google showed a total of 64,800 hits for Wilsonianism-not a particularly large number. Communism tallied 19 million; nationalism, 16.4 million; fascism, 13.5 million; and liberalism, 13.8 million. Wilsonianism is not even on a par with Maoism and Trotskyism, which record 511,000 and 400,000.

59. William Shakespeare, *Troilus and Cressida*, act 5, scene 3.

Afterword: Making Democracy Safe for the World

Anne-Marie Slaughter

If Woodrow Wilson were to give a major foreign policy address today, I wager that he would say: "Democracy must be made safe for the world." He would look out at the world and say, as he did say: Democracy must be defended where it exists and extended where possible. He would look at the political science supporting the democratic peace. But he would also look at the political science that says *democratizing* countries are more likely to go to war. Sudden suffrage all too often coincides with nationalism, fanaticism, extremism, and demagoguery. He would thus recognize that although it is democracy we want, as a matter of interest and ideals, it is the process of democratization that we must worry about.

We thus find ourselves in a position analogous to the old Maine joke, in which a traveler asks a Mainer, "Which way to East Vasselboro?" The answer: "You can't get there from here." But you can, of course, and we can help new democracies and transitional democracies navigate the perils on the road to mature liberal democracy. We can only do so, however, if we are prepared to redefine our destination and reappraise our modes of transport.

Our journey's end is not democracy but ordered liberty—what Wilson would have understood as constitutional government. Democracy is but an instrument to secure ordered liberty—perhaps the worst instrument imaginable, yet, in Churchill's immortal phrase, better than all the others.[1] Moreover, when Americans and other citizens of mature liberal democracies say "democracy," what they mean is *p*opular, *a*ccountable, and *r*ights-regarding government—a

This afterword was originally a lunchtime address at the Sesquicentennial Celebration at the Woodrow Wilson Center. It has been amended for publication by drawing substantially on *The Idea That Is America: Keeping Faith with Our Values in a Dangerous World*, by Anne-Marie Slaughter (New York: Basic Books, 2007).

government that is up to PAR. Finally, keeping our own governments up to PAR and working to help transitional and weak democracies achieve PAR in the first place cannot be any one country's task. As Wilson would have been the first to recognize, it must be a collective venture, one that engages countries in different regions around the world.

Securing Liberty Under Law

When Wilson wrote his classic text on government in the United States, he did not title it, following de Tocqueville, *Democracy in America*. He chose instead: *Constitutional Government in the United States*. He saw constitutional government as the highest form of government, the final stage in the modern evolution from autocracy to aristocracy to democracy. He defined constitutional government as "a government conducted upon the basis of a definite understanding, if need be a formal pact, between those who are to submit to it and those who are to conduct it, with a view to making government an instrument of the general welfare rather than an arbitrary, self-willed master, doing what it pleases—and particularly for the purpose of safeguarding individual liberty."[2] And indeed, our own Constitution is a pact among the people of the United States to "secure the Blessings of Liberty to ourselves and our Posterity."

What are those blessings? Throughout American history, we have been far better at proclaiming our devotion to liberty than examining precisely what we mean by it. That is in part because once we try to translate our rhetoric into reality, liberty is not so easy to define. Absolute liberty for all citizens, for instance, will quickly degenerate into chaos. Alternatively, liberty for some can soon mean oppression for others. To achieve anything resembling "liberty for all," individual liberty must be traded off against other values such as security, equality, justice, and tolerance. Wilson, indeed, defined political liberty in terms of perpetual adaptation: "the right of those who are governed to adjust government to their own needs and interests."[3]

Our Founders understood the need for these trade-offs and wrestled with them. Most fundamentally, they recognized the vital importance of *ordered liberty*, or liberty under law. As Thomas Jefferson wrote to a Greek patriot about the Greeks' revolt against their Ottoman rulers in 1823, America possessed the "*combined* blessings of liberty and order."[4] Jefferson and his fellow revolutionaries rejected order without liberty; that was the tyranny they had revolted against. But they understood equally that liberty without order would allow humanity's worst instincts to run unchecked. In George Washington's first inaugural address—the first presidential address by our first president—he counseled our young nation to attend to the supporting values that make liberty possible, among them "the eternal rules of order and right."[5]

Those grand-sounding "eternal rules" are far more likely in practice to be regulations as simple as traffic lights and as complex and technical as tax codes. What Washington had in mind was more likely the legal translations of the moral injunctions found in all great religions—thou shalt not kill or steal. But the order necessary for liberty to flourish includes the entire spectrum of the rule of law. Wilson concurred. "A constitutional government," he wrote, "is *par excellence* a government of law."[6] Law is the instrument by which the citizens of a constitutional government hold their government accountable and keep it to its promises. "For the individual, . . . who stands at the centre of every definition of liberty, the struggle for constitutional government is a struggle for good laws, indeed, but also for intelligent, independent, and impartial courts."[7]

Law is also the mechanism of perpetual adjustment that allows political liberty to flourish and adapt to changing circumstances across the centuries. But law cannot only apply only to the other guy—or to the other country. Everyone always sings the first verse of *America the Beautiful*: "O beautiful for spacious skies, for amber waves of grain." The second verse, however, has more to teach us today:

> O beautiful for pilgrim feet, whose stern, impassioned stress
> A thoroughfare for freedom beat across the wilderness!
> America! America! God mend thine every flaw,
> Confirm thy soul in self-control, Thy liberty in law!

Liberty requires restraint—self-restraint first, and then the capacity to restrain those who cannot exercise self-restraint. The entire concept of the rule of law is a collective precommitment to obey the law and to accept that if we violate it, it will be enforced against us. We enjoy liberty because we accept the necessity of ordered liberty.

An established order enshrines a particular definition of liberty at a particular time in a society's history—just as our Constitution secured liberty initially only for white men. Liberty is an ideal; its practical contours are continually, and imperfectly, defined and redefined both across time and across countries and cultures. But as American presidents have believed from Washington through Wilson, Roosevelt, Truman, Kennedy, Reagan, to the present, the best hope for all individuals to secure the conditions in which they can flourish is to establish a system of liberty under law.

Bringing Governments Up to PAR

In foreign policy, the encouragement and support of systems of liberty under law typically goes under the shorthand of "democracy promotion," not only for ease of reference but also for a more pernicious reason. It is often easier and faster to organize and hold elections than it is to build the necessary supporting institutions for stable constitutional government. As moving as it was to watch Iraqis hold up their purple thumbs to mark their vote in a free and fair election, both they and we had inflated expectations, and perhaps even dangerous ones, about what the election could accomplish in a landscape so physically and politically stunted. In Afghanistan, too, elections have proven to be no match for determined warlords.

Constitutional government is *hard*. Even in Germany and Japan, the Bush administration's poster children for the potential of democratizing despotic regimes, the road to liberal democracy took military defeat, lengthy occupation, economic renewal, the scrutiny and support of institutions like the nascent European Union and NATO, and constitutional disarmament—not to mention a long history of developed state institutions. Proclaiming the blessings and bounty of liberty under law without tempering expectations about the time frame and work necessary to achieve it and providing the sustained economic, political, and even military support the task may require is at best irresponsible and at worst immoral.

Wilson addressed these issues in the paternalistic language of the nineteenth century, but not without merit. He argued that self-government is not only a form of institutions, but also a "form of character":

> It follows upon the long discipline which gives people self-possession, self-mastery, the habit of order and peace and common counsel, and a reverence for law which will not fail when they themselves become the makers of law: the steadiness and self control of political maturity. And these things cannot be had without long discipline.[8]

Wilson went on to argue for the benefits of "giv[ing] the Filipinos constitutional government" until they could learn the habits necessary to govern themselves.[9] I will leave to others the determination of the extent to which such enlightened sentiments guided America's colonization of the Philippines until after World War II, as opposed to our strong need for naval bases in the Pacific. But as a statement of fact about the development of constitutional government,

Wilson's timetable concurs with the data of social scientists and the experience of prodemocracy groups around the world.

Building constitutional government requires sufficient security to live by the force of law rather than of arms; tolerance for social, ethnic, and religious divisions; and a culture of accountability for the spending of public funds. States that hold elections without the supporting constitutional infrastructure and conditions are likely to be unstable and prone to belligerent nationalism. On the flip side, states with the best prospects for sustaining constitutional government have reasonably strong domestic groups prepared to embrace the limits on power entailed by liberal democracy rather than use democracy to gain and maintain power. Representative government must deliver tangible benefits for the population as a whole, beginning with security and extending to at least modest prosperity.

Rereading our own history, from Washington to Wilson and from Wilson to the present, should make us much more attentive to the multiple dimensions of liberal democracy and the various metrics that track its progress. Three aspects need to be considered:

- *Popular government:* the extent to which a government actually represents its people through elected representatives, advisory councils, and other decision-making bodies designed to give different segments of the population a meaningful voice.

- *Accountable government:* the extent to which citizens can monitor the activities of their government (transparency, absence of corruption) and hold it responsible, through elections, votes of no confidence, or the courts, for failure to deliver on its promises or uphold the law.

- *Rights-regarding government:* the extent to which a government upholds and protects the rights of all its citizens, as guaranteed in a country's constitution, statutes, and treaties to which it is a party.

Thus, a government that is Popular, Accountable, and Rights-regarding is up to PAR as a liberal democracy. A government that is below PAR might well have free and fair elections but, through corruption or deception, might not be accountable to the people for its policies. Or it might consistently violate minority rights or the human rights of its citizens more generally. Or it might guarantee order under law and a degree of prosperity but deny its people the liberty to rule themselves. Or it might allow money to play such a large role in its elections that ordinary voters come to feel that they cannot make their voices heard.

Making democracy safe for the world means ensuring that democracies are up to PAR. That is likely to be a long, slow process. It is not one that the United States should try to undertake alone, nor one that should be focused only on other nations.

A Global PAR Index

In chapter 1 of this volume, John Milton Cooper emphasizes that Wilson used the passive voice very deliberately in proclaiming that the world "must be made safe for democracy."[10] Adopting that same voice, I argue that today Wilson would insist that "democracy must be made safe for the world." The construction, now as then, raises the question: By whom? *Not* by the United States alone. Equally important, however—*not* by others with the United States once again standing aloof. America should join other liberal democracies in the world to develop a global PAR index. Better yet, liberal democratic governments should come together and foster and facilitate the development of such an index by existing nongovernmental organizations and civil society groups in all their countries.

Much of the groundwork for developing such an index has already been laid; the nongovernmental organization Freedom House ranks all countries in the world according to whether they are free, partly free, or not free.[11] Transparency International, another civic organization based in Berlin, ranks countries on a corruption index that measures the prevalence of corruption and public attitudes toward it. Moreover, many human rights groups evaluate countries on their specific human rights records. A group of liberal democratic governments working with these nongovernmental groups could formulate a PAR index that would have broad legitimacy and could be used by these governments and groups in deciding whether and how to support democracy in countries with different rankings.

This process would allow advocates of democracy to gather and distill all the knowledge that governments and nongovernmental organizations have developed about what has worked in the many countries that have made successful transitions to democracy over the past three decades—as well as what has not worked. It would allow governments and citizens around the world to evaluate governments on a range of dimensions, thereby avoiding the black-or-white label of whether a country is a democracy or not. Such a cut-and-dried label is hard to apply and understandably generates tremendous resentment around the world from governments and citizens who find that our own American democracy is less than perfect (consider the Bush-Gore election and our system of campaign financing). Assessing whether a government is up to PAR would also break what often seems to the rest of the world like an obsession with elections, even when, as in Palestine, elections produce a Hamas government that openly supports terrorism.

Finally, a PAR index would acknowledge that successful liberal democracy comes in many forms. Some nations combine legislative and executive power in a single parliament led by a prime minister and cabinet. Democracies that have instead chosen to follow the U.S. model of a strong president separately elected from the legislature are often more vulnerable to coups. Some supreme courts exercise judicial review; others do not. Liberal democracies also differ significantly in the precise range of rights they protect. Some, for instance, restrict hate speech much more than in the United States but permit more of what the United States prohibits as pornography. European democracies typically restrict abortion more than most American states and do not have the death penalty. The South African Constitution requires its Supreme Court at least to find out what foreign and international courts think on important constitutional questions before issuing an opinion under South African law, while some U.S. Supreme Court justices reject that practice. America is not the only or even the best model for new democracies.

Governments below PAR—and no government should get a perfect score—could make progress in finding ways to increase popular participation in government, accountability, or human rights and be recognized and credited for such progress. For example, the Chinese government worries about the implications of handing the vote to 1.3 billion people who have never governed themselves before. The Egyptian government worries about the electoral power of radical Islamists. Both are worried even more about losing the privileges that political power has brought them. But both could nevertheless be encouraged or pushed to allow multiple parties in the elections that they do hold. Both could be brought to allow multiple currents of thought in their societies and politics. Both could develop mechanisms to combat corruption and improve the transparency of government decisions, and to improve their human rights records—all as part of an evolution not only toward democracy but also toward liberal democracy.

The PAR rankings would all be relative. The history of all liberal democracies, including our own, reveals the gap between the ideal of liberal democracy and the often checkered reality. Countries make progress, backslide, reform their systems, redefine their electorates, tie themselves to the mast of international human rights standards, and learn from other countries.

Such an enterprise would be deeply Wilsonian. Although Wilson's *Constitutional Government in the United States* has been printed and reprinted over the past century as a classic of American political science, his earlier work *The State* is much less well known. Writing in 1898, a decade before *Constitutional Government in the United States*, Wilson set about describing the governments not only of the United States but also of France, Britain, Italy, Belgium, Germany, Austria-Hungary, Serbia, Rumania, Bulgaria, Greece, Russia, Turkey, and Japan.[12] He certainly thought that the distinctively American form of constitutional government could be improved; his predilection for British parliamentary government was well known. A global PAR index would offer metrics for learning about and comparing governments around the world; it would also likely challenge the complacency of many mature liberal democracies, not least the United States. Wilson the political scientist would have liked that. Wilson the president, the reformer who reshaped the American political landscape by establishing institutions such as the Federal Reserve and the Federal Trade Commission, would have learned from it.

Embedding Democracy in Global Networks

Making the world safe for democracy and making democracy safe for the world are in many ways two sides of the same coin. In John Milton Cooper's reading, Wilson was insisting that individual nations be allowed to embark on the long journey toward constitutional government free of bullying and outright aggression from their neighbors. International sea-lanes had to be free to allow all nations to trade sufficiently to bring their citizens a decent standard of living. International rules had to be laid down and upheld to allow for the collective solution of common problems. The United States would help win the war and then would join with other nations to create the League of Nations to bring—as Wilson wrote in the 1918 edition of *The State*—"pressure to bear upon a state unmindful of its international obligations," thereby going far "towards supplying the sanction of regulated force which International Law has hitherto lacked."[13]

Today, a society seeking to become a polity capable of sustaining constitutional government will also require sustained international support, not only from institutions such as the United Nations, the World Bank and various regional banks, and the World Trade Organization but also from being directly linked to established liberal democracies through networks of regulators of all kinds, judges, and legislators.[14] Those networks can come through membership in regional institutions, above all the European Union, but also the Asia-Pacific Economic Cooperation, the Organization of American States, and the African Union. The countries belonging to all these organizations increasingly understand how dangerous fledgling or failed democracy can be for them—spilling conflict, people, disease, and poverty across borders and harboring insurgents, terrorists, and criminals of all sorts.

Strong, stable, and free nations make a strong and peaceful international order. A strong and peaceful international order can help make strong, stable, and free nations. The two together would be a genuinely Wilsonian world.

Notes

1. Winston Churchill, speech, House of Commons, November 11, 1947; quoted in *Winston S. Churchill: His Complete Speeches, 1897–1963*, ed. Robert Rhodes James (London: Chelsea House Publishers, 1974), vol. 7, 7566.

2. Woodrow Wilson, *Constitutional Government in the United States*, with a new introduction by Sydney A. Pearson Jr. (New Brunswick, N.J.: Transaction Publishers, 2006), 3.

3. Ibid., 4.

4. Thomas Jefferson to Admantios Coray, October 31, 1823, manuscript letter, Manuscript Division, Library of Congress, 204; http://www.loc.gov/exhibits/jefferson/jeffworld.html.

5. George Washington, First Inaugural.

6. Wilson, *Constitutional Government*, 17.

7. Ibid.

8. Ibid., 52.

9. Ibid.

10. See chapter 1 in this volume by John Milton Cooper.

11. For information on Freedom House (which has offices in New York City and Washington), see the organization's Web site, http://www.freedomhouse.org.

12. Woodrow Wilson, *The State: Elements of Historical and Practical Politics*, special ed., rev. to December 1918 by Edward Elliott (Boston: D. C. Heath, 1918; orig. pub. 1889).

13. Ibid., 86.

14. See Anne-Marie Slaughter, *A New World Order* (Princeton, N.J.: Princeton University Press, 2004).

Contributors

LLOYD E. AMBROSIUS is the Samuel Clark Waugh Distinguished Professor of International Relations and Professor of History at the University of Nebraska–Lincoln. He is the author of *Woodrow Wilson and the American Diplomatic Tradition: The Treaty Fight in Perspective*; *Wilsonian Statecraft: Theory and Practice of Liberal Internationalism during World War I*; and *Wilsonianism: Woodrow Wilson and His Legacy in American Foreign Relations*.

VICTORIA BISSELL BROWN is the L. F. Parker Professor of History at Grinnell College. Her books include *The Education of Jane Addams*; *Going to the Source: The Bedford Reader in American History*; and an edition of Jane Addams's *Twenty Years at Hull-House with Autobiographical Notes*. She has lectured widely on Jane Addams, the politics of the early twentieth century, and women's reform history. The Wisconsin Women's Network distributed her *Uncommon Lives of Common Women: The Missing Half of Wisconsin History* to all of Wisconsin's public schools and libraries. She was also a script adviser and on-screen contributor to the two-part television documentary *Woodrow Wilson* in the PBS *American Experience* series.

W. ELLIOT BROWNLEE is professor of history emeritus at the University of California, Santa Barbara, and a former fellow of the Woodrow Wilson International Center for Scholars. He is the author of *Federal Taxation in America: A Short History*, currently in its second edition; editor of *Funding the Modern American State, 1941–1995: The Rise and Fall of the Era of Easy Finance*; and coeditor of *The Reagan Presidency: Pragmatic Conservatism and Its Legacies*. Currently he is at work on two books, on the U.S. financing of World War I, and on taxation in Japan during the American occupation.

JOHN MILTON COOPER JR. is the E. Gordon Fox Professor of American Institutions at the University of Wisconsin, where he has taught history since 1970 and served as chair of the department. He is the author of *The Vanity of Power: American Isolationism and World War I*; *Walter Hines Page: The Southerner as American*; *The Warrior and the Priest: Woodrow Wilson and Theodore Roosevelt*; *Pivotal Decades: The United States, 1900–1920*; and *Breaking the Heart of the World: Woodrow Wilson and the Fight for the League of Nations*. He has served as a consultant to several television documentary programs that have aired in the PBS *American Experience* series, including *Woodrow Wilson*, for which he was chief historian. He is currently writing a biography of Woodrow Wilson.

GARY GERSTLE is the James Stahlman Professor of History at Vanderbilt University. He is the author of *Working-Class Americanism: The Politics of Labor in a Textile City, 1914–1960*, and *American Crucible: Race and Nation in the Twentieth Century*, which won the 2001 Saloutos Prize for the best book on immigration and ethnic history. He is also the coeditor of three books, including *The Rise and Fall of the New Deal Order, 1930 to 1980*, and *Ruling America: A History of Wealth and Power in a Democracy*. He is currently writing a book on the history of the American state.

MARK T. GILDERHUS is the Lyndon B. Johnson Chair in the Department of History at Texas Christian University. His books include *Diplomacy and Revolution: U.S.-Mexican Relations under Wilson and Carranza*; *Pan American Visions: Woodrow Wilson in the Western Hemisphere, 1913–1921*; *History and Historians: A Historiographical Introduction*; and *The Second Century: U.S.-Latin American Relations since 1889*. Currently, he is working on a study of U.S. diplomacy and warfare since 1914 and preparing a diplomatic profile of Secretary of State Robert Lansing. Gilberhus has also served as president of the Society for Historians of American Foreign Relations.

FRANK NINKOVICH is professor of history at Saint John's University in New York. His recent works include *The United States and Imperialism*; *The Wilsonian Century: U.S. Foreign Policy since 1900*; *Modernity and Power: A History of the Domino Theory in the Twentieth Century*; *U.S. Information Policy and Cultural Diplomacy*; *Germany and the United States: The Transformation of the German Question since 1945*; and *The Diplomacy of Ideas: U.S. Foreign Policy and Cultural Relations, 1938–1950*. He is currently working on a history of the emergence of a global outlook in the United States between 1865 and 1890.

EMILY S. ROSENBERG is professor of history at University of California, Irvine, specializing in American foreign relations. She is the author of *A Date Which Will Live: Pearl Harbor in American Memory*; and *Financial Missionaries to the World: The Politics and Culture of Dollar Diplomacy*, which received the Ferrell Senior Book Award from the Society for Historians of American Foreign Relations. She was an associate editor of *The Oxford Companion to American History*, and she is coeditor of the American Encounters / Global Interactions book series for Duke University Press.

ANNE-MARIE SLAUGHTER is the dean of the Woodrow Wilson School of Public and International Affairs and the Bert G. Kerstetter '66 University Professor of Politics and International Affairs at Princeton University. She writes and teaches broadly on global governance, international criminal law, and American foreign policy. Her most recent book is *The Idea that is America: Keeping Faith with Our Values in a Dangerous World*, published in 2007 by Basic Books. Her previous book, *A New World Order*, identified transnational networks of government officials as an increasingly important component of global governance. She is also the coauthor, with G. John Ikenberry, of the final report of the Princeton Project on National Security, *Forging a World of Liberty under Law: U.S. National Security in the 21st Century*.

GEOFFREY R. STONE, the Edward H. Levi Distinguished Service Professor at the University of Chicago, is also the former dean of the Law School and former provost of the university. His *Perilous Times: Free Speech in Wartime—From the Sedition Act of 1798 to the War on Terrorism* received awards from the John F. Kennedy School of Government at Harvard University, the *Los Angeles Times*, the Robert F. Kennedy Memorial, and the American Political Science Association. He is currently working on a volume titled *Sexing the Constitution*.

TRYGVE THRONTVEIT received his PhD in history in June 2008 from Harvard University, where he is now Lecturer on History for the 2008–9 academic year. He has taught courses on social thought in modern America, twentieth-century international history and U.S. foreign affairs, and the English Revolution. His dissertation, "Related States: Pragmatism, Progressivism and Internationalism in American Thought, 1880–1920," is an investigation into the influence of pragmatic ethics and Progressive reform thinking on Wilson-era domestic and foreign policy. He is the author of articles on William James's metaphysics and

Thorstein Veblen's aesthetics, and has delivered papers on Wilsonian politics and diplomacy at Harvard and Princeton universities.

MARTIN WALKER is editor in chief emeritus of United Press International and a senior scholar at the Woodrow Wilson International Center for Scholars. In his career as a journalist, he served as Moscow bureau chief, U.S. bureau chief, European editor, and assistant editor at *The Guardian* newspaper, and in 1997 he received Britain's "Reporter of the Year" award. He is a senior fellow of the World Policy Institute at the New School for Social Research in New York and a contributing editor of the *Los Angeles Times* "Opinion" section and of *Europe Magazine*. He has published seven nonfiction books and three novels, including *Waking Giant: Gorbachev and Perestroika*; *The Cold War: A History*; *Clinton: The President We Deserve*; and *America Reborn*.

Index